# Mastering
# New CLAIT

**Bernard
Kane**

Published in 2003 by:
Nelson Thornes Ltd
Delta Place
27 Bath Road
CHELTENHAM
GL53 7TH
United Kingdom

03  04  05  06  07 / 10  9  8  7  6  5  4  3  2  1

A catalogue record for this book is available from the British Library

ISBN  0 7487 7077 1

Illustrations by GreenGate Publishing Services and Derek Griffin
Page make-up by GreenGate Publishing Services

Printed and bound in Great Britain by Scotprint

# Contents

What you need to know about using a computer for New CLAIT • Computer systems and computer speak • A typical home or work computer system • What's inside your computer? • Switching on your computer • The Windows environment • The desktop • What are windows? • Using the mouse • Opening programs • Managing files • Setting up your filing structure • Using the files on your CD • Entering and editing text, numbers and symbols into a document • Using the mouse and pointer • Using the keyboard to navigate • Amending a document • Printing your work • Closing down your computer • Safe working practices • Practical assignment 1

What you need to know about wordprocessing for New CLAIT • Getting familiar with Word • Opening and using Word as a wordprocessing application • Understanding the Word screen • Understanding the menu bars and toolbars • Building a new document • Saving, recovering and renaming documents • Formatting and editing text in a document • Manipulating text in a document • Changing a page layout • Justifying text in a document • Printing your work • Exiting the application • Practical assignment 2

What you need to know about electronic communication for New CLAIT • What is electronic communication? • Using your e-mail software to send and receive mail • E-mail attachments • Printing e-mail messages and their attachments • Understanding the Internet and the World Wide Web • Navigating around the Internet and the World Wide Web • Practical assignment 3

## Acknowledgements

I would like to thank Rick Jackman and Fiona Elliott for their support and encouragement during the writing of this book, Katie Chester of GreenGate Publishing Services, Peterborough College of Adult Education, and in particular all the staff of the IT department, for the help and assistance offered during the development of the text, Amy Kane and Robin Morgan for advice in graphical design, The Microsoft Corporation for developing the Office suite of applications, and Denise MacDonald at The Business Café of Peterborough Cathedral.

## Dedication

To my wife, Wendy, whose belief in the project was only exceeded by her patience.

# Introduction

## Who is this book for?

This book has been written primarily to help you develop the skills needed to meet the assessment standards set by the Oxford, Cambridge and RSA Examination Board in its Level 1 Certificate for IT users, known now as New CLAIT. It is also designed to help anyone, even those not intending to take the formal qualification, to learn in a simple and practical way a little more about using computer hardware and software. The software referred to and used in this book is part of the Microsoft Office XP suite, but you will also find that much of the book can be used with most other versions of Microsoft Office. Also included are helpful tips on many additional features not specifically needed for the qualification but that may assist you in understanding more about the applications and how you can use them effectively at home or at work. You will learn what each application is used for and why things are done in particular ways.

## How to use this book

The book is presented in three parts. Part 1 looks at how to use a computer and gives general information on computer systems, the windows environment and file management. Part 2 covers the competences required in Microsoft Office applications for New CLAIT. Part 3 provides suggested solutions to the practical exercises, which you should complete in each unit to reinforce your understanding of the subject matter. The appendices include the syllabuses for the applications covered in the New CLAIT qualification, a useful list of keyboard shortcuts and a glossary of terms used in the book.

## Practical exercises

On the CD accompanying this book are a number of exercise files that have been produced for you to use with various Build-up and full practice exercises and Practical assignments throughout the book. When you have mastered the section on managing your files, you should copy these files to the appropriate folder on either your hard disk or a floppy disk.

## What is covered in each part?

Part 1 gives an overview of a computer system, introduces the windows environment and provides guidance on files and how to manage them. Part 1 also introduces the first formal requirements of New CLAIT about using a computer.

**Unit 1   Using a computer**

Part 2 looks at the requirements expected of students for New CLAIT in the following skills and applications:

Unit 2  **Wordprocessing using Word**
Unit 3  **Electronic communication**
Unit 4  **Spreadsheets using Excel**
Unit 5  **Databases using Access**
Unit 6  **Desktop publishing using Publisher**
Unit 7  **Graphs and charts**
Unit 8  **Computer art using Word**
Unit 9  **Web pages using FrontPage**
Unit 10 **Presentation graphics using PowerPoint**

Part 3 provides the solutions for the practical assignments at the end of each unit.

### Appendices

**Appendix 1:** details the full New CLAIT syllabuses.
**Appendix 2:** provides a range of shortcut keys for each application.
**Appendix 3:** contains a glossary of terms used in the book.

As you progress through each application, the skills that form part of the formal syllabus for New CLAIT will be identified clearly. You will also learn other functions which, although not part of the formal syllabus for this qualification, will give you a better understanding of the software and how it can be used. You can also reinforce skills learnt by completing hand-holding 'Try it out' exercises and then follow the progressive 'Build-up' exercises that lead to specific requirements for New CLAIT.

Shown below is a guide to the symbols used in the book:

This symbol indicates that the text that follows forms part of a formal requirement for the New CLAIT qualification.

After learning a new function or skill, this symbol invites you to reinforce what you have learnt with simple 'Try it out' practice exercises.

As you progress through the units of each section you will be invited to further reinforce your understanding by completing 'Build-up' exercises that are marked by this symbol.

Text in *italics* indicates that a new term is being used. Normally an explanation will follow or there is a brief explanation in the glossary in Appendix 3.

Words (other than headings) shown in **bold** invite you to perform an action with the mouse or keyboard.

## What is New CLAIT?

CLAIT stands for Computer Literacy and Information Technology. New CLAIT has been developed from the original qualification and incorporates a number of additional skills to help you meet the increasing demands of the modern workplace as software continues to develop. Both CLAIT and New CLAIT are nationally recognised qualifications and demonstrate an individual's skill in using a number of software applications at a practical foundation level. New CLAIT covers the standard generic software packages and also includes options for you to learn about electronic communications (or e-mail and using the Internet), web page design, charts and graphs, and computer art. To achieve Level 1 accreditation you must successfully complete the core unit on 'Using a computer' plus four optional units.

This book covers the requirements for accreditation for New CLAIT in *wordprocessing, electronic communication, databases, spreadsheets, desktop publishing, graphs and charts, computer art, web pages,* and *presentation graphics.* The box below shows briefly how applications covering these subjects are used.

| *How applications are used* | |
| --- | --- |
| Word | Creating documents and manipulating text |
| Microsoft Outlook and Internet Explorer | Electronic communications (e-mail) and the Internet |
| Databases | Storing data |
| Spreadsheets | Performing calculations |
| Desktop publishing (DTP) | Graphical and text design |
| Word | Creating artwork with images and text |
| Graphs and charts | Presenting information in charts, graphs and tables |
| Front Page | Web page design |
| PowerPoint | Creating presentations |

## How do I get New CLAIT assessments?

To achieve certification in an application students have to demonstrate competence in a series of assessment objectives, which are grouped together under a number of learning outcomes. These will become clear once you start working through the book. However, the advantage of New CLAIT is that you have the flexibility to complete the units towards accreditation at your own pace. In addition, you can decide whether to complete the whole qualification in one go, or receive certification on a unit-by-unit basis. At the beginning of each unit is a list of the skills needed for New CLAIT and also an explanation of all the skills covered in the unit. The syllabus shown in Appendix 1 provides full details for each of the required learning outcomes and assessment objectives.

You will be asked to work through a number of exercises, slowly building on your skills, until you decide you are ready to do a formal assessment. Each unit also covers a range of additional skills that are not part of the formal syllabus for the qualification but are designed to give you a better understanding of the software and how it can be used.

## What are learning outcomes and assessment objectives?

These terms refer to skills and concepts relating to applications or topics that you will be expected to understand to achieve accreditation. For instance, in Wordprocessing a learning outcome may be 'Use an input device to enter and edit text accurately'. This learning outcome will group a number of assessment objectives, such as:

- Enter text in paragraphs
- Insert text
- Move text
- Delete text.

This book takes you through each of the assessment objectives contained in the broader learning outcomes for each application or skill required by the awarding body.

Each unit is assessed by means of an assignment set by OCR. When you feel you are ready you can ask to do one of these assignments at your local college, school or other recognised training provider. You only need to undertake one assignment in any unit you decide to take as part of your overall certificate for IT users. You will be given two hours to complete each assignment.

The core unit, 'Using a Computer', is assessed externally by OCR. The optional units are centre-assessed and externally moderated by an OCR moderator.

That is all there is to it! Normally your tutor will be monitoring your progress and will have a good idea when you are ready to undertake an assignment. However, if you do not successfully complete all the elements of certification on the first occasion, you can do an assignment again.

# *Part 1*

## *The Windows environment*

| *Using a computer*

# Using a computer

**New CLAIT**

For New CLAIT there are a number of things about using a computer you will be expected to know, such as the basic components of a computer system, how to find and access data, how to manage your data files and print work you have prepared. As you progress through this unit each formal learning outcome is indicated by the New CLAIT symbol. However, also included in this unit are a number of additional features that you will undoubtedly find useful in understanding more about computers and computer systems.

## What you need to know about using a computer for New CLAIT

For New CLAIT you will need to know how to:

**Identify and use a personal computer workstation and system software**
- Switch on a computer and monitor safely.
- Use a personal computer and printer to produce a document.
- Know your way around the *operating system*.
- Load application software.
- Use an *input* device to enter data.
- Shut down an operating system.

**Locate and access data on a computer**
- Gain access to data using a login and/or password.
- Use file search facilities.
- Find a specified file.

**Input small amounts of unformatted text, numbers and symbols**
- Enter text.
- Enter numbers.
- Enter symbols.
- Amend an existing document.

**Print a document using the default printer settings**
- Switch on a printer safely.
- Load paper.
- Print a document.

**Manage documents and data**
- Create a new document.
- Open an existing document.
- Save an existing document.
- Save a document with a new filename.
- Close a document.

## Computer systems and computer speak

It is becoming increasingly difficult to get away from the fact that our lives are governed to a greater or lesser extent by computers. We use many common appliances such as washing machines, video recorders, music centres, cookers and other electrical goods, most of which rely to some degree or other on chips and processors similar to those found in modern computers. Indeed, we should not forget that as individuals we possess and use the most powerful computer known to mankind – the human brain. However hard humans strive, it will be many decades, even centuries, before man-made computer technology will be able to emulate the power and functionality of the human brain. Despite this, and the plethora of computer power at our disposal, many people never get round to using a personal computer (PC) for fear that the technology may be more than they can cope with, or simply because the jargon, or computer speak, puts them off. If you have bought this book then the chances are that you are prepared to have a go at learning how to use a PC. Even if you do not intend to take any formal qualifications, you will learn the basics of computer hardware and software that should make the PC an essential tool in your everyday life. So put aside any misgivings you might have and convince yourself that learning how to use a PC is child's play compared with using your brain for the numerous complex processes you carry out every day.

People talk of computer systems, but what are they?

### What is a computer system?

A computer system comprises the hardware users interact with physically, e.g. the keyboard, the central processing unit (CPU) or the visual display unit (VDU), and the software that ultimately results in something being displayed on the screen or printed on paper. Microsoft Office is software, as are Windows 95, 98, ME, 2000 and XP.

If you are considering buying a computer, what should you look for? Often the jargon used is off-putting for the beginner and can make choosing the right one very difficult. However, for most of us who want to use a computer at home for producing letters, playing computer games or perhaps monitoring household or personal finances etc., the choice is relatively straightforward. The computer market is a highly competitive one and most reputable dealers will want to keep your custom for the future by guiding you in buying the machine most suited to your needs. Before you buy your computer ask yourself why you want it. This will help the salesperson understand your needs and decide which machine will suit these best.

First we will look at the components of a PC computer system. Here you will learn what the terms mean and the function of each component.

## A typical home or work computer system

Most people are really only interested in being able to use a computer, and neither need nor want to know what is inside. Although it is useful to know what the parts inside do, it is not necessary to know in detail about how they work. However, some knowledge may help you when selecting a computer for yourself. When the salesperson talks to you about disk capacity, memory or processor speed he or she is probably trying to establish what specification of machine you need. The language of computers can be confusing to the beginner and manufacturers often assume a level of knowledge that most of us don't have. This unit will at least give you a few pointers and leave you feeling a little more confident when listening to someone using the many names things are called. First are the parts you can see, or in other words the hardware (see Figure 1.1).

**Figure 1.1** *A basic computer system*

### The parts of a typical basic system

These are the visible parts of your computer:
- a central processing unit (CPU)
- a visual display unit (VDU)
- a keyboard
- a mouse
- a printer.

**Figure 1.2a** *A tower case*

## The central processing unit (CPU)

The 'main box' of the computer is often referred to as the CPU, but when people call this the CPU they are technically incorrect as the actual CPU is a single component (chip) inside the case. The CPU determines the speed of your machine. For example, a 2 GHz chip is going to be faster than one that is only 333 MHz; the bigger the number the faster the processor. The box that houses the CPU can either be tower or desktop shaped. The shape is purely a matter of personal preference and available space. Some manufacturers are now designing computer systems with a more modern design, but the tower case shown in Figure 1.2a is still the more common style. The desktop case shown in Figure 1.2b now tends to be less common.

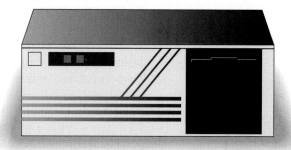

**Figure 1.2b** *A desktop case*

## The visual display unit (VDU)

The VDU, as its name suggests, allows you to see what is going on – it is like a TV screen. VDUs come in various sizes, usually between 15 inches and 17 inches. The screen size is measured (diagonally) according to the tube size and does not represent what you actually see, as the plastic case covers part of the tube (see Figure 1.3).

As technology advances different types of VDU become available. First, there are traditional screens, much like those of TV sets. If you can afford it, you can have a slimline LCD (liquid crystal display) monitor.

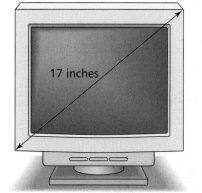

**Figure 1.3** *A standard monitor*

## The keyboard

The keyboard is an input device that allows the user to instruct the computer what to do. This can be inserting text, opening an application, formatting documents or using various keys known as function keys. Some of these function keys will be explained in detail later in the book. Figure 1.4 shows two styles of keyboard, both of which perform the same function.

## The mouse

The mouse (Figure 1.5) allows you to move around the screen. Once you have mastered the mouse you can scroll (or move) from one page to another, or select menu items or a piece of text. There are various styles and types of mouse, ranging from those that perform the basic movement functions, to more sophisticated ones that can be programmed to undertake a wide range of functions. For most of us the basic mouse is all that is usually needed.

**Figure 1.4a** *A standard keyboard*

**Figure 1.4b** *An ergonomic keyboard*

**Figure 1.5** *A standard two-button mouse*

## The printer

The printer is a device that allows you to transfer the text on your screen to paper, often referred to as hard copy. Printers come in a range of shapes and sizes. The most common types are the laser printers (see Figure 1.6a) and inkjet printers (see Figure 1.6b). Not surprisingly, the more sophisticated the printer the greater its cost. Unless you are looking for a truly professional finish or you need a very fast printer that will turn out many pages a minute, then the printers shown should be more than adequate for most people's needs.

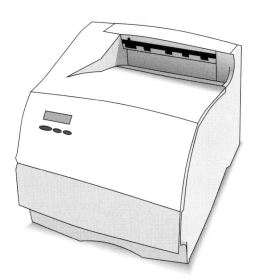

**Figure 1.6a** *A laser printer*

**Figure 1.6b** *An inkjet printer*

## Other devices

There are a variety of other devices to plug into your computer that allow you to do all sorts of exciting things. Scanners can add a whole new dimension to holiday snaps: you can scan all or part of a picture into a Word document, desktop publishing program or other application and send the results to friends or family.

**Figure 1.7** *An external modem*

More and more people are using the Internet and e-mail, which are covered later in this book. To access these you need a modem (which stands for modulator–demodulator (see Figure 1.7). Put very simply, a modem converts the computer's digital language into tones that can be transmitted down a cable (usually a telephone line), to be converted back into digital form at the other end. Some computers have a built-in modem while others need an external one, attached in much the same way as your mouse or keyboard.

Finally, you might want to listen to music while you are working, and for this you will need speakers. Most modern systems come complete with speakers.

## What's inside your computer?

To go into any great depth about the inside of your computer is beyond the scope of this book, but there are one or two basic terms that you may find useful when considering what is important when buying a new machine.

| What's inside your computer? | |
| --- | --- |
| RAM | This is a temporary storage area that your computer uses while it is running. Once you have switched your computer off, anything in RAM is lost. |
| BIOS | BIOS stands for basic input/output system. It is perhaps the most important program in your computer since it provides the instructions for running programs and also interprets keystroke actions on the keyboard. |
| Hard disk | This device allows your computer to store the work you have done permanently. Whereas RAM stores information temporarily (only while the computer is running), the hard disk stores your work until you delete it. |
| Cache | Cache is an area that your computer uses to store data that is used often. It is nowhere near as large as your main memory, but having cache memory allows your machine to work more efficiently. |
| Parallel port | This is a connector at the back of your machine that allows you to connect devices such as a printer. The parallel port has a 25-hole connector. |
| Serial port | This is another connector that allows you to connect other devices, such as a modem or mouse, to your computer. The serial port has a nine-hole connector. |
| USB | This stands for universal serial port and is a type of connector that can take the place of the more traditional connectors mentioned above. ▶▶ |

| PS/2 connector | The PS/2 is yet another type of connector that allows you to connect a mouse or keyboard to your machine. This connector has six holes and a round plug and socket. In many machines the mouse or keyboard is likely to have a PS/2 connector. |
| --- | --- |
| Motherboard | This is the main circuit board inside a computer housing the central processing unit, the BIOS chip, memory sockets, expansion slots and other components. |

## Storing data

Whether you are doing New CLAIT or simply using the computer for your own business or amusement, you will need to learn how to save your work. Indeed, knowing how to save and recover files is a formal requirement of New CLAIT.

Once you have typed a letter in a wordprocessing package, designed a spreadsheet or produced a poster using a desktop publishing package, you will want to keep your work to use later. To do this you save it. When you save work the application you are using creates a file and it is this file that is stored in one of the storage areas in your computer.

These files are generally saved on either a floppy disk (sometimes referred to as the 'A' drive). Also, nowadays more people have CD-writers and external Zip drives where data can be stored. Most computers have two or three disk drives. The first (and perhaps most important) is known as the hard drive. This storage disk is usually inside your machine and is often referred to as the 'C' drive.

You will learn how to save files later, but for now let's look at what is meant by the terms floppy and hard disks.

### The hard disk drive

A typical hard disk looks something like the one in Figure 1.8.

**Figure 1.8** *What a hard disk drive looks like inside the case*

Hard disk drives in modern computers can store extremely large quantities of information. You have probably heard of bytes, kilobytes, megabytes and gigabytes. In terms of drives or disks, these words describe the size of the storage capacity of a disk or the size of a file. For example, a floppy disk can contain 1.44 megabytes of data whereas a modern hard disk can store many gigabytes.

For example, when you type a character (e.g. 'a' or 'A' ) on your keyboard to display it on the computer screen, each character takes up one byte of storage area. In computer language, roughly 1000 bytes is known as a kilobyte. One million characters are known as a megabyte, and 1000 million characters is a gigabyte. If you have a hard disk that has the capacity to store 80 gigabytes, this is a very large storage capacity – 80,000 million bytes or characters. The figure below gives you a quick reference to size terms in computer speak. In decimal notation they are slightly larger.

| 1 byte | = | 1 character |
|---|---|---|
| 1 kilobyte | = | 1000 characters |
| 1 megabyte | = | 1 000 000 characters |
| 1 gigabyte | = | 1 000 000 000 characters |

### The floppy drive

The second type of drive we are going to look at is known as the floppy drive (or 'A' drive). It is normally accessed from the front of your machine, as shown in Figure 1.9.

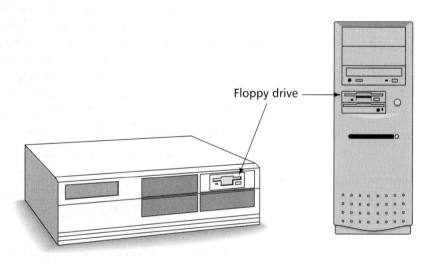

Floppy drive

**Figure 1.9** *Position of floppy drives*

The reason it is called the floppy drive dates back to the earlier computers when such drives used a 5.25-inch disk that was genuinely floppy. Most disks now are 3.5 inches square (Figure 1.10a) and the disk (while still floppy inside) is encased in a hard plastic cover. Although they seem sturdy (and they are certainly sturdier than the old floppies) they can nevertheless be damaged quite easily.

Always make sure you handle floppy disks with care, holding them by the label (Figure 1.10b). Never put them in hot places and make sure you keep them well away from magnets or anything containing a magnet such as a telephone handset.

**Figure 1.10a** *A 3.5 inch floppy disk*

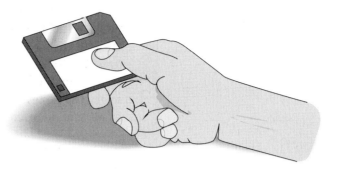

**Figure 1.10b** *Hold the disk like this*

To use the disk put it into the floppy drive at the front of your machine. Push the disk until you hear the click indicating it is in place.

Being able to save your data is one of the most important skills you need to know when starting to learn how to use a computer. It is also one required for New CLAIT and is covered later in this book.

## Switching on your computer

The first assessment objective for New CLAIT is to demonstrate your ability to switch a computer on.

First check that all the plugs attached to your machine are connected to the mains power supply. The number of plugs you have will depend largely on how many devices you have attached. On the system shown in Figure 1.1 on page 5 you will notice that there is the computer itself (which looks like a metal box), a monitor and a keyboard. This basic system is likely to have two normal 13-amp plugs, one for the computer and one for the monitor. Most systems also have a printer and often a scanner. The computer, monitor and printer are likely to have a switch with a symbol that looks something like this: ⏻

Make sure each plug is connected to the mains and then switch the mains socket to the on position. Then, and only then, should you switch on the individual switches for your computer and its devices. Normally the sequence would be:

- monitor first
- printer and other devices second
- computer box last.

Usually a small green light will show indicating that the power supply is on for each device.

### Boot-up

Once the switch on the main computer is pressed the machine will go through a boot-up (or start-up) sequence. You do not need to know what is happening, but in simple terms when you switch on the power your machine will look for its instructions relating to which system files and programs should be loaded.

*New CLAIT*

New CLAIT

## Windows as an operating system

Windows is an operating system. Operating systems manage the functions of your computer. You will only need to know the basic components and their functions. Being able to navigate around an operating system is a New CLAIT requirement. Windows 95, 98, 2000 or XP are all different versions of one type of operating system. There are many other operating systems such as Linux, Novell, Unix and Windows NT, but for now we are only concerned with Windows. In the following sections you will learn about the windows environment, the desktop, icons, command buttons, menus, the cursor and toolbars.

# The Windows environment

New CLAIT

## Logging on and using passwords

Maintaining the integrity of your data is important and should be taken seriously, whether it is to protect data at home or at work. Most companies have networks that require staff to login before they can use their computer. Even stand-alone computers (i.e. those not connected to a network) have facilities enabling you to set up user names and passwords to prevent unauthorised access to files. If you are intending to study for the New CLAIT qualification, you will be required to appreciate the need for security in the production of documents and the risks and consequences of unauthorised access to computers and networks. You will also need to understand simple login procedures and how to change a password, and be aware of good practice in selecting passwords. All this may seem complicated, but it is really quite straightforward.

Lets take it step by step; first the login procedure. The process of login requires two inputs; a user name (i.e. what you call yourself) and a password. On your home computer the user name will almost certainly be the one given to the software when it was first installed. In most Windows systems you can add or change the user name. If you have ever used e-mail you will already be familiar with the need to provide a user name and a password before you can access your mail. Passwords, like user names, can be changed but only by the person with access to the system information.

The version of Windows you are using will determine whether you are required to login or not. For example, if you are using Windows 98, after your computer has booted up a login dialogue box may appear. Providing this has not been set-up, pressing the Esc button will allow you to bypass the login procedure. If you are using Windows 2000 (which is built on network technology) you must login. After starting your computer you will be shown a dialogue box similar to Figure 1.11 (see opposite). The user name will, in most cases, already appear in the user name box. If you are working on a network the user name will probably show the last person who logged onto that computer. If this is the case then you need to simply overtype your own user name and press the Tab key on the keyboard to enter the password box.

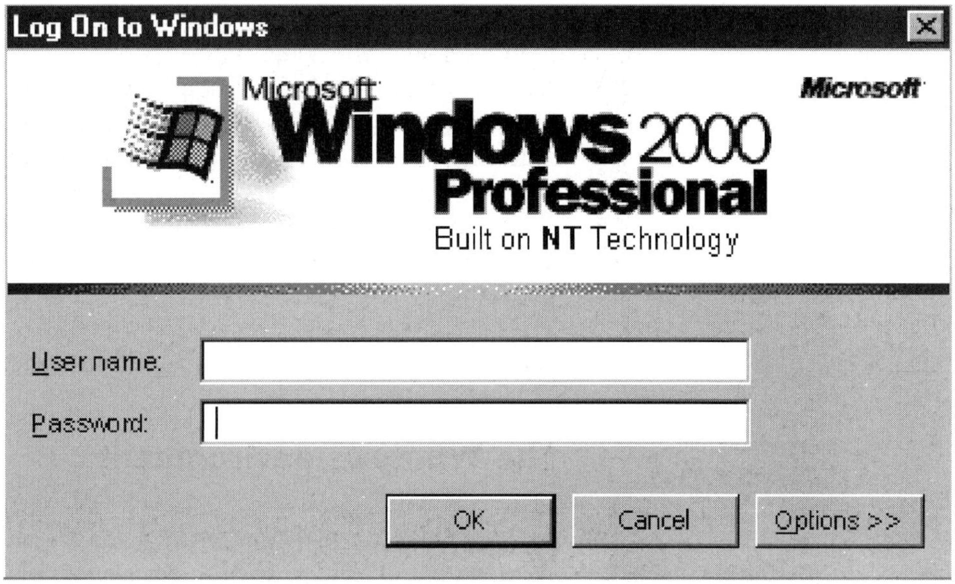

**Log On to Windows** ☒

**Microsoft**
**Windows** 2000
**Professional**
Built on **NT** Technology

*Microsoft*

Username: [                    ]

Password: [|                   ]

[ OK ]  [ Cancel ]  [ Options >> ]

**Figure 1.11** *Log on to Windows*

Passwords are without doubt the most important part of your security. In many instances it may be relatively easy to guess a user name, but it is essential that your password is known only to you and difficult to guess by other non-authorised persons. When you are deciding on a password to use there are a number of do's and don'ts that should be followed.

**Don't:**
- use names such as your children's, spouse's or friends' names
- use personal details such as a birthdates
- use number sequences like 12345
- write your password down in your diary or on the desk notepad
- tell anyone else your password
- type in your password when someone is looking over your shoulder.

**Do:**
- commit your password to memory
- use a password that is personal to you but is unknown to anyone else
- change your password immediately if you think it has been compromised
- change your password, preferably every three or four months.

## Changing your password

The version of Windows you are using, and also whether you are operating a stand-alone computer or working on a network, will determine how you change a password and what the password protects. Systems security is really beyond the scope of this book but for New CLAIT you are required to be able to change a password.

Passwords can be used to protect information at different levels. The next section looks at passwords at the start-up stage and also passwords used with a screen saver.

To change the password in Windows 2000 is very straightforward. First you need to ensure that the user login name for the password you want to change is the correct one and then, using Ctrl+Alt+Del and selecting the Change Password… option, type in the current password and then type in the new one. Let's try it.

## Try it out

**Press** Start on the bottom left of the screen.

**Select** Settings.

**Select** Control Panel.

A window similar to that shown in Figure 1.12 will appear.

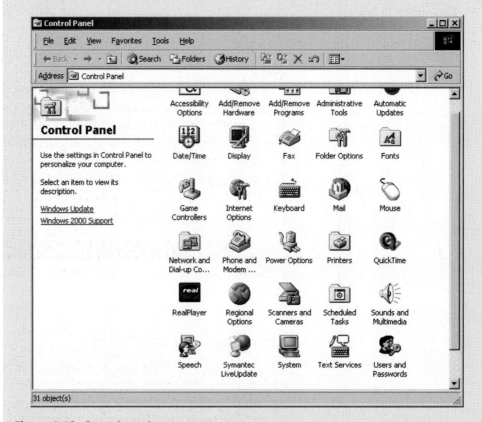

**Figure 1.12** *Control panel*

**Double-click** on the icon named Users and Passwords (Figure 1.13).

**Figure 1.13** *Enlarged control panel*

The dialogue box shown in Figure 1.14 will appear.

Double-click on Users and Passwords

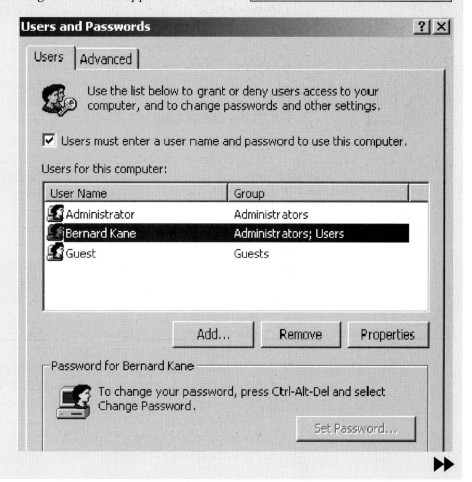

**Figure 1.14** *Users and Passwords*

Here you have the option of either creating a new user and setting the new user's password or, if you are already the user, changing your current password.

**Press** Ctrl+Alt+Del and select Change Password….

Check that the user name is correct.

**Type** in your old password.

**Type** in the new password.

**Type** in confirmation of the new password.

**Press** OK.

Another way of protecting your data is to make the screen saver password protected. Often the time you need protection is when you have been working on your machine and have left it to go and do something else while it is still switched on. After a set period (which you can set yourself) the screen saver will activate. The next time the keyboard is touched the screen saver will deactivate and you can continue working. If the screen saver is password protected you cannot continue to work unless the appropriate password is entered. However, this should be used with caution. If you forget the password it is not easy to regain control of your machine.

To set the screen saver password you will need to return to the control panel and select the icon called Display. Having selected the Screen Saver tab ensure the password-protected check box is enabled.

## The desktop

If you are new to Windows it is worth spending a little time getting to know the screen that is shown when the computer has finished its start-up sequence. This is known as the desktop and in many ways you can compare it with your normal desktop at home where you might have a place for pens or a tray for letters, perhaps even a rubber for rubbing out your mistakes. Another way is to consider the desktop as a main railway station. It can be seen as the starting point for all the places to which you might go. It has signposts showing where to go depending on what you want to do.

After starting your computer, the desktop is the first screen you will see. How this appears depends on how your computer is set-up and also the version of Windows being used. However, it will certainly be very similar to the screen shown in Figure 1.15 (see opposite).

On the desktop there will be a number of signposts known as shortcuts that are automatically loaded by Windows; examples are My Computer, My Documents and the Recycle Bin. At the bottom of the screen is a taskbar. This displays any windows or applications you have open and also has other icons (small pictures) that allow you to navigate around Windows. On the right of this bar are other icons such as a clock, volume control and possibly one showing the language in use or a mouse shortcut that allows you to change the way the mouse behaves. Again the taskbar will vary depending on how the computer is set up and all these icons can be changed. In the left-hand corner is a button named 'Start'.

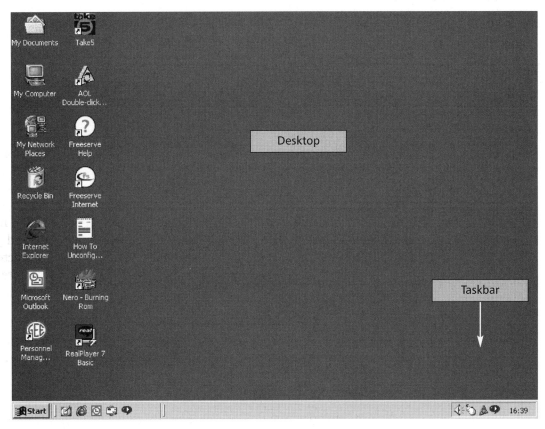

**Figure 1.15** *A typical Windows desktop*

If MS Office has been installed for you, it is likely that the Office toolbar will also be displayed on the desktop. We will be looking at toolbars a little later on, but for now it is sufficient to know that the icons on this bar allow you to access all the programs within Office.

### Shortcuts

Shortcut icons can be placed on the desktop at any time. They allow quick access to any applications or files you use regularly. Placing shortcuts on the desktop is not a New CLAIT requirement and you will not be studying this in any detail, but there is no doubt that shortcuts can be useful and if you want to place one on the screen to access a favourite program or file, guidance can be found in the help offered by Microsoft.

**Try it out**

*Finding help to add shortcuts to your desktop*

**Press** Start.

**Select** Help.

**Select** Index.

In the box saying 'Type in the keyword to find:'

**Type** Shortcuts.

All the options for shortcuts will be shown in the box immediately below.

**Double-click** with the left mouse button on 'adding to desktop'.

For now, use the Start button or Office's shortcut toolbar to locate the program(s) you want to work with. By pressing the Start button on the left of the screen, a menu list will appear. From this list you can access Program, Documents, or Help. Other shortcuts are also available from the Start button, some of which will be covered as you go through the book.

Alternatively, you can press the Start key on the keyboard.

## What are windows?

A *window* is a moveable and resizable area that contains information about the functions it can carry out. It is also an area where you, the user, can interact with the particular application in use.

The generic term 'window' should not be confused with Windows when the latter term is used in connection with operating systems such as Windows 98 or Windows 2000. An operating system runs the computer and controls both program software and the hardware attached to your computer (for example, the printer, mouse or modem).

Now let's have a look at a window.

**Try it out**

**Press** Start by placing the cursor over the button and clicking with the left-hand mouse button. Go to Programs by sliding the cursor up the menu list and clicking on Programs with the left-hand mouse button.

**Move** the cursor across to the next list (this is usually best achieved by sliding the pointer across from the main start list to the secondary list that appears when your pointer is over Programs).

**Select** Accessories. This will produce yet another list of options.

**Select** Notepad (Figure 1.16).

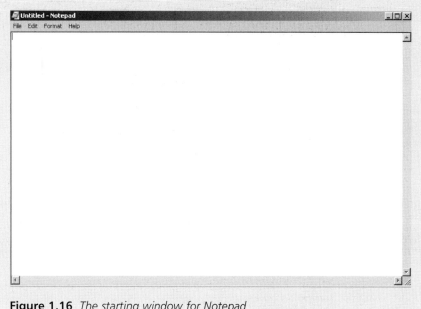

**Figure 1.16** *The starting window for Notepad*

Notepad is a simple text editor or, if you like, wordprocessor. Although it is not as sophisticated as Microsoft Word it can be used in a very similar way.

The names (e.g. File, Edit, Format) on the menu bar at the top of the window provide a *drop-down menu* list that allows you to start new documents, open existing ones, edit documents and even set margins and orientation in the Page Set-up... option under the File menu (Figure 1.17).

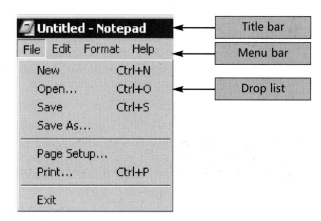

**Figure 1.17** *A drop-down menu in Notepad*

Here you are looking at it as simply another window that can be moved, sized and generally manipulated. At the top of the window in blue (if the default settings have not been changed) is the *title bar*. This tells you the name of the file and application (by default the filename is 'Untitled'). One of the main benefits of windows is the ability to have several windows open at the same time. You can move information from one window to another easily and view information in a number of different applications simultaneously. In Figure 1.18 you can see three windows.

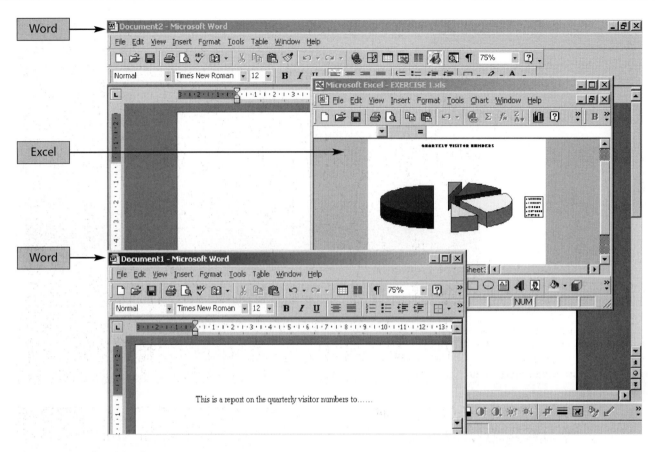

**Figure 1.18** *Three simultaneous windows*

Two of the windows in Figure 1.18 are Word windows and one is for Excel. The number of windows you can open at any one time depends largely on your computer's specification. Broadly speaking, the more memory available on your system the greater the number of open windows it can deal with. The windows do not have to be in view at the same time. If you have three applications open you can switch between them by pressing the Alt and Tab keys on your keyboard. The Alt key is pressed first and then the Tab key (often written 'Alt+Tab').

Alternatively if you look at the bottom of your screen, on the taskbar, you can see which programs are open. In Figure 1.19 (opposite) notice that Excel and Access are both open.

By clicking on its button, a program becomes active and will be placed in front of any others which are also open. This also applies if you have one program open but several files for the same program in use. The taskbar then shows you which files are open and in use.

## Moving windows

A window can be moved around the screen by placing the cursor on the title bar, clicking and holding down the left-hand mouse button then *dragging* the window around the main screen area. This window will remain where it is when the button is released.

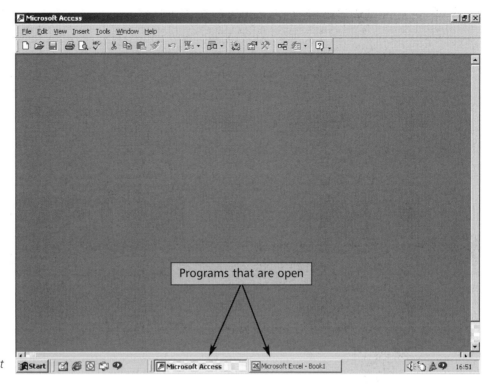

Programs that are open

**Figure 1.19** *The lower taskbar indicates that two programs are open, but only one is active at present*

### Try it out

**Move** the mouse pointer until it is over the title bar.

**Press** the left-hand mouse button.

**Hold** the left-hand mouse button down.

**Drag** the window a few centimetres to the right and then to the left.

## Resizing windows

In a similar way to moving the whole window, you can resize your window by placing the cursor over one edge of the window. The cursor will change shape to a double-headed arrow. Using the mouse button, the window can be resized by dragging left or right, up or down.

### Try it out

**Move** the cursor over to the right-hand edge of the window.

**Click** and hold down the left-hand mouse button.

**Drag** the window in and out.

### MOUSE TIP

You will know when the cursor is in the correct position because the pointer will change from an 'I' to a double-headed arrow ⟷.

Note that although you have used only one edge of the box you can also move the top, bottom and left-hand edge of the window.

### Scroll bars

*Scroll bars* are used when text (or other data) you are working on fills an area that cannot be viewed on the screen all at once. If you open Notepad, notice how the scroll bars are 'greyed out'. When something is 'greyed out' (as opposed to black) it means the function is *disabled*. If you think about it, this makes sense because the work area contains no information so there is nothing to scroll.

**Try it out**

**Move** the mouse pointer so that it is in the white working area.

**Press** the left-hand mouse button in the work area.

**Type** some letters across the screen until they disappear off the right-hand edge of the screen. As the letters disappear the scroll bar at the bottom of the screen becomes *enabled*.

**Click** on the scroll bar at the bottom of the window with the left-hand mouse button and, with the button still held down, drag the scroll bar left and right to see any text not visible in the window.

## Using the mouse

Most applications offer a variety of ways to complete a task. You will see this as you go through Unit 2 on Word. Many people find using a mouse for the first time quite difficult but, like learning most new skills, it is easily mastered with a little practice. If you are a touch typist and are worried about not being able to use the keyboard for the majority of your tasks, Microsoft Office provides keyboard shortcuts for nearly everything you can do with a mouse. A list of shortcuts is included in Appendix 2.

Most mice have two buttons, but there are many different types. Some have three buttons and others have two buttons with a wheel for scrolling. For now only the standard two-button mouse will be used. Generally speaking the left-hand mouse button is used to perform an action such as pressing one of the toolbar icons (e.g. underlining), printing or menu selection. You can also press the left-hand mouse button and hold it down to highlight text in order to change its format or drag it to a different location. You have already had some experience of this when you changed the size of the window earlier. The right-hand mouse button normally produces a pop-up menu with choices of what actions are available for you to perform.

## Opening programs

**New CLAIT**

Being able to load or open an application such as Word is an assessment objective for New CLAIT.

Programs can be opened by using either the Start button or the Microsoft Office shortcut toolbar:

**Try it out**

Start by opening Microsoft Word.

**Press** the Start button and a menu list will appear (Figure 1.20).

**Click** Programs and when the second menu list appears,

**Select** Microsoft Word (Figure 1.21).

**Figure 1.20** *The first menu, obtained by pressing Start*

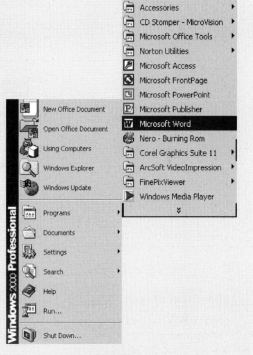

**Figure 1.21** *The secondary menu, obtained via Programs*

**MOUSE TIP**

Slide the cursor up the first menu and then directly across from Programs to the secondary list. If you move out of the blue line, the secondary list will either change to one of the other selection lists or disappear from view.

The list you see may be slightly different from that shown in Figure 1.21 as it will depend on the programs that have been installed onto your hard disk. You can open any of the programs shown on the list under Programs by simply placing the mouse over the program name and pressing the left-hand mouse button.

## Accessing help in Windows

Any good software program will offer you on-line help through its menu system. Some help systems are better than others but Microsoft has invested a substantial amount of effort in trying to ensure that both the experienced and the not so experienced user can get useful help on all aspects of their software. You can access help on Windows by pressing the Start button and then selecting Help.

**Try it out**

**Press** the Start button.

**Select** Help.

In the dialogue window at the top are four tabs. One tab will display the Contents of the complete Help file by broad topic. The Index tab allows you to be more specific by typing in a word related to the area you are interested in (Figure 1.22). The Search tab is similar, but here you type any word and the program will find topics that contain that word. If you find that you use a particular help topic on a regular basis you can add it to the box under the Favourites tab.

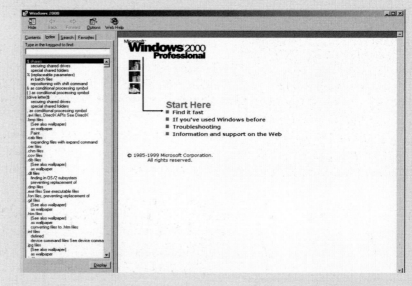

**Figure 1.22** *The Help dialogue window*

## Using help in programs

In the above example you were looking at help relating specifically to Windows. Microsoft also provides on-line help for all its software; it all works in fundamentally the same way, whatever the application.

For example, in Word the program's menu bar is an option named Help. If you click on the word Help it will display a drop-down menu list similar to that shown in Figure 1.23.

Help

[?] Microsoft Word Help    F1

Show the Office Assistant

[?] What's This?    Shift+F1

Office on the Web

WordPerfect Help...

Detect and Repair...

About Microsoft Word

**Figure 1.23** *A drop-down help menu*

Selecting the option labelled 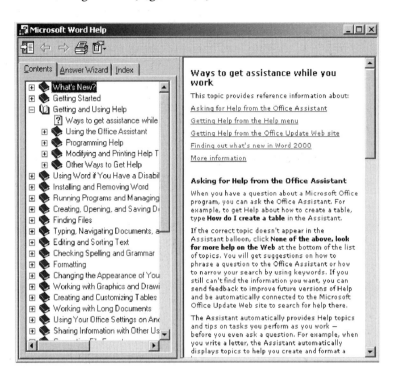 will bring up another dialogue box (Figure 1.24):

**Figure 1.24** *A help dialogue box*

Highlighting the content headings on the left by clicking on each one will produce further contents that are available to you in that area of help. The Answer Wizard lets you type a question in plain English. The system then looks at the words in your question and finds all the areas of help. Some may be appropriate, while others may not.

Alternatively, if you use the Index tab you will see the dialogue box shown in Figure 1.25. Here you can type in a word that describes the subject area in which you are interested.

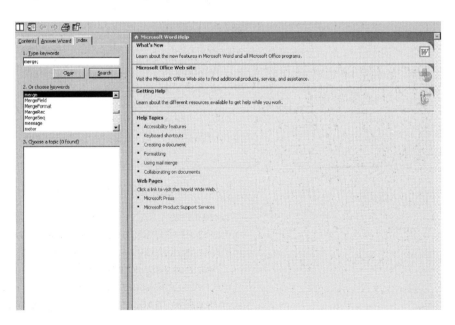

**Figure 1.25** *Accessing help using the Index tab*

After typing in the search word, Help will locate all relevant topics and list them in the bottom part of the dialogue box. On the right-hand side you will be given further options from which to select.

**Step 1**
Type word to search for or scroll list and select keyword

**Step 2**
Select topic from choices provided by keyword

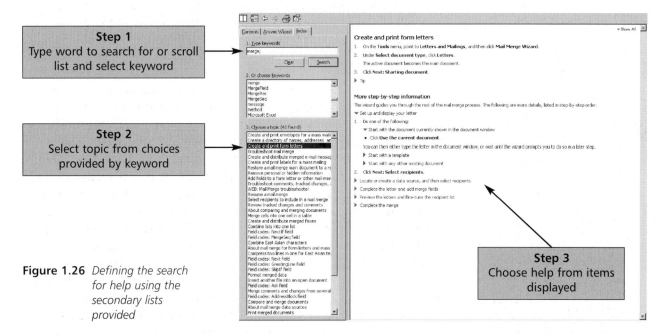

**Step 3**
Choose help from items displayed

**Figure 1.26** *Defining the search for help using the secondary lists provided*

Having completed the sequence the program will provide detailed help on the topic selected.

## Managing files

As you have already learnt (see page 9, Storing data), data is held on files, either on the hard disk or, when files need to be portable, on floppy disks. For New CLAIT you will be required, through a series of assessment objectives, to understand:

- how to locate data and files using the features of the system software
- generic document management terms and operations
- how to navigate filing systems from within generic open/save dialogues
- the need to save documents on a regular basis and the reasons for saving with a new filename
- how to delete a document using the chosen software or system software.

Don't worry at this stage about the meaning of these requirements as each element will be reviewed in detail through the next part of this unit.

File management is a subject in its own right and only the basics are covered at this stage. However, it is important to know how to create *folders* and this will help you to manage the data (or files) created.

Think of data as pieces of paper; how would you store them if you were not using a computer? You would probably use a filing cabinet like the one shown in Figure 1.27 (opposite).

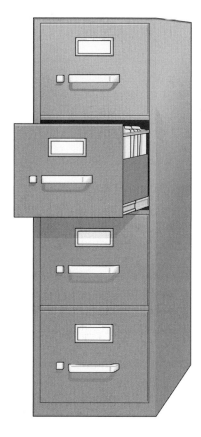

**Figure 1.27** *A traditional filing cabinet*

## Folders

A folder in computer terms is similar to one you would find in the filing cabinet shown in Figure 1.27. It is an area set aside for the storage of files (or documents created on your computer).

Think of the cabinet in terms of the hard disk of your computer. A real cabinet would have a number of drawers that correspond, in this analogy, to folders. Each draw has hanging containers to store files and letters. These hanging containers would represent sub-folders. The process is hierarchical, starting with the cabinet (your hard disk), then the drawer (a main folder), then a hanging folder that is a sub-category of the main folder (a sub-folder). Each hanging folder may have further folders inside and these would relate to sub-folders of the sub-folder. It may be easier to look at this in a diagram, still using the filing cabinet as the analogy for the hard disk drive. This is shown in Figure 1.28.

Both systems in Figure 1.28 show a hierarchical structure. Insurance as the main folder has two sub-folders called House and Contents. The Contents folder has two sub-sub-folders called China and Crystal. Remember that these folders are containers; they are not data. The data or files are placed into these containers. For the sake of argument, say you had an accident with a china bowl and wrote a letter to the insurance company. The letter when saved could be called Bowl_1. The letter Bowl_1 is the Word document file and it would be placed in the folder called China. To recover the letter in a manual system you would open the drawer called Insurance, pull out the folder called Contents and from that folder take out the third folder called China where the letter would be found. The principle is exactly the same when files are stored electronically.

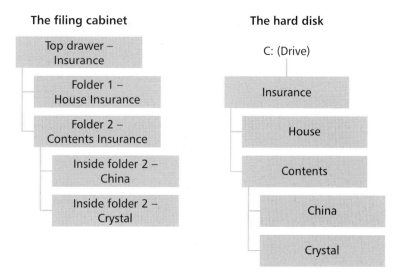

**Figure 1.28** *An analogy between normal and computer data storage*

Most Windows operating systems provide an application called Windows Explorer. Windows Explorer allows you to view the folder structure and add to it.

**Try it out**

Press the Start button.

Select Programs from the list.

Click Windows Explorer (sometimes kept under Accessories).

Select and click on My Computer from folder Search task pane to the left of the window.

Your screen will probably look a little different to the one shown in Figure 1.29 but will be very similar.

Depending on the version of Windows being used, the left-hand side will show the hierarchy of folders with the structure of the folders highlighted on the right. In Figure 1.29 My Computer is highlighted in the left pane and four disk drives and an icon saying Control Panel are shown in the right pane. As the capacity of hard disk drives increases, even modern operating systems find it difficult to cope with such vast areas and therefore it is sometimes necessary to split a disk into Partitions. Partitions are well beyond the scope of this book so it is only necessary to know that large disks often have more than one partition.

Each disk or partition is given a drive letter. In Figure 1.29 you can see we have an A Disk, a C Disk, a D Disk and an E Disk, where A is the floppy drive and D is the CD drive. In this case, C is the first hard disk and E is the second hard disk, although physically both these are on one disk. Confusing? Well don't worry about it at this stage. The chances are that your main drive will be the C drive. In this drive (or whichever is your main hard drive) you will find a folder called My Documents, and it is this folder that will be the main folder of your file structure.

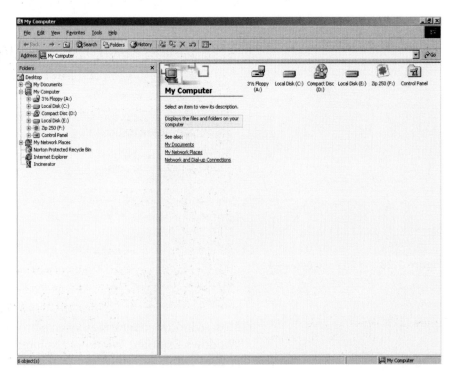

**Figure 1.29** *Windows showing file storage 'map'*

Since you are in the driving seat, you determine the structure you want. This book can give you guidance on how you might think about building a structure for your folders, but at the end of the day this is very much a matter of personal preference and what you find easiest to understand. However, before looking at building a structure it might be useful to look at the various types of files you might want to store. Again, this can only be an overview of the most common types, but it will give you some thoughts on how to construct your own filing system.

## File types and formats

All files have identifiers known as *file extensions* that distinguish their file type. Extensions come at the end of a filename separated by a full-stop, for instance 'MyLetter.doc'. Although you do not need to know what the file extensions of individual files are it can be useful in helping you to locate a file (or group of files) of a particular type or program. Modern search facilities make it much easier than it used to be to find a file. The list of file types is virtually endless but some standard ones used in the Office suite are shown in Table 1.1.

When you save a file for the first time you will be given the opportunity of selecting the default format for the application in use or choosing a different format. If, for instance, you are sending a letter electronically to a friend who you know only has WordPerfect (another wordprocessing package), Office allows you to save the work as a WordPerfect file.

In the Save As dialogue box under 'Save as type' there is an arrow to the right of the box, indicating that other selections are available. By clicking on the arrow and scrolling through the list you can select the file format you want (see Figure 1.30).

**Table 1.1** *Some commonly encountered file extensions*

| Application | File extension |
| --- | --- |
| Word | .doc |
| Access | .mdb |
| Excel | .xls |
| Powerpoint | .ppt |
| Publisher | .pub |
| Paint | .bmp |
| Outlook | .pst |
| Notebook | .txt |
| Wordpad | .rtf |

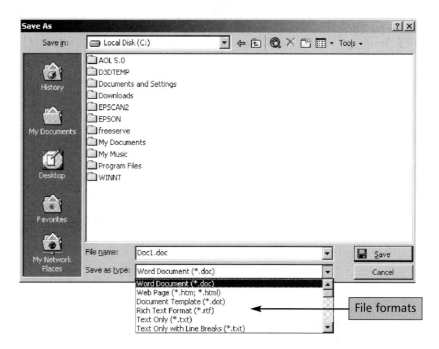

**Figure 1.30** *Selecting a file format other than the default selection*

What does all this mean? Perhaps the easiest way to start is by explaining the reasons for wanting to use different formats. You have just looked at one example, where a friend might have a different wordprocessing application to the one you use. However, more often you simply will not know what software the recipient is using. As a general rule most modern generic software packages can either read each other's formats or convert them into a form that can be read. The files that you will probably use most are various text formats. They are likely to be predominantly of three types:

- Word files
- Rich Text Format files
- text files.

## Word files

When you save a document in Word the application will automatically give it the extension '.doc'. When you press the Save button on the menu or toolbar you will see the dialogue box in Figure 1.31.

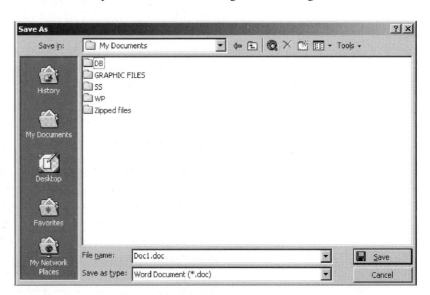

**Figure 1.31** *The Save As dialogue box in Word*

At the bottom of the box there is another box with a selection list, known as a *combo box*, showing the type of file that will be saved. In the example above this is a Word document (*.doc). Once you have saved your document you won't necessarily see the extension in Explorer or My Computer because Word is friendly enough to tell you that it is a Word document in the column headed 'Type'. In Windows 95, 98 and 2000, which use Windows Explorer, you can opt to see the file extension, but this is an option you must enable (or switch on) in the folder options under the Tools menu item.

## Rich Text Format files

Even if you are using the Microsoft Office suite of applications it does not follow that the people to whom you wish to send files have the same software. Rich Text Format files (.rtf) will save your work keeping the formatting, and enabling users of different programs to open and read or amend the document keeping the format you created in the original file.

### Text files

Saving your work as text files means that users of other programs will be able to open them but none of the formatting (such as bold, underlining and so on) will be saved with the file.

In Figure 1.32 you can see the various extensions of the saved text files.

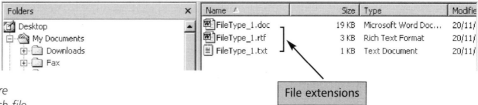

**Figure 1.32** *File extensions are appended to each file*

### Other application formats

In a similar way (with the exception of Access which operates slightly differently) other Office applications offer you a good choice of file formats in which to save work. For example, in Excel you can save an Excel spreadsheet in Lotus 1–2–3 format, in Microsoft Publisher (a desktop publishing package) or in Word (.doc) format, and so on.

The method is exactly the same as in Word. The only exception to this is Access where instead of saving the whole database in another file format you can save individual parts of the database (such as tables, queries or reports) in other formats.

### How much damage can I do?

The first question many people ask when they start to use a computer is 'How much damage can I do if I get it wrong?'. The simple answer to this is 'Not a lot'. It is true, you can cause yourself hours of frustration if you accidentally delete certain files, particularly those associated with programs, but generally speaking this usually means you simply have to re-install the software.

The secret is that if you are not sure, ask someone before deleting a file. Providing you have set-up your folders for your own work properly you will rarely, if ever, need to access files in other folders relating to programs.

### Restoring deleted files

Windows recognises that occasionally people make mistakes. When asked to delete a file it will therefore always give you a warning that you are about to delete a file (Figure 1.33).

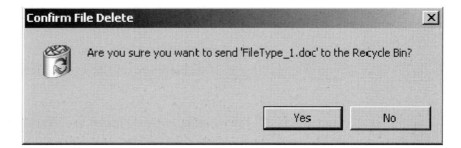

**Figure 1.33** *The software will normally ask you to confirm the deletion of a file*

If you reply 'Yes' the file will be sent to the Recycle Bin, which is where Windows temporarily stores all the files that you have deleted. If at some later stage you decide that you did not want to delete the file, it can be restored from the Recycle Bin. However, once the Recycle Bin has been emptied you can no longer recover the file. Windows has a shortcut for the Recycle Bin on the desktop that looks like this: If you are using Windows 98 the shortcut will look more like a rectangular waste-paper bin.

## Try it out

### Restoring a file

In this exercise you will:

- write a file in Notepad
- save it to the hard disk
- delete the file
- restore the file
- delete the file and empty the Recycle Bin.

**Press** Start.

**Select** Programs.

**Select** Accessories.

**Select** Notepad.

**Click** in the working space of Notepad and type the following:

'This is a practice exercise.'

**Select** File on the menu bar.

**Select** Save.

Check that the Save in: box shows the My Documents folder.

**Type** 'Ex1' in the box called 'File name:'.

**Click** the Save command button.

**Select** File on the menu bar.

**Select** Exit.

**Double-click** on the My Documents icon on the desktop.

**Press** the right-hand mouse button on the file Ex1.

**Select** Delete. When asked if you are sure you want to delete:

**Click** Yes.

**Double-click** on the Recycle Bin on the desktop.

**Select** Ex1.

**Select** Restore under the file menu.

▶▶

> **Double-click** the My Documents icon on the desktop and you will see that your file has been restored.
>
> Repeat this exercise up to where the file is in the Recycle Bin, but this time instead of restoring the file,
>
> **Click** on the file menu.
>
> **Click** Empty Recycle Bin. Your file has now been permanently deleted.

## Setting up your filing structure

Whether you are setting up a structure to save your files on a floppy or hard disk, the principle is the same. The key is to name the folder in your structure in such a way that the whole thing means something to you and represents the way in which you want to work and access your files.

If you were to open a new Word document and press the Save icon or use the Save or Save As... under the File menu option, the Save dialogue box automatically saves the file in the My Documents folder, as shown in Figure 1.34.

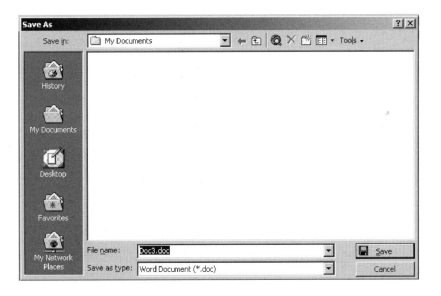

**Figure 1.34** *By default the programs will save files in the My Documents folder*

Technically there is nothing wrong in doing this, but let us say that you have been saving your work in the My Documents folder for several months; it is likely that you will have several hundred files to look through every time you need to find one. Also over a period of time you may well have been using other applications which will make searching for a particular Word document even harder.

How you eventually decide to keep track of your files is very much a matter of personal preference, but there must be some logic to the process. Look at Figure 1.35 (overleaf).

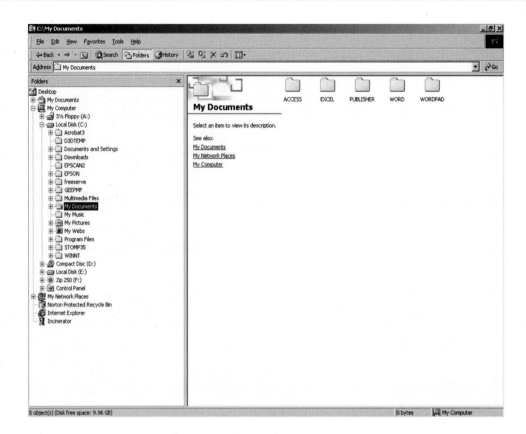

**Figure 1.35** *Example of a structure for storing files*

See how the structure on the right has been built with a folder for each application. Now think back to the section on saving your work and how there were individual sub-folders for subjects within the main folder. In this case the C drive has been substituted to show the actual structure under My Documents.

In the next Try it out exercise you are going to build a simple file structure in the My Documents folder on the C drive.

## Try it out

**Open** Windows Explorer.

**Click** on My Documents.

**Select** File, New, Folder from the menu bar.

When the new folder is displayed on the right-hand side of the Explorer dialogue box, overtype the highlighted words New Folder with Word. By just typing over words highlighted in blue, the text will be replaced.

**Highlight** My Documents again.

**Select** File, New, Folder.

When the next New Folder is displayed name it Excel.

Do this twice more. Call the next two folders Access and Publisher.

Your structure should now look something like the one in Figure 1.36.

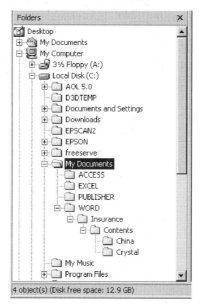

**Figure 1.36** *Creating a file structure using Windows Explorer*

Depending on which units you choose to do for New CLAIT you may wish to create folders for those units before continuing with the relevant units in this book.

## Using the files on your CD

If you have a CD writer on your computer you can store up to 650 MB of data on a CD and save valuable space on your hard disk. You may remember that with floppy disks you can only store up to 1.44 MB of data so using a CD gives you much more flexibility. Teaching you how to use a CD writer is beyond the scope of this book but you will need to know how to copy files from the CD accompanying this book and use them as you work through the exercises. Fundamentally, copying and using the files on the CD is as easy as using files on you hard or floppy disk but with one very important difference. When files are written to a CD their property is changed to 'read only': in other words you can look at these files but you cannot save any changes you may make to them unless you either save the file using the menu's Save As... option or alternatively copy the files to your hard or floppy disk and then change the 'read-only' property. Have a look at Figure 1.37.

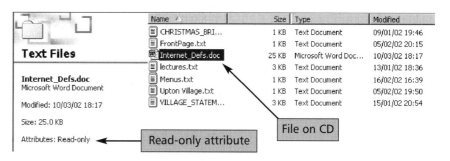

**Figure 1.37** *File with read-only attribute*

You can see that this file has a read-only attribute. To change this so that you can amend and save any changes to the file you will need to copy it to an appropriate directory and change the attribute.

## Try it out

Following the same procedures as you did when setting up your directory structure, add a new folder to your structure and call it 'CD Exercise Files'.

With your CD in the CD drive:

**Double-click** on the CD to see the files and folders.

**Select** all the folders.

**Drag** the folders (together with their files) across to the CD Exercise Files folder on your hard or floppy drive.

Your files will now have been copied to the new folder.

To change the attribute on a file:

**Right-click** on the file you wish to change.

**Select** 'Properties'.

**Uncheck** the '✓' in the read-only box.

**Press** OK.

You can now open any of the exercise files, modify them and save your changes.

### KEYBOARD TIP

To select all folders, click on the first folder to highlight it, then press the Shift key down and, while it is still pressed, click on the last folder to be selected. All folders will then be highlighted and can be copied or dragged to the new destination folder. To drag the files, simply click or hold down the left-hand mouse button and, while it is still held, drag the files, using the cursor to direct to the right destination.

## Entering and editing text, numbers and symbols into a document

### Entering text, numbers and symbols into a document

As part of the core unit for New CLAIT you will be expected to know how to undertake certain basic tasks associated with the creation of documents such as entering text, numbers and symbols. You will also be required to edit an existing document. This section covers some basic instructions for creating and editing a document. Both Notepad and WordPad are basic text editors, but WordPad is more sophisticated than Notepad and will be used in this section of the unit.

To open WordPad click on the Start button in the bottom left of the Windows screen:

**Start**

Click on the Programs menu item and from the secondary list click on Accessories, then select the WordPad option. Word Pad will open and will look similar to Figure 1.38. At the moment, don't worry about the various toolbars and function buttons.

When WordPad is opened with a new document you will notice a flashing 'I' at the top of the document. This is known as the cursor and is also the insertion point, indicating that WordPad is ready for you to start typing. Now try typing in some text.

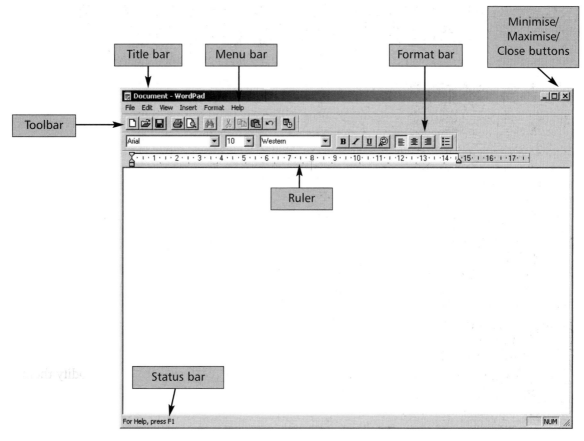

**Figure 1.38** *WordPad: a basic text editor*

## Try it out

**Open** WordPad.

**Type** in the following text:

'Text can be inserted into a document using the keys on a computer keyboard. Text can be typed in any of the fonts that have been installed onto the computer.'

**Save** the file as MyText.rtf using the same method as you used to save the Notepad Ex1 on page 32.

**Close** the file, by clicking on File and the Exit on the main menu bar.

### GENERAL TIP

To save the file select 'Save' from the File menu option. Locate the folder into which the file is to be saved. Type 'Mytext' in the Filename: box and press the OK button.

## Using the mouse and pointer

As you learnt earlier in the unit, there are a number of different styles of mouse from the very basic with a left-hand and right-hand button to those with three buttons and still others with a scroll wheel. In addition, there are roller-ball mice, where the user rolls the ball at the top of the mouse rather than moving the mouse itself. The more sophisticated the mouse the larger the range of functions it provides. For most users, however, a simple two-button mouse is more than adequate. Underneath the mouse (except infrared mice, which operate on an infrared signal) there is a ball which, as you will already have found, allows the pointer on the screen to be moved. By clicking on the document with the left-hand button the cursor is moved to that position. In the previous exercise you saw that when a new document is created the cursor is positioned at the top of the document page. Moving the mouse will move the pointer in sync with the mouse movement. By clicking the left-hand mouse button the cursor is repositioned to the location of the pointer. Have a look at Figure 1.39.

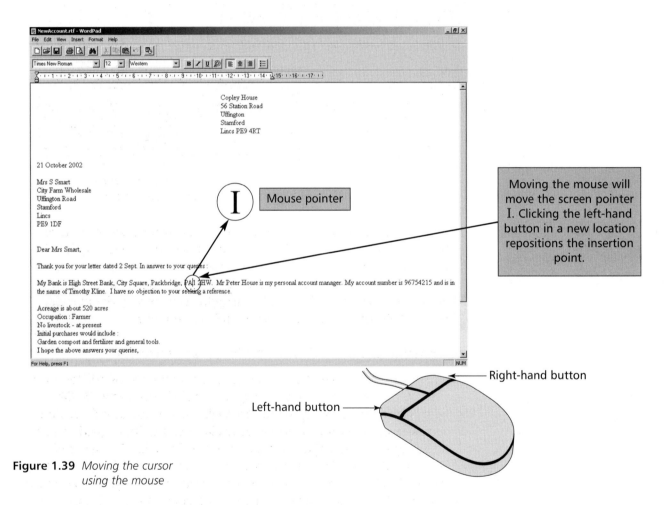

**Figure 1.39** *Moving the cursor using the mouse*

Once the cursor is at its new location you can highlight text using the mouse button in a number of ways:

- Double-clicking on the left-hand button selects the word over which the pointer has been placed.
- Triple-clicking on the left-hand mouse button selects the whole paragraph.
- By clicking and holding the left-hand mouse button you can drag the pointer down to highlight a block of consecutive text.

- By pressing and holding down the Ctrl key on the keyboard and then clicking on the left-hand mouse button you can select nonconsecutive text by releasing and re-clicking on the mouse button for each area of text that is to be highlighted.

## Using the keyboard to navigate

For those who prefer to use the keyboard to navigate around a document there are a number of keys that allow you to do this. In Figure 1.40 you can see four keys on the bottom row to the right side of the keyboard with arrows.

Arrow keys – move the cursor
up, down, left or right

**Figure 1.40** *Using the keyboard to navigate around a document*

By clicking on the screen and using one of the arrows you can move the cursor to any location. The up arrow moves the pointer up line by line; the down arrow similarly moves the cursor down line by line. The left and right arrows move the pointer left and right by one character at a time. Using a combination of keys changes the way the pointer reacts. A list of shortcut keys is shown in Appendix 2.

### Using search facilities to find a specific file

Earlier in this unit you learnt how to create a folder structure for your files. New CLAIT also requires that you can find files using the file search facilities in the software. Although you can use search facilities within most applications, Windows Explorer is usually as good as any to find specific files. You will already be familiar with the layout of Windows Explorer from earlier sections in the unit. On the standard toolbar in Explorer you will see a Search button (see Figure 1.41 on the next page). Clicking the Search button will show the Search task pane on the left of the window.

If you know the name of the file you are looking for then you can type the name in the 'Search for files or folders named:' box at the top of the task pane. More often than not you may not remember the full name. Underneath, in the 'Search for files or folders named:' box is a 'Containing text:' box. Here you can enter any text that you know may be in the file you are looking for. Finally, you can direct Windows Explorer to search in a particular part of your disk by using the 'Look in:' box.

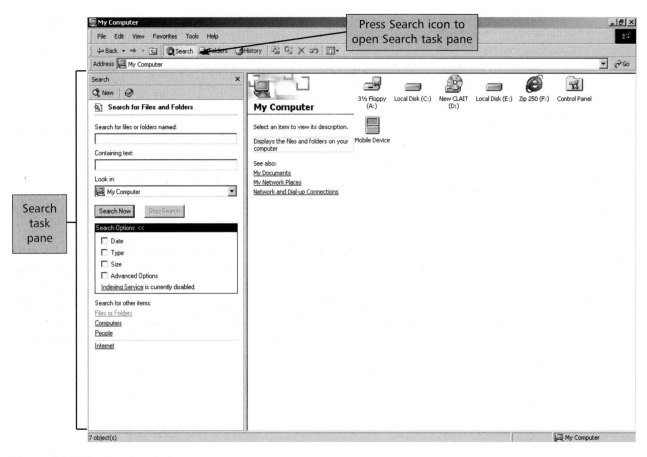

**Figure 1.41** *The Search task pane*

In the example shown in Figure 1.42, Windows Explorer has been asked to search for the text file MyText.rtf completed in the above 'Try it out' exercise.

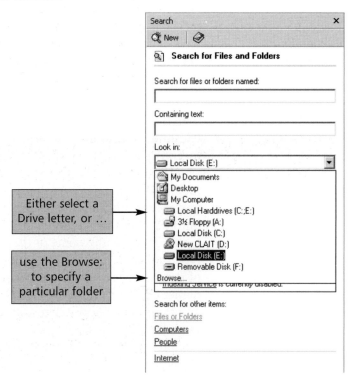

**Figure 1.42** *Using the 'Look in:' box to search a particular part of a disk*

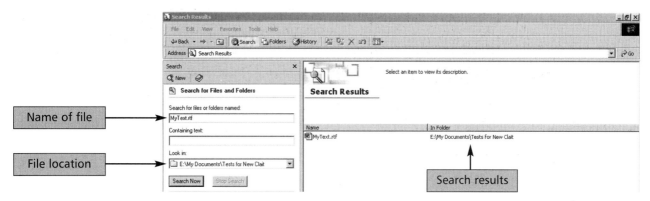

**Figure 1.43** *The Search Results window*

**Figure 1.44** *Using the Search Now button to conduct more advanced searches*

Once the name of the file has been entered in the 'Search for files or folders named:' and the location to search has been given in the 'Look in:' box, the Search Now button is pressed and the results of the search are shown in the Search Results window on the right (see Figure 1.43).

For more advanced searches the options below the Search Now button can be used to select by date, type, size and other advanced options (see Figure 1.44).

## Wild cards

Where you don't know the name or alternatively the file type, you can use the wild card '*' function to help you. For example, if you did not know the name of the file but you knew it was a Rich Text File (.rtf) you could use '*.rtf' and Windows Explorer would return the name of all your rich text format files in the area you asked it to search.

Now try searching for a file.

**Try it out**

**Open** Windows Explorer.

**Click** on the Search button on the toolbar.

**Type NewAccount.rtf** in the the 'Search for files or folders named:' box.

**Place** the accompanying CD in the CD drive.

**Select** the CD drive letter for your computer in the Look in: box.

**Click** the Search Now button.

You should now see the required file in the Search Results window.

## Using Shift and Return or Enter keys

As part of the accessibility package built into Windows, Microsoft provides an on-screen keyboard for those who find using the keyboard difficult. This function is also useful to remind yourself of the layout of the keyboard. To access the on-screen keyboard,

**Press**:
Start
Programs
Accessories
Accessibility
On-screen keyboard.

The keyboard will appear as shown in Figure 1.45.

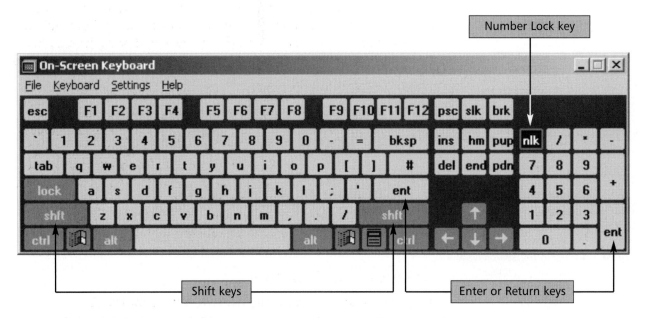

**Figure 1.45** *The On-screen keyboard*

Although there are some differences between the standard keyboard and the On-screen keyboard, the basic keys are virtually the same. Keyboards will vary depending on type and manufacture. For example, the keyboard shown in Figure 1.45 shows the shift key as 'shft', whereas it is often simply an arrow ⬆.

The shift key allows you to undertake a number of different functions. By default, characters are typed in lower case. You can change the case either by pressing the Caps Lock key on the left of the keyboard, (usually identified by Caps Lock on the key itself and shown in Figure 1.46) which will allow you to type upper case until you press the Caps Lock key a second time (this is known as a toggle key – one press is on; a second press switches it off). If you simply want to capitalize the first character of the sentence or an individual character you can achieve this by pressing the Shift key and then the required letter, while the shift key is still depressed.

**Figure 1.46** *Changing case using the Caps Lock key*

You will also notice on the keyboard that some keys have more than one symbol. For example, the number key '7' also has an '&' (called an ampersand). To type the symbol or number above the letter you use the shift key in conjunction with the key that has the symbol required. If you wanted to use an ampersand (&) you would press the shift key and then, with shift key held down, the number '7' key, which will then type an &.

The Enter key (also referred to as the Return key) allows you to create a new paragraph or line in your document. Most text editors 'wrap' text at the end of a line. This means that as soon as your typed text has reached the end of a line, the programme will automatically wrap to the next line. This is often referred to as a 'soft return'. If you want to create a new paragraph then you have to force a new line by pressing the Enter key. This is sometimes referred to as a 'hard return'.

To add a new paragraph to your document place the cursor at the place where the new paragraph is to be added and press the return or enter key. To add a further blank line simply press the enter key again.

## Amending a document

Being able to amend an existing document is a New CLAIT requirement. Earlier in the section you saw how the mouse and keyboard keys can help you move around a document and also reposition the cursor. Deleting or inserting characters is achieved using the Delete and Backspace keys shown in Figure 1.47.

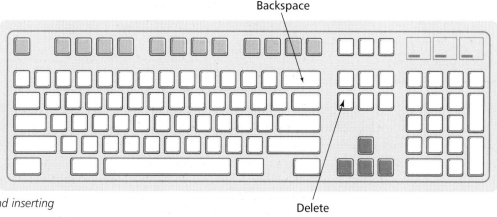

**Figure 1.47** *Deleting and inserting characters*

### Deleting text

First place the cursor at the place where a character, word or sentence is to be deleted. If the text to be deleted is to the left of the cursor press the backspace key; if it is to the right of the cursor press the delete key. You and can also use the mouse, as described above, to highlight a block of text. Pressing the delete key will then delete the highlighted text.

### Inserting text

To insert additional text place the cursor at the location where the text is to be added by clicking on the left-hand mouse button at the point of insertion and then simply type the required text.

Now try using some of these functions in a 'Try it out' exercise.

## Try it out

**Open** the MyText.rtf file in WordPad.

To open the file select File, Open from the menu and then locate the folder in which the file was previously saved.

**Position** the pointer in the document after the full stop of the second sentence, which ends '... onto the computer' and:

**Click** the left-hand mouse button to move the cursor to the new insertion point.

**Press** the enter key twice to give you a new paragraph and a blank line.

**Type** in the following text:

'You can navigate around the document by using either the mouse or arrow keys found on the keyboard. Pressing the up arrow will move the cursor up one line. Pressing the down arrow will move the cursor down one line. Press the left and right arrows to move the cursor left and right one character at a time.'

**Press** the enter key twice to create a new paragraph.

**Type** in the following text. (Note: to insert the symbols you will need to press and hold the shift key as you type the required symbol.):

'The symbols on the keyboard are accessed by pressing the Shift key and then the appropriate symbol. So, for example, these symbols may be used in a document:
!,",£,$,%,^,&,*,(,),_,+,|,<,>,?,@,:,{,},~.'

Using the mouse,

**Move** the cursor to the beginning of the last sentence in the second paragraph that starts: ' Press the left and ...'

**Insert** the following text:

'Holding down the up or down arrow will allow the cursor to continue to move until the button is released.'

**Press** the space bar (the long key in the bottom centre of the keyboard) to create a space between the last character of the new sentence (a full-stop) and the beginning of the next sentence.

**Save** the file. (Note: to save the file select File, Save from the menu or alternatively use the Save icon from the toolbar 💾.

**Close** the file.

## Saving an existing file with a new name

You have learnt how to save a file but there may be times when you want to keep the original file but make amendments to it and save it the with another name. To give a file a new name the 'Save As...' function is used. First select File, Save As... from the main menu and the dialogue box shown in Figure 1.48 appears.

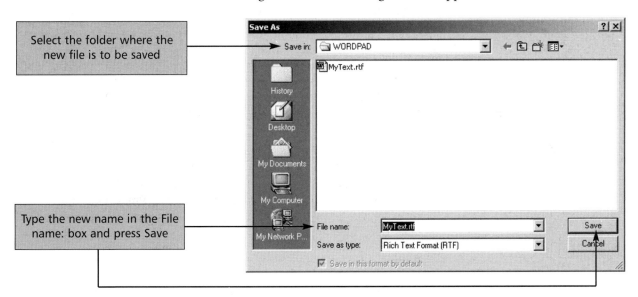

Select the folder where the new file is to be saved

Type the new name in the File name: box and press Save

**Figure 1.48** *Using the File, Save As function*

### Try it out

**Open** the file MyText.rtf.

**Save** the file as MyTextTwo.rtf in the same folder as the original.

If you now use the File, Save As... options again you will see both the original and the new file in the folder, as shown in Figure 1.49 on the next page.

▶▶

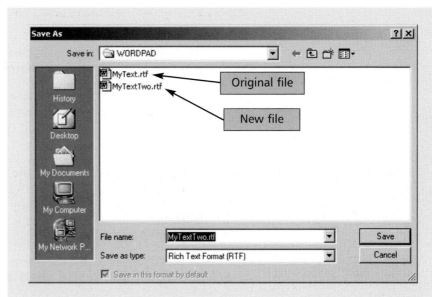

**Figure 1.49** *The new file is now saved in the folder next to the original file*

## Printing your work

For New CLAIT you are required to be able to load paper into a printer and then print a hard copy of your work.

### Printers

As described on page 7, printers come in a variety of type and sizes. However, laser and inkjet printers tend to be the most popular. Every printer has a paper tray, in which you load the paper. You should ensure that you know both where the tray is located and also how to open it. There are many different types of printer. Some have open trays where the paper is simply placed in the tray, whereas others have enclosed trays to accommodate a larger number of sheets. Figure 1.50 shows a printer with an open tray.

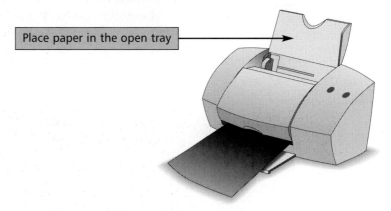

**Figure 1.50** *A printer with an open paper tray*

Make sure that your paper is kept dry (i.e. not in a damp room or area) and not crumpled. If the edges of the paper are not straight it is likely that it will not process through the rollers of the printer.

Once the paper has been loaded you are set to print your document. To print a document you can either select 'File, Print...' from the menu or alternatively click on the Print icon situated on the toolbar ![icon]. If you use the Print icon the printer will automatically print the current document without giving you any opportunity to change the print settings. Using the 'File, Print...' option will open the Print dialogue box shown in Figure 1.51.

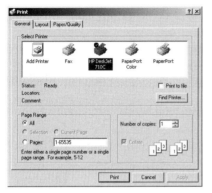

General options

Layout options

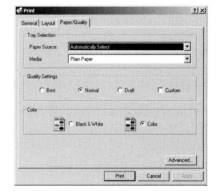

Paper/quality options

**Figure 1.51** *The Print dialogue box*

The Print dialogue box has three tabs. The first is the General tab and allows you to set the printer to be used, the pages to be printed and also the number of copies required.

The second tab, Layout, allows you to choose the orientation (i.e. portrait or landscape) and also the order of pages. There are also a number of advanced functions that you will not need to know for New CLAIT.

The third tab, Paper/Quality, allows you to select the paper source and the type of paper (Media:) being used. You can also set the quality settings (Best, Normal, Draft or Custom) and determine whether your hard copy (the printed copy) is to be printed in black and white or colour. Again, you can use the Advanced button to make further changes to the print but this is not required for New CLAIT.

**Try it out**

**Open** MyTextTwo.rtf.

**Select** File, Print... From the menu.

Do not change any of the default settings.

**Print** a copy of the document.

**Save** and close the file.

## Closing down your computer

When personal computers were less sophisticated and before Windows operating systems it was normal practice just to switch the computer off once the relevant files you might have been working on had been saved. In modern systems the Windows operating system operates differently to its predecessors. While Windows is working it stores data in its memory and, to ensure your system works properly the next time you use it, Windows needs to write (or save) certain data to the hard disk before it is turned off. By simply turning off the power Windows cannot save the information it needs, so it is important that you use the correct procedure to switch the computer off.

To 'Shut Down' your computer, select 'Shut Down...' from the Start menu. The dialogue box shown in Figure 1.52 will appear.

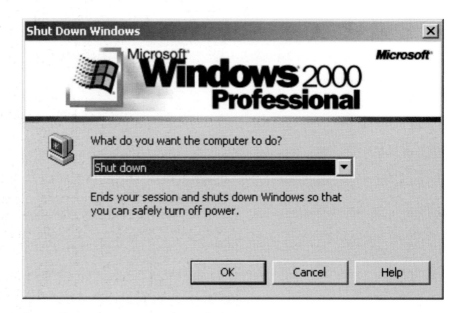

**Figure 1.52** *Shutting down your computer*

By pressing OK the system will close down safely. On some computers the system will close down and tell you it is safe to switch off your machine, while in others the system will automatically shut down and switch off.

## Safe working practices

As in most occupations there are accepted good and bad working practices. Using a computer, whether for enjoyment or work, is no different. There are specific areas you should watch out for to avoid the risk of damaging your health when using a computer on a regular basis:

## Health and safety tips

### Monitors

- The screen should be of a good size and the characters displayed must be clear.
- There should not be any flickering on the screen.
- The monitor should be capable of swivelling and tilting.
- The monitor should be positioned so that you do not get glare or reflections from windows.
- The monitor should be positioned so that the top line of text is just below eye level (see Figure 1.53).

**Figure 1.53** *A correctly positioned monitor*

### Keyboards

- Ensure that the keyboard's tilt can be adjusted.
- There must be sufficient room to rest your arms between the keyboard and the front of the desk. If possible use a wrist rest.

### Desk and chair

- Generally the desk and chair should be purpose-built, similar to, although not necessarily the same as, the one in Figure 1.54.

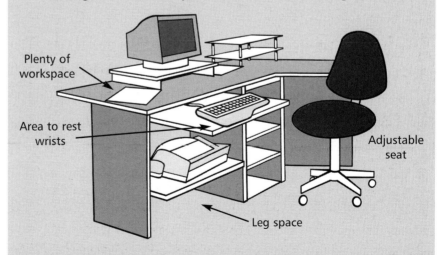

Plenty of workspace

Area to rest wrists

Adjustable seat

Leg space

**Figure 1.54** *A desk and chair suitable for use with a computer*

- Ensure that the work surface is sufficiently large to house all the required equipment.
- Wherever possible use a document holder.
- Make sure the desk is at a proper height.
- Distance from the eyes to the screen should be no more than 45–60 cm.
- The chair should be adjustable, normally for a height of between 42 and 54 cm, and be capable of supporting the lower back.

**Lighting**
- Lighting must be adequate, with a contrast between the screen and its surroundings.
- Where necessary use blinds or curtains to reduce glare.

Also remember that computer equipment generates a large amount of heat, so where you have a large number of computers or electronic equipment make sure that there is adequate ventilation.

In this unit you have covered all the main assessment objectives required for New CLAIT in the core unit Using a Computer. Now try this practical assignment to practice the skills you have learnt. A model solution can be found in Part 3.

**Practical assignment 1**

## Unit 1 Using a computer

### Scenario

Your computer has been set up for you and is ready to use. You have been given a password to gain entry to your data. (Use your own password for your computer.)

| Assessment objectives | Stage | |
|---|---|---|
| 1a | 1 | Switch on the computer and monitor safely. |
| 2a | 2 | Wait for the operating system software to load fully. |
| 1c 2b 2c | 3 | Using the operating system's 'find file' facility, find the text file **Meeting.doc**. (This file is on the accompanying CD. You will need to copy this file to your hard or floppy disk and then change its read-only attributes by unchecking the 'X' in the read-only box.) |
| 1c 1d 5b | 4 | Using an application (e.g. Word) that will allow you to read text files, open the file **Meeting.doc** in the application. |
| 1e 3a 3b 3d | 5 | Using the mouse and keyboard (or alternatives if available) add your name and today's date at the end of the document. |
| 5c | 6 | Save the document using the original filename, **Meeting.doc**. |
| 4a 4b | 7 | Switch on your printer and load a few sheets of paper. |
| 4c | 8 | Print the document using the default printer settings. |
| 5e | 9 | Close the **Meeting.doc** document. |
| 5a | 10 | Create a new text document using the same software as you used to edit **Meeting.doc**. |
| 1b 1e 3a | 11 | Enter the following data as shown, leaving a blank space between each line: (a) **Myname@ourbusiness.co.uk** |
| 3b | | (b) **Item JG/50: 60% discount** |
| 3c | | (c) **Your name and today's date.** |
| 5d | 12 | Save this document using filename **PE1_Print_2**. |
| 4c | 13 | Print the document using the default printer settings. |
| 5e | 14 | Close the document **PE1_Print_2**. |
| 1f | 15 | Exit the application software and shut down the operating system safely. |

# *Part 2*

# *Mastering New CLAIT through Microsoft Office*

*Wordprocessing using
  Word*
*Electronic communication*
*Spreadsheets using Excel*
*Databases using Access*
*Desktop publishing using
  Publisher*
*Graphs and charts*
*Computer art using Word*
*Web pages using FrontPage*
*Presentation graphics
  using PowerPoint*

# Wordprocessing using Word

**New CLAIT**

New CLAIT wordprocessing has five learning outcomes. Each learning outcome has a number of assessment objectives. A full list of all these is shown in Appendix 1. Additional information is offered in each unit over and above the formal elements of the qualification for a broader understanding of the application. Formal assessment objectives are indicated by use of a New CLAIT symbol.

## What you need to know about wordprocessing for New CLAIT

For New CLAIT you will need to know how to:

**Identify and use wordprocessing software correctly**
- Use appropriate application software.

**Use an input device to enter and edit text accurately**
- Enter text in paragraphs.
- Insert text.
- Move text.
- Delete text.
- Replace specified text.

**Select fonts and simple text formatting**
- Change font.
- Change font size.
- Emphasise text.
- Set text alignment/justification.

**Format basic paragraph and document properties**
- Set/amend margins.
- Insert paragraph breaks.
- Amend line spacing.

**Manage and print wordprocessing documents**
- Create a new document.
- Save a document.
- Save a document with a new filename.
- Print a document.
- Close a document.

*In this unit you will cover:*

- Getting familiar with Word
- Understanding the Word screen
- Understanding the menu bars and toolbars
- Building a new document
- Saving, recovering and renaming documents
- Formatting and editing text in a document
- Manipulating text in a document
- Changing a page layout
- Justifying text in a document
- Printing your work
- Exiting the application

## Getting familiar with Word

The purpose of this unit is to help familiarise you with the main elements of Word. The unit covers all the competencies required for New CLAIT and also includes additional information on the software to give you a better understanding of the versatility of the Word package.

## Opening and using Word as a wordprocessing application

Some Windows basics were explained in Unit 1, but if you are already familiar with Windows you may have decided to skip that section. However, one of the competencies of New CLAIT is to be able to identify and use wordprocessing software correctly, so as it is part of the formal syllabus it is covered again here briefly.

First you must know how to switch on your machine. On most machines the on/off (or power) button is at the front and is normally marked 'power' or with an on/off symbol ⏻ .

When you press the power button your machine will boot up. This is a technical term used to describe the process that occurs when a computer is switched on and looks for its instructions on which system files and programs should be loaded. Once the boot-up process has finished the Windows start-up screen will appear. When you press the Start button, a pop-up menu will appear. Your menu may look slightly different to the one in Figure 2.1, depending on what programs are on your machine.

By sliding the mouse pointer up to the Programs item a second menu will appear displaying, with icons, all the programs that are available for you to use. Among these is the Microsoft Word icon:

Microsoft Word

Click on this and Word will load (or open) and you should see the screen shown in Figure 2.2.

**Figure 2.1** *A typical start-up screen*

Your screen may appear slightly different depending on what toolbars are being displayed. The screen shown in Figure 2.2 on page 58 has three toolbars displayed – standard, formatting and drawing. Toolbars can be switched on and off from the menu bar, as you will see later.

## Understanding the Word screen

The screen may seem a little confusing at first, but things will become clearer as the elements are explained. Each area has a name and Table 2.1 names each area and describes its function.

**Table 2.1** *Areas of the Word screen and their functions*

**Document window**   This is the most important part. It is the area where all your work is really done. You can type in your text, insert objects and format your document. You will see the efforts of your labours in this part of the window.

**Title bar**   This is always the bar at the top of your application and tells which application you are running and, in the case of Word, the name of the document you are working on.

**Menu bar**   These two are grouped together. The bar is simply the object that holds the menu items. It can be customised and moved, as can any other toolbar.

**Minimise\maximise**   These panels allow you to enlarge or shrink the application or document window.

**Close buttons**   As the name suggests, this lets you close the application, or if in the document window, the document itself.

**Toolbar**  Microsoft provides a large number of *shortcut* buttons to make life easier. You can decide which of these pre-formatted toolbars you wish to use. You do not have to use any and can rely entirely on the *menu* bar. The toolbars can also be customised to suit individual needs.

**Scroll bar**  Sometimes your document will be larger than can be seen on the screen all at once. The scroll bars allow you to move to different parts of your document for viewing purposes.

**Status bar**  This tells you where the cursor is located in your document.

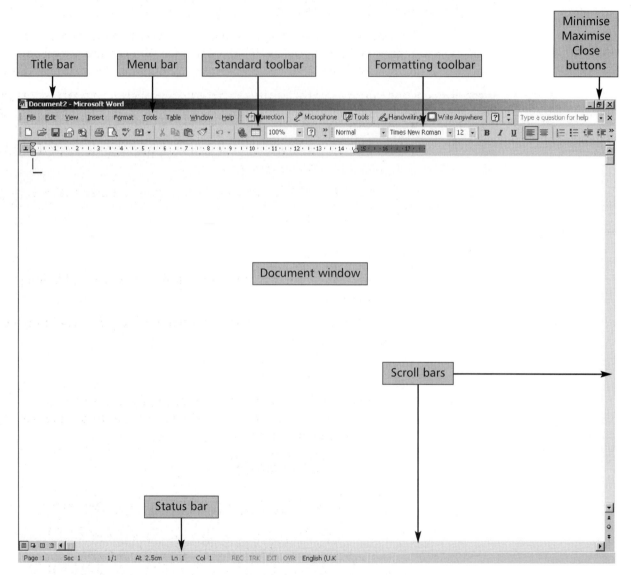

**Figure 2.2**  *The screen seen when Word is first opened*

All functions in Word (and other applications) are accessed either through the drop-down menu bars, toolbars or via the keyboard. Think of the menu bar as an index in a book, guiding you to the various parts you want to read. Some of the menus are particularly user friendly as they not only give the name of the item but often show you the toolbar icon and also the keyboard shortcut key. Toolbars contain icons (shortcuts) that indicate what the underlying command button is used for. For example, the **B** on the menu bar is a quick way of turning the bold function on and off. When you press a toolbar button its background changes to a lighter colour, signifying that the function (in this case bold) is switched on.

If you are new to the Windows environment it is worth spending a little time understanding the screen. The toolbars shown are optional and can be either displayed or not as required. The following is an example of a menu bar:

| File | Edit | View | Insert | Format | Tools | Table | Window | Help | English (U.S.) ▾ Speech | | Type a question for help ▾ ✕ |

In Windows there is always more than one way to perform the same operation. Take, for example, opening a file. You can use a toolbar button, keyboard shortcut or the Open... option on the main menu bar.

## Try it out

### Option 1: The toolbar

**Press** the Open File icon 🗁 on the standard toolbar to bring up the Open File dialogue box.

**Press** the Esc key on the keyboard to close the dialogue box.

(Do not open a file at this stage.)

### Option 2: The keyboard

**Press** and hold down the Ctrl key and then, while still holding the Ctrl key:

**Press** the character 'o' on the keyboard: again, this will bring the dialogue box into view.

### Option 3: The main menu

**Select** File, Open... on the main menu. If you use this option notice in Figure 2.3 how Word also shows you the alternative methods mentioned above.

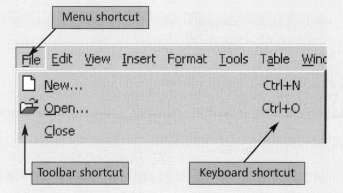

**Figure 2.3** *Using the main menu, Word shows any shortcuts that could have been used to achieve the same purpose*

Which method you use is a matter of preference.

## Understanding the menu bars and toolbars

You can access the drop-down menus in two ways. First, by placing the cursor over the menu item (e.g. Format) and pressing the left-hand mouse button. The menu will then expand to show you the options available.

The second method is by using the keyboard shortcut. Each of the menu options has an underlined letter. By pressing the Alt key and, while holding it down, tapping the underlined letter, a drop-down menu will come into view. Figure 2.4 shows the drop-down menu for Format.

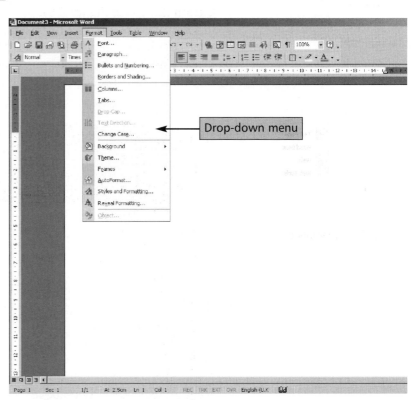

**Figure 2.4** *Format drop-down menu*

---

**Try it out**

### Option 1: The main menu

**Move** your cursor over a menu item.

**Press** the left-hand mouse button.

**Repeat** this for each of the menu items.

### Option 2: The shortcut key

**Press** and hold down the Alt key.

**Press** the underlined letter for the desired menu (e.g. Alt+I).

Again, **repeat** this for each of the menu items.

Notice how some of the sub-menu items are greyed out; this means they are not available to you at this time. For example, under the Table sub-menu most of the items are greyed out (or *disabled*). If you think about it, this makes sense since there is no table being used.

### How to change toolbar options

You may find that the default toolbar has either more shortcuts on it than you need or not enough. With Microsoft Office's applications you are given an option to customise any of the toolbars or even make new ones that suit your working style and the tasks being done.

By pressing the Alt+V keys the View drop-down menu appears. In the secondary drop-down menu under toolbars is a menu item called Customise… (see Figure 2.5).

Customise allows you to access the dialogue box. This box has three tabs – Toolbars, Commands and Options. Select the Toolbars tab; it will show which of the toolbars are currently in use. You can select or deselect any of these by clicking in the check box (see Figure 2.6).

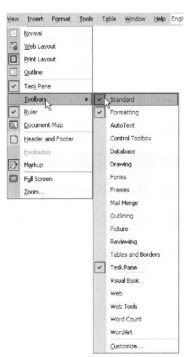

**Figure 2.5** *Toolbar menu*

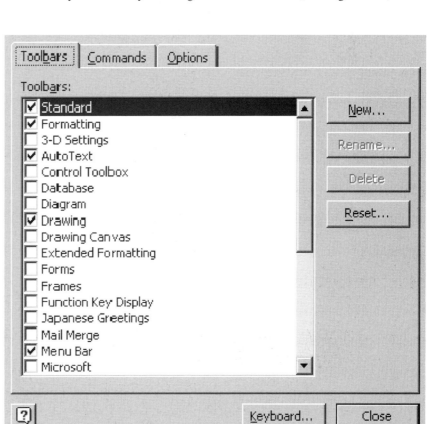

**Figure 2.6** *Toolbars/standard menu*

Notice also that the Toolbars option, under the main menu of View, shows which toolbars are active by displaying a small tick to the left of each toolbar name. Again, if you decide you want an additional toolbar, simply click on the toolbar's name. If, on the other hand, you no longer need a toolbar click in its box and the toolbar will disappear (along with its tick). It really does not matter which of these methods you use.

*Try it out*

**MOUSE TIP**

When selecting a menu item you need only press the left-hand mouse button once. You do not need to double-click.

*Option 1*

**Select** View on the main menu.

**Select** Toolbars.

**Deselect** the standard toolbar by clicking that option on the list.

Notice how this toolbar is no longer visible on the screen.

Repeat the process by selecting the standard toolbar option and the toolbar reappears.

*Option 2*

**Select** View on the main menu.

**Select** Toolbars.

**Select** Customise....

**Select** the Toolbars tab.

**Deselect** one of the toolbar options, e.g. Formatting.

Notice how the toolbar disappears from the screen.

Reselect the toolbar and it will reappear on the screen for you to use.

**Press** Close and you are returned to the Word screen.

### Customising your toolbar

Adding and removing icons from a toolbar is very straightforward.

By selecting Toolbars under the View menu option and then selecting Customise... at the bottom of the list, you can bring up the same dialogue box you used in the exercise above. This time, however, select the Commands tab (Figure 2.7). To add an icon to your screen toolbar select the menu item you want from the Categories box. Press the icon displayed in the Commands section. Notice how the Description button on the bottom left of the box is enabled when a selection is made. By pressing the Description button you will see a description of the item you have selected (see Figure 2.8).

When you have found the item that you want to be displayed on the toolbar, press and hold down the left-hand mouse button and simply drag the icon onto the appropriate toolbar.

To remove an icon from your toolbar, simply select the icon on the toolbar while the Customize dialogue box is open, and drag it off the toolbar. Don't worry that it has disappeared – you can always restore it later by reversing the process. Have a go at adding and then removing an icon on the toolbar.

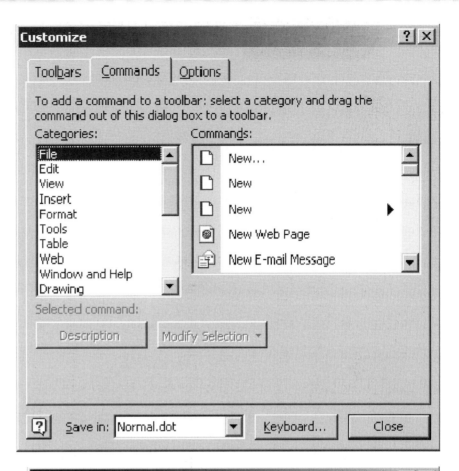

**Figure 2.7** *Customise menu, Commands tab*

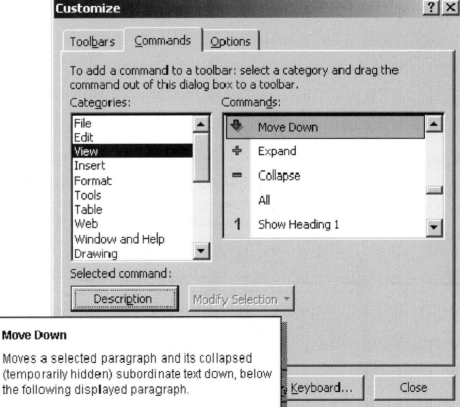

**Figure 2.8** *Customise menu, Description button*

**Try it out**

*Adding an icon*

Make sure the formatting toolbar is visible on the screen.

**Select** the <u>V</u>iew option on the main menu.

**Select** <u>T</u>oolbars.

**Select** Customi<u>s</u>e....

**Select** the <u>C</u>ommand tab (if it is not already selected).

**Select** Format from Categories:

**Scroll** down the list on the right, and

**Select** $x^2$ Superscript.

**Press** the Description box button and read the description.

**Select** and Drag $x^2$ Superscript from its location in Comman<u>d</u>s onto the formatting toolbar.

*Removing an icon*

**Open** the Customi<u>s</u>e... dialogue box.

**Press** the $x^2$ Superscript button and, with the mouse button still pressed,

**Drag** the icon off the toolbar.

You should now be able to:

- find your way around the Word screen
- use menus and toolbars
- change toolbar options
- customise a toolbar.

## Building a new document

To start a new document use the <u>F</u>ile, <u>N</u>ew option on the menu bar, press the new blank file shortcut □ located on the standard toolbar or use the keyboard shortcut (Crtl+N). If you use either of the last two options Word will automatically assume you want to open a normal, blank, text document. Depending on your version of Microsoft Office, the <u>F</u>ile, <u>N</u>ew option from the main menu will give you the opportunity to select one of Word's other *templates* such as a memo, Report Wizard, fax, etc. Office 97 or 2000 will open a dialogue box similar to that shown in Figure 2.9a. If you are using Office XP the options appear as a separate window on the right of your screen (Figure 2.9b). Although these look slightly different they both do the same job. If you are using XP, then by selecting General Templates from the New From Template option you will see the same dialogue box as that shown in Figure 2.9a.

New from template

Weathervane Cottage.dot

General Templates...

For New CLAIT you will only be using the blank document template, so you can use any of the shortcuts. However, you might find it useful to try the other templates to gain experience of what is on offer. Also, although it is beyond the scope of this book, you can build your own templates and customise them for either home or office use.

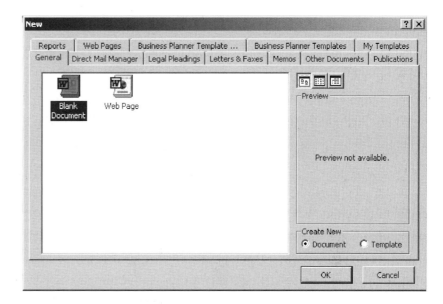

**Figure 2.9a** *The Template dialogue box*

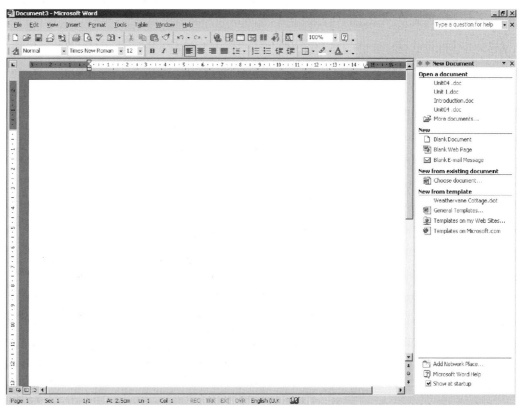

**Figure 2.9b** *Templates dialogue menu in Office XP*

As the normal template is used the most often it is always the default option offered by Word. Word opens a new document based on the normal template shown on the toolbar (Figure 2.10).

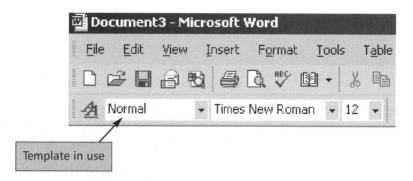

**Figure 2.10** *The Normal template*

Template in use

## Entering text in paragraphs

**New CLAIT**

As you learnt earlier, the white area in a new document is where all the work is done.

There are some basic rules of accuracy you must follow if you intend to complete the New CLAIT assignments. You may find the list of paragraph and punctuation rules below useful as you go through this unit.

### Important rules for CLAIT Word assignments

**Paragraph and punctuation rules when completing New CLAIT assignments:**

- There must be at least one space after a comma (,) or semicolon (;) and no more than two.
- Normally two spaces occur after a full-stop (.), question mark (?) or colon (:), but you will not be penalised for one space. However, you will be penalised for using more than two spaces.
- In modern wordprocessors you do not need to press the Return key for the next line as the software automatically word wraps when you get to the end of a line. Only use the Return key when you want to start a new paragraph.
- There must be either one or two clear line spaces between paragraphs. Although you will not be penalised for inconsistent spacing, you will if you add more than two spaces or have no spaces between paragraphs.
- Names and proper nouns must have initial capital letters. Also, upper-and lower-case text must be used where indicated.

### Learning about the keyboard

There are various keyboard layouts and although they may differ slightly, in general they follow similar styles and all are known as qwerty keyboards. This is because the first six alphabetic characters on the third line of the keyboard spell qwerty. The most common style is the standard keyboard shown in Figure 2.11, although as you saw earlier (Figure 1.4b) there are other types such as the ergonomic keyboard.

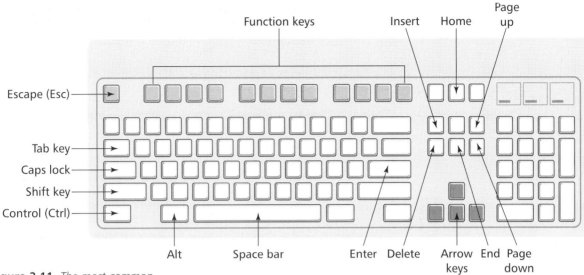

**Figure 2.11** *The most common pattern of Qwerty keyboard*

When a new document is opened, the cursor will be positioned at the top of the document, awaiting user input. The cursor will look like this: **I** (known as the insertion point).

If you want to type in lower-case letters simply make sure the Caps Lock light is not on. To make a capital letter press the Shift key, and while pressing it press the letter you want to capitalise. When you release the Shift key you will be returned to normal lower case. If you want to type a series of capital letters press the Caps Lock key, located on the left of your keyboard. You will know if it has been selected because a green light will show on the keyboard, sometimes (but not always) with the letter 'A' above it indicating it relates to characters. The Caps Lock key is known as a *toggle button* and only switches off when you press it a second time.

If you want to change your text characters from normal text to italics press the Ctrl+I keys. First press the Ctrl key and then tap the I, then release both.

The rules governing punctuation, word and line spacing must be adhered to for New CLAIT. However, sometimes it is not always obvious by looking at the screen whether there are two spaces or one between words, and it is even more difficult to see whether a *hard return* has been put in where it should be a word-wrapped line (*soft return*).

Similarly, you may sometimes find the cursor will not do what you want it to, and this is very often because you have a return or some other *non-printable character* where one should not be. Do not worry; help is at hand. On the toolbar you will see a symbol like this ¶ (referred to as the 'Show/Hide' button). If you press this symbol it will show you all the non-printable characters such as tabs, paragraph marks, page breaks and hidden text. You will find this helpful when checking your work for paragraph and spacing accuracy. When the 'Show all' toolbar option has been enabled the formatting is displayed by a full-stop between words (spaces) and the ¶ symbol at the end of a paragraph (i.e. when a hard return has been made). Pressing the Enter key (see the keyboard in Figure 2.11) produces a new line. Normally Word and most other wordprocessing packages insert a soft return at the end of a line. This is known as word wrapping. Figure 2.12 explains how this works.

The fat bird watched as the worm slid past him and made no attempt to pick it up with his beak.

The bird had been feasting himself on breadcrumbs thrown down by passers by and had no appetite left for worms – even fat juicy ones.

**Figure 2.12a** *Text as seen with the Show all option not activated*

**Figure 2.12b** *The same text as in Figure 4.12a, but with the Show all option activated to show non-printing characters*

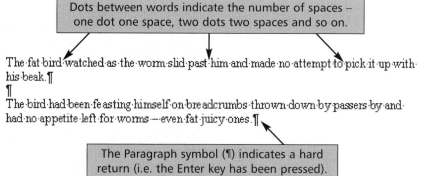

Dots between words indicate the number of spaces – one dot one space, two dots two spaces and so on.

The·fat·bird·watched·as·the·worm·slid·past·him·and·made·no·attempt·to·pick·it·up·with·his·beak.¶
¶
The·bird·had·been·feasting·himself·on·breadcrumbs·thrown·down·by·passers·by·and·had·no·appetite·left·for·worms·–·even·fat·juicy·ones.¶

The Paragraph symbol (¶) indicates a hard return (i.e. the Enter key has been pressed).

---

### Basic keyboard navigation rules

Before doing some exercises in Word it will be helpful for you to learn some of the rules for moving around a document. A more comprehensive list of shortcuts is given in Appendix 2.

- Pressing the End key takes the cursor to the end of a line.
- Pressing the Home key takes the cursor to the beginning of a line.
- Pressing the Delete key deletes characters to the right of the cursor.
- Pressing the Backspace key (←) deletes characters to the left.
- The up arrow (↑) moves the cursor up line by line.
- The down arrow (↓) moves the cursor down line by line.
- The left arrow (←) moves the cursor left along the line.
- The right arrow (→) moves the cursor right along the line.

## Saving, recovering and renaming documents

### Saving a document

On page 34 you saw how you can create folders or directories on either the A or C drive. Having created the directories, the next stage is to create and save a document (or file).

When Word opens a new document it provides a default filename for the document. This is usually simply 'Document' with a number immediately following it (Document1, Document2, etc.). Although the title bar says Document1 this has not yet been saved to your hard or floppy disk.

**Try it out**

**Create** a new Word document.

**Type** the following words into your new document:

'The little boy went to the river bank and placed his bright red sailing boat on the water.'

**Select** File, Save on the main menu or alternatively press the Save icon on the standard toolbar 🖫. The dialogue box shown in Figure 2.13a will appear.

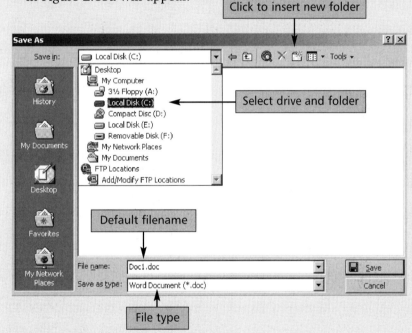

Figure 2.13a *The Save As dialogue box*

**Double-click** on the drive you want to save the file to (e.g. C or A).

**Press** the New Folder icon.

**Type** in a name for your new folder (use 'Test' in this case).

**Press** OK.

**Type** the name of your new file in the File name: box (use 'Test1', in this case).

**Press** the Save button and you will then be returned to the document window. Notice how in the title bar at the top of the screen the default filename Document1 has been replaced with your new name, Test1.

**Select** File, Close.

### Recovering a saved Word document

Recovering a saved Word document is not formally a New CLAIT requirement, but is implicit because of the actions you are required to undertake in assignments.

**Try it out**

**Select** the File option on the menu.

**Select** Open... and a very similar dialogue box to the one on the previous page will be shown (see Figure 2.13b).

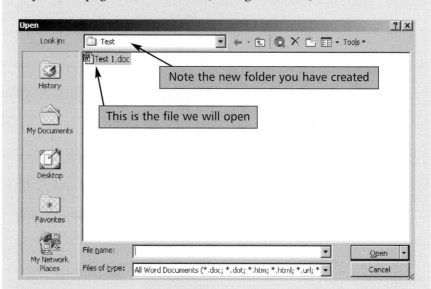

**Figure 2.13b** *Open menu*

Make sure the Test folder is shown in the Look in: box. If it is not, then:

**Highlight** the drive and folder where the file is stored (Test).

**Double-click** on the file (Test1) or Press the Open command button.

### Saving a document with a new filename

If you are working on a fairly large document make sure you save it at regular intervals – say every 10–15 minutes. This means that if you have a power cut or a computer problem you will only lose the work you have done since the last save.

To save further work done on a file that has already been saved once, simply press the Save icon. This will save the file you are working on without the need to go back to the menu and use the File, Save options. However, this will only save work done on the current file. If you want to save your file as something else (for example if you want two copies of a document, each slightly different), then you will need to use the File, Save As... option.

Instead of selecting the Save option on the menu or pressing the Save icon on the toolbar, go to the File, Save As... option on the main menu. Now go through the same process as when you saved the original file but this time give the file a new name in the File name: box.

You should now be able to:

- create a new Word document
- enter text into a document
- find your way around the keyboard
- move to different parts of a document
- save and recover a document
- save a document with a new filename.

## Build-up Exercise 1: Stage 1

**Create** a new document.

**Type** the text shown in the box below into the document window.

You will notice that there are a number of mistakes in the text. Word underlines by default any word it decides is spelt incorrectly with a red wiggly line. Where Word thinks the grammar is wrong it underlines with a green wiggly line. Type in the text as it is shown, complete with errors.

> Peter and Mary Get Their New Car
>
> Peter and Mray had been saving to buy a new car for about two years and the day had finally arrived when it would be delivered to their local garrage. Peter had spent a long time going through all the road reports he could find.
>
> He had decided that he needed a car which would not only provide a satisfactory performnnce but most importantly one that had plenty of space in the boot for his golf clubs. Petrol consumtion was also important and the saloon he had chosen was suposed to give him at least 56 miles to the gallon. For Mary, on the other hand, it was more important that the shape and colour were to her liking. She had spent many hours looking at the many different colours availbe on the market. When she went shopping she would watch all the cars in the car park to decide which shape she liked best.
>
> When both Peter and Mary arrived at the garage their new car was sittting on the forecourt. They both immediately fell in love with their new purchase. The boot was cavernous, the shape was round and appealing and the colour was just right. After filling in the paperwork they drove off and waved goodbye to the garage owner.

**Save** your work as 'BU1a' in a new folder on either your hard disk drive or a floppy disk. Call the new folder 'Word Exercises'.

**Press** the ¶ symbol on the toolbar. You should see that the paragraph symbols only show where a return has been made.

Your text should look like this:

> Peter·and·Mary·Get·Their·New·Car¶
> ¶
> Peter·and·Mray·had·been·saving·to·buy·a·new·car·for·about·two·years·and·the·day·had·
> finally·arrived·when·it·would·be·delivered·to·their·local·garrage.··Peter·had·spent·a·
> long·time·going·through·all·the·road·reports·he·could·find.··¶
> ¶
> He·had·decided·that·he·needed·a·car·which·would·not·only·provide·a·satisfactory·
> performnnce·but·most·importantly·one·that·had·plenty·of·space·in·the·boot·for·his·golf·
> clubs.··Petrol·consumtion·was·also·important·and·the·saloon·he·had·chosen·was·
> suposed·to·give·him·at·least·56·miles·to·the·gallon.··For·Mary,·on·the·other·hand,·it·
> was·more·important·that·the·shape·and·colour·were·to·her·liking.··She·had·spent·many·
> hours·looking·at·the·many·different·colours·availbe·on·the·market.··When·she·went·
> shopping·she·would·watch·all·the·cars·in·the·car·park·to·decide·which·shape·she·liked·
> best.··¶
> ¶
> When·both·Peter·and·Mary·arrived·at·the·garage·their·new·car·was·sittting···on·the·
> forecourt.··They·both·immediately·fell·in·love·with·their·new·purchase.··The·boot·was·
> cavernous,·the·shape·was·round·and·appealing·and·the·colour·was·just·right.··After·
> filling·in·the·paperwork·they·drove·off·and·waved·goodbye·to·the·garage·owner.¶

## Formatting and editing text in a document

New CLAIT

### Emphasising text

Emphasising text normally means making it bold or italic or perhaps underlining something like a heading. Being able to emphasise text is a requirement of New CLAIT.

Headings are normally in bold, often with capitals. The heading in our example in the Build-up exercise is not, therefore you will first *format* the heading so that it is entirely in capitals and bold text. Whilst emphasising text is a New CLAIT requirement, being able to change the case (i.e. changing the letters from lower case to upper case and vice versa) is not. It is included in this section to give you a broader understanding of formatting text generally.

### Highlighting text to be formatted

Before any text can be changed to a different format you must first tell Word which text is to be altered. You have already seen that in Windows software there are usually a number of ways of solving problems. Here you will be shown the most popular method for highlighting text.

To highlight text, first put the cursor at the beginning or end of the text to be highlighted. In the exercise this means the P of Peter in the heading. Next, with the left-hand button held down, drag the cursor across the heading until it is all highlighted and then let go.

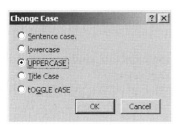

**Figure 2.14** *The Change Case dialogue box*

## Build-up Exercise 1: Stage 2

Using file BU1a:

**Highlight** the heading of your text.

Your heading should now look like this:

Peter and Mary Get Their New Car

### Changing case

You will not be surprised to learn that Word's formatting options allow you to change the case of any text without the need to retype it. To access this option you need to select the Format drop-down menu and then select Change Case... . The dialogue box in Figure 2.14 will appear.

### KEYBOARD TIP

If you would rather use the keyboard than the mouse to format text, place the cursor at the beginning of the text you want to format, hold down the Shift key and, with the Shift key still held down, press the End key (Shift+End). If you are unfamiliar with the keyboard buttons have a look back at the keyboard picture in Figure 2.11 on page 67. Although keyboards can differ slightly you will find the buttons are roughly in the same place for each type.

## Build-up Exercise 1: Stage 3

Using file BU1a and with the heading highlighted:

**Select** Format on the main menu.

**Select** Change Case....

**Select** Upper case.

**Press** OK.

**Save** the file.

Your heading should now look like this:

PETER AND MARY GET THEIR NEW CAR

**New CLAIT**

### Underlining text

Underlining text can be achieved by using the keyboard, the Underlining icon on the formatting toolbar or the Font... dialogue box under the Format menu option. The keyboard and toolbar options tend to be most popular. To use the keyboard method simply highlight the text to be underlined and press Ctrl+U on the keyboard. Now have a go at the Build-up exercise below to investigate the remaining two options.

## Build-up Exercise 1: Stage 4

Make sure the heading on the exercise BU1a is highlighted:

Try each of the options shown below. After trying the option, click outside the highlighted text to deselect it and, having viewed the results, re-highlight the text to try the next option.

*Option 1: Toolbar*

**Press** the U button ⊔ on the toolbar (the U stands for underlining).

*Option 2: Menu*

**Select** Format on the main menu.

**Select** Font A .

**Select** the underline option available in the combo box shown in Figure 2.15.

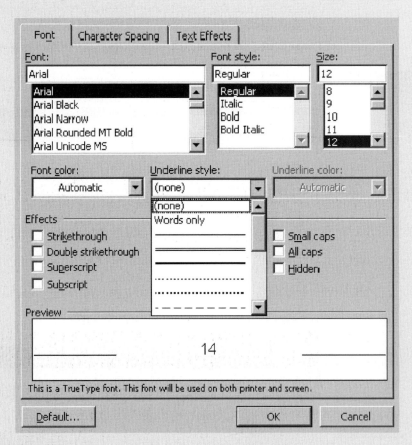

**Figure 2.15** *Font window*

**Press** OK.

Your underlined heading should now look like this:

PETER AND MARY GET THEIR NEW CAR

**Save** your work using either the File, Save option on the menu bar or pressing the Save icon on the toolbar.

**New CLAIT**

## Centring text

Centring text is another aspect of text formatting covered in the New CLAIT syllabus; it is very straightforward. By placing the cursor in front of the text to be centred you can use either the Centring icon ☰ on the formatting toolbar or the keyboard shortcut. Where a paragraph is to be centred, simply use the Centring icon and, provided the cursor is placed within the paragraph, the whole of the paragraph will be centred. Try it out on file BU1a in the following Build-up exercise.

### Build-up Exercise 1: Stage 5

With file BU1a open:

> **Place** the cursor at the beginning of the heading.
>
> **Press** the Centre Text icon on the toolbar or Press Ctrl+E.
>
> **Save** the file.

**New CLAIT**

## Emboldening text

Emboldening text is also a requirement of New CLAIT. Making text bold helps to emphasise it. Emboldening text is very straightforward using similar toolbar or keyboard techniques.

### Build-up Exercise 1: Stage 6

Using file BU1a, **highlight** the heading as in previous stages but this time:

> **Place** the cursor at the beginning of the heading.
>
> **Press** down the Shift key and while still holding the Shift key down,
>
> **Press** the End key.

This will highlight the heading in much the same way as you did for underlining.

> **Press** the **B** command button.

Your heading should now look like this:

**PETER AND MARY GET THEIR NEW CAR**

**Save** your work as BU1b using the Save <u>A</u>s… option on the <u>F</u>ile menu.

## New CLAIT

### Deleting text

Once you have got to grips with the idea of highlighting text to perform an action you can do almost anything as far as formatting is concerned.

A popular way to delete text is by using the highlighting technique then pressing the Delete key on the keyboard. If you only want to delete a few characters at a time then place the cursor in the position where you want to start deleting. If you want to delete characters to the right of the cursor then press the Delete key. If you want to delete characters to the left of the cursor press the Backspace key (see Figure 2.11 on page 67 for key positions).

## New CLAIT

### Moving text

Moving text around from one part of a document to another or copying chunks of text to use in another document are competencies required by New CLAIT. These actions are normally called cutting and pasting, and as you can by now imagine, Word makes this type of work easy.

### Build-up Exercise 1: Stage 7

Suppose you wanted to move the second sentence of text in file BU1b to the end of the second paragraph. The process is very much the same as formatting.

**Highlight** the following text using the left-hand mouse button as in the previous exercise.

> Peter had spent a long time going through all the road reports he could find.

*Option 1: Keyboard*

**Press** Ctrl+X and the text will disappear from view.

What has actually happened is that the text has been cut from the paragraph and Word has placed it on what is known as the *clipboard* – a sort of storage area in the memory. Had you pressed the Delete button you would have seen the same effect, but the deleted text would not have been placed on the clipboard and could not have been pasted back into the document.

Because this sentence is at the end of the paragraph the space between the first and second paragraph will have closed up. To reinstate the space,

**Press** the Enter key.

**Place** the cursor where the text is to be pasted.

In this case it will be after the full-stop following ' ... boot for his clubs' and immediately in front of the 'P' for Petrol.

When you are happy that the cursor is in the right place,

**Press** Ctrl+V and the sentence reappears in the right position.

*Option 2: Mouse drag and drop*

Cutting and pasting is not the only way to move text around. The 'drag and drop' option using the mouse is fast, effective and easy to master. Have a go at dragging and dropping text.

## Build-up Exercise 1: Stage 8

**Copy** the text you typed in the previous exercise by highlighting it.

**Press** Ctrl+X to cut the text from the page and send it to the clipboard.

**Open** a new Word document (to do this press Ctrl+N, use the New Document icon or alternatively use the File, New option from the main menu bar).

**Paste** the copied text into the new document using Edit and Paste from the menu options or use Ctrl+V on the keyboard. Now you are ready to move some text using the drag and drop method.

**Highlight** a chunk of text by pressing and holding down the left-hand mouse button. It really does not matter what text you use but let's use the passage 'When both Peter and Mary arrived at the garage their new car was sitting on the forecourt'.

With the left mouse button still depressed:

**Move** the cursor over the highlighted text and with the mouse button still held down,

**Drag** the highlighted text to another position, e.g. the end of the first paragraph.

**Release** the left-hand mouse button.

See how effortlessly the text has moved.

**Save** the amended file as BU1c.

You should now be able to:

- edit text in a document
- format text
- change the case of text
- align text as specified
- emphasise text as specified
- cut, copy and delete text
- move text as directed.

## New CLAIT

## Changing fonts and font sizes

### What are fonts?

Modern wordprocessing and other text-based software packages provide a bewildering array of fonts. It may surprise you to know that there are literally thousands of fonts that are available to you. In Word alone there are dozens of different fonts that you can choose to work with. Strange as it may seem, 'fonts' is quite a large topic in its own right. There are various types of font, styles and so on. A font is a typeface style and most are known as TrueType fonts. In essence this means that what you see on the screen is what will be printed on paper. This is often referred to as *WYSIWYG* (pronounced wisiwig): '**W**hat **Y**ou **S**ee **I**s **W**hat **Y**ou **G**et'. There are three basic types of font. Serif fonts have strokes or 'handles' at the ends of the letters. This is a scrif font: **F**. Sans-serif fonts do not have strokes or handles. This is a sans-serif font: **F**. The third type of font is a special font called a symbol or script font. This is a symbol font: ©.

For most of your work you will be using two fonts: Times New Roman and Arial. If you look on your toolbar you will see the font that is currently selected for the actual document. The figure below shows the toolbar font selection box:

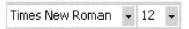

The box on the left allows you to select a style of font and the one on the right allows you to select the size of the font.

## Try it out

**Open** a new Word document.

**Type** in the following text:

'The captain eased the boat up to the jetty and one of the crew tied up and waited for the passengers to arrive.'

**Highlight** all the text.

**Select** a font from the Font Styles drop-down box.

**Change** the size of font in the second box using the drop-down selection box. (You can also type in the desired size if the font selected is a sizeable font and then press Enter.)

## Using the spell checker

Although New CLAIT does not require you to be able to use the spell checker it does call for text to be entered with no more than three data accuracy errors. In other words you must check your work thoroughly for errors. More often than not your errors will be those minor spelling mistakes that we all make from time to time. While the spell checker is not necessarily infallible it will identify most spelling mistakes and is included in this section as another tool you can use to help make life a little easier.

Word helps you to see at a glance where typing has led to spelling mistakes. Microsoft is an American product and it is therefore important that you are using the English (UK) version of the spell checker dictionary. Used with caution, the checker can remedy the vast majority of mistakes.

### Identifying the dictionary in use

In Office XP, Microsoft has made selecting your dictionary very easy. If you select Language from the Tools option on the main menu and then on the second drop-down menu select Set Language... you will see the dialogue box shown in Figure 2.16a.

**Figure 2.16a** *The Language window*

Simply select the language you want to use and press the Default button. You will be asked if you want to make this the default language. Press the OK button and that's all there is to it.

Now spell check the work you saved on file BU1c.

**Spell check caution!**

When using the spell checker you need to be aware that Word checks for spelling errors and not whether you have used the right word. For example, you may have typed the word 'their' but meant to type 'there'. To Word both spellings are correct.

## *Build-up Exercise I: Stage 9*

**Open** file BU1c.

**Select** Tools on the main menu.

**Select** Spelling and Grammar....

Whether you use the menu, the icon or the F7 key, once you have selected the Spelling and Grammar option, the following dialogue box will appear (Figure 2.16b).

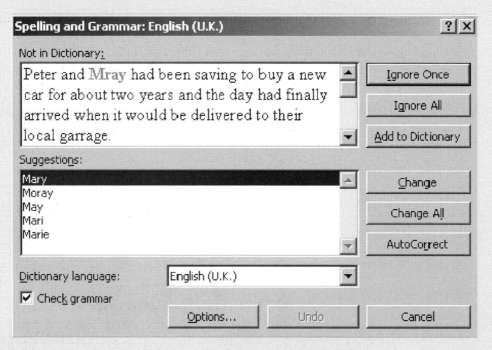

**Figure 2.16b** *Spelling and Grammar window*

Notice that the spell checker has found the first spelling error immediately after the place where the cursor was left. In this case it is 'Mray'. The checker gives you a variety of options, including a suggested alternative. All you need to do is check the alternative and, if you think it is right, press the Change command button. The checker will continue to go through the document until it has reported all the errors. At this point you will get the following message:

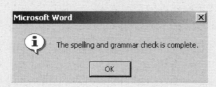

**Press** OK and return to your document.

As the checker goes through your work it will also look for grammatical errors and suggest alternatives where it can. You can choose to accept these or ignore them.

**Save** your file as BU1d.

You should now have a perfectly acceptable document that is nearly ready for printing. It should look something like the one shown below.

---

### PETER AND MARY GET THEIR NEW CAR

Peter and Mary had been saving to buy a new car for about two years and the day had finally arrived when it would be delivered to their local garage. When both Peter and Mary arrived at the garage their new car was sitting on the forecourt.

He had decided that he needed a car which would not only provide a satisfactory performance but most importantly one that had plenty of space in the boot for his golf clubs. Peter had spent a long time going through all the road reports he could find. Petrol consumption was also important and the saloon he had chosen was supposed to give him at least 56 miles to the gallon. For Mary, on the other hand, it was more important that the shape and colour were to her liking. She had spent many hours looking at the many different colours available on the market. When she went shopping she would watch all the cars in the car park to decide which shape she liked best.

They both immediately fell in love with their new purchase. The boot was cavernous, the shape was round and appealing and the colour was just right. After filling in the paperwork they drove off and waved goodbye to the garage owner.

---

## Manipulating text in a document

### Amending line spacing

It is a requirement of New CLAIT that you are able to amend line spacing and, even if you are not intending to do the qualification, this is another Word function that is extremely useful to know. There are occasions when you will want to increase the line spacing of your work so that you, or someone else reading the work, can make handwritten amendments more easily. For some people it also makes reading the text easier.

## *Build-up Exercise 1: Stage 10*

**Open** file BU1d.

*Option 1: Menu*

**Click** in the first line of the last paragraph.

**Select** Format on the main menu.

**Select** the Paragraph option. The dialogue box in Figure 2.17 will appear.

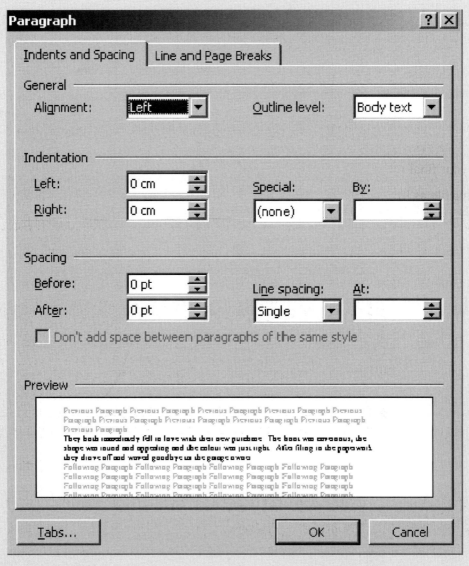

**Figure 2.17** *Paragraph window*

A little over halfway down the box towards the right-hand side you will see a combo box (that's the one with a down arrow to the right of the box) with Line Spacing: above it. By default it shows single spacing.

**Press** the arrow to drop down the options available.

**Select** Double.

**Press** OK.

Notice how your spacing has changed to double. Now change the paragraph back to single spacing using the same technique.

Another way of displaying the Paragraph Format dialogue box is to put the Paragraph Formatting icon ▤ on your format toolbar. By pressing the icon the dialogue box will appear.

*Option 2: Keyboard*

Line spacing can also be amended by using the keyboard.

**Highlight** the last paragraph again.

**Press** Ctrl+2.

The line spacing has changed to double. To change back to single line spacing simply press Ctrl+1 while the paragraph is highlighted.

Make sure your final paragraph is in double spacing.

**Save** your file as BU1e.

---

**New CLAIT**

### Inserting text

To insert a piece of text at a particular point in a document, click the cursor at the point where you want to put the new text. Now type the word (or words) you want to enter. Make sure that the Insert key (see the keyboard picture in Figure 2.11) has not been accidentally switched on. If the key is switched on it will replace any text that is in front of the cursor. This may sometimes be exactly what you want to do, but for now you want to add text rather than replace it.

## Build-up Exercise 1: Stage II

**Open** file BU1e.

**Place** your cursor at the end of the first sentence in paragraph 1.

**Type** the following sentence after the first sentence of the first paragraph:

'They rose early that morning and, after a good cooked breakfast, got the local bus down to the garage.'

Your text should now look like this:

---

### PETER AND MARY GET THEIR NEW CAR

Peter and Mary had been saving to buy a new car for about two years and the day had finally arrived when it would be delivered to their local garage. They rose early that morning and, after a good cooked breakfast, got the local bus down to the garage. When both Peter and Mary arrived at the garage their new car was sitting on the forecourt.

He had decided that he needed a car which would not only provide a satisfactory performance but most importantly one that had plenty of space in the boot for his golf clubs. Peter had spent a long time going through all the road reports he could find. Petrol consumption was also important and the saloon he had chosen was supposed to give him at least 56 miles to the gallon. For Mary, on the other hand, it was more important that the shape and colour were to her liking. She had spent many hours looking at the many different colours available on the market. When she went shopping she would watch all the cars in the car park to decide which shape she liked best.

They both immediately fell in love with their new purchase. The boot was cavernous,

the shape was round and appealing and the colour was just right. After filling in the

paperwork they drove off and waved goodbye to the garage owner.

---

**Save** your file as BU1f.

---

**New CLAIT**

### Inserting paragraph breaks

By now you should be relatively familiar with entering text. However, sometimes on looking back at your work you realise the paragraphs are too long and you want to split them up to make the text easier to read.

To insert a paragraph break is simplicity itself. Place the cursor where you want the new paragraph to start and press the Enter key twice.

---

## Build-up Exercise 1: Stage 12

**Open** file BU1f.

**Place** your cursor in front of the sentence starting 'For Mary, on the other hand, it was more …'

**Press** the Enter key twice.

**Save** your file as BU1g.

### Finding and replacing text

Being able to find and replace text in a document is not only a New CLAIT requirement; it is also a very useful tool if you work with long documents. It allows you to replace a word or words throughout the text.

Imagine that you have just typed a long report on birds in your local area which runs to more than 50 pages. You suddenly realise that where you have typed in 'cuckoo' you should actually have typed 'woodpecker'. There are about 30 occurrences of the word 'cuckoo' and finding each one will not only take an age but you will also run the risk of missing one. As you might expect, Word has a solution.

On the Edit option of the main menu under Replace... there is a dialogue box that allows you to search for the word you want and replace it with another word or words (see Figure 2.18).

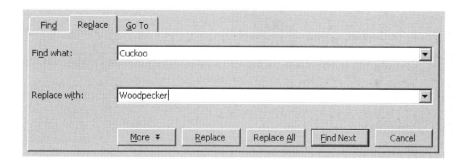

**Figure 2.18** *Replace window*

**KEYBOARD TIP**

You may have noticed on the menu that you can also call up the Find and Replace dialogue box by pressing Ctrl+H.

In the Find what: box you type the word or words you want to replace – in the example above this would be 'cuckoo'. Next, in the Replace with: box you type the new word that is going to replace 'cuckoo'. In this example it would be 'woodpecker'. Word then offers you the choice of either replacing all occurrences of the found word at once or visiting each occurrence separately so you can decide if you want to replace it. The second method can be useful if there are certain places where the original word should be kept. If you use the option that replaces all the occurrences at once you may be faced with the problem of having to then go through the document manually to find the places where you want to revert to the original word.

## Build-up Exercise 1: Stage 13

With file BU1g open:

**Select** Edit on the main menu.

**Select** Replace....

**Type** 'car' in the Find what: box.

**Type** 'vehicle' in the Replace with: box.

▶▶

There should be five occurrences of the word 'car' (or 'cars) in all. Your text should now look like this:

---

### PETER AND MARY GET THEIR NEW VEHICLE

Peter and Mary had been saving to buy a new vehicle for about two years and the day had finally arrived when it would be delivered to their local garage. They rose early that morning and, after a good cooked breakfast, got the local bus down to the garage. When both Peter and Mary arrived at the garage their new vehicle was sitting on the forecourt.

He had decided that he needed a vehicle which would not only provide a satisfactory performance but most importantly one that had plenty of space in the boot for his golf clubs. Peter had spent a long time going through all the road reports he could find. Petrol consumption was also important and the saloon he had chosen was supposed to give him at least 56 miles to the gallon.

For Mary, on the other hand, it was more important that the shape and colour were to her liking. She had spent many hours looking at the many different colours available on the market. When she went shopping she would watch all the vehicles in the vehicle park to decide which shape she liked best.

They both immediately fell in love with their new purchase. The boot was cavernous,

the shape was round and appealing and the colour was just right. After filling in the

paperwork they drove off and waved goodbye to the garage owner.

---

**Save** your file as BU1h.

You should now be able to:

- understand fonts
- spell check a document
- change the line spacing in a document
- insert text
- insert paragraph breaks
- find and replace specified text.

## Changing a page layout

### Changing margins

Changing margins is a New CLAIT requirement.
Word sets its margins by default, according to the template you are using. Although you can easily change these settings you will normally want to do so only for the document you are working on at the time.

To see the screen margin settings on a document you need to be in the Print Layout view mode. You can access this through the View menu option. There are basically four views available, accessed by the following icons:

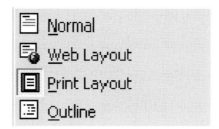

Figure 2.19 shows the page layout view with left, right, top and bottom margins.

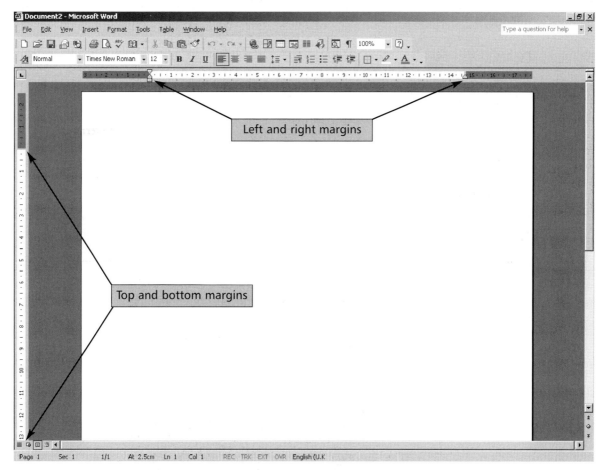

**Figure 2.19** *Page layout view*

Your screen may vary slightly depending on the version of Office you are using, but whether you are using Office 97, Office 2000, Millennium Edition or Office XP the layout will be virtually the same.

There are a number of different ways you can change margins. You can use the Page Set-up option under the File menu item, or you can drag the margins on the screen with your mouse. The method you choose depends to some extent on the level of accuracy you want to achieve and personal preference.

### Option 1: Mouse

Because the tabs that change indents and margins are close together you need to take care that you are actually changing the margins and not the indents when using the drag method. A double-headed arrow will appear when the cursor is in the correct position to change the margin. You can see on the screen in Figure 2.20 where the Margin tabs are relative to the Indent tabs.

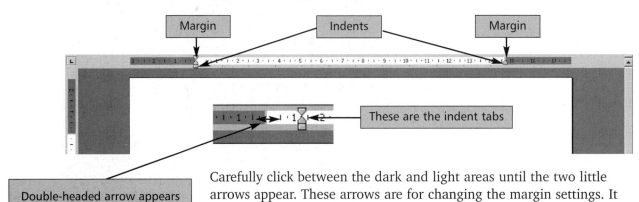

Margin    Indents    Margin

These are the indent tabs

Double-headed arrow appears when margin is selected

**Figure 2.20** *Margins and indents*

Carefully click between the dark and light areas until the two little arrows appear. These arrows are for changing the margin settings. It can be tricky to find the right position to move the margins rather than the indents, so it is sometimes easier to use the Page Set-up... option described next.

### Option 2: Menu

The Page Set-up... option allows you to enter a specific margin setting. To access the Page Set-up... dialogue box use File, Page Set-up... on the main menu.

The dialogue box shown in Figure 2.21a and Figure 2.21b may initially look complicated but for New CLAIT you are only interested in the third and fourth field boxes down, those for left and right margins. Figure 2.21a is for those who are still using Office 97 and Office 2000. If you are using Office XP your Page Set-up dialogue box will look like that in Figure 2.21b. Although they look slightly different they are basically the same and certainly do the same job.

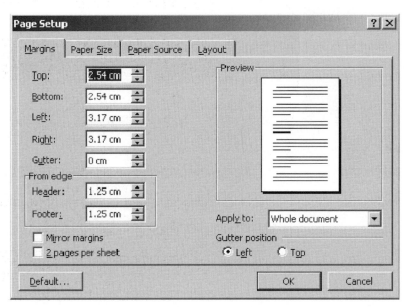

**Figure 2.21a** *The Page Setup dialogue box for Office XP, Margins tab activated*

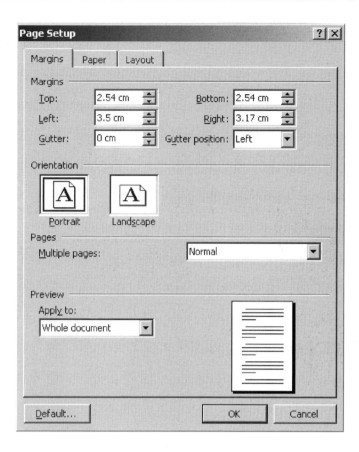

**Figure 2.21b** *Page Setup dialogue box in Office XP*

To increase the left or right margin simply click in the appropriate box and insert the number you want, either by typing the number in directly or by using the arrows to the right of the box. Remember that increasing the margin decreases the printed area of the page. If you want to decrease the margin (i.e. make the typing area larger) then insert a lower number in the appropriate box. For example, the default for left and right margins is usually 3.17 cm. To increase the margins by 2 cm the 3.17 should be changed to 5.17 cm.

## Build-up Exercise I: Stage 14

With file BU1h open:

**Select** File Page Set-up....

**Select** the Margins tab.

**Add** two centimetres to the left-hand margin.

**Add** two centimetres to the right-hand margin.

**Press** OK.

You will be returned to your document. Notice how both margins have moved towards the centre of the page.

## Changing the unit of measurement

The unit of measurement used can also be changed and this is done using Tools, Options... from the main menu. Units available are centimetres, inches, points and picas. When the dialogue box is displayed select the General tab and change to one of the settings offered in the combo box as shown in Figure 2.22.

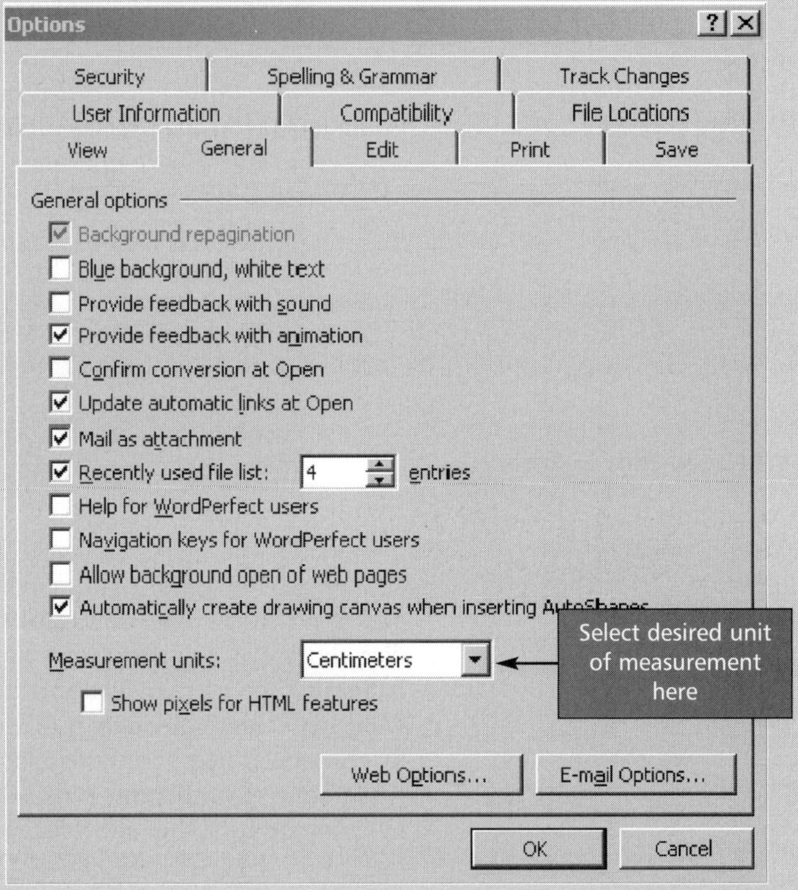

**Figure 2.22** *Options window*

## Using the Undo function

There will be occasions when you make a typing or formatting mistake. Although you are not required to know about the Undo function for New CLAIT it is a very handy little trick to have up your sleeve. To undo the previous action (or actions) you can use the Undo icon on the toolbar, which looks like a bent arrow pointing backwards, or use the Undo option of the Edit menu from the main menu.

Try this out by undoing the margin changes you have just done for Exercise 1. You can then practise using the drag method for changing the margins.

## Build-up Exercise 1: Stage 15

**Press** the Undo icon to undo your margin changes.

**Drag** the margins in by the same amount as before using the mouse.

**Save** your file as BU1i.

## Page size and orientation

While looking at the options in the Page Setup dialogue box, notice the opportunities you have to change the page size and orientation, although these are not New CLAIT requirements. If you are using Office XP the opportunity for changing the orientation from portrait to landscape is given on the Margins tab. If you are using an earlier version of Office this option is given on the tab named Paper Size. Have a look again at Figures 2.21a and 2.21b.

You can select the size of paper you want to use and also the orientation of the paper (i.e. portrait or landscape).

### Try it out

**Select** File, New to open a new document.

**Select** Page Set-up… from the File menu options.

If you are using Office 97 or 2000:

**Select** the Paper Size tab.

**Click** the radio button (the little round one in the orientation box) that says landscape.

If you are using Office XP then simply select the appropriate picture for portrait or landscape.

**Press** OK.

Your page will be changed from portrait to landscape.

## Justifying text in a document

### Justifying text

You will have noticed that the paragraphs in some books have straight edges on both the left-hand and right-hand sides. This is known as 'fully-justified text'. In other words it is aligned on both its left and right edges. You can, of course, have the text aligned to the right or aligned to the left or even aligned in the centre. For New CLAIT you are only required to be able to fully justify or left justify text, but for completeness both right and centre justification are included here.

Have a look at the examples below:

### Left-aligned text

Pressure of work has become synonymous with stress but is this really the case? The expression 'if you want something doing give it to a busy person' does not necessarily mean that the busy person is stressed. It may well be that some people can cope with and thrive on greater amounts of work than others without being stressed. Stress is a mental and physical condition that changes the way we live and enjoy life. There is some evidence that a little stress is good for us, but too much stress can be damaging.

### Right-aligned text

Pressure of work has become synonymous with stress but is this really the case? The expression 'if you want something doing give it to a busy person' does not necessarily mean that the busy person is stressed. It may well be that some people can cope with and thrive on greater amounts of work than others without being stressed. Stress is a mental and physical condition that changes the way we live and enjoy life. There is some evidence that a little stress is good for us, but too much stress can be damaging.

### Centred text

Pressure of work has become synonymous with stress but is this really the case? The expression 'if you want something doing give it to a busy person' does not necessarily mean that the busy person is stressed. It may well be that some people can cope with and thrive on greater amounts of work than others without being stressed. Stress is a mental and physical condition that changes the way we live and enjoy life. There is some evidence that a little stress is good for us, but too much stress can be damaging.

### Justified text

Pressure of work has become synonymous with stress but is this really the case? The expression 'if you want something doing give it to a busy person' does not necessarily mean that the busy person is stressed. It may well be that some people can cope with and thrive on greater amounts of work than others without being stressed. Stress is a mental and physical condition that changes the way we live and enjoy life. There is some evidence that a little stress is good for us, but too much stress can be damaging.

To achieve any of the above results, first highlight the text you want to change, then click on the appropriate icon on the toolbar shown in Figure 2.23. If the Paragraph Format icons are not present by default, you may need to place them on the toolbar using the guidance given on pages 62 and 63.

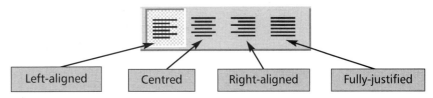

**Figure 2.23** *The Text Alignment buttons on the formatting toolbar*

Alternatively you can use the Paragraph Formatting dialogue box shown in Figure 2.24.

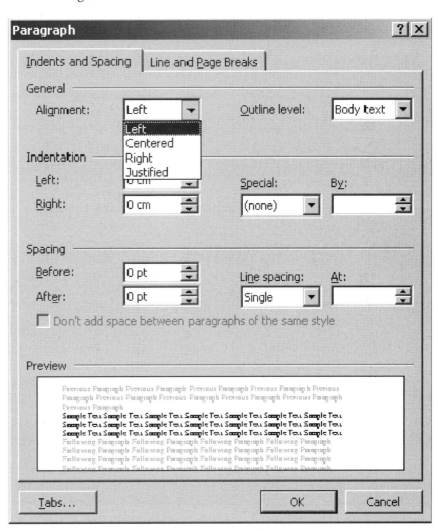

**Figure 2.24** *Paragraph window*

To access this dialogue box go to Format on the menu bar and then select Paragraph. Looks familiar, doesn't it? Well, of course it is, because this is the same box you used to change the line spacing. By now you should be getting familiar with changing the options in the various combo boxes and this is no different to previous ones. Once again, you can also use the Paragraph Formatting icon on the toolbar.

## Build-up Exercise I: Stage 16

**Open** file BU1i if it is not already open.

**Select** Edit, Select All from the main menu.

**Press** the Fully-Justified icon on the formatting toolbar.

Your text should now be fully-justified.

### PETER AND MARY GET THEIR NEW VEHICLE

Peter and Mary had been saving to buy a new vehicle for about two years and the day had finally arrived when it would be delivered to their local garage. They rose early that morning and, after a good cooked breakfast, got the local bus down to the garage. When both Peter and Mary arrived at the garage their new vehicle was sitting on the forecourt.

He had decided that he needed a vehicle which would not only provide a satisfactory performance but most importantly one that had plenty of space in the boot for his golf clubs. Peter had spent a long time going through all the road reports he could find.

Petrol consumption was also important and the saloon he had chosen was supposed to give him at least 56 miles to the gallon.

For Mary, on the other hand, it was more important that the shape and colour were to her liking. She had spent many hours looking at the many different colours available on the market. When she went shopping she would watch all the vehicles in the vehicle park to decide which shape she liked best.

They both immediately fell in love with their new purchase.

The boot was cavernous, the shape was round and appealing

and the colour was just right. After filling in the paperwork

they drove off and waved goodbye to the garage owner.

**Save** your file as BU1j.

You should now be able to:

- change the margins of a document
- change the unit of measurement
- use the Undo function

- change the page size and orientation of a document
- justify text.

## Printing your work

### Understanding the print options

Printing your work is very straightforward. On the File menu item select Print... and the dialogue box shown in Figure 2.25 appears.

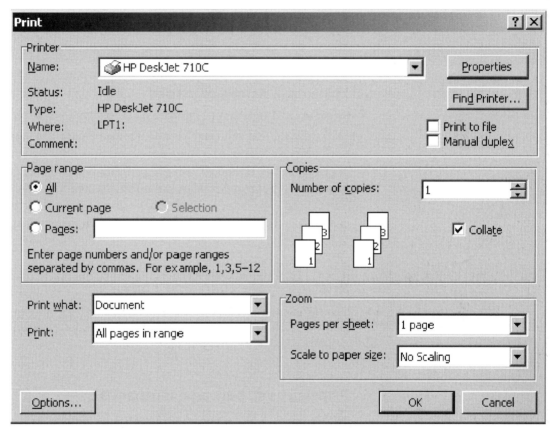

**Figure 2.25** *Print window*

In Office XP, this dialogue box differs slightly from that in earlier versions, but not enough to confuse you as at Level 1 you will not need the additional options offered by Office XP, and they are not covered in this book.

### Selecting a printer

It is perhaps worth spending a little time looking at the Print dialogue box. The name of the printer is shown in the first combo box. This tells you the present default printer; it should be the one you are currently using. If it is not, then click on the arrow to the right of the box and choose your printer from the others in the selection. If your printer is not shown it means it has not been installed on your machine and if this is the case you will need some help to install it.

### Printer set-up

The Properties command button to the top right of the Print dialogue box gives you a variety of options regarding the set-up of the printer and the quality of print. The selections given are self-explanatory. The box underneath tells you whether the printer is in use or idle.

### Print to a file

To the right of the Comment field, a dialogue box gives you the option of printing *to file*. This allows you to save a file and print to another printer at a later time.

### Printing a range of pages

In the Page Range field you can choose to print your entire document (All), just the current page or a selection of pages. It may be that you have amended parts of a long document and only want to print those pages you have edited. If you are printing a number of consecutive pages use a hyphen between the numbers, like this: '2–19'. If, on the other hand, you want to print a selection of pages that are not consecutive then use a comma between each number, like this: '2,5,8,10'.

### Printing more than one copy

The Copies option asks how many copies of your document you want to print, and this section also allows you to collate copies of a document more than one page long.

### Printing just odd or even pages

The Print what box gives you a number of options, but it is unlikely you will need these at present. On the right is a combo box that allows you to choose between printing all the pages in the range, odd pages or even ones.

### New CLAIT

### Printing the document

Once you have reviewed all the options in the Print dialogue box you can make your selections and print your document. To print the whole document, simply ensure that 'All' is selected and then press OK. Alternatively you can press the Print icon 🖨 located on the standard toolbar.

## Build-up Exercise 1: Stage 17

Now print the file BU1j:

**Open** file BU1j if it is not already open.

**Select** File, Print....

**Press** OK.

**Close** the document.

### Exiting the application

There are two standard ways to exit (or close) your application and this applies to nearly all applications as well as Word.

#### Option 1: Menu

The first method is to go to the File, Exit option on the main menu, selecting Exit.

#### Option 2: Toolbar

The second method is to use the Close button next to the Minimise and Maximise buttons on the toolbar of the application:

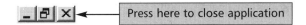
Press here to close application

You should now be able to:

- understand the print options available
- understand how to select a printer
- understand some of the printer set-up options
- print a range of pages
- print multiple copies of a document
- print odd or even pages of a document.

You have now covered all the assessment objectives required for New CLAIT wordprocessing, plus a number of additional features of the software that you should find useful when working with Word.

Now put everything you have learnt for New CLAIT wordprocessing together in one exercise. Once you have completed this assignment you can check your completed version against the solution in Part 3 towards the end of the book.

*Practical assignment 2*

## Unit 2 Wordprocessing using Word

### Scenario

You are a newly appointed manager for a corporate hospitality and seminar centre and you have been asked to prepare a report on your marketing ideas for the coming year.

| Assessment objectives | Stage | |
|---|---|---|
| 1a 5a | 1 | Create a new wordprocessing document. |
| 4a | 2 | Set the left and right margins to 2.5 cm. |
| 2a 3d | 3 | Enter the following text with an unjustified right margin and a left justified margin. |

Marketing Report – 2002

The Caster Seminar Centre opened in June 2002 and despite a slow start in attracting new business to the centre there has, over the last two months, been a significant upturn in both enquiries and bookings.

Returns on our internal questionnaire reveal that there are a lot of companies who have chosen to use their conference and meetings room space for additional office space rather than relocating. This is partly due to the significant increase in rented commercial accommodation.

There is clearly a market for our service and providing we target our publicity material effectively the centre should be able to increase its turnover by at least 50% over the coming year. With sales, excluding hospitality, running at £3,000 per month this would offer the opportunity of increasing our take to £4,500 by June 2003.

The plan is to prepare a professional flyer advertising our services and send it to over 800 companies in the local area. The survey conducted on the accommodation we currently use indicated that at least 10% of local companies would be prepared to use the Caster Seminar Centre for training and meetings. Our present clientele only covers around 30 companies or 3.75% of the potential market.

Our competitors, who offer an inferior service, are attracting between 5% and 10% of the market so there is an opportunity to increase market share. We are now working on a formal marketing plan, which will be available for review in about three weeks.

| | | |
|---|---|---|
| 2a | 4 | Enter your name and today's date below the text leaving a least one blank line. |
| 3b | 5 | Format the heading so that it is larger than the rest of the text. |
| 5b 5d | 6 | Save your report with the filename **PE2_Print_1** and print one copy. |

Having shown your report to the boss she has asked for a number of changes.

| | | |
|---|---|---|
| 4b | 7 | Insert a paragraph break and one clear line space in the final paragraph after the words '...opportunity to increase market share.' |
| 2b | 8 | Insert the following text as the last sentence of the fourth paragraph, after the text, '... of the potential market': |
| | | Early indication from our surveys suggests the 'Service' and 'Professional' sectors are the most likely companies to use our facilities. |
| 2c | 9 | Move the first sentence of the fourth paragraph: |
| | | 'The plan is to prepare a professional flyer advertising our services and send it to over 800 companies in the local area.' |
| | | to become the last sentence of the third paragraph. |
| 2d | 10 | In the second paragraph, which begins 'Returns on our internal questionnaire reveal...' delete the sentence, |
| | | 'This is partly due to the significant increase in rented commercial accommodation.' |
| | | Ensure you maintain the paragraph spacing between the second and third paragraph. |
| 2e | 11 | Replace all occurrences of the word 'companies' with the word 'organisations' (five times in all). |
| 3a | 12 | Change the heading 'Marketing Report – 2002' to a different sans-serif font and set it to point size 14. |
| 3c 3d | 13 | Embolden and centre the heading 'Marketing Report – 2002'. Make sure that the rest of the text in not emboldened. |
| 3d | 14 | Fully justify all text apart from the heading. |
| 4c | 15 | Set the fourth paragraph only in double line spacing. |
| 4a | 16 | Change the left and right margins from 2.5 cm to 2 cm. |
| 5c | 17 | Save the report with the new filename **PE2_Print_2**. |
| 5d | 18 | Print a final copy of the report. |
| 1a 5e | 19 | Close the document and exit the application securely. |

# UNIT 3

# Electronic communication

The New CLAIT electronic communication Unit has five required learning outcomes. Each of the learning outcomes has a number of assessment objectives. As with other units, each assessment objective is linked to specific aspects of knowledge and understanding. Unit 3 of this book addresses all requirements of New CLAIT for electronic communication and provides additional information over and above that required for the qualification to give you a broader understanding of electronic mail and web browsing.

## What you need to know about electronic communication for New CLAIT

For New CLAIT you will need to know how to:

**Identify and use e-mail and browsing software**
- Use appropriate application software.

**Transmit and receive e-mail messages and attachments**
- Create a new message.
- Access an incoming message.
- Reply to a message.
- Forward a message.
- Copy a message.
- Access an attached file.
- Attach a file to an e-mail message.
- Recall a stored e-mail address.

**Navigate the World Wide Web**
- Access specific web page(s).
- Navigate the World Wide Web using hyperlinks.

**Use search techniques to locate data on the Web**
- Use a site-specific (local) search engine.
- Use a general web search engine.
- Locate web page(s) containing required data.
- Save data from a web page.

**Manage and print electronic documents**
- Store a web address (URL).
- Delete an e-mail message.
- Store an e-mail address.
- Store an e-mail attachment.
- Print message(s) and attachment(s).
- Print web pages.

---

> ## *In this unit you will cover:*
>
> - What is electronic communication?
> - Using your e-mail software to send and receive mail
> - E-mail attachments
> - Printing e-mail messages and their attachments
> - Understanding the Internet and the World Wide Web
> - Navigating around the Internet and the World Wide Web

## What is electronic communication?

So that you are not put off from the outset, you need to be clear about what is meant by 'electronic communication' and what it means in relation to New CLAIT. In general terms, electronic communication means the transmission of data down a phone line (or similar) through a modem or other suitable device. For most of us, however, the term means such things as e-mail or browsing the Internet. This is also what it means as far as New CLAIT is concerned. In this unit you will learn how to use some of the software available and how to complete some basic tasks relating to the use of electronic mail (e-mail) and the Internet. You will also learn about some of the terms used, such as World Wide Web (WWW) and Universal Resource Locator (URL or address). There are many more than this, but there are only a few that you will ever need for day-to-day use.

### E-mail

Electronic mail, or e-mail, has revolutionised the way we communicate with each other over short or long distances. You no longer need to go down to the post box and see when the next collection is or if there are collections over bank holidays. Being able to use the e-mail service allows you to send personalised messages all over the world at any time of day or night. From a business point of view you can e-mail important business information in one time zone ready for it to be received in another anywhere in the world. You can send not only simple messages but also other documents you have been working on or graphics. It is an extremely efficient and effective form of communication.

In this unit you will learn how to create and send messages, send attachments and save important messages. You will also learn how to open and read e-mails from friends and colleagues, print messages and store e-mail addresses, avoiding the need to retype an address every time you use it.

E-mail and the Internet brings with it a whole new language that can initially be off-putting. Jargon is prolific in IT, particularly in electronic communication, however, once you have used it yourself a few times you will find you are as good as the next person at reeling it off.

In Appendix 3 are a few of the terms you will come across while using the Internet or e-mail. You are not expected to know all these terms for New CLAIT but you may find it useful to have a basic understanding of what some of them mean. There are literally hundreds of jargon words used in relation to the Internet. A very useful glossary of terms is available through the BBC Webwise program. Also there are many websites devoted to definitions for both the Internet and other aspects of computing and IT.

### Software you can use to send e-mails

Before you can send or receive e-mail messages you will need to set up an e-mail account. Being able to set up an account is not a New CLAIT requirement. If you are following a New CLAIT course with a training provider they will already have accounts set up for you. However, if you want to use e-mail at home you will need to set up your own account before you can send or receive mail. Most large commercial *Internet Service Providers* (ISPs) such as Freeserve, Virgin, AOL, BT and so on will provide you with a CD that allows you to set up both your *browser* and e-mail facilities. Setting up the account usually requires you to simply place the CD provided into your CD drive and follow the instructions. For most people just starting to use e-mail, there are two questions on their minds:

- Which is the best account for me?
- How much will it cost?

There is no simple answer to the first question. Many of the major ISPs offer very similar services and all are effective, simple to use and stable. Some, like AOL, use their own Internet e-mail program while others may use programs such as Microsoft's Outlook Express. As far as costs are concerned, many ISPs now provide a free service and use advertising revenue to cover the costs of providing the service to you. Some providers will charge a monthly fee, depending on the services you want, though you need to remember that your phone line costs will probably be additional to any charges you pay to your Internet provider. Although unrestricted, 'no additional' access is becoming more popular, like most things in life, you get what you pay for!

Have a look at Figures 3.1a, 3.1b and 3.1c. Figure 3.1a shows the screen you would use to write a new mail in Outlook Express. Figure 3.1b is the screen provided by BlueCarrots which you can subscribe to free on the Internet, and Figure 3.1c is NeoMail, an Internet service provided through an ISP. The point is that all of these require the same or similar input to compose a new e-mail message. Each has a place to put the address you are sending the mail to. For example, 'bernard.kane@bksolutions.co.uk'. Similarly each has a place for a copy address and each has a main area where the text of the message is written. As is often the case, the provider you choose to use is largely a matter of personal preference, as is the way in which you use e-mail.

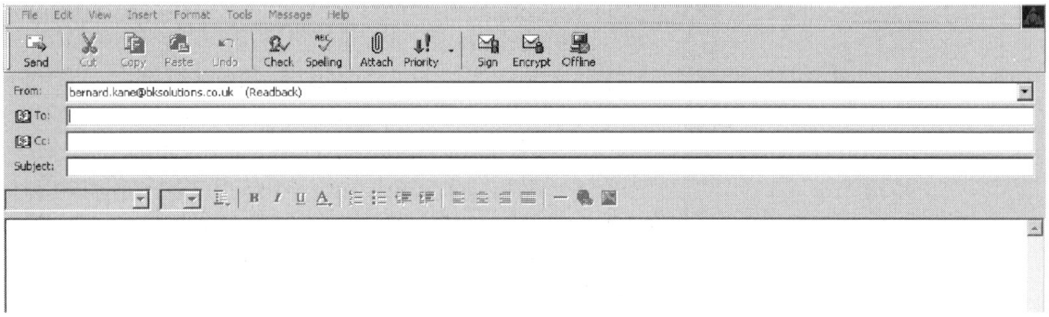

**Figure 3.1a** *New mail Message screen*

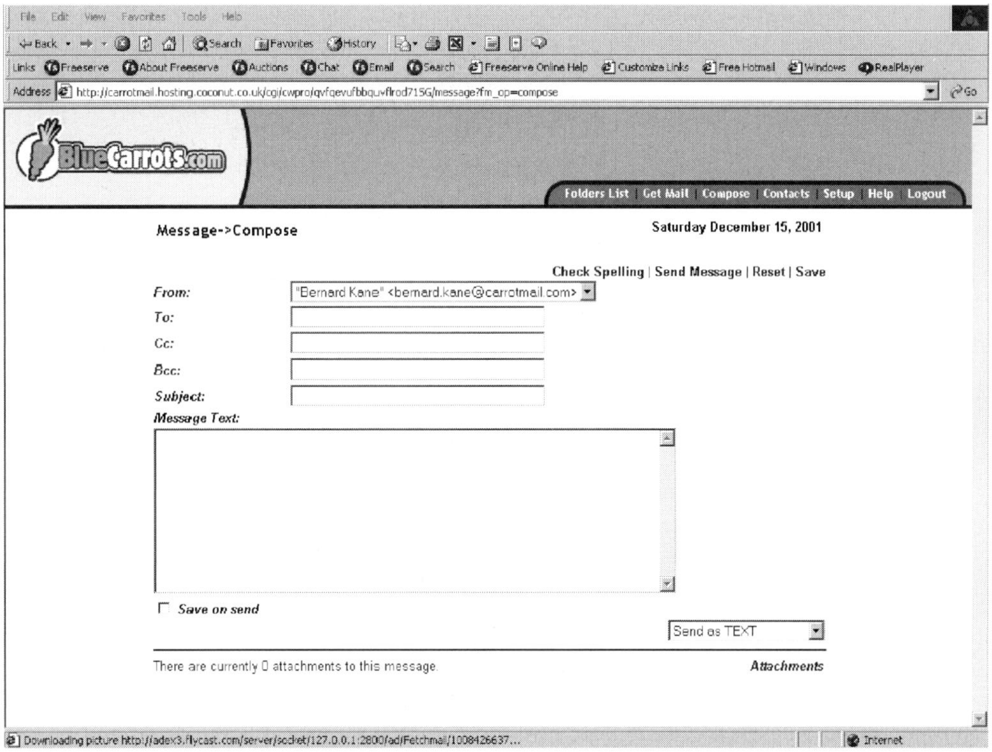

**Figure 3.1b** *BlueCarrots screen*

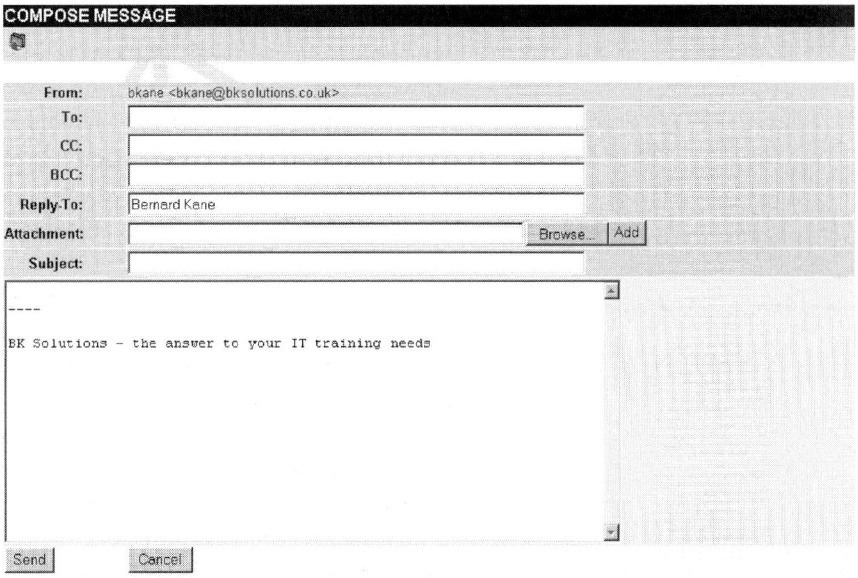

**Figure 3.1c** *NeoMail screen*

**New CLAIT**

## Using your e-mail software to send and receive mail

### Creating a new e-mail message

For the purposes of this unit you will be using Outlook Express. Have a look at Figure 3.2 below.

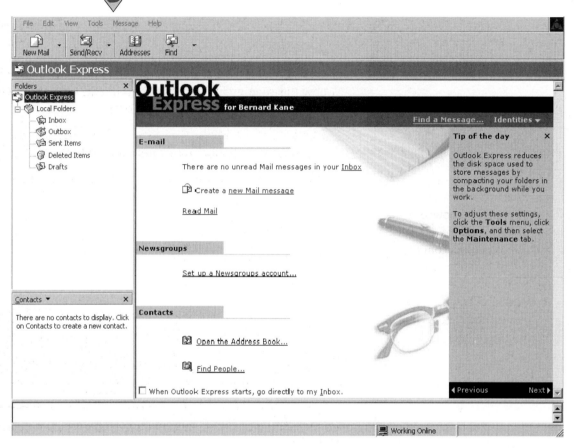

**Figure 3.2** *The Outlook Express screen*

If you are starting with a new computer at home, when you first open Outlook Express it will guide you through a Wizard that helps you set up your e-mail account. The main screen of Outlook Express is fairly self-explanatory. In the top left is a section called Folders. Here you will see a main folder called Outlook Express. Then there will be a sub-folder called Local Folders. The sub-folders of Local Folders are what you are really interested in. There will initially be five sub-folders of local folders named:

- Inbox
- Outbox
- Sent Items
- Deleted Items
- Drafts.

Below the Folders box is one called Contacts. At first this will state that there are no contacts to display. This must be true, since you have yet to set up any contacts.

In the main screen to the right of the Folders and Contacts boxes you are provided with a number of options, from creating a new mail message to reading mail and setting up new contacts.

This section of the unit assumes that you have organised a provider and set up an e-mail address and account. If you have not yet done this then you should do so before completing the unit.

Now try to create and send a new message through a Try it out exercise.

## Try it out

**Open** Outlook Express.

**Select** the Inbox folder. You may well see that you already have a new message giving you information and help about Outlook Express sent automatically by Microsoft.

**Click** on the New Mail icon on the toolbar [New Mail]. A dialogue box similar to that shown in Figure 3.3 will appear.

**Click** in the To: box and enter your own e-mail address.

**Click** in the Subject: box.

**Type** 'Test Message'.

**Click** in the Message window.

**Type** 'This is my first e-mail'.

### GENERAL TIP

You will have been asked to provide an e-mail address as part of the set-up for your ISP. This will usually start with your name followed by the server address. So bernard.kane@aol.com or bernikane@fsnet.co.uk or bernard.kane@bksolutions. co.uk could all be legitimate e-mail addresses.

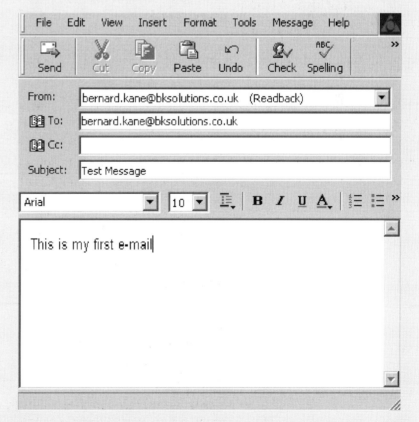

**Figure 3.3** *This is my first e-mail*

**Press** the Send button on the toolbar .

The first time you press the Send icon a dialogue box will appear telling you that your mail will be placed in the Outbox. You can choose not to have this notification each time by checking the 'Don't show me this again' box.

Depending on how your Outlook Express is set up, and whether or not you are already 'on-line', sent mail will be placed in the Outbox and either delivered as soon as you connect to the network or after pressing the Send/Recv icon [Send/Recv].

If you are planning to write a number of e-mails, you don't really want your telephone bills mounting up while you compose them. It is usually better to write all your e-mails first and then send them together. As you complete each message and press the Send button your e-mails will be placed in the Outbox. Some ISPs now offer a monthly fee service that includes calls, and if you have chosen one of these accounts it is clearly less important how long you are on-line.

Whether your Outlook Express is set up to send mail immediately or not, it will send mail after pressing the Send/Recv icon and a connection has been made.

If you are not connected you will first be asked if you want to 'go on-line'. You will then see the Dial-up Connection box shown in Figure 3.4.

---

**E-MAIL TIP**

If you are planning to write a number of e-mails and want to send them as a batch, if you are already on-line you can instruct Outlook Express only to send mail when you are ready. Under Tools on the main menu select Options... and then the Send tab. Uncheck the 'Send messages immediately' box. Mail will then be sent only when you next press the Send/Recv icon on the toolbar [Send/Recv].

---

**Figure 3.4** *Dial-up connection box*

**Enter** your user name and password.

When you open Outlook Express, and before you go on-line, you can check whether there are messages to be sent as the Outbox displays the number of unsent messages in brackets (see Figure 3.5).

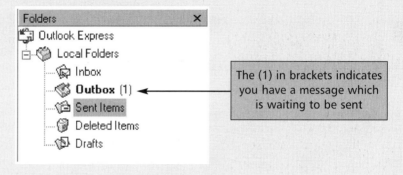

The (1) in brackets indicates you have a message which is waiting to be sent

**Figure 3.5** *Outbox unsent messages display*

## New CLAIT

### Accessing incoming e-mail messages

You could be forgiven for asking why you were asked to send an e-mail to yourself, and how is it possible to do this. In the first place it is an easy way to get practice in sending and receiving mail and secondly it is possible because of the way in which e-mail communication works. Have a look at the picture in Figure 3.6.

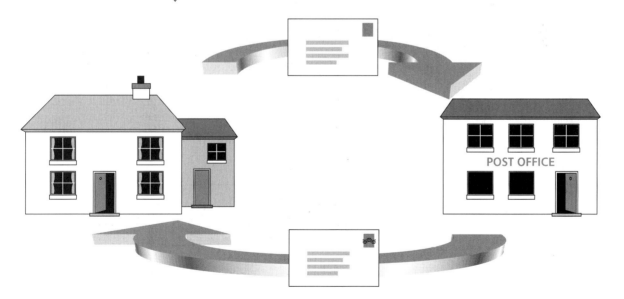

**Figure 3.6** *The traditional paper-based postal system*

There is nothing to stop you sending a letter from your own home to yourself. The letter leaves the house and is sent to the Post Office for sorting. The letter is then collected and delivered back to your house. E-mail works in a very similar way. Have a look at Figure 3.7.

Your computer

ISP

e-mail leaves your computer to ISP's server

olivetti

**Figure 3.7** *An ISP server*

ISP server identifies address and forwards

The normal mail delivery is very similar to the electronic system. All that is different is that the mail is sent electronically rather than manually.

### Opening and reading your mail

As you saw above, the Outbox will always show you whether there is mail waiting to be sent. In a similar way, the Inbox will display e-mails that have not yet been read by enclosing a number in brackets after the word 'Inbox' under Folders. It also displays who the unread e-mails are from, their subject matter and the date they were sent. Some providers offer a range of ways to tell you that there is mail waiting to be read. For example, AOL will display something like 'You have mail'; others will automatically display all the messages, one underneath the other, or say simply 'You have no messages'.

**Try it out**

**Open** Outlook Express.

**Press** the Send/Recv icon on the toolbar.

When the Dial-up dialogue box appears,

**Enter** your user name and password.

**Press** Connect.

Once the connection has been made you should see one e-mail in the Inbox (see Figure 3.8). ▶▶

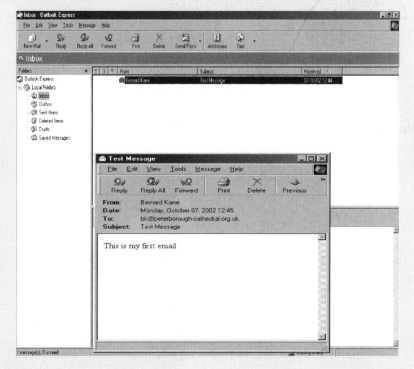

**Figure 3.8** *Inbox waiting messages display*

**Double-click** on the message to read your mail (see Figure 3.9).

**Figure 3.9** *E-mail message display*

## Using the Address Book

When you created your first e-mail you typed the address (in this case your own) directly into the To: box. However, say you were sending a whole series of individual e-mails to a number of different people. It would be extremely laborious to have to type the address in each time you wanted to send an e-mail to a particular person. Microsoft provides a facility called the Address Book where you can store all your frequently used e-mail addresses. The Address Book is accessed by pressing the Address Book icon on the toolbar

or by using the <u>T</u>ools, Address <u>B</u>ook option on the main menu.
A dialogue box similar to Figure 3.10 will appear.

**Figure 3.10** *E-mail Address Book*

This box allows you to see the names and addresses already in your Address Book. When you first use the Address Book there will, of course, be no names to see. Adding addresses is very straightforward. Do this now through a simple Try it out exercise.

**Try it out**

**Open** Outlook Express.

**Click** on the Address icon.

**Click** on the New icon.

**Select** New Contact (the dialogue box shown in Figure 3.11 will appear).

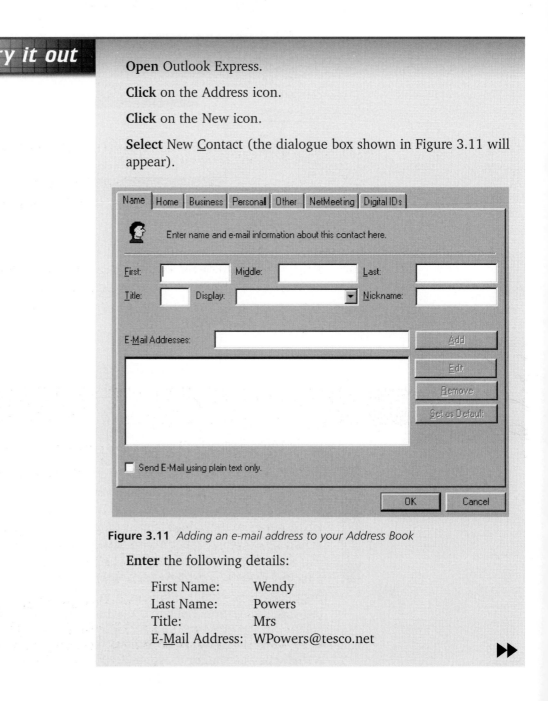

**Figure 3.11** *Adding an e-mail address to your Address Book*

**Enter** the following details:

| | |
|---|---|
| First Name: | Wendy |
| Last Name: | Powers |
| Title: | Mrs |
| E-Mail Address: | WPowers@tesco.net |

We could, of course, now go on to fill in all Wendy's other details such as her home and business addresses, spouse's name and so on. For now, the above will be enough.

**Press** OK.

Your new name will now appear in the address list.

Now **enter** a second name:

First Name:      Bernard
Last Name:      Powers
Title:               Mr
E-Mail Address:  BPowers@tesco.net

**Press** OK.

### Copying a message

For New CLAIT you will need to know how to send a copy (cc) of a message to a third party. There are two ways to copy a message.

- carbon copy (cc)
- blind carbon copy (bcc)

By using the 'cc' box the main addressee will see and know who the message has been copied to, however if you use the 'bcc' box the main addressee will not see who has also had the message.

### Try it out

**Open** Outlook Express.

**Create** a New Mail message by pressing the New Mail icon.

**Click** on the Address icon to bring up the address box.

**Select** Wendy Powers.

**Press** the To:-> button.

**Select** Bernard Powers.

**Press** the Cc:-> button.

Wendy Powers will be displayed in the To:-> message recipients.

Bernard Powers will be displayed in the Cc:-> message recipients as the carbon copy recipient of the message (Figure 3.12). ▶▶

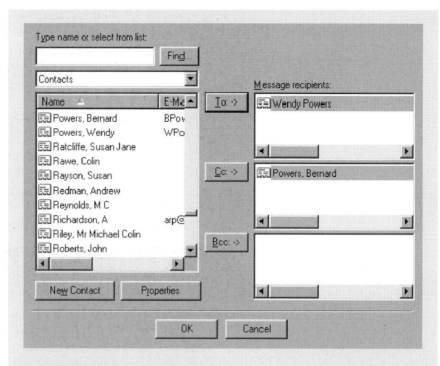

**Figure 3.12** *Copying a message*

**Press** OK.

Complete the message as shown in Figure 3.13.

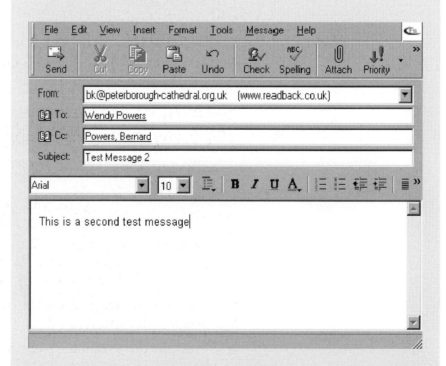

**Figure 3.13** *E-mail message window*

**Press** Send.

Remember that by pressing Send you are sending your mail to the Outbox. The actual message will not be sent to the recipient until you go on-line. Since this is a fictitious e-mail address there is no point in sending it so you will delete the message.

### Deleting a message

To delete a message from either the Inbox or the Outbox simply select either Inbox or Outbox. Use the right-hand mouse button and click on the message. From the drop-down menu select <u>D</u>elete.

Now put some of the skills you have learnt into practice in a Build-up exercise. In this exercise you will enter the details of your e-mail address into the Address Book, create a message, send a message to yourself, access and read your message and finally delete your message.

### Build-up Exercise 2: Stage 1

**Open** Outlook Express.

**Open** the Address Book and enter the following details:

First name
Last name
Title
e-mail address

If you don't yet have your own e-mail account use the following: 'yourname@somewhere.co.uk'

When you have completed all these details,

**Press** OK to close the Address Book.

### Build-up Exercise 2: Stage 2

**Create** a new message addressed to yourself and include the following details:

To:         Your own e-mail address
            (e.g. me@somewhere.co.uk)
Subject:   A message to me
Message:   This message is to help me understand how to create and send e-mail messages.

**Send** your message to the Outbox.

If you are using a proper e-mail address and account, make a connection using the Dial-up Connection dialogue box and send your e-mail.

If you are using a dummy address you do not need to dial-up a connection.

## Build-up Exercise 2: Stage 3

If you send an e-mail with your own address through a live connection:

**Check** you have a dial-up connection.

**Press** the Send/Recv icon or use the Send and Receive option on the main menu.

**Check** you have received the message sent in Stage 2.

**Open** the message in the Inbox.

**Delete** the message in your Inbox.

If you used a dummy e-mail address,

**Open** the Outbox.

**Delete** the message 'A message to me'.

You should now be able to:

- create a new e-mail message
- send an e-mail
- open and read new e-mail
- create an address in the Address Book
- copy a message to someone else
- delete an e-mail.

### New CLAIT

### Forwarding an e-mail

In addition to copying an e-mail you can also forward a message received from someone else. Forwarding a message is very similar to sending an original one and New CLAIT includes this skill as a requirement in its syllabus. To forward a message open the message you want to forward and click on the Forward icon  .

The dialogue box should look familiar. Type in the e-mail address you want to forward the message to and press the Send button.

Have a go at forwarding a message.

### Try it out

**Open** Outlook Express.

With the Inbox selected,

**Press** the New Mail icon.

**Enter** your e-mail address in the To: field.

**Enter** 'Forwarding Messages' in the Subject: field.

▶▶

**Type** the following message: ' I am forwarding this message to myself for practice'.

**Press** the Send icon to put the message in the Outbox.

**Press** the Send/Recv icon, and if you are off-line:

**Enter** your user name and password.

**Press** Connect to get a dial-up connection.

**Open** your Inbox, and

**Double-click** on the new message with the subject 'Forwarding Messages'.

This time notice that there is a Forward icon on the toolbar .

**Press** the Forward icon.

**Insert** your e-mail address.

**Press** the Send icon.

**Press** the Send/Recv icon.

This time when you receive your new mail the message will be prefixed by **Fw:**, indicating that this message has been forwarded by someone else.

## New CLAIT

## E-mail attachments

From time to time either people will send you attachments in the form of text files or graphics or you may wish to send attachments to someone for information. New CLAIT requires you to be able to understand how to attach, access, store, and print e-mail attachments.

### How do I know if I have an e-mail with an attachment?

When your Inbox shows that you have new mail, the preview window on the right-hand side of the window will display a small paperclip next to any e-mails that have one or more attachments (see Figure 3.14).

Paperclip shows e-mail has an attachment

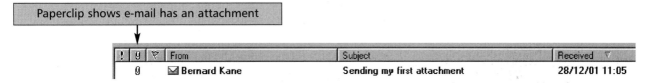

**Figure 3.14** *E-mail attachment bar*

### Accessing and saving e-mail attachments

When the Inbox displays a new message, open the message in the normal way by either double-clicking on it or highlighting it and selecting File, Open on the main menu. This time you will see the text of the message and the dialogue box also indicates that there is an attachment waiting for you to view or save (see Figure 3.15).

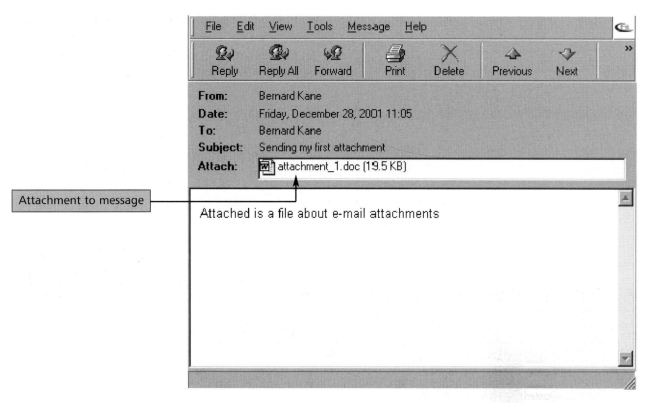

Attachment to message

**Figure 3.15** *E-mail attachment message*

Helpfully, Outlook Express shows that the attachment is a Word file and so by double-clicking on it the file will automatically open in Microsoft Word and save your document in the normal way.

Alternatively, you can store (or save) your attachment to view later by using the File, Save Attachments... option on the menu bar. The dialogue shown in Figure 3.16 appears.

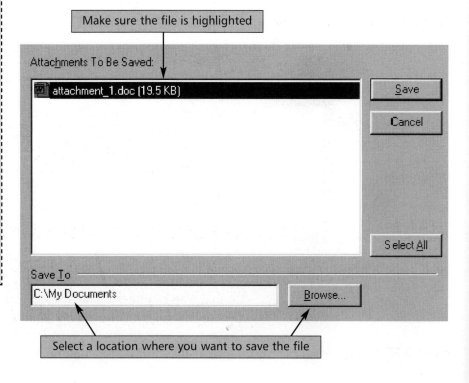

Make sure the file is highlighted

Select a location where you want to save the file

**Figure 3.16** *Attachments to be Saved window*

Using the <u>B</u>rowse… command button select the folder where you want to save your file. Once you are happy that you have the correct folder in the Save <u>T</u>o: box, press the <u>S</u>ave button. You can now retrieve this file whenever you want as it is saved on your hard disk.

## Sending an attachment

Sending an attachment with an e-mail message is almost as easy as receiving one. First you create a New Mail message. Include the address, any copy addresses and the subject. Enter the text for your message. Before pressing the Send button go to the Insert option on the menu and then select File <u>A</u>ttachment… . Follow the stages shown in Figure 3.17.

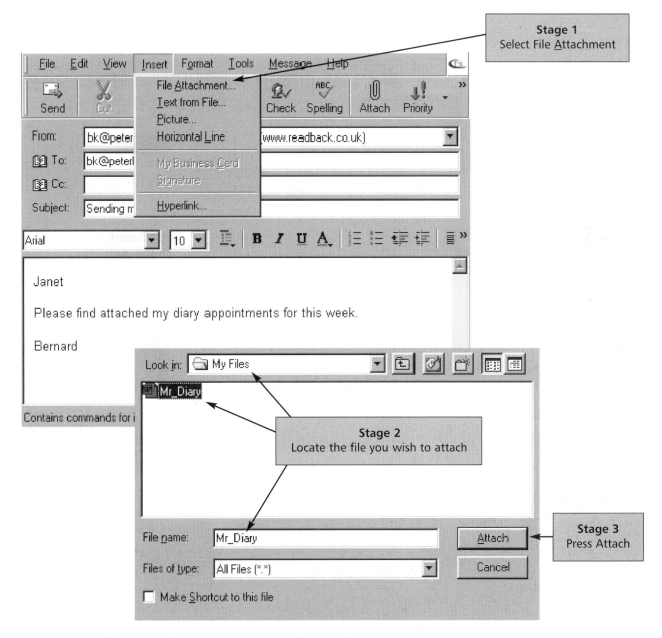

**Figure 3.17** *Sending an attachment*

When the Insert Attachment dialogue box appears, first locate the file you wish to attach. Then, making sure this is shown in the File _name:_ box, press the _A_ttach button. You are now returned to your new mail but this time you have a new attachment showing in the Attach: field (see Figure 3.18).

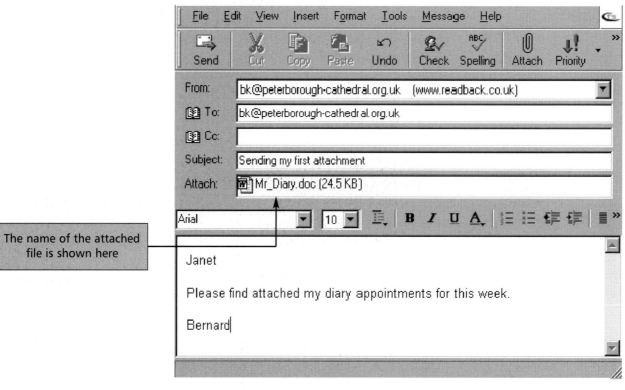

The name of the attached file is shown here

**Figure 3.18** _New mail showing name of attachment_

Now you can send your e-mail in the normal way by pressing the Send button and then the Send/Recv icon when you are ready to send the message.

As Outlook Express searches for any new mail and also any mail to send, it will show you graphically how far it has got in the process (see Figure 3.19 on page 120).

Now have a go at a Build-up exercise to give you practice at attachments.

**GENERAL TIP**

E-mail messages with attachments take longer to send than messages without attachments. The length of time it takes to send the message will largely depend on the size of the file attached to it. Text files will tend to transfer fairly quickly, whereas graphic files are normally larger and will take a little longer.

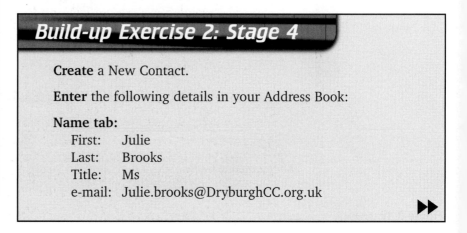

**Build-up Exercise 2: Stage 4**

**Create** a New Contact.

**Enter** the following details in your Address Book:

**Name tab:**
    First:    Julie
    Last:    Brooks
    Title:    Ms
    e-mail:  Julie.brooks@DryburghCC.org.uk

**Business tab:**

| | |
|---|---|
| Company: | Dryburgh City Council |
| Street Address: | West Street |
| City: | Dryburgh |
| State/Province: | Cambs |
| Zip Code: | PE3 1SE |
| Job Title: | Community Group Leader Co-ordinator |
| Department: | Community Services |
| Phone: | 01743-648452 |
| Fax: | 01743-648453 |
| Web Page: | http://www.DryburghCommunityCentre.org.uk |

**Create** a new message using your own e-mail address with the following information:

| | |
|---|---|
| To: | your e-mail address |
| Subject: | Dryburgh Community Centre – Bookings |

In the main message section:

**Type:**

'Please find attached details concerning the arrangements for booking the above centre.

Julie Brooks

Community Group Leader Co-ordinator'

From the CD accompanying this book:

**Attach** the Word file named **Attachment.doc**.

**Press** the Send button to send your message to the Outbox.

If you are working off-line:

**Press** the Connect button on the Dial-up dialogue box.

**Press** the Send/Recv button to send your e-mail message and attachment.

**Press** the Send/Recv button a second time to receive the message you have just sent.

**Save** the file **Attachment.doc** to your hard or floppy disk.

## Printing e-mail messages and their attachments

New CLAIT requires students to be able to print e-mail messages and any attachments that form part of the e-mail. Printing the attachment is very straightforward. Simply open the attachment as explained above and then print the document in the normal way. So, for example, in the previous Build-up exercise you would open attachment_2 by either double-clicking on it and printing it in Word or, if you saved the file to disk, open Word and then the Word file in the usual way.

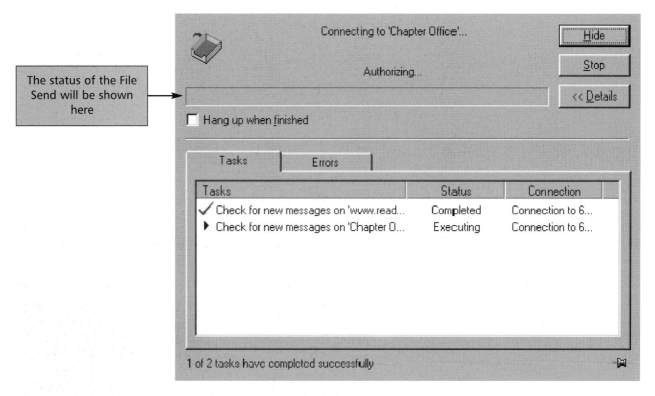

The status of the File Send will be shown here

**Figure 3.19** *Status of the messages file*

To print a message, first open the message, by either highlighting it in the Inbox and selecting File, Open from the main menu or double-clicking on the message. From the message's box select the File, Print from the menu as shown in Figure 3.21.

Your printout will show you who the message was sent from, who the recipient is, the date and time the message was sent, the name of any attachment files, the subject matter and the message itself.

Have a go now at printing the message you received from Julie Brooks (albeit from yourself).

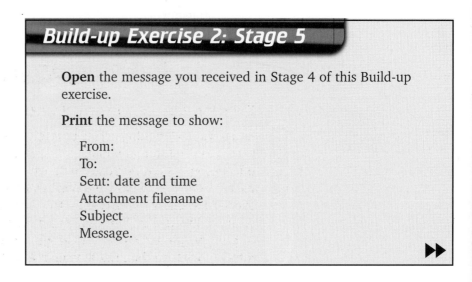

## Build-up Exercise 2: Stage 5

**Open** the message you received in Stage 4 of this Build-up exercise.

**Print** the message to show:

    From:
    To:
    Sent: date and time
    Attachment filename
    Subject
    Message.

Once you are happy with your printout, which should look similar to Figure 3.20,

> **Delete** the message from your Inbox.

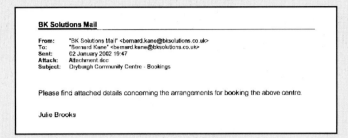

Figure **3.20** *E-mail printout*

**Remember:** to delete a message click on the Inbox and then, with the right-hand mouse button, click on the message to be deleted and select Delete.

Select File... →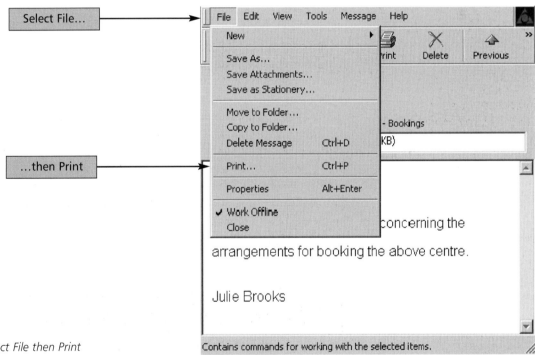

...then Print →

**Figure 3.21** *Select File then Print*

## Printing copies of sent items

In addition to printing copies of received e-mail correspondence you may also want to retain hard (printed) copies of mail you have sent to other people. Printing items you have sent as opposed to those you have received is virtually the same as printing received e-mail messages except that instead of accessing the Inbox mail the Sent Items folder is selected. In the Sent Items folder simply select the messages you wish to print and, as for received messages, select File, Print... from the menu or click on the Print icon on the toolbar.

You should now be able to:

- forward an e-mail message
- understand about e-mail attachments
- save an attachment
- print messages received and sent
- print attachments.

You have now covered all the requirements in New CLAIT for electronic mail. The next section looks at the World Wide Web – one part of the Internet.

## Understanding the Internet and the World Wide Web

The chances are that if you are reading this book you will have heard of the Internet and the World Wide Web, but what are they? Many people talk of the Internet and the World Wide Web as if they are one and the same – they are not. The Internet is a physical thing; it is a network of networks. When computers are linked together they form a *network*. There are various different types of network, from those of a very local nature to others that cover a wide geographical area. The Internet is a vast network of computers all linked together through telephones, cables and satellites. Have a look at Figure 3.22.

**Figure 3.22** *The Internet*

Put simply, the Internet is a series of computers linked physically and is fundamentally a transportation system allowing vast amounts of information to be transported from one computer to another anywhere on or above the globe. No one really knows how many computers form the entire Internet but it runs into countless millions. In the last section you looked at electronic mail – this is a service provided through the Internet.

## The World Wide Web (WWW or W3)

The World Wide Web (or WWW or W3 as it is variously known) is another service provided on the Internet. Earlier in this unit you were given a number of definitions for some of the jargon used. The basis of the World Wide Web is a programming language called Hypertext Markup Language (HTML) and it is this language that allows you to use hypertext. Web pages are written in HTML. If you have used Help in any of your Microsoft applications you will have noticed some words are in blue and are underlined. These are links to other pages or documents and are known as hyperlinks (see Figure 3.23).

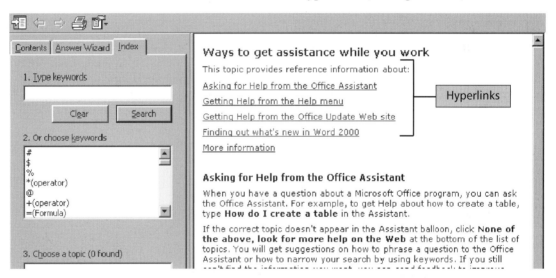

**Figure 3.23** *Hyperlinks in the Microsoft Help menu*

If you click on a word or a series of words in this format it will take you to the underlying address for that web page or document. You will be pleased to learn that for New CLAIT you do not need to know (unless you intend to cover web pages) how HTML or hypertext work but simply that they exist and what they are for.

## Internet browsers

In this unit you will be using Microsoft's Internet Explorer to logon to the Internet. This software is known as a browser and allows you not only access to the Internet but also to view all the documents on the World Wide Web. There are a number of browsers available for you to use but the two most common are Netscape and Internet Explorer. These are known as 'graphic browsers' because they facilitate your being able to view images, videos and other forms of graphic files. You will cover Microsoft's Internet Explorer in a little more detail shortly.

### Search sites (engines and directories)

As the name suggests, these allow users to search for information on the World Wide Web. If the actual address is known, or the *URL* for the web page being searched, this can be entered straight into the address field on your browser. However, with literally millions and millions of addresses available on the Web, it would be impossible for anyone to know all of them so search engines are used to help find web pages that contain words or phrases that are of interest. Without these search facilities it would be virtually impossible to find the required relevant information quickly. There are primarily two types of search site that you are likely to come across; search engines and site or web directories. A search engine will ask you to key in a word or phrase that helps to find the range of information sought and it will search its own database of websites that contain that word or phrase and take you directly to a website or page. Site directories are similar but provide a list of sites organised by headings such as arts, computers, entertainment, travel, finance and so on. Usually these sites are broken down into sub-headings to allow you to refine your information needs. For example, 'computing' may be broken down into software, hardware, Internet, sales and products, etc. Nowadays many search engines are a mixture of the two.

Examples of search engines for both categories are:

- http://www.google.com
- http://www.yahoo.com
- http://www.infoseek.com
- http://www.hotbot.com
- http://www.altavista.com
- http://webcrawler.com
- http://www.excite.com
- http://www.about.com

There are, of course, many more. Again, which you use is very much down to personal preference, in terms of both the one that has the best links for what you are looking for and also style, speed of search and ease of use.

### Understanding URLs

A URL is an address that identifies a document on the Web. URLs have a common format and each part of the address has a particular relevance to finding a document. Take a look at this address:

http://www.msn.com/

The first part of the address – http:// – identifies the fact that you are looking for a web server (as opposed to a mail server, for example). The www.msn.com identifies the actual computer on which the document is stored, and anything after the final / identifies the actual document and its type. A URL is to the Internet what a full address is to a house or company.

### Getting to know Internet Explorer

Microsoft Windows provides a browser called Internet Explorer (IE) for you to use. To launch Internet Explorer you can use the IE icon on your desktop, the toolbar icon or use the Programs, Internet Explorer option from the Start button as shown in Figure 3.24.

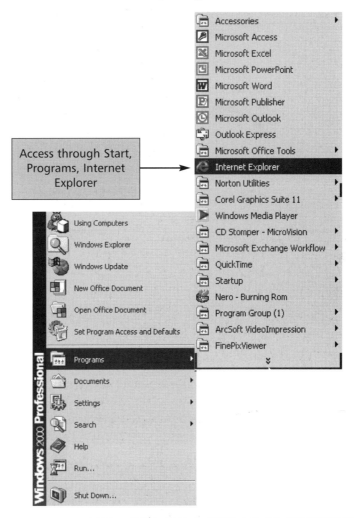

**Figure 3.24** *Launching Internet Explorer*

---

## Try it out

**Press** Start.

**Select** Programs.

**Select** Internet Explorer.

**Press** Connect in the Dial-up Connection box to connect to the Internet.

Explorer will open on the web page that has been set for the default Home Page option. The Home Page is set up through the Internet Options dialogue box, which can be found under Tools on the main menu. In the example shown in Figure 3.25 the Home Page default is the MSN UK Home Page with the URL: http://www.msn.com.

Your opening page may differ depending on what default has been set.

**Figure 3.25** *MSN Home Page*

You should now be able to:

- understand the concept of the World Wide Web (WWW)
- have an understanding of Internet browsers
- understand what search engines are
- understand what URLs are
- open Internet Explorer

**New CLAIT**

## Understanding the Internet Explorer window

Having opened Internet Explorer lets have a look at the layout. The layout for Explorer is a little different from other windows you may be used to, so this will be looked at in some detail (Figure 3.26).

### The Internet Explorer window

**Address box:** This is probably the most important part of Internet Explorer's window and is where you put the URL (address) of where you want to go.

**Main menu:** Much of this will be familiar, but notice on the menu that there is an item called Favourites (also called Bookmarks in other browsers, such as Webscape Navigator). This allows you to add favourite sites that you visit often to a favourites list. This will be covered later.

▶▶

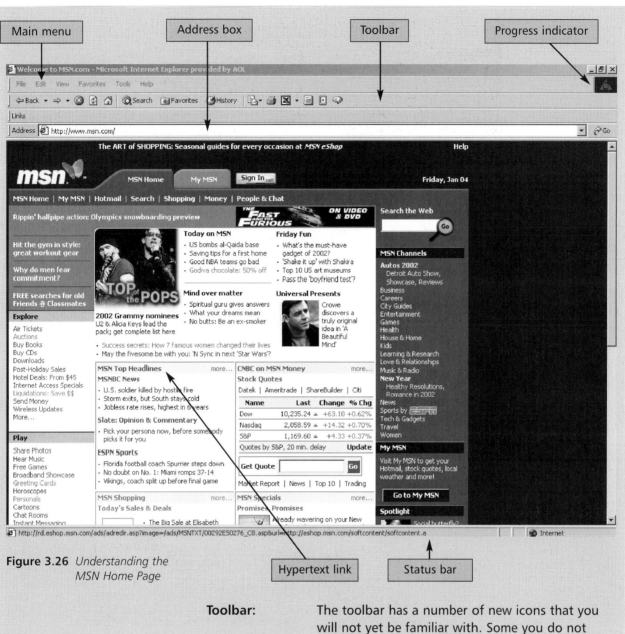

**Figure 3.26** *Understanding the MSN Home Page*

| Toolbar: | The toolbar has a number of new icons that you will not yet be familiar with. Some you do not need to know about now, but those shown below are important: |
|---|---|

The History icon is a toggle switch and allows you to look at the sites you have visited recently so that you can return to them without necessarily placing them in your favourites list. Clicking on the icon will show the list and clicking on it a second time will hide the list.

The Favourites icon is also a toggle switch and by clicking on this the favourites folder will be displayed on the left of your screen. Look at Figures 3.26 and 3.27.

▶▶

Favourites button off

Favourites button on

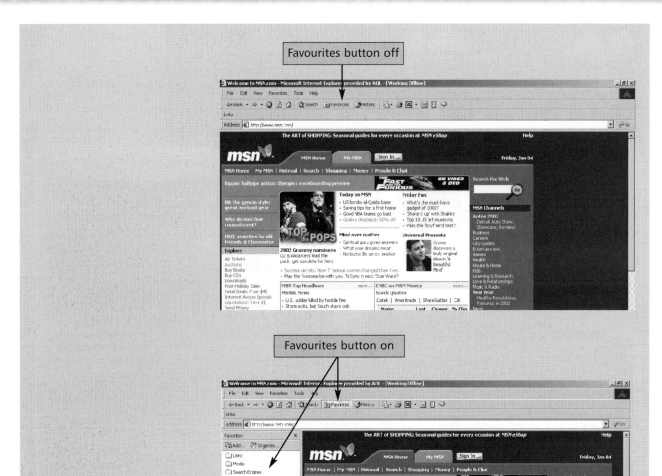

**Figure 3.27** *Favourites button on and off*

| Progress indicator: | The progress indicator graphic will vary depending on the ISP you are using. If you are Microsoft only this will be an 'E' for Explorer. In Figure 3.26 it is the AOL symbol. Whichever symbol is displayed it will animate by rotating or spinning while the browser is searching for a site, downloading information or completing some other task. When no activity is taking place, the symbol will be motionless. |
| --- | --- |
|  | The Search icon is also a toggle button which, when pressed, presents you with a search field to the left of the browser window. See Figure 3.28. |

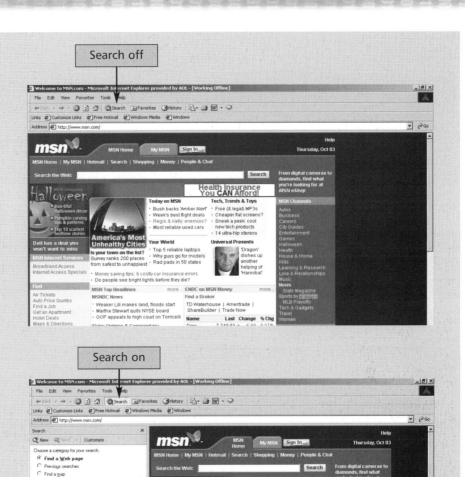

**Figure 3.28** *Search button on and off*

**Hypertext link:** Hypertext links are underlined text that provide a link to different parts of the same website or other websites. As you move the cursor over a piece of hypertext the cursor changes to a hand.

**Status bar:** This shows the name of the file or document that is being downloaded. When the browser is working hard you will notice a lot of activity going on in the status bar. By running the cursor over hypertext in the web page, the status bar will indicate the URL of that link.

The Home icon loads the starting page. Until closed, each page viewed remains in memory. You may find you have moved through several pages of the same website and then want to return to the starting page.

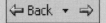

The Back icon allows you to return to the previously viewed pages, and similarly the Forward icon allows you to move forward to pages you have already viewed.

**Try it out**

**Press** the Internet Explorer icon or use the Start menu option to launch Internet Explorer.

When prompted, if you are not on-line,

> **Press** the Connect button to connect to the Internet.
>
> **Press** the Favourites icon on the toolbar.
>
> **Click** in the Address box, and
>
> **Type** www.nelsonthornes.com. The text will be highlighted.
>
> **Press** Enter.

Notice how Internet Explorer automatically places the http:// in front of the www.

> **Select** the Add button (see Figure 3.29).

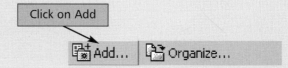

**Figure 3.29** *Select the Add button*

When used for the first time,

In the Add Favourite dialogue box:

> **Press** New Folder....
>
> **Click** Create In....
>
> **Enter** the new folder's name 'Publishers' (see Figure 3.30).

**Figure 3.30** *Naming a new folder*

In the Name: field of the Add Favourite dialogue box:

**Type** Nelson Thornes.

**Press** OK.

Your new favourite website under the folder Publishers has now been added to the favourites list, as shown in Figure 3.31. Each time you want to visit this site, all you need to do is select Publishers in your favourites folder and click on Nelson Thornes. Obviously you do not have to put anything in the favourites folder. You could enter the address of the site you want to visit in the Address box of your browser each time you use the Internet. However, using the favourites folder is a time saver and also means you don't need to remember the address every time you use a certain site.

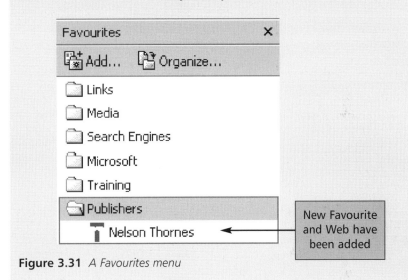

**Figure 3.31** *A Favourites menu*

### Changing your default Home Page

Sometimes you will find that you use one Home Page more than others and in this case it makes sense to change the default page to the one you use most regularly. For example, let's say you normally used www.google.com as your search engine and each time you used Internet Explorer you wanted it to open at the Google website. You can do this by changing the default Home Page address. Under Tools on the main menu you select Internet Options.... Re-type the address of the site you want to use as your default in the Address: field. Have a look at Figure 3.32.

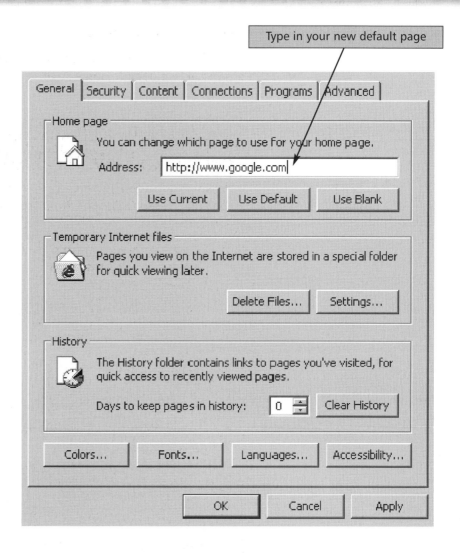

Type in your new default page

**Figure 3.32** *Changing the default Home Page address*

## Try it out

**Open** Internet Explorer and connect to the Internet.

**Select** Internet Options from Tools on the main menu.

**Type** http://www.google.com in the Address: field.

**Press** OK.

**Close** Internet Explorer but don't disconnect.

**Re-open** Internet Explorer.

This time, instead of http://www.msn.com (or whatever default you had initially), the Google search engine has become your default.

**Repeat** the exercise but, this time, replace Google with your original default address.

### ADDRESS TIP

If you are unfamiliar with URLs and think you may not be able to remember your original default setting, write the address down before you change it.

You should now be able to:

- understand the Internet Explorer window
- change the default Home Page.

---

## Build-up Exercise 3

You are going to create a new folder in favourites called 'Search Engines'. In the folder you will include the following search engines:

> http://www.about.com
> http://www.google.com
> http://infoseek.com
> http://www.lycos.com
> http://www.webcrawler.cpm
> http://www.yahoo.com
> http://www.altavista.com

**Open** Internet Explorer.

**Create** a new sub-folder of favourites and call it Search Engines.

If you are not already on-line, make a connection to the Internet.

**Open** the first search engine to be added to the favourites list – www.about.com.

**Hint:** Enter the address in the Address box field and press Enter.

**Press** the Favourites button.

**Select** Add....

**Click** on your new Search Engines folder.

Accept the default name in the Name: box.

**Press** OK.

Now add the remaining search engines following the same procedure as above. The names in your folder for each search engine should be as follows:

> http://www.google.com – Google
> http://infoseek.com – Infoseek
> http://www.lycos.com – Lycos
> http://www.webcrawler.com – Webcrawler
> http://www.yahoo.com – Yahoo
> http://www.altavista.com – Altavista

Your Search Engine folder should now look similar to Figure 3.33.

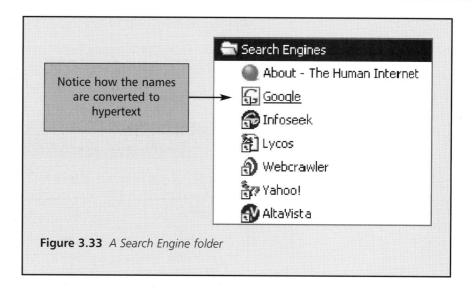

**Figure 3.33** *A Search Engine folder*

## Navigating around the Internet and the World Wide Web

**New CLAIT**

### Using a general search engine to find specific information

Now that you are happy with Internet Explorer and you have set up a number of search engines in your favourites folder, it is time to learn how to use search engines to find specific data. For New CLAIT you will be expected to be able to instigate a search for specified information by navigating the WWW using a general search engine and then understanding how to use the links contained in the site to 'drill down' to find information on specific subject matter. You will also be expected to locate a specified website and select material from that site based on a local search.

**Try it out**

### Scenario

You have decided that you want a short break in November to Rome. Using the following information find out how much a flight to Rome will cost.

| | |
|---|---|
| Date out: | 1 Nov 02 |
| Date return: | 7 Nov 02 |
| Departure: | Any London Airport |
| Passengers: | 1 adult |

**Open** Internet Explorer and dial-up a connection to the Internet.

**Select** The Google search engine from your favourites list.

**Type** Flights + Europe + ebookers in the search field (Figure 3.34).

▶▶

**Figure 3.34** *Selecting flights using the Google search engine*

**Press** Enter.

**Click** on any hyperlink that indicates ebookers.com.

The ebookers site should appear on the screen (Figure 3.35).

**Figure 3.35** *ebookers window*

**Click** on Flights at the bottom of the page in the ebookers site.

**Enter** the details for the required flight.

**Press** Enter.

**Print** your results.

**Note:** Companies are constantly updating their websites and the information contained in them. The figures in this exercise are for illustration and may be different from those you access. However, the principles will remain the same.

Having input your required details, ebookers will search for the answers to your flight query and then show the results of the search. Figure 3.36 illustrates the type of return you might expect.

▶▶

**Figure 3.36** *Flight window*

## Using a site-specific (local) search engine

New CLAIT requires that you are able to locate relevant data from a specific website using a site-specific (local) search engine. In this case you are going to follow a simple Build-up exercise to locate specific information about a book using the Nelson Thornes URL www.nelsonthornes.com.

### Build-up Exercise 4: Stage 1

*Scenario*

You are a Learning Assistant in the local college and one of the tutors has rung you and asked if you can find out about a book on CLAIT and IBT II by an author with the surname Kane. He doesn't know the full name of the book but thinks it begins with Mastering. He does know it is published by Nelson Thornes publishers. He would particularly like to know the ISBN. Your task is to find the details of the book, and print the page with the details of the book. He has also heard that Nelson Thornes advertises job vacancies on the site and has asked if you would access this page and send him a sample of some of these in a text file via e-mail.

**Open** Internet Explorer and make a connection to the Internet.

**Type** www.nelsonthornes.com in the Address box of your browser.

**Press** Enter.

Using the search facility for products:

**Search** for the book by author, with the name Kane.

**Print** the page with details of the book.

---

**SEARCH TIP**

Select the Jobs tab at the top of the home page.

## Build-up Exercise 4: Stage 2

**Search** for the page on the website that refers to jobs.

**Select** The Nelson Thornes employer.

**Save** the details of the first page as a text file in an appropriate folder or on a disk to access later.

**Hint:** Use File, Save As.... In the Same As Type... box press the arrows on the right of the box and select the text file (*.txt) option.

**Close** Internet Explorer.

---

## Build-up Exercise 4: Stage 3

**Open** Outlook Express.

**Create** a new e-mail message with the following details:

| | |
|---|---|
| To: | use your own e-mail address |
| Subject: | Mastering Office 2000 through CLAIT and IBT II |
| Message: | Further to your request, the name of the book you were interested in is called *Mastering Office 2000 through CLAIT and IBTII* by Bernard Kane. The ISBN is 0-7487-6501-8. I have also attached a text file of the first page of job vacancies advertised at Nelson Thornes. |
| | Yours sincerely |

**Enter** your name at the end of the message.

**Attach** the saved job text file.

**Send** the e-mail to the Outbox.

**Send** your e-mail from the Outbox to its recipient.

> ### Build-up Exercise 4: Stage 4
>
> **Press** the Send/Recv icon to receive the e-mail.
>
> **Open** the attached file in Word.
>
> **Save** the attachment – give it a different name from the original.
>
> **Print** both the message and the attached file.
>
> **Close** Outlook Express and the dial-up connection.

## Saving an image from the web

In addition to saving text files from the web, for New CLAIT you will also need to know how to save images from web pages or sites. The process is fairly straightforward. First find the image you want to download and save. With the right-hand mouse button, click on the image and a menu appears similar to that shown in Figure 3.37.

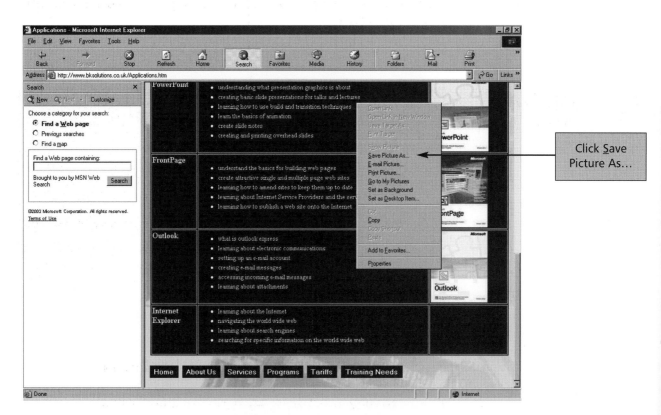

**Figure 3.37** *Saving an image from a web page*

There are a number of options to choose from but you are interested in the 'Save Picture As…' item. Clicking on this will open the Save Picture dialogue box shown in Figure 3.38.

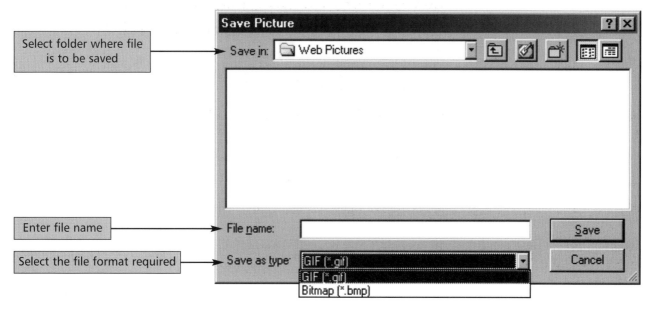

**Select folder where file is to be saved**

**Enter file name**

**Select the file format required**

**Figure 3.38** *The Save Picture dialogue box*

The options you have for the format will usually be either GIF or Bitmap. First select the folder to which the picture is to be saved and then enter the name you wish to call the image. After selecting the file format, press Save.

## Try it out

**Connect** to the Internet using your normal browser.

Using your right-hand mouse button:

**Click** on one of the images in the default web page.

**Select** Save Picture As.

**Save** the picture to your hard or floppy disk using one of the file formats available.

**Close** the browser and Internet connection.

You should now be able to:

- use a general search engine to find specific information
- use a site-specific search engine
- save an image from a website to your hard/floppy disk.

This completes all the skills you will need for the electronic communication unit of New CLAIT. Now have a go at Practical Assignment 3. Once you have completed this assignment check your work against the solution in Part 3 towards the end of the book.

**Practical assignment 3**

## Unit 3 Electronic communication

### Scenario

You are a medical secretary working in a large local hospital for one of the consultants. You have impressed on your boss the need for more IT training for both yourself and others in the department. Your job is to advise the selected training company of your needs.

| Assessment objectives | Stage | |
|---|---|---|
| | | The first thing you need to do is e-mail your colleagues and ascertain what their needs are so that you can establish what training is needed and the cost. |
| 1a<br>2a | 1 | Create a new e-mail message. (Note: for practical reasons, you will be sending the e-mail to yourself.)<br><br>To: Your e-mail address<br>Subject: IT Training<br><br>Message:<br><br>Dear Colleague<br><br>The Personnel Department has agreed that we can submit a request for IT training following the installation of our new computers and software. Please see the attached document and let me have your views.<br><br>Your Name |
| 2g | 2 | Attach the file **Training.doc** (on the CD) to your message.<br>Now send this e-mail to yourself. |
| 2b<br>2d<br>2f<br>5e | 3 | Open the Inbox in your mail software and open the new message you sent.<br>Open the attachment and save it with a different filename (e.g. **Training2.doc**) to your hard or floppy disk.<br>Print both the e-mail message and the attachment.<br>With the saved attachment open, fill in the form and save the file. |
| 1a<br>2g | 4 | Create a new message (again to yourself).<br><br>Message:<br><br>Thank you for your e-mail and request for information on training. Please find attached my response to your request.<br><br>Enter your name at the bottom of the message.<br><br>Attach the completed training form and send the message. |

### Scenario

You have now received all the forms from your colleagues and see that many of them are seeking help with tables, mail merge and creating presentations for the talks given by the consultants. You pass your findings to the Personnel Manager who asks you to investigate who you might get to put together a suitable training programme and how

*Practical assignment 3 (cont.)*

much it might cost. You have estimated that a two-day course should be all that is needed. You have also heard of a training company called BK Solutions, who think they may be able to help.

| 3a 4a | 5 | Make a connection to the Internet.<br>Type in the following URL (web address): www.bksolutions.co.uk<br>Once you have located the site find the page called 'tariffs'.<br>Copy the table giving the tariff details and paste it to a new Word document.<br>Save this new document as **Tariffs** to your hard or floppy disk. |
|---|---|---|

### Scenario

In two of the replies you received from colleagues there was some interest in learning about definitions relating to the Internet. You decide that although this would not be suitable to include in the general training it might be helpful to provide those who were interested, with a list of Internet definitions.

| 4b 4c 4d 5a 5f 6 | 6 | Make a connection to the Internet.<br>Using one of the general web search engines, locate a web page that has Internet Definitions.<br>Once you are satisfied with the page selected, add the page to your favourites folder.<br>Copy the information and paste it to a new Word document and save the document as **Internet_defs**.<br>(For the purposes of the exercise do not copy more definitions than would fill one half of an A4 page.)<br>Print the web page containing the definitions. |
|---|---|---|
| 2a 2e 2g 5c | 7 | Create a new e-mail message:<br><br>To: Personnel@myhospital.org.uk<br>Copy to: ConsultantA@myhospital.org.uk<br>Subject: IT Training<br>Message:<br>For Mrs Jones<br><br>Dear Mrs Jones<br><br>I have now consulted with all my colleagues concerning the proposed IT training. The general consensus is that training in a variety of Word functions and PowerPoint presentations would be most useful.<br><br>My research indicates that we would need two days' training at a cost of £1,000 for ten of us. That equates to £50 per day each, which seems very reasonable.<br><br>I have attached relevant details of costs from the company.<br><br>Your name |
| | 8 | Send the e-mail to the outbox (you should work off-line). |
| 5e | 9 | Print both the e-mail message and attachment. Make sure that details (To, CC, From, Date, Subject) are shown and also that details of attachments are shown. |

# Spreadsheets using Excel

New CLAIT's unit on spreadsheets has five learning outcomes and each of these has several assessment objectives. As in other units, each assessment objective is linked to specific aspects of knowledge and understanding. Unit 4 of this book addresses all requirements for New CLAIT in respect of spreadsheets and provides additional information over and above that required for the qualification to give you a broader understanding of spreadsheets and how they work.

## What you need to know about spreadsheets for New CLAIT

For New CLAIT you will need to know how to:

### Identify and use spreadsheet software correctly
- Use appropriate software.

### Use an input device to enter and edit data accurately
- Insert text and numerical data.
- Insert a row or a column.
- Delete a row or a column.
- Amend text and numerical data.

### Insert, replicate and format arithmetical formulae
- Use formulae that produce correct results.
- Replicate formulae (fill).
- Recalculate data.

### Use common numerical formatting and alignment
- Align text.
- Align numerical data.
- Display numerical data as an integer (i.e. to zero decimal places).
- Display numerical data as a decimal to two decimal places.
- Display as currency (to include £ sign).

### Manage and print spreadsheet documents
- Create a new spreadsheet.
- Save a spreadsheet.
- Save a spreadsheet with a new filename.
- Print a spreadsheet with formulae showing in full.
- Print a spreadsheet with data showing in full.
- Close a spreadsheet.

## In this unit you will cover:

- What are spreadsheets?
- Working with data
- Navigating around worksheets
- Layout and changing column widths
- Saving a spreadsheet
- Entering, displaying and replicating numerical data and formulae
- Automatic recalculation of data
- Using common numerical formatting and alignment
- Printing a spreadsheet display

When you are completing the New CLAIT spreadsheet assignments you are not allowed any numerical data errors or errors in calculated totals, so 100% accuracy is essential. Although this may seem harsh, if you think about it the requirement makes a lot of sense. If you type a letter and make a couple of spelling mistakes it will not necessarily alter the meaning of the letter. However, if you incorrectly enter the wrong data (or numbers) into cells that you then add up, the answer will be wrong. Things in spreadsheets are either right or wrong – there is nothing in between. However, you are allowed three errors in text, but clearly it is best to try and avoid any errors if at all possible.

## What are spreadsheets?

Spreadsheets are essentially sophisticated calculators. They were initially used as accounting aids to carry out mathematical calculations on rows and columns of figures. Today the worksheet is still primarily an electronic calculator, but modern spreadsheets allow you not only to perform simple and complex arithmetical calculations but also to create 'what if' scenarios, and much more.

### Using Excel for the first time

To open Excel use Start, Programs, Microsoft Excel, or alternatively use the Excel shortcut icon on the Microsoft Office shortcut toolbar.

**Try it out**

**Press** Start.

**Select** Programs.

**Select** Microsoft Excel.

### The Excel window

When you have opened Excel, the applications window will look either like Figure 4.1a or Figure 4.1b, depending on which version of Office you are using. Figure 4.1b is basically the same as 4.1a although when you initially open the application you have a number of options on the right-hand side of the page, which do not appear in Excel 97 or Excel 2000. These options are available to you from the main menu in these earlier versions.

If you are using Microsoft Office XP click on the Close icon as indicated in Figure 4.1b. You will then see that both versions are more or less identical. The first thing to notice is that the screen is very similar to Word except that there is a grid where your document window would normally be.

Since Excel uses some different terminology from other applications, the box below shows a number of new terms you will come across later in this unit.

### Spreadsheet terms used in Excel

| | |
|---|---|
| **Address** | The address is the location referred to in terms of a cell. For example, A1, B2 or F7. |
| **Cell range** | A cell range is a range of selected cells. For example, this could be A1 to D4. If you are using Excel XP, 2000 or Excel 97 there are 256 columns and 65,536 rows per worksheet. If you are using an earlier version you will have a smaller range. When using a range, the start and end point is distinguished by a colon, e.g. B4:D9. |
| **Column heading** | A column heading describes or defines the cells within a given column of a spreadsheet, e.g. column A, column B, column C and so on. |
| **Formula bar** | This displays the location and contents of the current cell (i.e. where the cursor is located). It also shows any formula used in the cell. |
| **Sheet tabs** | These allow you to display different spreadsheets within your workbook and to move between worksheets. By default, the tabs are called Sheet 1, Sheet 2 and Sheet 3. The default name can be changed, for example to Company A, Company B and Company C. For New CLAIT you do not need to know about different sheets. |
| **Workbook** | A workbook is a file holding a collection of worksheets. When a new document is created in Excel it automatically has the default name Book 1, Book 2, etc. This is equivalent in Word to the default name Document 1, Document 2, etc. |
| **Worksheets** | Worksheets are the basic building blocks of a spreadsheet. They are comprised of a number of cells used for the storage of data. Usually cells are linked, which allows you to analyse the data contained in a range of cells. |

**Figure 4.1a** *The screen that appears when you open a new worksheet in Excel – versions prior to Office XP* ▶

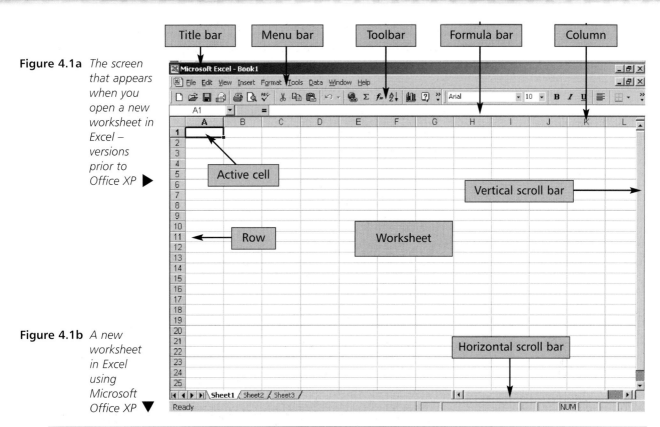

Title bar | Menu bar | Toolbar | Formula bar | Column

Active cell

Vertical scroll bar

Row

Worksheet

Horizontal scroll bar

**Figure 4.1b** *A new worksheet in Excel using Microsoft Office XP* ▼

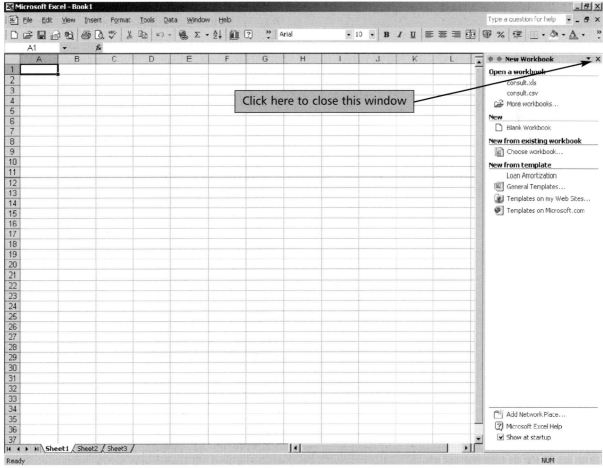

Click here to close this window

## Working with data

### Data types

Before starting to work with data you will need to understand the types of data that Excel supports.

Excel supports four basic data types:

- values (e.g. numbers)
- text (e.g. headings, notes, etc.)
- functions (e.g. Sum, Average, Count)
- formulae (these can be simple formulae such as '=A1+B1' or a combination of numbers, text and functions).

Excel recognises the type of data you input by the characters you use, for example:

- **Numbers:** digits (e.g. 1, 2, 3, 4, 5), a decimal point (1.23), a hash sign (#), a percentage sign (%), a plus sign (+) or a minus sign (–).
- **Text:** any string of characters (e.g. A1, 7FG, :8, etc.)
- **Formulae:** formulae are always preceded by an equals sign (=).

### Cell alignment

Text and numerical data are aligned differently by default. Numbers in cells are right justified and text is left justified. As you type numbers into a cell they appear on the left of the cell until you click outside the cell you are working on or press the Enter key. Default alignments can be changed, as you will see later in this unit.

### Inserting text and numerical data

Being able to enter data is a New CLAIT requirement. You can enter data in two ways: directly or using the formula bar.

### Direct entry

By placing the cursor where you want to enter the data and clicking on the relevant cell you can type in the required data. The information can be seen both in the cell and in the formula bar.

### Using the formula bar

First click on the cell to where the data is to be stored. Then click in the formula bar and type in the text, numbers or a formula and it will automatically be reproduced in the cell where the cursor is located. Conversely, you can type numbers or a formula directly into a cell and the formula bar will automatically show you the contents of that cell.

Have a go at entering some data into a new worksheet.

**Try it out**

**Open** Excel.

*Numerical data*

**Option 1: Typing data into the spreadsheet cell**

**Click** in cell A1.

**Type** in the number 45.

**Click** outside the cell for Excel to accept the entry.

**Click** the cursor in cell B1.

**Type** in the number 34.

**Click** outside the cell to accept the entry.

**Click** the Undo icon twice.

**Option 2: Typing data into the formula bar**

**Click** the cursor in cell B1.

**Click** in the formula bar.

**Type** in the number 62.

**Click** the cell B2.

**Type** in the number 89.

**Click** outside the cell to accept the entry.

**Close** the file without saving.

*Text data*

**Open** a new workbook.

If you are using Office 97 or 2000 go to File New... on the menu or press the new workbook icon.

If you are using Office XP then either press the New Workbook icon or the Blank Workbook option offered on the right-hand side of the screen, which is displayed after the File New... option is selected from the main menu.

| New |
| --- |
| ☐ Blank Workbook |

**Option 1: Typing data into the spreadsheet cell**

**Click** the cursor in cell A1.

**Type** The Book.

**Click** outside the cell or press Enter for the text to be accepted.

**Option 2: Typing data into the formula bar**

**Click** the cursor in cell B1.

**Click** in the formula bar.

**Type** The Boat.

**Click** outside the cell or press Enter.

You should now be able to:

- distinguish between types of data
- understand the default alignment of data types
- insert numerical and text data directly into a worksheet
- insert numerical and text data using the formula bar.

## New CLAIT

### Amending text and numerical data

Being able to delete data is a New CLAIT requirement. If you have entered numerical or text data incorrectly you will need to understand how to delete or amend any mistakes you have made. Deleting text (or numbers) is very straightforward. Once data has been entered, by clicking back on the cell and pressing the Delete key Excel will remove the cell contents. However, if the cell is formatted deleting will not remove these features.

(**Note:** a cell can be formatted in a number of ways. For example, numbers in cells can be formatted to a required number of decimal places, or as currency or percentages. Cells can be formatted in terms of the alignment of text and numbers, font style or borders.)

To remove all contents including formatting you need to use the Clear, All option on the Edit menu. It is easier to demonstrate this with a Try it out exercise.

### Try it out

**Open** a new worksheet.

**Click** in cell A1.

**Type** in the number 40 and press Enter.

Note that the cursor has automatically moved down to the next cell.

**Type** in the number 40 in cell A2.

**Press** Enter.

**Click** in cell A2 again.

**Select** Format, Cells from the main menu.

> **Select** Number in the Category: box. Make sure Decimal places: is set to '2'.

Notice how your original '40' changes to '40.00'.

> **Highlight** cells A1 and A2.

> **Press** the Delete key.

The contents of the cells will disappear.

> **Re-enter** the number 40 in both cells A1 and A2.

Notice how the formatting of A2 is still set to two decimal places.

> **Repeat** the above steps, but instead of pressing the Delete key use the Clear, All on the Edit menu.

When you re-enter the numbers, the formatting in cell A2 has reverted to the default (without decimal places).

## Navigating around worksheets

So far you have only used very small parts of a worksheet, typically cells at the top of the sheet in the A or B columns. Potentially a worksheet can have tens of thousands of rows and many dozens of columns. You could well be working on a worksheet created by someone else and not know how big it is. Knowing how to move around a worksheet can be extremely useful although this is not a formal New CLAIT objective. Moving around a worksheet is not that dissimilar to moving around a Word document. Either move the cursor using the mouse and click in the cell where you want to be or alternatively use the arrow keys on the keyboard to move from one location to another.

In large worksheets you can use the 'GoTo' shortcut commands. These are either F5 or Ctrl+G. These are, incidentally, the same for Word documents.

**Try it out**

> **Press** F5 and type AB6000 in the Reference box.

> **Press** OK and the cursor will relocate itself to the nominated cell.

> **Press** F5 and return to cell A1.

Repeat this exercise using the Ctrl+G command.

### Moving between worksheets

If your workbook has a number of worksheets you can move between them by either using the tabs at the bottom of the worksheet or, if you prefer, using the keyboard shorcuts Ctrl+Page up or Ctrl+Page down.

**New CLAIT**

## Layout and changing column widths

Every time you open a new workbook Excel automatically gives you a blank worksheet into which you can start entering data. However, if you were preparing a presentation for someone on paper you would not start writing something down before you had given some thought to its layout. This is no different from designing a new workbook.

Here are a couple of examples (Figures 4.2 and 4.3).

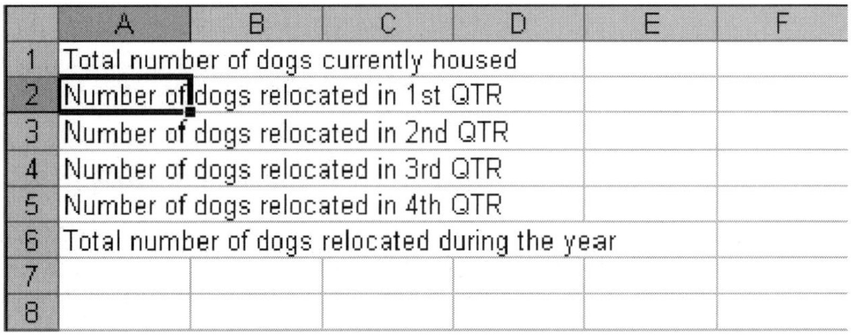

| | A | B | C | D | E | F |
|---|---|---|---|---|---|---|
| 1 | Total number of dogs currently housed | | | | | |
| 2 | Number of dogs relocated in 1st QTR | | | | | |
| 3 | Number of dogs relocated in 2nd QTR | | | | | |
| 4 | Number of dogs relocated in 3rd QTR | | | | | |
| 5 | Number of dogs relocated in 4th QTR | | | | | |
| 6 | Total number of dogs relocated during the year | | | | | |
| 7 | | | | | | |
| 8 | | | | | | |

**Figure 4.2** *Excel spreadsheet*

In column A, rows 1–6 display the row headings.

Data relating to each row heading is placed in cells B1–B6.

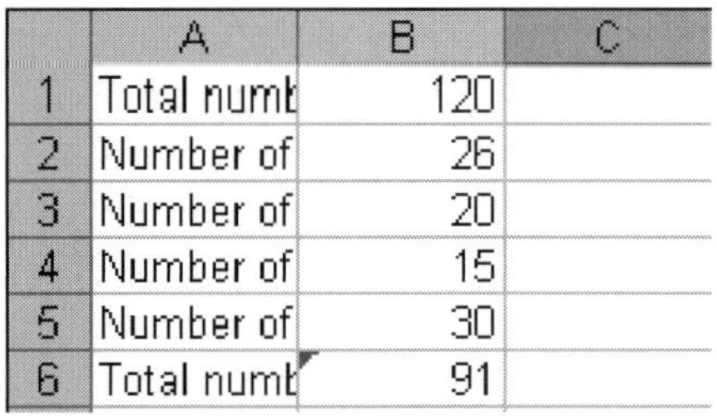

| | A | B | C |
|---|---|---|---|
| 1 | Total numb | 120 | |
| 2 | Number of | 26 | |
| 3 | Number of | 20 | |
| 4 | Number of | 15 | |
| 5 | Number of | 30 | |
| 6 | Total numb | 91 | |

**Figure 4.3** *Excel spreadsheet, with data cut off in column A*

In Figure 4.3 you can see that the text in column A is cut off because it flows into the cells of column B. (Note: this would be OK if column B did not have any data in it as the text would simply move across into that column.) However, since column B is not blank part of the text in rows A1–A6 is hidden. Clearly it would be difficult, if not impossible, for someone looking at the worksheet to understand from the text in view what the data represented.

It would be far better if the data were moved to the first blank column as it would then be unaffected by column B; in this case, looking at Figure 4.2, the first column unaffected by the row headings is F. Placing the data in column F could be one solution but this would leave columns C, D and E unused. Technically there is nothing wrong with this approach but it is not really good practice. Another solution would be to change the width of column A. One way of doing this is by placing the cursor between the columns until the cursor changes to a double-headed arrow and then holding the left mouse button down and dragging the column to the desired width (Figure 4.4).

Alternatively, place the cursor on the line between the two columns (A and B) and double-click. Column A will expand to the width of the largest cell.

---

### KEYBOARD TIP

An alternative to dragging the column to the correct width is to place the cursor between the columns and then double-click with the left-hand mouse button. The column will expand to accommodate the widest cell.

| | A | B |
|---|---|---|
| 1 | Total number of dogs currently housed | 120 |
| 2 | Number of dogs relocated in 1st QTR | 26 |
| 3 | Number of dogs relocated in 2nd QTR | 20 |
| 4 | Number of dogs relocated in 3rd QTR | 15 |
| 5 | Number of dogs relocated in 4th QTR | 30 |
| 6 | Total number of dogs relocated during the year | 91 |

**Figure 4.4** *Excel spreadsheet, with column A expanded*

Being able to adjust column widths is a New CLAIT requirement.
One of the most common mistakes people make is in not ensuring that columns are wide enough to display the cell contents after the data has been placed in a cell.

## Try it out

**Open** a blank workbook.

**Enter** the following data in cell A1:

'Sales Returns for the Eastern Region'

**Place** the cursor between columns A and B (see Figure 4.5).

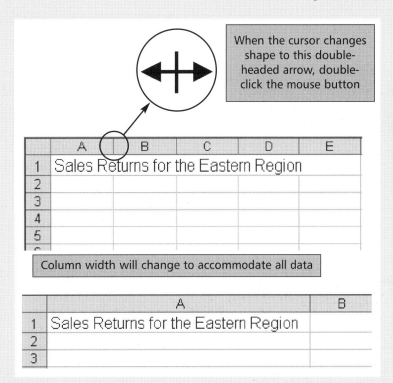

When the cursor changes shape to this double-headed arrow, double-click the mouse button

Column width will change to accommodate all data

**Figure 4.5** *Altering the column width*

**Double-click** using the left-hand mouse button.

Notice how the column width has changed to accommodate all the new data.

New CLAIT

## Saving a spreadsheet

Saving a spreadsheet file is no different from saving a Word file. As you saw in the section on types of files, Excel saves files with an '.xls' extension (whereas Word uses the extension '.doc').

When you looked at setting up a file structure in Unit 1 you created folders for some of the applications in this book. When working through the Build-up exercises in this unit use the Excel folder you created. If you did not complete this exercise then review Unit 1 and create a folder to hold your exercise files or your floppy or hard disk.

You should now be able to:

- amend text and numerical data
- navigate around a worksheet
- understand layout and changing column widths
- save a spreadsheet.

## Build-up Exercise 5: Stage 1

If you have not already got Excel open, then open it now. A new workbook should be opened waiting for you to enter some data.

**Click** in cell A1 and enter the following: BOAT NAME.

**Click** outside the cell to accept the entry.

Now enter the data shown in Table 4.1:

**Table 4.1** *Data for entry into an Excel spreadsheet*

| cell A2 | MAYFLY |
|---------|--------|
| cell A3 | JAYJAY |
| cell A4 | PETER PAN |
| cell A5 | JOSSE |
| cell A6 | TINKERBELL |
| cell A7 | HILLSTREAM |
| cell A8 | JUNKERS |

Widen the column to accommodate the full name of each boat and heading.

**Save** your worksheet as 'BU5a'.

## Entering, displaying and replicating numerical data and formulae

### Entering data using AutoFill

Using AutoFill is not a formal New CLAIT requirement but it is a useful and simple-to-use function that Microsoft provides and one that can save you time and effort in entering data. For example, if you had a spreadsheet that was dealing with figures from January to December you could type in each of the twelve months or alternatively you could enter the first month, January, and get Excel to complete the remaining months. This is known as a series and Excel has a number of these that you can use.

**Try it out**

**Open** a new workbook.

**Type** 'January' in cell A1.

**Press** Enter.

**Click** on cell A1.

**Move** the cursor to the bottom-right of box, over the small black square, and the cursor will change shape to a thin, black cross (Figure 4.6).

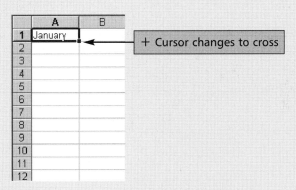

**Figure 4.6** *The small, black square used to autofill cells*

**Drag** cursor to A12.

Sometimes you may want to fill a series that is not part of Excel's standard package. The Edit, Fill, Series… option from the menu bar can provide help.

**Try it out**

**Open** a new workbook.

**Type** '1' in cell A1.

**Highlight** cells A1 to A20 and then from the main menu select Edit, Fill, Series….  ▶▶

The following dialogue box will appear (Figure 4.7):

**Figure 4.7** *The Series box*

Excel has noted that the series is in a column.

> **Select** Linear, if it is not already selected.

> **Set** the Step value at 1 (you could make the step value anything you wanted).

> **Press** OK.

Notice how Excel fills the highlighted cells A1:A20 with numbers 1 to 20. Remember that you must tell Excel the starting value. In this case it was 1. If you had started with 8 and changed the step value to 4 the resulting series would have increased by 4 at each step, to the end of the highlighted section. Try this by entering 8 in B1 and 4 in the Step value: box. Highlight B1:B10, and follow the same procedure as above to see the result.

Now return to Build-up Exercise 5.

## Build-up Exercise 5: Stage 2

**Open** BU5a.

**Enter** the data in Table 4.2. You can enter the data directly or use the AutoFill function.

**Table 4.2** *Further data for entry using AutoFill*

| cell B1 | RACE 1 |
|---------|--------|
| cell C1 | RACE 2 |
| cell D1 | RACE 3 |
| cell E1 | RACE 4 |

Once you have completed this series, complete the title line of the spreadsheet.

**Enter** the following data:

| cell F1 | WEIGHTING |
|---------|-----------|
| cell G1 | WEIGHTED TIME |

Your worksheet should now look like Figure 4.8.

| | A | B | C | D | E | F | G |
|---|---|---|---|---|---|---|---|
| 1 | BOAT NAME | RACE 1 | RACE 2 | RACE 3 | RACE 4 | WEIGHTING | WEIGHTED TIME |
| 2 | MAYFLY | | | | | | |
| 3 | JAYJAY | | | | | | |
| 4 | PETER PAN | | | | | | |
| 5 | JOSSE | | | | | | |
| 6 | TINKERBELL | | | | | | |
| 7 | HILLSTREAM | | | | | | |
| 8 | JUNKERS | | | | | | |

**Figure 4.8** *Entering data into an Excel spreadsheet*

**New CLAIT**

### Inserting numerical data

Being able to enter numerical data is a New CLAIT requirement. You have already entered numbers in cells when you did the exercise above. Now enter the numeric data for Build-up Exercise 5.

## Build-up Exercise 5: Stage 3

**Open** file BU5a.

Enter the numerical data in Table 4.3 into your worksheet.

**Table 4.3** *Numerical data for entry into the spreadsheet*

| BOAT NAME | RACE 1 | RACE 2 | RACE 3 | RACE 4 | WEIGHTING | WEIGHTED TIME |
|-----------|--------|--------|--------|--------|-----------|---------------|
| MAYFLY | 25 | 24 | 26 | 23 | 1.09 | |
| JAYJAY | 28 | 27 | 27 | 26 | 1.08 | |
| PETER PAN | 32 | 31 | 30 | 29 | 1.01 | |
| JOSSE | 22 | 24 | 22 | 21 | 1.15 | |
| TINKERBELL | 29 | 25 | 28 | 27 | 1.06 | |
| HILLSTREAM | 31 | 28 | 27 | 30 | 1.05 | |
| JUNKERS | 33 | 32 | 34 | 32 | 1.01 | |

▶▶

**Click** on cell B2.

**Type** the first number.

**Type** all numbers in the cell range B2:F8.

Your worksheet should look like the one in Figure 4.9.

|   | A | B | C | D | E | F | G |
|---|---|---|---|---|---|---|---|
| 1 | BOAT NAME | RACE 1 | RACE 2 | RACE 3 | RACE 4 | WEIGHTING | WEIGHTED TIME |
| 2 | MAYFLY | 25 | 24 | 26 | 23 | 1.09 | |
| 3 | JAYJAY | 28 | 27 | 27 | 26 | 1.08 | |
| 4 | PETER PAN | 32 | 31 | 30 | 29 | 1.01 | |
| 5 | JOSSE | 22 | 24 | 22 | 21 | 1.15 | |
| 6 | TINKERBELL | 29 | 35 | 28 | 27 | 1.06 | |
| 7 | HILLSTREAM | 31 | 28 | 27 | 30 | 1.05 | |
| 8 | JUNKERS | 33 | 32 | 34 | 32 | 1.01 | |

**Figure 4.9** *Entering numerical data into an Excel spreadsheet*

**Save** your worksheet.

**Close** the worksheet.

## New CLAIT

### Inserting and deleting columns and rows

Being able to insert and delete columns and rows is a requirement for New CLAIT. Under <u>I</u>nsert on the main menu are two items; <u>R</u>ows and <u>C</u>olumns. You can insert either a column or a row by placing the cursor in the position where you want the column or row to be inserted.

## Try it out

**Open** a new workbook and enter the data in Table 4.4.

**Table 4.4** *Data for extra columns in the spreadsheet*

| GAMES | TEAMS | PLAYERS |
|---|---|---|
| CRICKET | 8 | 135 |
| SQUASH | 15 | 220 |
| BASEBALL | 6 | 105 |
| FOOTBALL | 25 | 450 |
| TENNIS | 10 | 32 |
| SNOOKER | 14 | 60 |

You are going to insert a new column between TEAMS and PLAYERS and call it LEAGUES.

**Click** in cell C1.

**Select** Insert, Columns from the main menu.

A new column appears to the left of PLAYERS.

**Type** a new heading in cell C1 'LEAGUES'.

**Enter** the data in Table 4.5 for the number of leagues:

**Table 4.5** *Inserting a new column of data*

| Cell | LEAGUES |
| --- | --- |
| C2 | 2 |
| C3 | 2 |
| C4 | 1 |
| C5 | 3 |
| C6 | 2 |
| C7 | 2 |

**Click** in Cell A5.

**Select** Insert, Rows from the main menu.

A new row will appear above FOOTBALL.

**Enter** the data In Table 4.6 for the new row.

**Table 4.6** *Inserting a new row of data*

| GAMES | TEAMS | LEAGUES | PLAYERS |
| --- | --- | --- | --- |
| GOLF | 3 | 1 | 12 |

**Save** your worksheet as SPORTS.

**Close** the workbook.

That's all there is to inserting rows and columns.

Deleting columns and rows is equally straightforward. Click in the cell where the column or row is to be deleted, select Edit, Delete… from the main menu and the dialogue box shown in Figure 4.10 appears.

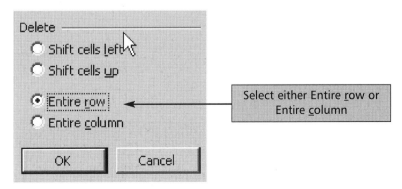

**Figure 4.10** *Deleting columns and rows in Excel*

Select either Entire row or Entire column, press OK and the row or column will disappear. Try it out on the worksheet you have just created.

**Try it out**

**Open** SPORTS.

**Click** in cell A2 'CRICKET'.

**Select** Edit, Delete... from the main menu.

**Select** Entire row.

**Press** OK.

**Click** in cell D1 'PLAYERS'.

**Select** Edit, Delete... from the main menu.

**Select** Entire Column.

**Press** OK.

You should now be able to:

- enter data using AutoFill
- insert numerical data
- insert and delete columns and rows.

**New CLAIT**

## Using formulae

Being able to use a formula to produce correct results for various calculations is a New CLAIT requirement. Entering a formula sounds complicated, but once you understand what a formula is, it is no different from entering normal text or data. What, then, is a formula? If you wanted to add up a series of numbers on a piece of paper you would first write down the numbers. Then you might add the numbers together and place the total at the bottom of the number series, like this:

$$20$$
$$30$$
$$40$$
$$10$$
Total 100

In this case you have mentally added up the figures and written down the result. A formula to do this would be: $20+30+40+10=100$. In Excel a formula is always preceded by an equals sign ($=$).

Try entering a formula into a cell on a new worksheet.

**Try it out**

**Open** a new workbook.

**Enter** the data in Table 4.7:

**Table 4.7** *Further data for entry using AutoFill*

| cell A1 | 25 |
|---------|----|
| cell A2 | 32 |
| cell A3 | 45 |
| cell A4 | 54 |

In cell A5 enter the following:

=A1+A2+A3+A4

**Press** Enter or click outside the cell.

Your worksheet should look like Figure 4.11.

| A5 | ▼ | *fx* | =A1+A2+A3+A4 | |
|----|---|------|------|---|
| | A | B | C | D |
| 1 | 25 | | | |
| 2 | 32 | | | |
| 3 | 45 | | | |
| 4 | 54 | | | |
| 5 | 156 | | | |

**Figure 4.11** *Using a formula in an Excel spreadsheet*

Notice the formula appears in the formula bar and the result of the formula '156' in cell A5.

Formulae are not restricted to adding up numbers – you can use any of the mathematical operators such as subtraction (–), division (/) or multiplication (∗). Excel also provides many special formula functions that can be used in more complex calculations. You may come across some of these if you decide to take your learning further. However, the basic operators are all you will need for New CLAIT.

In the Build-up exercise that follows you will insert a new column and then use a formula to add up all the minutes for each boat in the worksheet built earlier – BU5a.

## Build-up Exercise 5: Stage 4

**Open** BU5a.

**Insert** a column to the left of the column headed WEIGHTING and call your new column TOTAL TIMES.

> **Enter** the following formula in cell F2:
>
> =E2+D2+C2+B2
>
> **Press** Enter.
>
> You should now have a total of 98.
>
> **Save** your worksheet.

Other methods of entering a formula to add up a range of figures are available. For example, in the exercise you have just done, instead of typing out '=E2+D2+C2+B2' you could have used a formula such as =SUM(B2:E2). Excel offers an even simpler way of performing this calculation known as the AutoSum function. On your toolbar you will see the AutoSum symbol which looks like this Σ. It is in fact the Greek symbol called sigma. By placing the cursor where the result of the calculation is to go and then clicking on the Σ symbol, Excel will complete the calculation for you. It will look at the relevant row or column and suggest a range of figures to add up. You can change the suggested range by clicking on the first cell in the range you want and then drag the cursor to the end of the range to be calculated. Have a go at first typing in the range and then using the AutoSum function.

**Try it out**

**Open** a new workbook.

**Enter** the data shown in Table 4.8.

Table 4.8 *Data for the AutoSum feature*

| STREET | HOUSES |
| --- | --- |
| STREET 1 | 35 |
| STREET 2 | 40 |
| STREET 3 | 33 |
| STREET 4 | 36 |
| STREET 5 | 38 |
| STREET 6 | 37 |
| STREET 7 | 42 |
| STREET 8 | 48 |
| STREET 9 | 54 |

**Click** in cell B11.

**Enter** the following formula:

=SUM(B2:B10)

**Press** Enter (or click outside the cell).

As mentioned before, all formulae are preceded by the = sign. The SUM indicates that we wish to add up a range of numbers. Ranges are shown by having the start of the range you want to calculate (in this case B2) separated from the end of the range (in this case B10) by a colon ':'.

Now **delete** (or clear) cell B11.

**Click** in cell B11 again (which should now be empty).

**Press** the AutoSum symbol on the toolbar.

Excel will now show you the range the AutoSum function expects to add up (Figure 4.12).

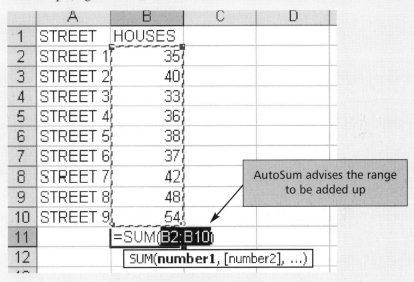

**Figure 4.12** *Using the AutoSum function*

**Press** Enter to accept the range.

**Save** your worksheet as House_Occupants.

Now return to Build-up Exercise 5 where you recently inserted a new column and the total time for the boat MAYFLY using a manually typed formula.

## Build-up Exercise 5: Stage 5

**Open** BU5a.

Using the AutoSum function,

**Calculate** the total time in F3 for the boat JAYJAY.

**Save** your worksheet.

**Close** the worksheet.

**New CLAIT**

### Replicating formulae

Being able to replicate formulae is a New CLAIT requirement. Replicating a formula is just as the name suggests. Instead of typing in the same formula for each line of your worksheet you can get Excel to replicate the formula in as many rows or columns as you need. Excel looks at the cell information in the formula you want to replicate and then repeats that formula for each line or row you specify. To do this Excel uses something called *relative referencing*. Don't worry, it's not as complicated as it sounds. First try it out and then you will be given an explanation of what has happened.

**Try it out**

**Open** your file House_Occupants.

**Add** a new column with the heading AVERAGE OCCUPANTS.

**Enter** the data in Table 4.9:

**Table 4.9** *Data for relative referencing*

| AVERAGE OCCUPANTS |
| --- |
| 3 |
| 2.5 |
| 4 |
| 3 |
| 2 |
| 3 |
| 3 |
| 4 |
| 2 |

**Enter** the following formula in Cell D2:

=C2*B2

Here Excel is being asked to multiply cell C2 by cell B2.

**Press** Enter (or click outside the cell).

Your worksheet should now look like Figure 4.13 on the following page.

Next you are going to replicate the formula placed in cell D2 to cells D3:D10.

**Click** in cell D2 again. Notice how the cell has a thick black line around it with a small square box in the bottom right corner (see Figure 4.14).

|    | A | B | C | D | E |
|----|---|---|---|---|---|
| 1 | STREET | HOUSES | AVERAGE | OCCUPANTS | |
| 2 | STREET 1 | 35 | 3 | 105 | |
| 3 | STREET 2 | 40 | 2.5 | | |
| 4 | STREET 3 | 33 | 4 | | |
| 5 | STREET 4 | 36 | 3 | | |
| 6 | STREET 5 | 38 | 2 | | |
| 7 | STREET 6 | 37 | 3 | | |
| 8 | STREET 7 | 42 | 3 | | |
| 9 | STREET 8 | 48 | 4 | | |
| 10 | STREET 9 | 54 | 2 | | |
| 11 | | 363 | | | |

**Figure 4.13** *An Excel spreadsheet, using the multiplication function*

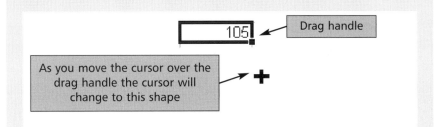

**Figure 4.14** *Replicating a formula from cell to cell*

When the cursor changes shape drag the box down to cell D10 (see Figure 4.15).

|    | D | E | F | G |
|----|---|---|---|---|
| | \GE OCCUPANTS | | | |
| 3 | 105 | | | |
| 2.5 | 100 | | | |
| 4 | 132 | | | |
| 3 | 108 | | | |
| 2 | 76 | | | |
| 3 | 111 | | | |
| 3 | 126 | | | |
| 4 | 192 | | | |
| 2 | 108 | | | |

- ⦿ Copy Cells
- ○ Fill Formatting Only
- ○ Fill Without Formatting

**Figure 4.15** *Replicating formulae in an Excel spreadsheet*

### Relative referencing

When you started this exercise you entered the formula =C2*B2. If you now click in cell D3 you will find that the formula has changed to C3*B3, cell D4 reads C4*B4 and so on down to D10 which now reads C10*B10. When you replicate a formula Excel automatically adjusts the references in the new cell based on the relative position of the formula. Excel makes the assumption that you want to use the reference of the new cell rather than the original cell and will continue to do this until the end of the range. This is known as relative referencing.

We can now return to Build-up Exercise 5 and replicate the total time for each boat.

## Build-up Exercise 5: Stage 6

**Open** BU5a.

**Click** in cell F3.

**Replicate** the formula in F3 to F4:F8.

Your worksheet should now look like Figure 4.16.

| | A | B | C | D | E | F | G | H |
|---|---|---|---|---|---|---|---|---|
| 1 | BOAT NAME | RACE 1 | RACE 2 | RACE 3 | RACE 4 | TOTAL TIM | WEIGHTING | WEIGHTED TIME |
| 2 | MAYFLY | 25 | 24 | 26 | 23 | 98 | 1.09 | |
| 3 | JAYJAY | 28 | 27 | 27 | 26 | 108 | 1.08 | |
| 4 | PETER PAN | 32 | 31 | 30 | 29 | 122 | 1.01 | |
| 5 | JOSSE | 22 | 24 | 22 | 21 | 89 | 1.15 | |
| 6 | TINKERBELL | 29 | 25 | 28 | 27 | 109 | 1.06 | |
| 7 | HILLSTREAM | 31 | 28 | 27 | 30 | 116 | 1.05 | |
| 8 | JUNKERS | 33 | 32 | 34 | 32 | 131 | 1.01 | |

**Figure 4.16** *Using a replicated formula in an Excel spreadsheet*

**Save** the worksheet as BU5b.

## Automatic recalculation of data

A really useful function of a spreadsheet is that once you have inserted all the formulae you need to calculate the results you want, there is then no need to make any further changes to the formulae if you need to change the underlying data on which the formulae are based. So if you take a simple example, say calculating the sum of the range A1:A10, and the formula to do this is in A11, no matter what changes you make to the numbers in cells A1:A10 the result will always be calculated for you by the formula in cell A11.

This can easily be demonstrated with the following Build-up exercise.

### Build-up Exercise 5: Stage 7

If it is not already open,

> **Open** BU5b.

You have just received information that TINKERBELL was penalised 10 minutes into RACE 2 for going round a buoy the wrong way.

> **Amend** the 25 minutes previously recorded to read 35.

Notice how TINKERBELL's Total time has automatically increased from 109 minutes to 119 mintues.

> **Save** your worksheet.

You should now be able to:

- insert a simple formula
- use the AutoSum function
- replicate a formula
- understand how automatic recalculation works.

## Using common numerical formatting and alignment

Understanding and being able to appreciate some of the more common conventions for the display of data in a spreadsheet is a New CLAIT requirement. You will need to know how to align text in a cell, column or row. You will also need to know how to display either numbers with no decimal places (integers) or numbers that are shown on your worksheet to two decimal places. Similarly, numbers are not always simply integers or decimals, they can also be displayed in a currency format or even as a percentage. You will also need to appreciate that sometimes what you see on the screen is not always the number entered. If you are using integers, for example, Excel will round your number up or down to the nearest whole number, although in a calculation the actual number you entered will be used.

Have a look at Figure 4.17, where there are two columns of figures. The figures in column B are formatted to zero decimal places (integers). The figures in column C are formatted to one decimal place. Look at the Total line. Column B says the total is 6 whereas the total for column C is only 5.7.

|   | A | B | C |
|---|---|---|---|
| 1 | No1 | 1 | 1.4 |
| 2 | No2 | 2 | 1.5 |
| 3 | No3 | 1 | 1.2 |
| 4 | No4 | 2 | 1.6 |
| 5 | Total | 6 | 5.7 |

**Figure 4.17** *Formatting to decimal places*

Perhaps with so little data this would not make a huge difference but just imagine if this spreadsheet was used in a bank and there were tens of thousands of rows.

With a large spreadsheet the rounding factor could be considerable. There are ways around the problem, but they are beyond the scope of this book. At this stage, it is sufficient for you to be aware of the potential problem when presenting figures.

### Aligning text

You may recall that at the beginning of this unit it was stated that, by default, text was always left aligned and numbers were always right aligned. However, you can change this alignment whenever you wish.

Have a look at the file BU5b. At present the headings are all left aligned (because this is the default alignment for text). However, you may feel that with the numbers right aligned the overall appearance of the worksheet would be enhanced by right aligning the headings.

## Build-up Exercise 5: Stage 8

With BU5b open,

> **Highlight** the headings in columns B to H.

Using the Alignment icon on the toolbar,

> **Press** the Right Alignment icon.

> **Save** your worksheet.

### Other text formats

New CLAIT only requires you to understand left, right and centring of text. However, there are other styles of formatting that you may find useful. Earlier you inserted a new column with a heading of TOTAL TIMES. Because there was a column immediately to the right of this new column the full heading text was cut off and not visible. As you have seen, one way of overcoming this is to extend the width of the column; however, this may make the worksheet look unbalanced with different width columns. Another way of overcoming the problem is by using the word wrap function.

## Build-up Exercise 5: Stage 9

**Open** BU5b.

**Click** in cell F1.

**Select** <u>F</u>ormat, C<u>e</u>lls... from the main menu. The dialogue box in Figure 4.18 appears.

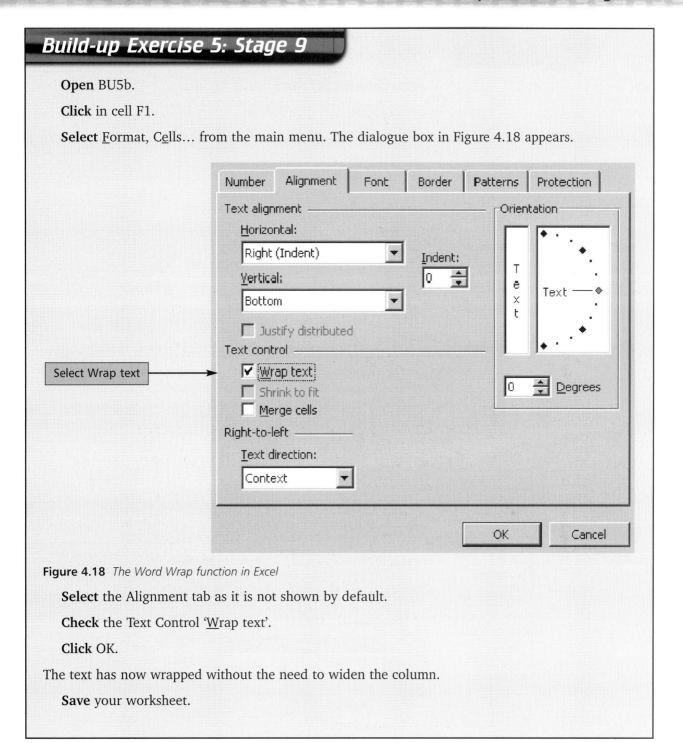

Select Wrap text →

**Figure 4.18** *The Word Wrap function in Excel*

**Select** the Alignment tab as it is not shown by default.

**Check** the Text Control '<u>W</u>rap text'.

**Click** OK.

The text has now wrapped without the need to widen the column.

**Save** your worksheet.

### Formatting numerical data

By default Excel formats numbers in cells with a General format. This means that there is no specific number format. So, for example, if you entered 1.1 into a cell it would appear just like that – not 1.10 or 1.

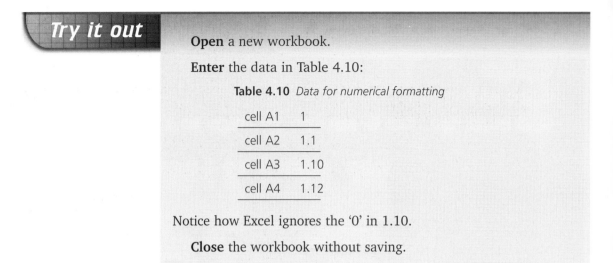

**Try it out**

**Open** a new workbook.

**Enter** the data in Table 4.10:

**Table 4.10** *Data for numerical formatting*

| cell A1 | 1 |
|---------|------|
| cell A2 | 1.1 |
| cell A3 | 1.10 |
| cell A4 | 1.12 |

Notice how Excel ignores the '0' in 1.10.

**Close** the workbook without saving.

More often than not you will want, or indeed need, to format cells in a specific way. This could be as integers (i.e. no decimal places), or with a specific number of decimal places, or as currency. Excel provides a wide variety of number format options. Have a look at Figure 4.19.

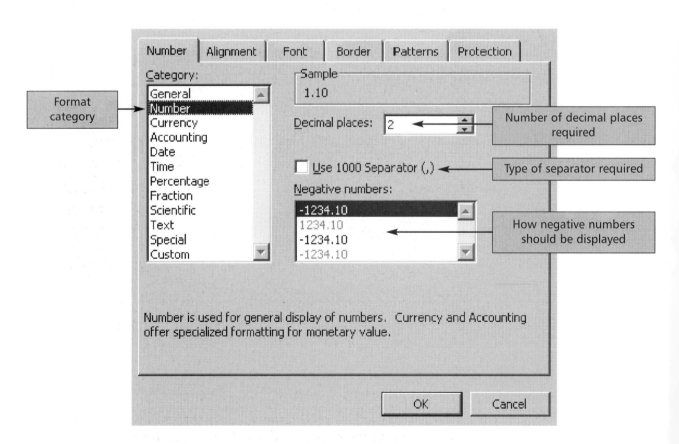

**Figure 4.19** *Format category options in Excel*

On the left-hand side you can see the category types. These range from numbers to customising your own format. Have a go at formatting some numbers in the following Try it out exercise.

**Try it out**

**Open** a new workbook.

**Enter** the data shown in Table 4.11.

**Table 4.11** *Data for formatting adjustments*

| CLUB SETS | STOCK | AVG WGT | COST |
|---|---|---|---|
| CALLAWAY | 12 | 1.2 | 649 |
| TAYLOR MADE | 15 | 1.05 | 575 |
| DUNLOP | 10 | 1.02 | 380 |
| WILSON | 10 | 1.06 | 369 |
| FAZER | 25 | 1 | 145 |

**Select** columns B, C and D.

Using the Number category option in the Formatting box, make the following formatting adjustments to your worksheet: (Remember that before formatting can be completed, the relevant column or cell must be highlighted.)

Columns B, C and D – heading right-aligned
Column B – no decimal places
Column C – 2 decimal places
Column D – currency to 2 decimal places

Your worksheet should now look like Figure 4.20.

| | A | B | C | D |
|---|---|---|---|---|
| 1 | CLUB SETS | STOCK | AVG WGT | COST |
| 2 | CALLAWAY | 12 | 1.20 | £649.00 |
| 3 | TAYLOR MADE | 15 | 1.05 | £575.00 |
| 4 | DUNLOP | 10 | 1.02 | £380.00 |
| 5 | WILSON | 10 | 1.06 | £369.00 |
| 6 | FAZER | 25 | 1.00 | £145.00 |

**Figure 4.20** *Making formatting adjustments to an Excel spreadsheet*

**Close** your worksheet and save, giving it a suitable name.

You should now be able to:

■ use common numerical formatting and alignment
■ understand the principles of rounding up and down
■ align text in a worksheet.

Now return to the Build-up exercise and put some of the new skills you have learnt into practice.

## Build-up Exercise 5: Stage 10

**KEYBOARD TIP**

If you want to highlight cells that are not adjacent (e.g. B3:D7 and F3:F7) press the Ctrl key and highlight the first series and then, keeping the control key pressed, highlight the second series.

**Open** BU5b.

**Enter** a formula into cell H2 that calculates the WEIGHTED TIME for each boat.

**Tip:** TOTAL TIMES * WEIGHTING

**Replicate** the formula to cells H3:H8.

**Format** columns B:F as Number to no decimal places (i.e. integers).

**Format** columns G and H as Number to 2 decimal places.

**Format** the column headings and the boat names to **bold**.

**Save** your worksheet as BU5c.

Your worksheet should now look like Figure 4.21.

| | A | B | C | D | E | F | G | H |
|---|---|---|---|---|---|---|---|---|
| 1 | BOAT NAME | RACE 1 | RACE 2 | RACE 3 | RACE 4 | TOTAL TIMES | WEIGHTING | WEIGHTED TIME |
| 2 | MAYFLY | 25 | 24 | 26 | 23 | 98 | 1.09 | 106.82 |
| 3 | JAYJAY | 28 | 27 | 27 | 26 | 108 | 1.08 | 116.64 |
| 4 | PETER PAN | 32 | 31 | 30 | 29 | 122 | 1.01 | 123.22 |
| 5 | JOSSE | 22 | 24 | 22 | 21 | 89 | 1.15 | 102.35 |
| 6 | TINKERBELL | 29 | 35 | 28 | 27 | 119 | 1.06 | 126.14 |
| 7 | HILLSTREAM | 31 | 28 | 27 | 30 | 116 | 1.05 | 121.80 |
| 8 | JUNKERS | 33 | 32 | 34 | 32 | 131 | 1.01 | 132.31 |

**Figure 4.21** *Formatting an Excel spreadsheet to different numbers of decimal places*

**Close** your workbook.

## Printing a spreadsheet display

Printing a spreadsheet is reasonably straightforward and for the most part the same as printing a Word document. However, before pressing the Print button there are a couple of decisions you need to make:

- **Orientation** – do you want your work in landscape or portrait format?
- **Area to print** – do you want to set the print area for later use?

## Orientation

Page orientation was mentioned briefly earlier. A page can be in either a portrait or a landscape orientation. To see the difference look at Figure 4.22.

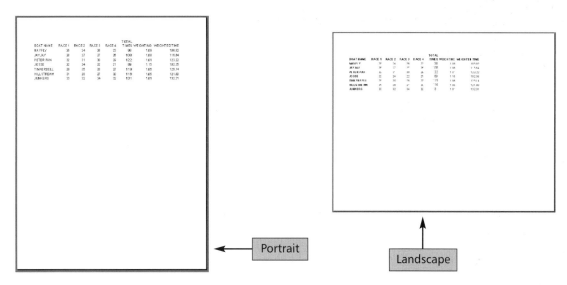

**Figure 4.22** *Portrait/landscape orientation*

In spreadsheets you will probably find that you use landscape more often than portrait. By default Excel selects portrait format. If you want landscape you need to give your printer the orientation information before printing your work. You can always check how the printout will look by using the Print Pre<u>v</u>iew option on the <u>F</u>ile menu.

### Try it out

**Open** file BU5c.

**Select** Print, Print Pre<u>v</u>iew on the <u>F</u>ile menu bar.

**Press** <u>S</u>et-up….

**Change** the radio button option to landscape.

**Click** OK.

Your page will change from portrait to landscape (see Figure 4.23 overleaf).

### Setting the print area

There will be occasions when you only want to print part of a spreadsheet. Excel offers you the opportunity to tell the printer which part of your spreadsheet you want to print. If you decide not to identify a print area Excel will print the whole spreadsheet where there is data, and normally this is all you will need for New CLAIT.

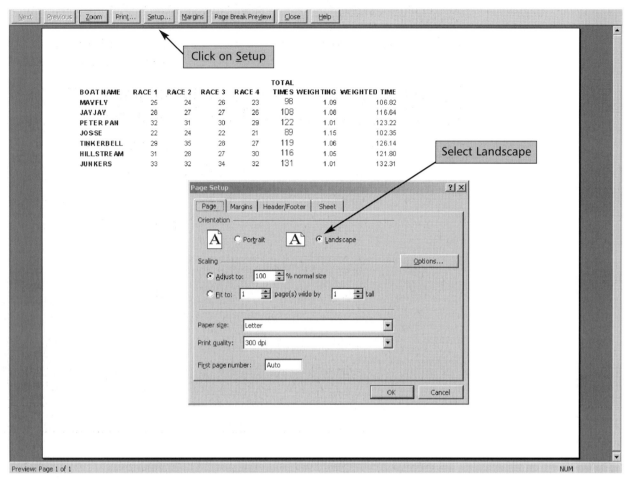

**Figure 4.23** *Changing the orientation of a spreadsheet*

## Try it out

### Setting print area

**Open** file BU5c.

**Type** 'This is my spreadsheet' in cell A10.

**Highlight** cells A1:H10.

**Select** File, Print Area, Set Print Area.

**Select** File, Print Preview.

Notice how your text called 'This is my spreadsheet' is incorporated.

### Clearing print area

**Select** File, Print Area, Clear Print Area.

Now repeat the above exercise, but this time highlight cells A1:H8. This time when you use Print Preview the text is excluded from the print.

### Printing the spreadsheet

Having decided on the data to be printed, the spreadsheet's orientation and the print area, you can now print your work (called 'hard' copy).

---

## Build-up Exercise 5: Stage II

**Delete** the text you entered in cell A10 of file BU5c.

**Set** the area to be printed as A1:H8.

**Select** File, Print....

**Press** the Preview button on the bottom of the Print dialogue box .

**Press** Set-up....

**Change** the radio button option to Portrait.

**Press** OK.

**Press** Print....

**Save** file Bu5c.

**Close** file Bu5c.

---

### Printing headers on your spreadsheet

Although headers and footers are not a formal requirement for New CLAIT you will need to put your name and the task you are doing on each printout you are asked to complete in an assignment. You can, of course, write this by hand, but it is also very easy to automatically put a header containing your name and the task on the printed version of your work. This will make it look more professional and neater.

## Try it out

**Open** file BU5c from the Build-up exercise.

**Select** File, Print Preview, Set-up....

**Press** the Header/Footer tab of the dialogue box.

**Press** Custom Header... and the dialogue box in Figure 4.24 appears.

**Type** your name in the Left section: and the exercise number in the Right section: box.

**Press** OK on the Header dialogue box and then the Page Set-up box.

**Print** your spreadsheet. Your name appears on the left and the exercise number on the right.

That is all there is to it.

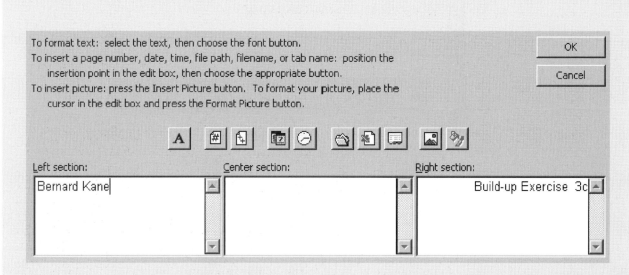

**Figure 4.24** *Formatting headers/footers on an Excel spreadsheet*

## New CLAIT

### Displaying and printing formulae

Being able to show and print the formulae used in a spreadsheet is a New CLAIT requirement. From time to time you may find it necessary to display the formulae embedded in your spreadsheet. This is likely to be so if you are reviewing the results of calculations and they appear to be incorrect. Excel does not make mistakes, so if the answers to your formulae look wrong it is likely that you have entered something incorrectly. You can check this by displaying your formulae. When formulae are displayed, columns become wider and text and numerical data take on a different alignment.

To change the view of your spreadsheet so that the formulae are displayed is simply a matter of changing an option in the Options... window under the Tools menu.

**Note:** When the display is changed to show the formulae, Excel automatically widens the columns to display the formula and at the same time changes the alignment of number cells so that they become left-aligned. When the view is changed back to normal, the alignment and column widths revert to their original settings.

### Try it out

**Open** file BU5c.

**Select** Tools.

**Select** Options... and the dialogue box in Figure 4.25 appears.

**Click** in the Formulas check box.

**Press** OK and return to the spreadsheet.

Notice how the spreadsheet now displays the formulae you have used.

**Print** the spreadsheet as described on pages 170–4.

Now return your spreadsheet to its normal view by using the same procedure but this time uncheck the Formula box.

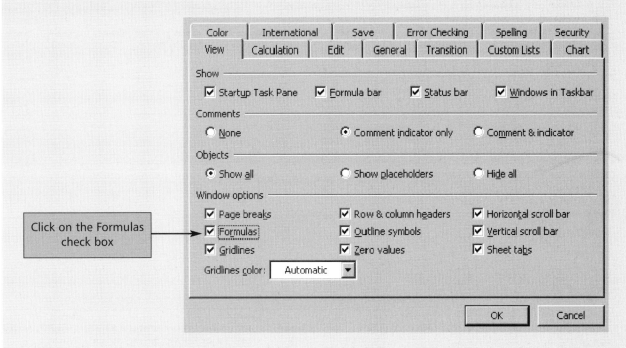

Click on the Formulas check box

**Figure 4.25** *Displaying formulae in Excel*

### Hiding columns and rows

Earlier in this unit you learnt how to delete columns and rows from a spreadsheet. Deleting a column or row is a permanent change to the spreadsheet but sometimes you may wish simply to hide a column or row, mainly for viewing or printing purposes.

To hide a column first click in the cell(s) that references the relevant column(s) or row(s). Next select Format, Column (or Row) from the main menu and then select Hide. The column or row will disappear from the screen view but you will notice that the column or row headings will indicate clearly that the column or row is there but not visible. For example, if you have a spreadsheet that had columns A–K and you hide all columns D–F, then on the column headings you would see the sequence go from A, B, C to G, H, I, J, K. To 'unhide' the column or rows, highlight the cells across the hidden column or row and then select Unhide from the menu option. Have a look at Figure 4.26.

In this example columns H and I have been hidden but the formula in column J, which relies on the closing stock figure of column H, is not affected. When the columns are Unhidden the cells between columns G and J are highlighted and then Unhide is selected, as shown in Figure 4.27.

| | A | B | C | D | E | F | G | H | I | J |
|---|---|---|---|---|---|---|---|---|---|---|
| 1 | ITEM | Opening Stock | Value per Item | Sales 1st Qtr | Sales 2nd Qtr | Sales 3rd Qtr | Sales 4th Qtr | Closing Stock | Sales Value | Closing Stock Value |
| 2 | WIDGET 1 | 2000 | 45 | 147 | 156 | 154 | 123 | 1420 | 26100 | 63900 |
| 3 | WIDGET 2 | 2100 | 48 | 156 | 145 | 114 | 115 | 1570 | 25440 | 75360 |
| 4 | WIDGET 3 | 3500 | 52 | 205 | 253 | 223 | 254 | 2565 | 48620 | 133380 |
| 5 | WIDGET 4 | 2510 | 32 | 140 | 187 | 191 | 187 | 1805 | 22560 | 57760 |
| 6 | WIDGET 5 | 1478 | 65 | 236 | 269 | 289 | 301 | 383 | 71175 | 24895 |
| 7 | WIDGET 6 | 2360 | 49 | 425 | 456 | 515 | 451 | 513 | 90503 | 25137 |
| 8 | WIDGET 7 | 4781 | 14 | 569 | 601 | 552 | 584 | 2475 | 32284 | 34650 |
| 9 | WIDGET 8 | 5325 | 58 | 241 | 235 | 261 | 289 | 4299 | 59508 | 249342 |
| 10 | WIDGET 9 | 4157 | 78 | 224 | 201 | 220 | 261 | 3251 | 70668 | 253578 |
| 11 | WIDGET 10 | 2541 | 25 | 156 | 169 | 178 | 190 | 1848 | 17325 | 46200 |
| 12 | Totals | | | 2499 | 2672 | 2697 | 2755 | 20129 | 464183 | 964202 |

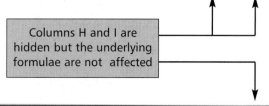

Columns H and I are hidden but the underlying formulae are not affected

| | A | B | C | D | E | F | G | J |
|---|---|---|---|---|---|---|---|---|
| 1 | ITEM | Opening Stock | Value per Item | Sales 1st Qtr | Sales 2nd Qtr | Sales 3rd Qtr | Sales 4th Qtr | Closing Stock Value |
| 2 | WIDGET 1 | 2000 | 45 | 147 | 156 | 154 | 123 | 63900 |
| 3 | WIDGET 2 | 2100 | 48 | 156 | 145 | 114 | 115 | 75360 |
| 4 | WIDGET 3 | 3500 | 52 | 205 | 253 | 223 | 254 | 133380 |
| 5 | WIDGET 4 | 2510 | 32 | 140 | 187 | 191 | 187 | 57760 |
| 6 | WIDGET 5 | 1478 | 65 | 236 | 269 | 289 | 301 | 24895 |
| 7 | WIDGET 6 | 2360 | 49 | 425 | 456 | 515 | 451 | 25137 |
| 8 | WIDGET 7 | 4781 | 14 | 569 | 601 | 552 | 584 | 34650 |
| 9 | WIDGET 8 | 5325 | 58 | 241 | 235 | 261 | 289 | 249342 |
| 10 | WIDGET 9 | 4157 | 78 | 224 | 201 | 220 | 261 | 253578 |
| 11 | WIDGET 10 | 2541 | 25 | 156 | 169 | 178 | 190 | 46200 |
| 12 | Totals | | | 2499 | 2672 | 2697 | 2755 | 964202 |

**Figure 4.26** *Viewing and hiding columns in spreadsheets*

Select the cells across the hidden columns

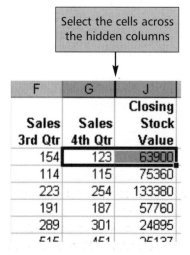

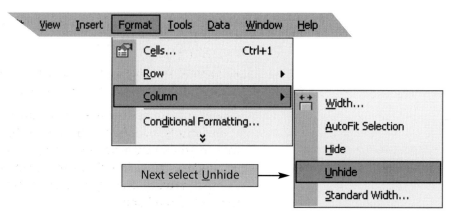

Next select Unhide

**Figure 4.27** *Selecting Unhide*

**Try it out**

**Open** a new workbook in Excel.

**Enter** the data, as shown in Figure 4.28.

| | A | B | C | D |
|---|---|---|---|---|
| 1 | **Month** | **Red Wine** | **White Wine** | **Rose** |
| 2 | **Jan** | 520 | 698 | 401 |
| 3 | **Feb** | 546 | 871 | 456 |
| 4 | **Mar** | 982 | 925 | 563 |
| 5 | **Apr** | 1025 | 1205 | 687 |
| 6 | **May** | 1250 | 1462 | 963 |
| 7 | **Jun** | 1350 | 1952 | 985 |
| 8 | **Jul** | 1455 | 1546 | 1025 |
| 9 | **Aug** | 1253 | 1475 | 1125 |
| 10 | **Sep** | 1547 | 1698 | 1258 |
| 11 | **Oct** | 1471 | 1756 | 1247 |
| 12 | **Nov** | 1369 | 1258 | 1542 |
| 13 | **Dec** | 2201 | 2500 | 1897 |

**Figure 4.28** *Using the 'Unhide' feature in Excel*

**Highlight** cells A5:A10.

**Select** Format, Row, Hide from the main menu.

You should now only be able to see rows A1:A13.

Now **unhide** these rows.

**Highlight** cells A4:A11.

**Select** Format, Row, Unhide from the main menu.

The rows will appear on the screen again.

You should now be able to:

- change the page orientation for printing
- set the print area
- insert headers
- display formulas in the worksheet and print them
- hide columns and rows before printing a spreadsheet.

That completes all the elements required for New CLAIT on spreadsheets, together with some additional features that were covered to give you a better understanding of the application.

Now complete Practical Assignment 4. Once you have completed this assignment, check your work against the solution in Part 3 towards the end of the book.

## Unit 4 Spreadsheets using Excel

### Scenario

You work for a small charity. Part of the charity's income comes from dividends from investments. Your manager has asked you to prepare a spreadsheet showing the charity's investments so that she can watch their progress on the market.

| Assessment objectives | Stage | |
|---|---|---|
| 1a 5a | 1 | Create a new spreadsheet. |
| 2a | 2 | Enter the following data, leaving the VALUE column blank. |

| STOCK | HOLDING | CURRENT PRICE | COST | DIVIDEND | PAYMENT DATES | VALUE |
|---|---|---|---|---|---|---|
| BAE SYSTEMS | 270 | 4.25 | 341.05 | 2.1 | NOV | |
| PERSIMMON | 1250 | 2.07 | 3308 | 6 | OCT | |
| UNILEVER | 332 | 4.4175 | 1614.99 | 3.1 | DEC | |
| BAA | 397 | 5.615 | 2255.27 | 1.9 | JAN | |
| NATIONAL GRID | 520 | 5.565 | 3000 | 2.8 | JAN | |
| BARCLAYS | 160 | 17.12 | 3186 | 6.7 | OCT | |
| LLOYDS | 240 | 6.425 | 2256 | 3.7 | OCT | |

| Assessment objectives | Stage | |
|---|---|---|
| 2a | 3 | Enter your name and the date in cells three rows below the data. |
| 3a 3b | 4 | The VALUE column is completed by multiplying the HOLDING by the CURRENT PRICE. Insert a formula to calculate the VALUE of the BAE SYSTEMS stock. Replicate this formula to show the VALUE for each STOCK in the portfolio. |
| 5b | 5 | Save your worksheet report with the filename **PE4_Print_1** and print one copy, showing the figures not the formulae. Make sure that all the data are displayed in full. |
| 2b | 6 | Insert a new column entitled COST PRICE between CURRENT PRICE and COST. |
| 3a 3b | 7 | COST PRICE is calculated by dividing COST by HOLDING. Insert a formula to calculate the COST PRICE for BAE SYSTEMS. Replicate this formula to show the COST PRICE for each HOLDING. Having reviewed the current position your manager has decided to make some changes to the portfolio. |
| 2c | 8 | Delete the row containing the NATIONAL GRID stock. |
| 2d | 9 | Make the following amendments to the worksheet: (a) The CURRENT PRICE for BAE SYSTEMS has gone up to 4.55. (b) You increase your UNILEVER holdings to 500. (c) The dividend for BARCLAYS has gone up to 7%. (d) The heading STOCK should be changed to STOCK HELD. Your manager has asked you to format the worksheet. |

| | | |
|---|---|---|
| **4a** | **10** | Apply alignment as follows: |
| | | (a) The STOCK HELD column and all data in it should be left-aligned. |
| | | (b) The remaining column headings should be right-aligned. |
| | | (c) All numeric values should be right-aligned. |
| | | (d) PAYMENT DATES should be right-aligned. |
| | | (e) All column headings should be in bold. |
| **4c** | **11** | Format the data as follows: |
| **4d** | | |
| **4e** | | (a)  The CURRENT PRICE, COST PRICE, COST and VALUE data should be displayed as currency to 2 decimal places. |
| | | (b) The DIVIDEND data **only** should be displayed in integer format (to zero decimal places). |
| **5c** | **12** | Save your worksheet using the filename **PE4_Print_2**. Print one copy, showing figures not formulae. Make sure that all the data are displayed in full. |
| **5e** | | |
| **5d** | **13** | Print the worksheet with all the formulae showing. Make sure that all formulae are displayed in full (**PE4_Print_3**). |
| **1a** | **14** | Save and Close the worksheet and exit the software securely. |
| **5f** | | |

# UNIT 5

# Databases using Access

The New CLAIT database unit has five required learning outcomes. Each learning outcome has several assessment objectives. As with the unit for Word, each assessment objective is linked to specific aspects of knowledge and understanding. Unit 5 of this book addresses all requirements of New CLAIT for databases and provides additional information over and above that required for the qualification to give you a broader understanding of databases and how they work.

## What you need to know about databases for New CLAIT

For New CLAIT you will need to know how to:

**Identify and use database software correctly**
- Use an appropriate application software package.

**Use an input device to enter and edit data accurately**
- Create new records.
- Enter data.
- Delete a record.
- Amend data.
- Replace specified data.

**Create simple queries/searches on one or two criteria**
- Select data on one criterion.
- Select data on two criteria.
- Present only selected fields.

**Present selected data sorted alphabetically, numerically and by date**
- Sort data alphabetically.
- Sort data numerically.
- Sort data by date.

**Manage and print database files**
- Open an existing database.
- Save data.
- Save a query or filter.
- Print results of a query/filter and data in a table.
- Close a database.

> ### In this unit you will cover:
>
> - What is a database?
> - What is Microsoft Access and why do I need it?
> - What are the basic components of a computerised database?
> - Getting familiar with Access
> - The Access screen
> - Building your first database
> - Changing data in a table
> - Interrogating and sorting data through queries
> - Printing queries and tables
> - Sorting records numerically and by date

Although New CLAIT does not require you to build a database (a requirement in the original CLAIT programme), students are expected to have a broad understanding of database concepts. It is difficult to understand these without having some knowledge of what a database is, its uses and how to develop the essential building blocks that form the overall structure of a database. In addition to the skills you are required to know, this unit will also show you a number of aspects of database technology that should help you to understand the general concepts behind these skills. In this unit you will learn how to build a simple database. For the more formal exercises that form part of the New CLAIT syllabus you will use the database file on the CD.

## What is a database?

There is nothing new or magical about databases. You have probably used them for years but have not realised that something you use on a daily basis is, fundamentally, a database.

A database is nothing more than a collection of data and is used to store information on a topic or subject. At some time or another you have probably used an address book or a card index in the office or at home. These are both databases. Take the address book. A person's name, their initials and the parts of their address (house name, street, town and postcode) form the data of your database. You store this data and then use it to find out different things from it. So if, for example, you want to send a letter, you use your address book to collect the data and find a full address to put on the envelope. In short, you retrieve the data to provide information for the postman, as shown in Figure 5.1.

Earlier in this book we looked at spreadsheets and you learnt that spreadsheet software can also store data. Sometimes it is difficult to determine whether it is better to use a database application or a spreadsheet for a particular job. In its simplest terms, a spreadsheet helps you to perform complex calculations on numeric data. It also allows you to ask 'What if' questions. Databases, on the other hand, while still able to perform calculations, are really designed to store large quantities of data that can be queried in a variety of ways. If you are dealing with small amounts of data it is sometimes easier to use a spreadsheet rather than design a database. However, at the end of the day, these are personal choices you will need to make depending on what you want or are asked to do.

**Figure 5.1** *An address book is a traditional example of a manual database*

## What is Microsoft Access and why do I need it?

You will sometimes hear people talking about a *database management system* (or *DBMS*). This is the system that stores and retrieves information in a database. It is, if you like, the filing cabinet or, in the above example, the blank address book.

Sometimes, however, you may want to keep data that has a range of different aspects and components. For example, you may not want to keep just names and addresses in your address book but also information about your friends' children, their interests, birthdays, dates when you met them or what they gave you for Christmas; the list could be endless. As you see, the data becomes more complex to store and manipulate, and although not impossible to do manually, it is often easier to use a computer.

Access is known as a *relational database management system* (*RDBMS*). Consider the difficulty a large gas company would have in keeping all its records manually. The resources the company would expend every time it billed its customers would be enormous. Similarly, a bank would have great difficulty in advising customers each month of the balance of their accounts without the assistance of a computerised system.

Normally organisations like these commission software developers to build specially designed databases based on sophisticated database application software such as Paradox, Open Insight, Oracle or some other heavyweight database-programming application. Smaller companies (and homes) do not need expensive bespoke programs, that can cost from many thousands to millions of pounds. This is where

Access comes to the rescue. However, do not get the idea that it is lightweight. Some very sophisticated databases have been built in Access (as well as very basic ones). Access is easy to use, friendly and very flexible. Its great advantage is not only the speed with which you can build a simple database but also the ease with which data captured can be queried and reported using very professional-looking reports. As Access is part of the Microsoft Office suite it is easy to export your data to any of the other applications in the suite, such as Excel, Word or PowerPoint.

## What are the basic elements of a computerised database?

### Tables

At the heart of any database are objects known as *tables*. These are the containers that store the data you want to keep. You may also come across the term 'table' in Word and other wordprocessing applications. Although there are some differences, the tables in Access are substantially the same. Indeed, you can use the tables in Word to store data to produce mail-merged letters and forms. A complex relational database may have dozens of tables, all related to one another, but the basic premise remains: it is the table that ultimately stores the data and is the source of information. Tables contain *records* and these records are made up of *fields*. Have a look at Figure 5.2. A complete record may be:

> MR H J CASTER HUGH

The individual fields that go to make up the record would be:

> (Title): MR, (Initials): H J, (Surname): CASTER,
> (Firstname): HUGH.

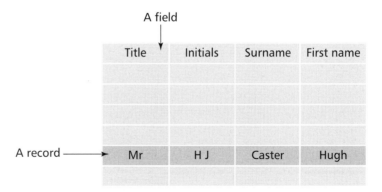

**Figure 5.2** *A record containing several fields*

### Queries

Once all the data has been entered into a table you will want (eventually) to *query* it, to draw out specific records or parts of records. For example, let us suppose you had also included in the table above the following three fields: Date of birth; Sex; Town.

Had you entered, say, 2000 records each containing all this data, it would now be difficult to select particular records with specific details that may be required for a list.

Suppose you wanted to find all those people who were female, under 25 and lived in Birmingham. You could question the database and ask it to give only those records that fitted these requirements.

The processes just described are the two basic functions of databases you need to know for achieving certification in New CLAIT.

## Getting familiar with Access

### Using Access as an application

By now you will be fairly familiar with opening any of the Office applications. However, with Word and Excel, you are taken directly to a working window that allows you to start working straight away. Access gives you a number of options to choose from before you can build a new database. To understand this process complete the following 'Try it out' exercise.

### Try it out

**Press** Start.

**Select** the Programs icon.

**Select** [ Microsoft Access ]. The version of Office you are using will determine how the initial screen will look. Figures 5.3a and 5.3b show the initial screen for Office 97/2000 and Office XP, respectively.

**Figure 5.3a** *Starting a database in Access, using Office 97/2000*

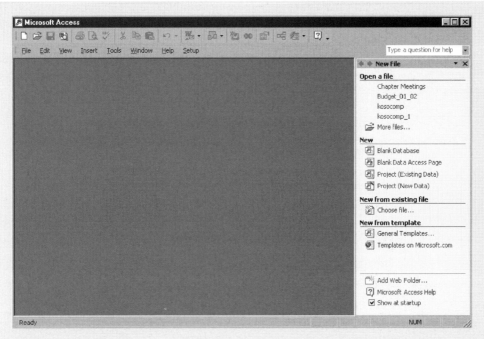

**Figure 5.3b** *Starting a database in Access, using Office XP*

In both versions Access is giving you the option of:

- starting a new <u>B</u>lank <u>D</u>atabase
- using the <u>D</u>atabase Wizard (from General templates in the XP version)
- opening an existing database.

  **Select** the <u>B</u>lank Database.

  **Press** OK.

You will see the screen shown in Figure 5.4.

**Figure 5.4** *Naming your new database*

This dialogue box is the same whichever version of Office you are using.

Here Access is asking you to name your database. If you set up an Access folder when you covered 'setting up your filing structure' in Unit 1, open the folder in the Save in: field and name your database 'Presents'. If you have not created this folder, do so now, using the techniques shown on page 34.

Now you are in Access, so have a look at the screen that is on display(see Figure 5.5).

## The Access screen

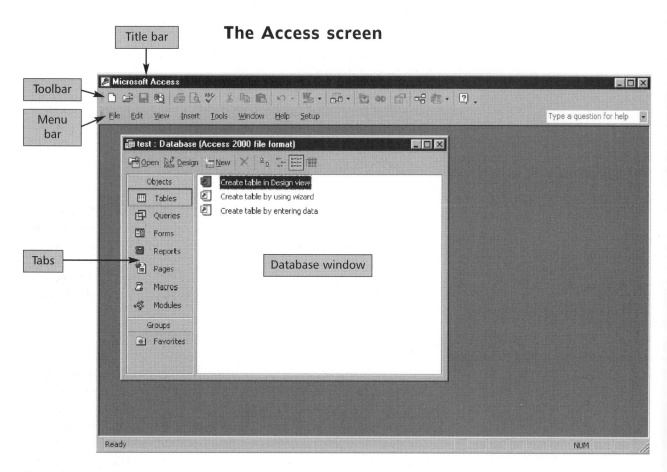

**Figure 5.5** *The Access screen and Database window*

So far there is nothing too worrying. With the exception of the *database window*, you have come across all the other parts of the window in Word. Let's have a look in a bit more detail at the database window. Although there are obviously differences from Word, it is nevertheless fairly straightforward.

Each of the buttons on the left of the database window shown in Figure 5.5 represents a database object. Tables have already been described, but what are the other features shown? Although you will only need the Query tab for New CLAIT, here is an overview of what the other buttons do.

## Queries

The query is an essential tool in any database. A query is the means by which you sort and select groups of records against your own defined set of criteria. For example, you may say 'let me know all the children in my database whose birthdays fall between 1 January and 1 February'. Queries are covered in more depth later in this unit.

## Forms

Next on the tabs list is *forms*. Forms are the main interface between the user and the application and are found in any computerised database. Although they are not essential in terms of allowing your database to work, they help make the whole application more user friendly. They make it easier to enter data into tables and at the same time make things clearer for users who may not be very familiar with computer hardware and software.

## Reports

*Reports* allow you to interrogate the data and get useful information out in a printed format.

## Macros

Often (but not necessarily always) a macro is a function provided in most applications to automate actions you might otherwise do through the keyboard. For example, having built a form you could use a macro to open it either by pressing a button or as part of an *event procedure*. The buttons on your toolbars all have macros behind them. Access makes it very easy even for a novice to create macros using the Macro Wizard.

## Modules

*Modules* can be tricky and unless you really want to learn about them you should leave these well alone until you have more experience in building databases or in programming. You can build a very effective and professional looking Access application without having to go anywhere near a module or writing any programming at all. For the more adventurous, Access has its own built-in programming language based on Visual Basic; it is called 'Access Visual Basic for Applications', or VBA for short.

# Building your first database

## Creating a record structure

Being able to build a record structure (or table) is not a New CLAIT requirement and OCR will provide the basic data table for you to use. However, as was mentioned earlier, tables are the very building blocks of a database and it is useful to know how they are created.

The easiest way to learn about record structures (tables) is by building one; you can do so using the Try it out exercises that follow.

**Try it out**

**Open** your database file 'Presents', if it is not already open.

**Select** the Tables tab in the Database window.

At the top of the dialogue box you will see three command buttons. One says Open and the other Design. The third button says New.

**Press** the New button and the screen should look like Figure 5.6.

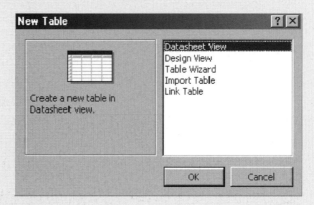

**Figure 5.6** *The New Table dialogue box*

Access now gives you five options:

- Open a new table in Datasheet view.
- Open a new table in Design view.
- Build a new table using the Table Wizard.
- Import a table from elsewhere.
- Link a table from another database.

For now you want to start a new table in Design view so:

**Highlight** Design View.

**Press** OK.

Your screen now changes to the one shown in Figure 5.7:

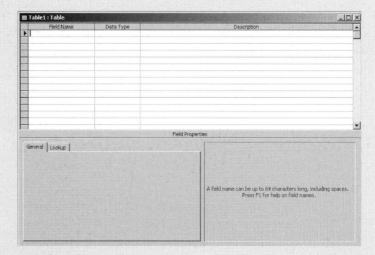

**Figure 5.7** *The Design view screen*

There are three columns: Field Name, Data Type, Description.

Notice that when you click in the first Field Name box, Access provides some basic help in the box on the bottom right. Indeed, if you click in the other two columns you can get help for those too. Try doing that now.

You are going to build a table called tbl_PRESENTS_RECORD. These are the fields you need in the table:

RECIPIENT

PRESENT

WHERE_BOUGHT

DATE_BOUGHT

OCCASION

COST

In the first column type in your field names. When you have finished it should look like Figure 5.8.

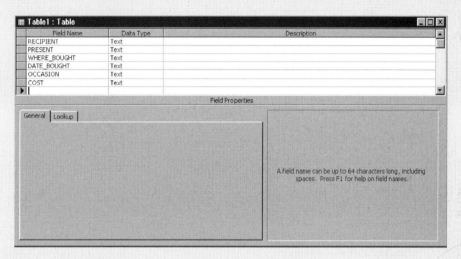

**Figure 5.8** *Table in Design view*

Now you need to change some of the data types in the second column. By default Access first makes all the data types 'Text'. If you click in the first box of the second column and press the small arrow, Access tells you what other data types you can have. For example, if you look at Figure 5.9 you will see you can have Memo, Number, Date/Time, Currency, and so on. Most of the time you will be using Number, Text or Date/Time.

**Figure 5.9** *Field name/data type shown in Access*

Looking at the table, the type of data you need is fairly straightforward. Now go into each field and change the data type as shown below. Your database table should now look like Figure 5.10.

| RECIPIENT | Text |
| --- | --- |
| PRESENT | Text |
| WHERE_BOUGHT | Text |
| DATE_BOUGHT | Date/Time |
| OCCASION | Text |
| COST | Currency |

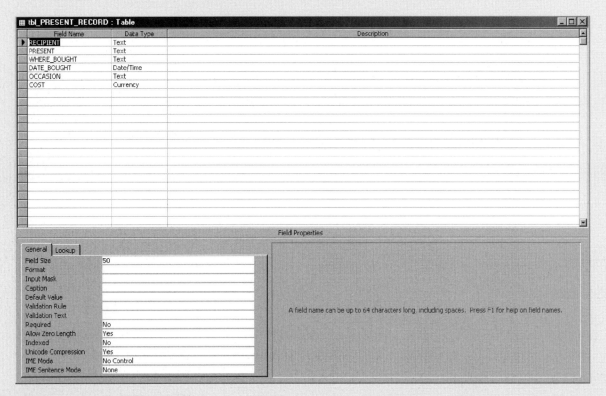

**Figure 5.10** *Changing the data type*

As you click on a field, notice a further box is enabled below the field names. This box allows you to modify the properties of the fields created. For example, as you highlight the PRESENT field you will see its data type is text. In the bottom of the Field Properties box Access has given this a size of 50. This means that you can put up to 50 characters worth of data (text or numbers – known as *alphanumeric characters*) in that field of the table. If you think your data will require more than 50 characters, increase 50 to the desired amount (up to a maximum of 255 characters). However, remember that the larger the size of field you create the more storage space your database will take up on your disk. Always try to keep the size to the minimum needed.

Numeric fields have a number type. In most cases you will use either Long Integer or, if you want to have decimal places, Double. Integer and Long Integer fields house whole numbers and do not allow for decimal places. If you are dealing with fields that relate to money then the Currency data type might be more appropriate. You can change the number type by clicking on the down arrow to the right of the Field Size combo box (see Figure 5.11).

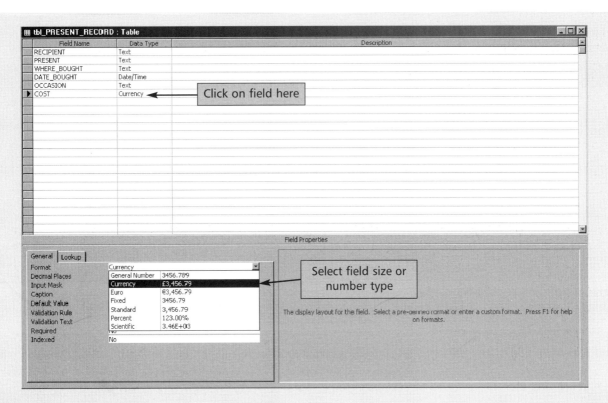

**Figure 5.11** *Changing the property of a numeric field*

You do not need to concern yourself at this stage with the other properties displayed in the bottom box.

Now **save** the table.

**Select** File, Save from the main menu.

The dialogue box shown in Figure 5.12 appears on the screen.

**Figure 5.12** *Save As window*

**Type** 'tbl_PRESENT_RECORD' in the Table Name box.

You may ask why tbl_PRESENT_RECORD and not just PRESENT_RECORD?

Ask ten different developers what the convention for naming objects is and you will probably get ten different answers. However, it is as well to have some consistency in your naming technique and this is just one way. The 'tbl' part identifies the object type, in this case a table. As you will see, when queries are covered, the prefix 'qry' is used.

The main reason for using conventions becomes clearer when you start to develop more complex databases containing tables, queries, forms, reports, macros (and even modules!). There may well be occasions when you want to give a table and a query or report the same name, and it becomes easier to identify these objects if they are prefixed with an identifier, such as 'tbl' or 'qry'.

**Press** OK.

The message in Figure 5.13 will be displayed:

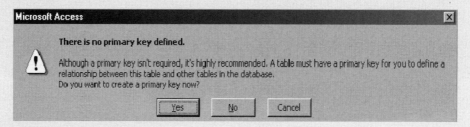

**Figure 5.13** *Microsoft Access – no primary key defined*

## What are primary keys?

Understanding what *primary keys* are and being able to use them is not a New CLAIT requirement. However, as you saw in Figure 5.13, Access will always ask you if you want a primary key, and therefore you may find it helpful to know what these are.

A primary key is where the value of a record is uniquely identified. Take the table 'tbl_PRESENT_RECORD'. You could have included a field before RECIPIENT to hold a number, unique to each particular record, the primary key, for example:

| RECIPIENT-ID | |
| --- | --- |
| 1 | UNCLE JACK |
| 2 | TOM PEACOCK |
| 3 | SARA |

Primary keys are important when your database has more than one table and you need to build a relationship between two or more tables.

### Try it out

Returning to tbl_PRESENT_RECORD:

**Press** the No command button.

**Close** the Design view of your table and return to the main database window where you will see your saved table (Figure 5.14).

### GENERAL TIPS

Once the table has been saved, close the Design view by clicking the Close icon on the top right of the Table Design window: ✖

If you are using Access 97 your database window will be slightly different, with the database object tabs along the top as in Figure 5.15

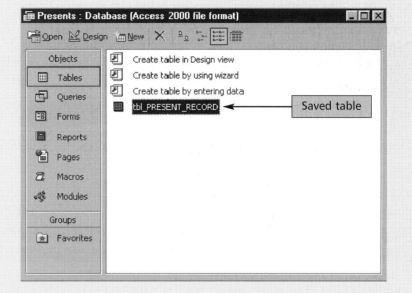

**Figure 5.14** *Saving a table in Access*

### Entering data into a table

**New CLAIT**

The ability to enter data into a record structure (table) is a New CLAIT requirement.

Now that you have saved your table, notice how the name of your table has been added to the database window (Figure 5.15).

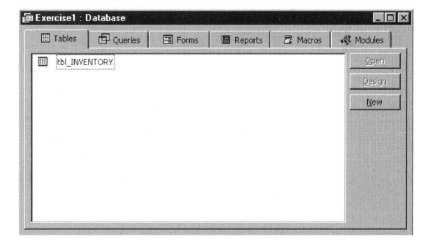

**Figure 5.15** *The database window you will see if you are using Access 97 (the table name is illustrative only)*

### KEYBOARD TIP

In the following 'Try it out' exercise, if an entry in one row is the same as that in the next (e.g. BIMBLES in Figure 5.17) then when you enter the next blank field, press Ctrl+' and the item from the line immediately above it will be reproduced. Alternatively, you can cut and paste or retype the data into the field.

There are basically two ways you can enter data into a table. The first is through a form. Since forms are not covered in New CLAIT, this option is not used. The second method of entering data into a table is directly into the table itself. When a table has been created and opened using the Open button, rather than Design, this is known as the Datasheet view.

**Try it out**

**Highlight** the table name.

**Press** Open and you will see the empty table waiting for data to be entered (Figure 5.16).

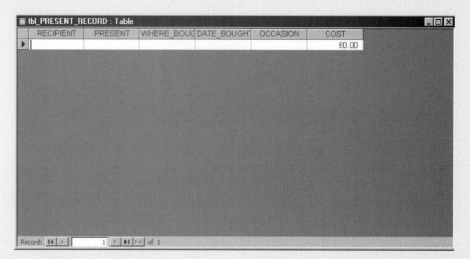

**Figure 5.16** *Empty table awaiting data*

**Click** in the first row of the table under RECIPIENT.

**Enter** the data shown in Figure 5.17 below.

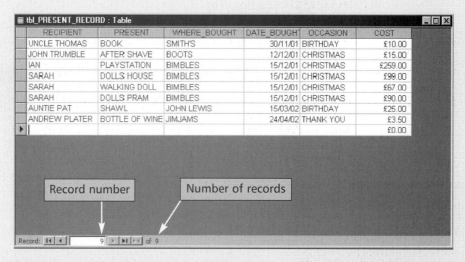

**Figure 5.17** *Entering data into the Access table*

Notice how at the bottom of the table there is a record counter showing the number of records entered in the table and also a box that indicates the current record.

You should now be able to:

- understand the Access screen
- create a table
- understand what primary keys are
- enter data into a table.

## Changing the width of columns in tables

As you saw in the exercise above some data you input was too long for the width of the column in the table and as a consequence not all the data was in view after it had been inputted. A requirement in New CLAIT is that all data must be displayed in full on each of your printouts. When you are asked to print a table, or the results of a query in table format, you will be penalised in a New CLAIT assignment if the text in the column is not visible. It is therefore important that you are able to adjust the width of a column.

The easiest way of achieving this is to place the cursor over the line between two columns and, holding down the left mouse button, drag the column to the width required. Alternatively you can double-click on the mouse button and the column will adjust to the widest entry in that column. When the mouse is correctly positioned between columns the pointer shape will change to that shown in Figure 5.18.

> Cursor changes to double-headed arrow

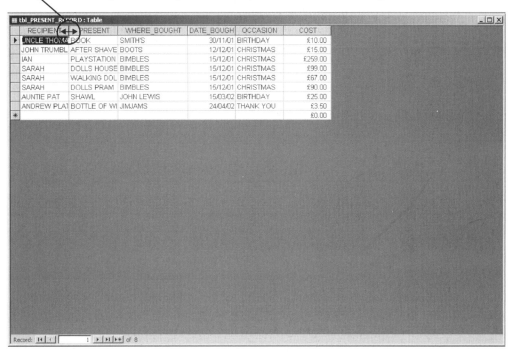

**Figure 5.18** *Cursor changes to double-headed arrow to adjust the width of a column*

### Try it out

**Open** your file tbl_PRESENT_RECORD, if it is not already open.

**Place** the cursor between the columns RECIPIENT and PRESENT.

**Drag** the column to a width where all the items in the table are visible.

**Close** the table.

**Save** the table layout when prompted to do so.

New CLAIT

## Saving your data

Saving data is a New CLAIT requirement.

Unlike saving a text file in Word, Access automatically saves the data you have entered and it is therefore safe to close the table. If you have made any changes to the table's layout (such as changing the width of the columns) Access will prompt you to save any changes you have made.

New CLAIT

## Changing data in a table

Although New CLAIT does not require you to be able to build a database structure nor enter the basic data, you will be expected to add records, amend existing records, delete and replace specified data in a prepared data file. The earlier Try it out exercise gave you practice at entering data. You will now use the file created for you on the CD which accompanies this book.

(**Note**: Remember that when you are asked to work on some of the pre-prepared files on the CD you will need to first copy it to your hard or floppy disk and change its read-only attributes).

## Build-up Exercise 6: Stage 1

*Scenario*

You are the manager of an animal welfare centre where unwanted, injured and lost animals are looked after and for whom new homes have to be found. You have a database for the dogs in your care and you realise that since no one else has the IT skills, you will need to maintain the database as new dogs arrive and others leave.

**Copy** the database file called **Dogs.mdb** from the CD to the folder you created earlier and uncheck the 'read-only' attribute.

**Open** the database called **Dogs.mdb**.

**Open** tbl_DOGS.

**Add** the following new records (Table 5.1):

**Reminder:** To add a new record, click in the first column of the table in Datasheet view and type the data shown. Then tab, using the tab key, to the next field and type the next part of the record. Alternatively, when you have typed the data in the last column of the current record, pressing the New Record button  will take you to a new record (i.e. to the first field in the next row of the table).

▶▶

**Table 5.1** *Adding new data records*

| NAME | BREED | AGE | SEX | COLOUR | DATE_ADMITTED | TEMPERAMENT | HOUSE_TRAINED | ADMIN_CHARGE |
|------|-------|-----|-----|--------|---------------|-------------|---------------|--------------|
| PUMPKIN | LABRADOR | 1 | M | GOLDEN | 25/04/02 | FRIENDLY | YES | £10.00 |
| TODD | RETRIEVER | 2 | M | GOLDEN | 13/05/02 | ACTIVE/FRIENDLY | YES | £7.50 |
| REX | COLLIE | 1 | M | BLACK & WHITE | 20/04/02 | ACTIVE/PLAYFUL | YES | £10.00 |

tbl_DOGS should now look like Figure 5.19.

| NAME | BREED | AGE | SEX | COLOUR | DATE_ADMITTED | TEMPERAMENT | HOUSE_TRAINED | ADMIN_CHARGE |
|------|-------|-----|-----|--------|---------------|-------------|---------------|--------------|
| CHLOE | MONGREL | 2 | F | BLACK | 12/05/02 | ACTIVE/FRIENDLY | YES | £10.00 |
| JACK | GERMAN SHEPHERD | 1 | M | BLACK & TAN | 25/03/02 | TOLERANT | YES | £12.00 |
| JEPS | COLLIE | 1 | M | BLACK & WHITE | 12/06/02 | ACTIVE | YES | £7.00 |
| BIMPY | LURCHER | 6 MTHS | F | TAN & WHITE | 14/06/02 | PLAYFUL | NO | £10.00 |
| NUTS | BASSETT | 2 | M | LEMON & WHITE | 16/04/02 | IMPISH | YES | £10.00 |
| TOM | MONGREL | 1 | M | BLACK | 25/05/02 | FRIENDLY/PLAYFUL | YES | £5.00 |
| KERRY | TERRIER | 3 MTHS | F | GREY | 20/05/02 | ACTIVE | NO | £10.00 |
| SUSIE | COCKER SPANIEL | 1 | F | BLACK | 12/06/02 | QUIET | YES | £10.00 |
| FLASH | WHIPPET | 2 | M | TAN | 20/04/02 | ACTIVE/FRIENDLY | NO | £10.00 |
| SONIE | ENGLISH SETTER | 1 | M | GOLD | 30/04/02 | ACTIVE/GOOD NATURED | YES | £15.00 |
| PUMPKIN | LABRADOR | 1 | M | GOLDEN | 25/04/02 | FRIENDLY | YES | £10.00 |
| TODD | RETRIEVER | 2 | M | GOLDEN | 13/05/02 | ACTIVE/FRIENDLY | YES | £7.50 |
| REX | COLLIE | 1 | M | BLACK & WHITE | 20/04/02 | ACTIVE/PLAYFUL | YES | £10.00 |
| | | | | | | | | £0.00 |

Record: 13 of 13

Your new records will be at the end of the table

**Figure 5.19** *Adding new records to a database*

### Deleting, amending and replacing record data

Being able to delete or replace data is a New CLAIT requirement.

### Deleting records

To delete records in a table is straightforward. First the record to be deleted is highlighted and then the Delete key on the keyboard is pressed. Access will advise you that you are about to delete a record (or records) and gives you the opportunity of changing your mind. Unlike other delete functions, once a record has been deleted you cannot undo the deletion.

## *Build-up Exercise 6: Stage 2*

If it is not already open, open the **Dogs.mdb** database.

### *Scenario*

You are delighted that Jack, the German Shepherd, and Nuts, the Bassett Hound, have just been found new homes. You will need to delete these records from your database.

**Place** the cursor in the Record Selector box next to the NAME field for the record relating to Jack (Figure 5.20).

| | NAME | BREED |
|---|---|---|
| | CHLOE | MONGREL |
| ▶ | JACK | GERMAN SHEPHERD |
| | JEPS | COLLIE |
| | BIMPY | LURCHER |
| | NUTS | BASSETT |
| | TOM | MONGREL |
| | KERRY | TERRIER |
| | SUSIE | COCKER SPANIEL |
| | FLASH | WHIPPET |
| | SONIE | ENGLISH SETTER |
| | PUMKIN | LABRADOR |
| | TODD | RETRIEVER |
| | REX | COLLIE |
| ✱ | | |

Select record here →

**Figure 5.20** *Deleting records from a database*

**Press** the Delete key on the keyboard.

**Repeat** the process for Nuts.

Notice how the record number at the bottom of the table has changed to show the new number of records.

### Amending data

However careful you are, from time to time you may enter data incorrectly or even find that some of the data in a record needs updating and changing. Amending data is quite straightforward. In the scenario of the animal welfare centre you have decided that it would be useful simply to have codes for the dogs' temperaments. The codes to be used are:

| Temperament | Code |
|---|---|
| ACTIVE | AC |
| FRIENDLY | FR |
| PLAYFUL | PL |
| GOOD NATURED | GN |
| QUIET | QU |

To change the data in the field you must first open the table in Datasheet view (i.e. where you can see all the data in the table). Then click in the field that you want to change, highlight all the text and then overtype with the changes you want to make.

## Build-up Exercise 6: Stage 3

With your **Dogs.mdb** database open,

**Open** tbl_DOGS in Datasheet view.

**Click** in the first record of the TEMPERAMENT field.

**Change** ACTIVE/FRIENDLY to the codes AC/FR.

**Repeat** this exercise for each of the other records, using the appropriate code.

Your table should now look like Figure 5.21.

| NAME | BREED | AGE | SEX | COLOUR | DATE_ADMITTED | TEMPERAMENT | HOUSE_TRAINED | ADMIN_CHARGE |
|------|-------|-----|-----|--------|---------------|-------------|---------------|--------------|
| CHLOE | MONGREL | 2 | F | BLACK | 12/05/02 | AC/FR | YES | £10.00 |
| JEPS | COLLIE | 1 | M | BLACK & WHITE | 12/06/02 | AC | YES | £7.00 |
| BIMPY | LURCHER | 6 MTHS | F | TAN & WHITE | 14/06/02 | PL | NO | £10.00 |
| TOM | MONGREL | 1 | M | BLACK | 25/05/02 | FR/PL | YES | £5.00 |
| KERRY | TERRIER | 3 MTHS | F | GREY | 20/05/02 | AC | NO | £10.00 |
| SUSIE | COCKER SPANIEL | 1 | F | BLACK | 12/06/02 | QU | YES | £10.00 |
| FLASH | WHIPPET | 2 | M | TAN | 20/04/02 | AC/FR | NO | £10.00 |
| SONIE | ENGLISH SETTER | 1 | M | GOLD | 30/04/02 | AC/GN | YES | £15.00 |
| PUMPKIN | LABRADOR | 1 | M | GOLDEN | 25/04/02 | FR | YES | £10.00 |
| TODD | RETRIEVER | 2 | M | GOLDEN | 13/05/02 | AC/FR | YES | £7.50 |
| REX | COLLIE | 1 | M | BLACK & WHITE | 20/04/02 | AC/PL | YES | £10.00 |
| * | | | | | | | | £0.00 |

Record: 11 of 11

**Figure 5.21** *Changing data in a table*

### New CLAIT

### Replacing data

Replacing data can be achieved in very much the same way as amending data. However, suppose your database had 2000 entries. Searching through each record to find the data you wanted to replace would be an extremely tedious and laborious process. Microsoft Access provides a very useful tool that allows you to find and replace any data that you want to change. The simplest way of showing you how to do this is through a Try it out exercise.

### Try it out

**Open** the database called **Cars.mdb** (remember to copy **Cars.mdb** from the CD to your hard or floppy disk and uncheck its 'read-only' attributes).

**Open** the table called tbl_CARS in Datasheet view.

The make of car is to be coded. Use the following codes for the individual makes:

| | | | |
|--------|-----|------------|-----|
| FORD | FRD | BMW | BMW |
| TOYOTA | TYA | VOLKSWAGON | VWG |
| JAGUAR | JAG | VOLVO | VLO |
| NISSAN | NSN | | |

With the table open in Datasheet view:

**Select** Edit on the main menu and then Replace....

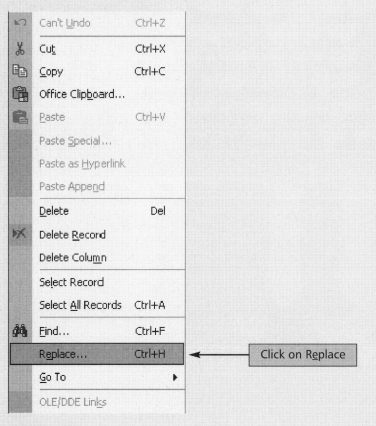

**Figure 5.22a** *Edit/Replace selection*

A new dialogue box will appear (see Figure 5.22a) similar to the one you saw in Figure 2.18 (page 85), when you looked at the find and replace option in Word. This dialogue box is slightly different but the principles are fundamentally the same. Have a look at Figure 5.22b. Check that the word selected to find is the one you want. In the Replace With: box enter the word that will replace the original one. In this case change FORD to FRD (see Figure 5.22b). Check that you are searching in the correct table, which will be shown in the Look in: field.

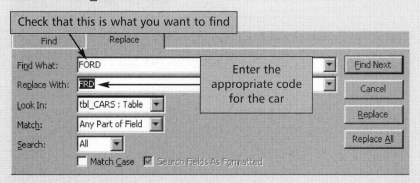

**Figure 5.22b** *Find What/Replace With dialogue box*

**Enter** FRD in the Replace With: box.

Access gives you the option (as was the case in Word) to replace that particular occurrence or to replace all occurrences of FORD with FRD.

**Press** the Replace <u>A</u>ll option.

Access now gives you the chance to change your mind. Once the replacement has been carried out it cannot be undone.

**Press** OK.

Now **replace** the remaining makes of car with the appropriate code.

Your table should now look like Figure 5.22c.

| MAKE | MODEL | COLOUR | YEAR |
|------|-------|--------|------|
| FRD | FIESTA | BLUE | 1998 |
| BMW | 518SE | WHITE | 1992 |
| FRD | CAVALIER | PURPLE | 1991 |
| TYA | CORROLLA | YELLOW | 1987 |
| FRD | MONTEGO | BLACK | 1999 |
| FRD | KA | BLUE | 2000 |
| VWG | BEETLE | BLUE | 2001 |
| JAG | XJ6 | GREEN | 1989 |
| VWG | BORA | BLUE | 1999 |
| VLO | 780 ESTATE | BLACK | 1989 |
| NSN | MICRA | BLUE | 1997 |
|  |  |  |  |

**Figure 5.22c** *Replacing data in a spreadsheet*

You should now be able to:

- change the column widths of a table
- save your data
- add records to a table
- delete records from a table
- amend data in a table.

## Build-up Exercise 6: Stage 4

Return to the **Dogs.mdb** database.

You have noticed that in one record, the English Setter is described as GOLD but in the new records these dogs are described as GOLDEN.

**Replace** all occurrences of GOLDEN with GOLD.

Your table should now look like Figure 5.22d.

| NAME | BREED | AGE | SEX | COLOUR | DATE_ADMITTED | TEMPERAMENT | HOUSE_TRAINED | ADMIN_CHARGE |
|------|-------|-----|-----|--------|---------------|-------------|---------------|--------------|
| CHLOE | MONGREL | 2 | F | BLACK | 12/05/02 | AC/FR | YES | £10.00 |
| JEPS | COLLIE | 1 | M | BLACK & WHITE | 12/06/02 | AC | YES | £7.00 |
| BIMPY | LURCHER | 6 MTHS | F | TAN & WHITE | 14/06/02 | PL | NO | £10.00 |
| TOM | MONGREL | 1 | M | BLACK | 25/05/02 | FR/PL | YES | £5.00 |
| KERRY | TERRIER | 3 MTHS | F | GREY | 20/05/02 | AC | NO | £10.00 |
| SUSIE | COCKER SPANIEL | 1 | F | BLACK | 12/06/02 | QU | YES | £10.00 |
| FLASH | WHIPPET | 2 | M | TAN | 20/04/02 | AC/FR | NO | £10.00 |
| SONIE | ENGLISH SETTER | 1 | M | GOLD | 30/04/02 | AC/GN | YES | £15.00 |
| PUMPKIN | LABRADOR | 1 | M | GOLD | 25/04/02 | FR | YES | £10.00 |
| TODD | RETRIEVER | 2 | M | GOLD | 13/05/02 | AC/FR | YES | £7.50 |
| REX | COLLIE | 1 | M | BLACK & WHITE | 20/04/02 | AC/PL | YES | £10.00 |
| | | | | | | | | £0.00 |

Record: 10 of 11

**Figure 5.22d** *Using the data replacement feature in Access*

## Interrogating and sorting data through queries

**New CLAIT**

### Building a new query

As explained on page 187, an essential function of a database is the ability the user has to search for specific records against given criteria or carry out other functions such as sorting records into a desired order. This is called querying your database, and being able to build and use queries is a New CLAIT requirement. If you have never built a query before the Design view of the query screen can be quite daunting at first sight. In reality, like most windows, once you have had the chance to understand it, it is fairly straightforward. The easiest way to understand how to use queries is to have a go at building one and that is what you will do now in this simple Try it out exercise.

### Try it out

In this exercise you will sort the make of cars in the CARS database into alphabetical order.

**Open** the **Cars.mdb** database.

*Option 1*

In the Database window:

**Select** the Queries tab.

**Select** New (see Figure 5.23).

**Select** Design view.

or

*Option 2*

In the Database window:

**Select** the Queries tab.

**Double-click** on Create query in Design view.

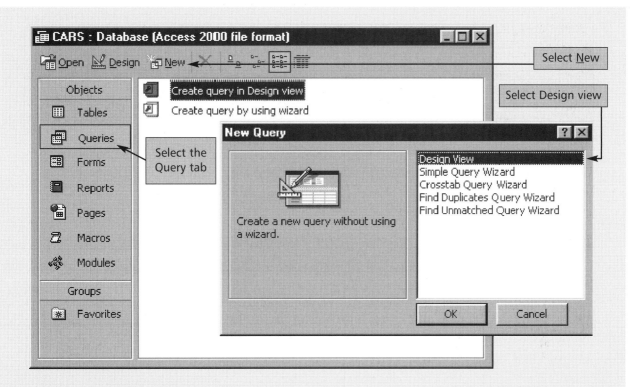

**Figure 5.23** *Building queries in Access*

Your screen will now look like Figure 5.24.

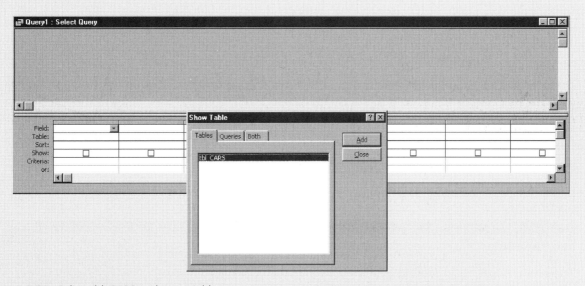

**Figure 5.24** *Select tbl_CARS and press Add*

The small dialogue box shows the objects that are available for you to use in the query. You can see three tabs at the top of the box: Tables, Queries, Both. The Tables tab will be highlighted and shows the only object currently in the database, which is tbl_CARS.

**Press** the Add button (or you can double-click on the tbl_CARS).

This adds a list of field names from the table to your query and these will be used in the query.

**Press** the Close button.

The Selection dialogue box will disappear leaving you with just the query grid and the box showing the table fields (see Figure 5.25).

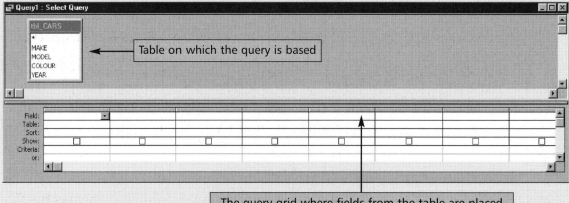

**Figure 5.25** *The Query grid in Access*

The top part of the box houses the objects that you will work with. In this case it is the table containing all the information on the cars – tbl_CARS. In the lower part of the box the fields to be used are placed in the query. For the purposes of this simple exercise you will use all the fields.

There are a number of ways in which fields can be placed in the grid. Here are three of the options:

### Option 1

Using the drag and drop method,

**Click** and hold down the left-hand mouse button on the field MAKE.

**Drag** the field into 'Field' in the first column.

### Option 2

**Double-click** on the MODEL field in the table. This will automatically place the field in the next available position in the grid. If this is the first field it will go to the first column, the second to the second column and so on until you have selected each field you want to use in the query.

### Option 3

**Click** in the Field box on the grid. As you click in the box an arrow will appear to the right of it.

**Press** the arrow and select the field to be used (see Figure 5.26).

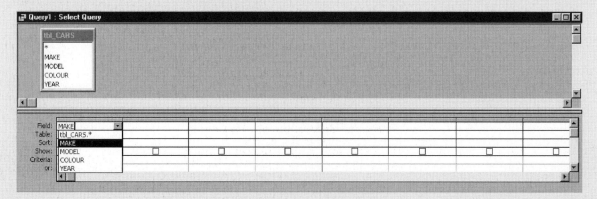

**Figure 5.26** *Selecting the fields to use*

Depending on which of the above options you have chosen to use, now place the rest of the field in the grid. Try to use a different option for each field.

Your query grid should now look like Figure 5.27a.

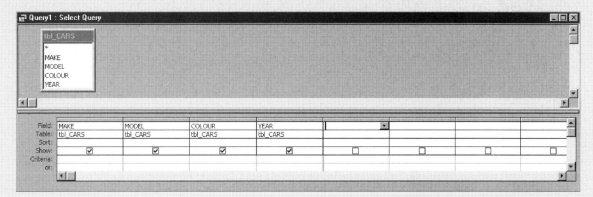

**Figure 5.27a** *The Query grid in Access*

To run the query, click on the Run icon on the main menu. See Figure 5.27b.

**Figure 5.27b** *Running the query in Access*

To return to the Design view of the query,

> **Click** on the Design view icon also shown in Figure 5.27b. When you have run your query it should look almost identical to the tbl_CARS when it is open. You now need to sort the MAKE of car into alphabetical order.

Return to the Design view of the query.

In the grid just below the point where you placed the first field, the third row is titled 'Sort'. As you click in the Sort box, an arrow appears on the right-hand side. If you click on the arrow you will be given the opportunity of sorting in ascending, descending or 'not sorted' order (Figure 5.27c).

> **Select** Ascending.

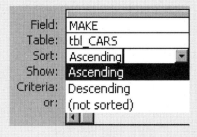

**Figure 5.27c** *Selecting how data will be sorted – Ascending/Descending or not sorted*

> **Run** the query.

You should now find that all the cars have been sorted by MAKE in alphabetical order (see Figure 5.27d).

| MAKE | MODEL | COLOUR | YEAR |
|------|-------|--------|------|
| BMW | 518SE | WHITE | 1992 |
| FRD | KA | BLUE | 2000 |
| FRD | MONTEGO | BLACK | 1999 |
| FRD | CAVALIER | PURPLE | 1991 |
| FRD | FIESTA | BLUE | 1998 |
| JAG | XJ6 | GREEN | 1989 |
| NSN | MICRA | BLUE | 1997 |
| TYA | CORROLLA | YELLOW | 1987 |
| VLO | 780 ESTATE | BLACK | 1989 |
| VWG | BORA | BLUE | 1999 |
| VWG | BEETLE | BLUE | 2001 |

Record: 1 of 11

**Figure 5.27d** *The data has now been sorted*

**Save** your query as qry_CARS_SORTED_BY_MAKE.

Notice how the query name is prefixed with 'qry'. If you can't remember why this is so, go back and review page 191.

## Selecting records using criteria

*New CLAIT*

You will recall that a further requirement of New CLAIT is that you can select specific records using one or more criteria. Using the same database, we are going to amend our query so that it will give only BLUE cars.

### Try it out

If it is not already open,

**Open** your **Cars.mdb** database and the query you have just made in Design view.

In the third column along, headed COLOUR, find the row which is called Criteria.

**Click** in the box on this row under the COLOUR column.

**Type** the word 'BLUE' (see Figure 5.28a).

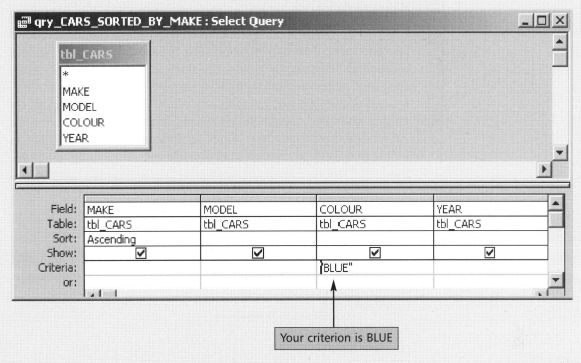

**Figure 5.28a** *Using criteria to return specific data*

Notice how Access will automatically recognise BLUE as text and will place quotation marks around the entry.

**Run** the query.

See how, in Figure 5.28b, the query has only selected those records where the car is BLUE.

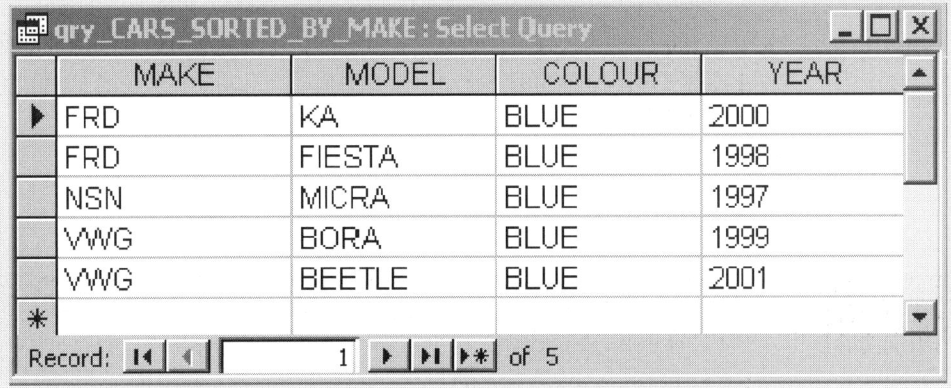

**Figure 5.28b** *Records selected using the criterion 'Blue'*

**Save** your query as qry_CARS_SORTED_BY_MAKE_COLOUR.

New CLAIT

### Selecting records using more than one criterion

For New CLAIT you will need to be able to select specific records by one and more than one criterion. The principle for selecting records by more than one query is exactly the same as it is for one. Where more than one criterion is selected the query will look at the first criterion on the left of the grid and work its way along until it has found all the criteria you have stipulated. More often than not you will use things called *comparison operators*. Don't let this name put you off. The box below may help you understand these better. These are the comparison operators you may have to use in a formal New CLAIT assessment.

---

#### Comparison operators

| | |
|---|---|
| < | less than |
| <= | less than or equal to |
| > | greater than |
| >= | greater than or equal to |
| = | equal to |
| <> | not equal to |

---

### Try it out

In this exercise you are going to extend the original query to select only those cars with a manufacture date after 1999.

**Open** your query qry_CARS_SORTED_BY_MAKE_COLOUR in Design view.

In the Criteria row under the YEAR column,

**Type** >1999.

**Run** the query.

You should now see only two records, as shown in Figure 5.28c.

| | MAKE | MODEL | COLOUR | YEAR |
|---|---|---|---|---|
| ▶ | FRD | KA | BLUE | 2000 |
| | VWG | BEETLE | BLUE | 2001 |
| * | | | | |

Record: 14 ◀ | 1 | ▶ ▶I ▶* of 2

**Figure 5.28c** *Extending the query criterion*

**Save** your query as qry_CARS_SORTED_BY_COLOUR_DATE.

New CLAIT

### Presenting only selected fields in a query

There will be occasions when you are building a query when you need to include fields from a table or other query because they will be used when entering criteria. So, for example, taking the last Try it out exercise (Figure 5.28b), suppose you only wanted to show in a report the MAKE, MODEL and COLOUR of the car. You will still need to use YEAR in the query because this field is where the criterion younger than 1999 is specified. However, you do not necessarily want to display the year itself. To achieve this is very simple.

### Try it out

**Open** the **Cars.mdb** database.

**Open** qry_CARS_SORTED_BY_COLOUR_DATE in Design view.

Notice that under the row called 'Sort' there is another row called 'Show'. This row has check boxes with ticks in them indicating that when the query is run these fields will be shown. If you uncheck the box(es) then those fields that are not checked will not be shown when the query is run.

**Uncheck** the Show check box in the YEAR column.

**Run** your query.

The query will now only show MAKE, MODEL and COLOUR (see Figure 5.28d).

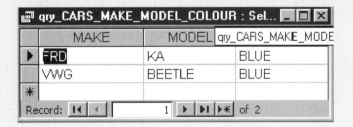

**Figure 5.28d** *Query: Make, model and colour; with year not shown*

**Save** your new query as qry_CARS_MAKE_MODEL_COLOUR.

### Saving the query as a form or report

As has already been mentioned building forms is not a New CLAIT requirement. However, Access provides a very useful function that allows you to save tables and queries as forms. Forms are a user-friendly way of allowing data to be input to a table.

**Try it out**

Open qry_CARS_SORTED_BY_MAKE in Design view.

Select Save As... from the File menu.

The dialogue box shown in Figure 5.29 appears.

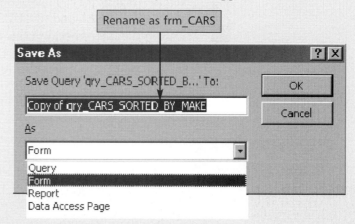

Figure 5.29 *Saving a new query*

Amend the name in the top field to frm_CARS.

Select Form in the As box.

Press OK.

Access will build a form based on the fields contained in the query. The properties of the form can be changed as required at a later time.

## Understanding object properties

The need to understand an object's property is not, you will be pleased to learn, a requirement for New CLAIT. However, sometimes it is useful to know why something looks or acts the way it does. There is an old saying 'you don't know what you don't know'. Understanding a little about properties will help you see why objects appear as they do.

Access is known as an object-orientated database. This is because, like other Windows-based databases, its tables, queries and forms are all objects. You will know from everyday life, objects have properties. Windows in a house have properties; they are made of glass, they can be seen through, they are fragile, the edges of the glass are sharp and so on. These are all properties of a window. In a similar sort of way, a table or form has properties. For example, a form will be a certain height, it will have a name, the text in the form will have a certain style (Arial 12 points).

You can change the properties of an object very simply. Have a look at the form created in the last Try it out exercise (see Figure 5.30a). Notice how the caption at the head of the form has the same name as the query on which the form was based: qry_CARS_SORTED_BY_MAKE. The caption can be changed to make the form look a bit more sensible and user friendly.

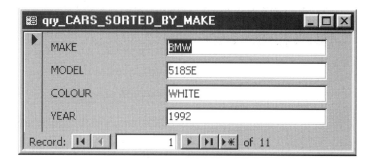

**Figure 5.30a** *Changing a caption*

---

**Try it out**

**Open** frm_CARS in Design view.

This will look somewhat different to other Design views you have seen. Figure 5.30b shows some of the parts of the form.

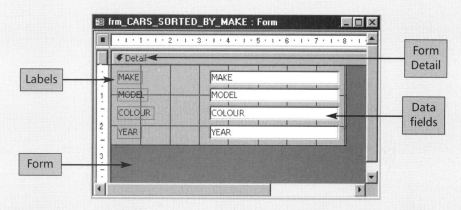

**Figure 5.30b** *Query in Design view*

**Right-click** in the shaded grid area of the form.

**Select** Properties at the bottom of the drop-down menu box.

The properties box will appear as shown in Figure 5.30c on the following page.

At this stage don't worry about what all the properties mean. A little way down the list of properties is one called Caption. If you have been following this exercise it is currently reading qry_CARS_SORTED_BY_MAKE.

**Highlight** the text and replace it with CARS IN STOCK.

Now change to Form view using the icon on the toolbar  or the menu option under View.

Notice how the form heading has now changed to CARS IN STOCK.

**Save** the changes you have made to your form and exit the database.

▶▶

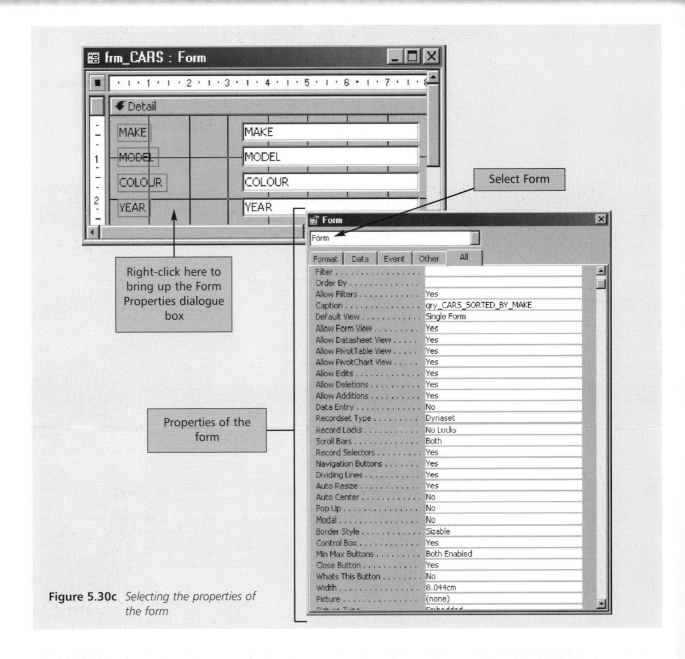

**Figure 5.30c** *Selecting the properties of the form*

You should now be able to:

- build a query
- select records using one criterion
- select records using more than one criterion
- present only specified fields in a query
- understand a little about properties.

## Printing queries and tables

Being able to print the results of your query is a New CLAIT requirement. Printing a query is very similar to printing a document in Word. In the following Try it out exercise you are going to print the results of the query qry_CARS_SORTED_BY_MAKE_COLOUR.

**Try it out**

**Open** your **Cars.mdb** database.

**Open** the file qry_CARS_SORTED_BY_MAKE_MODEL_COLOUR.

To print the results of your query go to File, Page Set-up....

**Select** the Page tab.

**Click** in the Landscape radio button.

**Press** OK.

**Select** File, Print.

**Press** OK.

**Close** qry_CARS_SORTED_BY_MAKE_MODEL_COLOUR.

## Sorting records numerically and by date

Before reinforcing the skills you have learnt with some Build-up exercises, there are two final assessment objectives you have to meet for New CLAIT. These require you to be able to sort data both numerically and by date. These objectives are dealt with at the end of this section because both elements are much the same as sorting data alphabetically. They will also provide an opportunity for you to amend a table structure, add new data and modify an existing query.

**Try it out**

**Open** the **Cars.mdb** database if it is not already open.

**Open** tbl_CARS in Design view.

The cars arrive from auction sales and you need to record the numbers arriving and the date of the delivery from the auction.

After the YEAR field enter two new fields: STOCK and DATE IN. The data type for STOCK is to be Number and DATE IN is to be Date/Time.

**Change** to Datasheet view.

**Add** the following STOCK and DATE IN data from Table 5.2 on the next page.

**Table 5.2** *Amending a table structure*

| MAKE | MODEL | COLOUR | YEAR | STOCK | DATE IN |
|------|-------|--------|------|-------|---------|
| FRD | FIESTA | BLUE | 1998 | 2 | 23/04/02 |
| BMW | 518SE | WHITE | 1992 | 1 | 20/05/02 |
| FRD | CAVALIER | PURPLE | 1991 | 3 | 10/06/02 |
| TYA | CORROLLA | YELLOW | 1987 | 1 | 12/05/02 |
| FRD | MONTEGO | BLACK | 1999 | 2 | 03/04/02 |
| FRD | KA | BLUE | 2000 | 2 | 01/06/02 |
| VWG | BEETLE | BLUE | 2001 | 1 | 05/04/02 |
| JAG | XJ6 | GREEN | 1989 | 1 | 09/04/02 |
| VWG | BORA | BLUE | 1999 | 1 | 26/06/02 |
| VLO | 780 ESTATE | BLACK | 1989 | 1 | 26/06/02 |
| NSN | MICRA | BLUE | 1997 | 3 | 02/05/02 |

**Open** the query qry_CARS_SORTED_BY_MAKE in Design view.

**Add** the two new fields (STOCK and DATE IN) to your query grid.

Remember that Access will action your criteria requests starting from the left-hand side of the grid. In this instance we no longer want to sort by MAKE so change the ascending order in the Sort cell for this field by clicking in the field and selecting 'not sorted'.

**Sort** STOCK in ascending order.

Using the File, Save As... menu option,

**Save** your query as qry_CARS_SORTED_BY_STOCK.

Now repeat this exercise, but this time sort DATE by ascending order and save your amended query as qry_CARS_SORTED_BY_DATE.

Your queries should now look the same as Figure 5.31a and b.

| MAKE | MODEL | COLOUR | YEAR | STOCK | DATE IN |
|------|-------|--------|------|-------|---------|
| VLO | 780 ESTATE | BLACK | 1989 | 1 | 26/06/02 |
| VWG | BORA | BLUE | 1999 | 1 | 26/06/02 |
| JAG | XJ6 | GREEN | 1989 | 1 | 09/04/02 |
| VWG | BEETLE | BLUE | 2001 | 1 | 05/04/02 |
| TYA | CORROLLA | YELLOW | 1987 | 1 | 12/05/02 |
| BMW | 518SE | WHITE | 1992 | 1 | 20/05/02 |
| FRD | KA | BLUE | 2000 | 2 | 01/06/02 |
| FRD | MONTEGO | BLACK | 1999 | 2 | 03/04/02 |
| FRD | FIESTA | BLUE | 1998 | 2 | 23/04/02 |
| NSN | MICRA | BLUE | 1997 | 3 | 02/05/02 |
| FRD | CAVALIER | PURPLE | 1991 | 3 | 10/06/02 |
| * | | | | 0 | |

Record: I◀ ◀ [ 1 ] ▶ ▶I ▶* of 11

**Figure 5.31a** *Sorting records numerically: qry_CARS_SORTED_BY_STOCK*

| MAKE | MODEL | COLOUR | YEAR | STOCK | DATE IN |
|------|-------|--------|------|-------|---------|
| FRD | MONTEGO | BLACK | 1999 | 2 | 03/04/02 |
| VWG | BEETLE | BLUE | 2001 | 1 | 05/04/02 |
| JAG | XJ6 | GREEN | 1989 | 1 | 09/04/02 |
| FRD | FIESTA | BLUE | 1998 | 2 | 23/04/02 |
| NSN | MICRA | BLUE | 1997 | 3 | 02/05/02 |
| TYA | CORROLLA | YELLOW | 1987 | 1 | 12/05/02 |
| BMW | 518SE | WHITE | 1992 | 1 | 20/05/02 |
| FRD | KA | BLUE | 2000 | 2 | 01/06/02 |
| FRD | CAVALIER | PURPLE | 1991 | 3 | 10/06/02 |
| VLO | 780 ESTATE | BLACK | 1989 | 1 | 26/06/02 |
| VWG | BORA | BLUE | 1999 | 1 | 26/06/02 |
| * | | | | 0 | |

Record: 14 ◄ [ 1 ] ► ►I ►* of 11

**Figure 5.31b** *Sorting records by date: qry_CARS_SORTED_BY_DATE*

You should now be able to :

- print your queries
- sort data both numerically and by date.

Now consolidate what you have learnt in the last few pages by completing some Build-up exercises covering some of the formal objectives for New CLAIT. If you can't remember any particular aspect then refer back to the relevant part in this section. In this series of Build-up exercises you will be:

- creating a simple query
- selecting data on one criterion
- selecting data on more than one criterion
- sorting data numerically and by date
- presenting only selected fields
- replacing data using the search and replace function available
- printing your work.

## Build-up Exercise 6: Stage 5

First you will create a query that sorts data by date, which is a New CLAIT requirement.

**Open** the **Dogs.mdb** database.

**Create** a new query based on tbl_DOGS.

**Include** all fields in the query.

**Save** your query as qry_ALL_DOGS_AWAITING_HOMES.

Your query should look like Figure 5.32 on the following page.

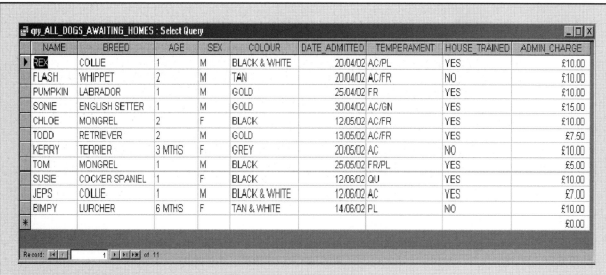

**Figure 5.32** *Presenting only selected data fields in Datasheet view*

**Close** your query.

## Build-up Exercise 6: Stage 6

**Create** a new query based on tbl_DOGS.

**Include** all fields in the query.

**Set** the criteria on BREED so that MONGRELS are not included.

**Sort** the data by DATE_ADMITTED in ascending order (i.e. earliest admission date first).

**Run** your query.

**Save** your query as qry_NOT_MONGRELS.

Your query should look like Figure 5.33.

| NAME | BREED | AGE | SEX | COLOUR | DATE_ADMITTED | TEMPERAMENT | HOUSE_TRAINED | ADMIN_CHARGE |
|------|-------|-----|-----|--------|---------------|-------------|---------------|--------------|
| REX | COLLIE | 1 | M | BLACK & WHITE | 20/04/02 | AC/PL | YES | £10.00 |
| FLASH | WHIPPET | 2 | M | TAN | 20/04/02 | AC/FR | NO | £10.00 |
| PUMPKIN | LABRADOR | 1 | M | GOLD | 25/04/02 | FR | YES | £10.00 |
| SONIE | ENGLISH SETTER | 1 | M | GOLD | 30/04/02 | AC/GN | YES | £15.00 |
| TODD | RETRIEVER | 2 | M | GOLD | 13/05/02 | AC/FR | YES | £7.50 |
| KERRY | TERRIER | 3 MTHS | F | GREY | 20/05/02 | AC | NO | £10.00 |
| SUSIE | COCKER SPANIEL | 1 | F | BLACK | 12/06/02 | QU | YES | £10.00 |
| JEPS | COLLIE | 1 | M | BLACK & WHITE | 12/06/02 | AC | YES | £7.00 |
| BIMPY | LURCHER | 6 MTHS | F | TAN & WHITE | 14/06/02 | PL | NO | £10.00 |
| * | | | | | | | | £0.00 |

Record: 1 of 9

**Figure 5.33a** *Sorting data by date in Datasheet view*

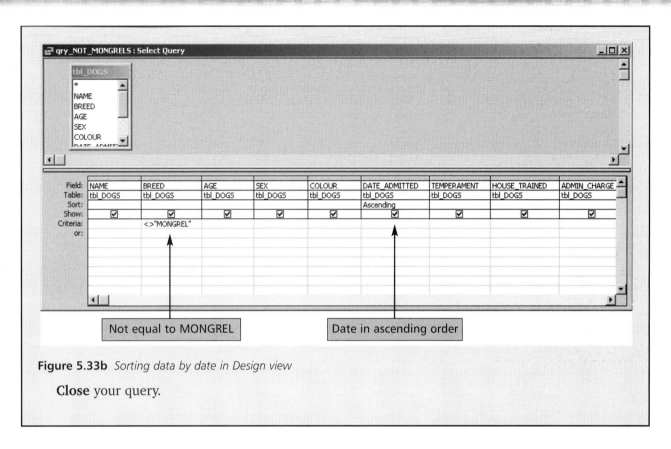

**Figure 5.33b** *Sorting data by date in Design view*

**Close** your query.

## Build-up Exercise 6: Stage 7

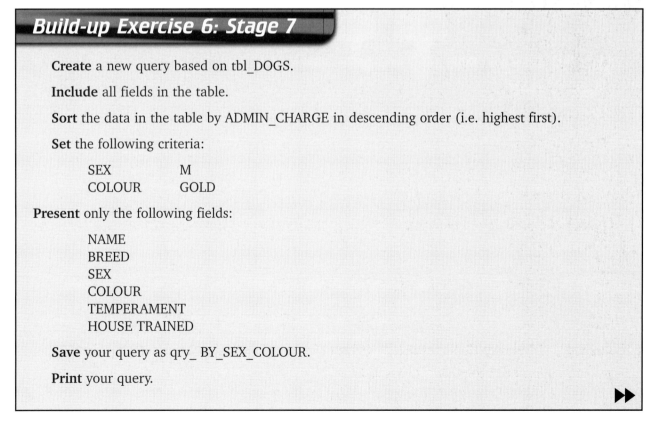

**Create** a new query based on tbl_DOGS.

**Include** all fields in the table.

**Sort** the data in the table by ADMIN_CHARGE in descending order (i.e. highest first).

**Set** the following criteria:

    SEX        M
    COLOUR    GOLD

**Present** only the following fields:

    NAME
    BREED
    SEX
    COLOUR
    TEMPERAMENT
    HOUSE TRAINED

**Save** your query as qry_ BY_SEX_COLOUR.

**Print** your query.

▶▶

Your query should look like Figure 5.34.

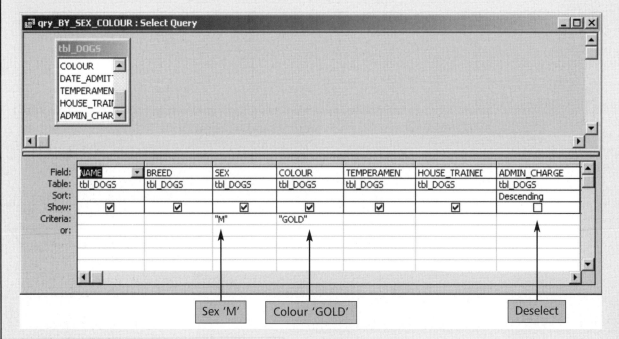

| NAME | BREED | SEX | COLOUR | TEMPERAMENT | HOUSE_TRAINED |
|---|---|---|---|---|---|
| SONIE | ENGLISH SETTER | M | GOLD | AC/GN | YES |
| PUMPKIN | LABRADOR | M | GOLD | FR | YES |
| TODD | RETRIEVER | M | GOLD | AC/FR | YES |

Record: 1 of 3

**Figure 5.34a** *Sorting and presenting data using specific criteria in Datasheet view*

**Figure 5.34b** *Sorting and presenting data using specific criteria in Design view*

**Close** the query.

That completes all that you need to know for New CLAIT about database applications.

Now have a go' at putting together everything you have learnt for New CLAIT databases by completing Practical Assignment 5. Once you have completed the assignment you can check the completed version against the solution in Part 3 towards the end of the book.

You will be using the database called COMPUTERS which you can find on the CD accompanying this book.

## Unit 5 Databases using Access

### Scenario

You are a local computer consultant who advises people on what is on the market and the best deals around. You have set up a database that includes all the national and local deals and prices.

You have just finished reviewing a number of local papers, advertisements and the national press and have found a number of new deals that you want to enter in the database.

| Assessment objectives | Stage | |
|---|---|---|
| 5a<br>2a<br>2b | 1 | (a) Copy the database **Computers.mdb** from the CD onto your hard drive or a floppy disk and change the 'Read only' attribute.<br>(b) Open the database. |
| 2c | 2 | Add new records for the following deals you have found: |

(a) COMPAQ has just offered a deal for a PC with a Pentium 4 processor; a 256 MB RAM, a 21 inch CRT display monitor and a 50 GB hard disk drive; all for the price of £999.00. There are 20 machines in stock. The deal will be valid until 10/07/02.

(b) COMPAQ's second deal is for a PC with an Intel 1.2 GHz processor, 512 MB of RAM, a 17 inch SVGA monitor and a 60 GB hard disk drive for £1099.00. There are 20 machines in stock. This deal is also valid until 10/07/02.

(c) IBM has brought out another laptop to add to its series currently on offer. It has an 800 MHz processor, 128 MB of RAM, a 12.1 inch TFT display screen and 20 GB of hard disk drive for £2205.00. There are 10 machines in stock. The deal is valid until 20/07/02.

(d) A local man you know builds computers in the back room of his house. They are reliable and well built. The prices are not as keen as the main dealers but being local the support is excellent. He trades under the name ALLBITS. He can provide a PC with a 1 GHz processor, 256MB of RAM, a 17 inch CRT monitor and 40 GB hard drive. The price of this package is £899.00 and he will honour this price for any orders before 31/08/02. He has two machines in stock.

(e) Time Computers has decided to withdraw its laptop with the Pentium III processor, 256 MB RAM and 15 inch TFT screen. Delete this entire record.

You have decided that instead of using the full words for 'personal computer' and 'laptop', it would be simpler to use codes.

| | | |
|---|---|---|
| 2e | 3 | In the TYPE field, replace the existing data as follows:<br><br>(a) PERSONAL COMPUTER should be replaced with PC.<br>(b) LAPTOP should be replaced with LT. |
| 5d | 4 | Print all the data in **Computers.mdb** in table format. |

| 2d | 5 | On reviewing your data you notice a couple of mistakes. Make the following amendments to the data in your table. |

(a) COMPAQ'S Pentium 4 PC should have a 40 GB hard disk and not 50GB.

(b) COMPAQ'S 1.2 GHz PC should have a 21 inch SVGA monitor, not a 17 inch one.

## Scenario

You have had a number of enquiries from people who will be looking for new computers after 20 June 2002. You decide to send a simple flyer out with some basic information.

| 3a 4a 3c | 6 | Set up the following database query: |

(a) Select all computers where the deal ends after 20 June 2002.
(b) Sort the data alphabetically by MAKE.
(c) Display only MAKE, TYPE, RAM, HARD DISK and PRICE.

Save the query.
Print the results of the query in table format.

## Scenario

You decide to promote all the laptops on your database that cost less than £2000.00 since most of your local clients want their machines for home use and would not be willing to pay more than this.

| 3b 4b 3c | 7 | Set up the following database query: |

(a) Select all computers that have a laptop TYPE.
(b) Select laptops costing less than £2000.00.
(c) Sort the HARD DISK in descending order of size.
(d) Display only MAKE, PROCESSOR, HARD DISK and PRICE.

Save the query.
Print the results of the query in table format.

| 3b 3c 4b | 8 | Set up the following database query. |

(a) Select all computers where the supplier has 10 or more computers. in STOCK and the MAKE is either TINY or TIME.
(b) Display on the following fields: MAKE, TYPE, PROCESSOR, STOCK, VALID TILL.
(c) Sort STOCK in ascending order.

Save the query.
Print the results of the query in table format.

| 1a 5b 5e | 9 | Exit the software with all updated data saved. |

# UNIT

# 6

# Desktop publishing using Publisher

**New CLAIT**

This unit will help you understand some of the main concepts of desktop publishing and also learn the requirements for producing and printing simple publications by using Microsoft's desktop publishing package – Publisher. Although you do not necessarily need to have undergone any pre-training to complete this unit you may find it helpful to complete Unit 1 on using a computer and Unit 2 on Wordprocessing.

## What you need to know about desktop publishing for New CLAIT

For New CLAIT you will need to know how to:

**Identify and use appropriate software correctly**
- Use appropriate application software.

**Set up a standard page layout and text properties**
- Set the page size and orientation.
- Set margins.
- Create text areas and text frames.
- Set column widths and spacing.
- Use serif and sans-serif fonts.
- Use multiple font sizes.

**Import and place text and image files**
- Import text file(s).
- Import image(s).
- Enter a heading.
- Use lines or border features.

**Manipulate text and images to balance a page**
- Apply alignment and justification.
- Set paragraph spacing and/or first line indent.
- Move and resize an image.
- Resize text.
- Fit the headline text to the page width.
- Balance columns.

**Manage publications and print composite proofs**
- Create a new publication.
- Save a master page/template.
- Save a publication.
- Print composite proof(s).
- Close a publication.

---

*In this unit you will cover:*

- Getting familiar with Publisher
- What is desktop publishing?
- Preparing your first publication
- Formatting a publication
- Displaying text effectively
- Using graphic files
- Manipulating text and images
- Formatting lines and borders
- Setting up a publication template
- Printing your work

---

## Getting familiar with Publisher

OCR requires that you use only desktop publishing or a suitable wordprocessing software package to complete this unit. While it is acceptable to produce the necessary documents using a wordprocessing package, such software does have a number of limitations – particularly when it comes to some of the more complex tasks associated with importing text or graphics. The main difference between a wordprocessing and a desktop publishing (DTP) package is that in the former you enter text directly into the working page; with software such as Publisher, which is designed specifically to produce desktop published material, all inputs, whether they are text, images or other objects, are managed in frames. If you are using an earlier version of Publisher than XP your screens will look a little different to the ones in this book, but the principles are exactly the same, and you should have no difficulty in following the requirements for New CLAIT.

## What is desktop publishing?

Desktop publishing packages (Publisher is just one of many) allow you to manipulate text and graphics to design professional-looking documents such as magazine articles, newsletters and advertisements where the visual appearance of the document is as important as the content. Modern wordprocessors have a degree of sophistication that will allow you to do almost everything that can be done in DTP, but they are not quite as flexible or easy to use as DTP packages that are specially built for the purpose. Microsoft Publisher forms part of the Office professional suite of applications. You don't have to be a design specialist to quickly learn how to produce very eye-catching material using the Publisher application.

When you first open Publisher a screen appears that may look somewhat confusing if you are completely new to this type of work. Publisher comes packed with hundreds of pre-prepared design layouts that you can change using the Wizard. Being able to use the Wizard is not a requirement for New CLAIT but you may wish to take a little time to look at the vast array of layouts available.

### The Microsoft Publisher catalogue

When you load (or open) Publisher the first screen shows you a catalogue of design layouts that have been pre-prepared. Figure 6.1 gives an indication of the range of layouts offered.

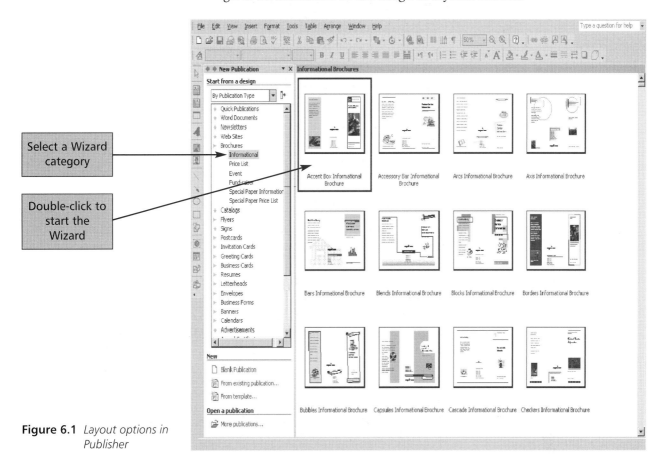

Select a Wizard category

Double-click to start the Wizard

**Figure 6.1** *Layout options in Publisher*

**Try it out**

**Select** the type of publication you want.

**Double-click** on the publication.

**Press** Next> and then follow the Wizard guidance pages.

## Preparing your first publication

### Preparing an A4 page layout

Office provides a range of different blank publication templates, from web pages, postcards and business cards to posters, banners and tent cards. To choose a blank publication style (or template) select the 'By Blank Publications' option from the list offered under the 'Start from a design' drop-down menu list.

(**Note:** If you are using Publisher 2000 click on the Blank Publications tab to bring up the template options.)

Figure 6.2 shows the Publisher screen options.

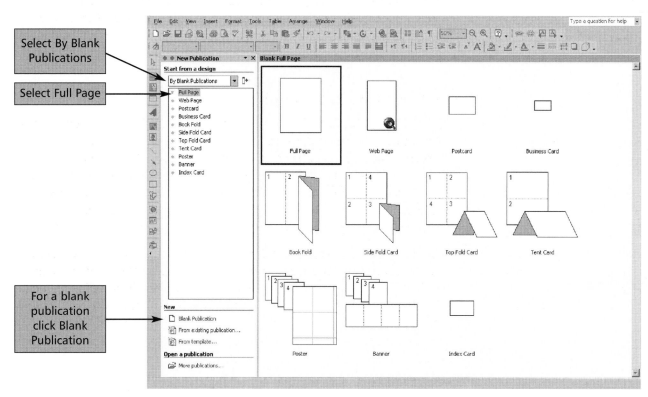

**Figure 6.2** *Publisher screen options*

Being able to prepare an A4 page layout with an appropriate page orientation is a New CLAIT requirement. Click on the Blank Publication hypertext shown in Figure 6.2. To change the default to an A4 page layout use the File, Page Set-up… on the main menu. Select Printer & Paper and then ensure Paper Size is set to A4 (see Figure 6.3).

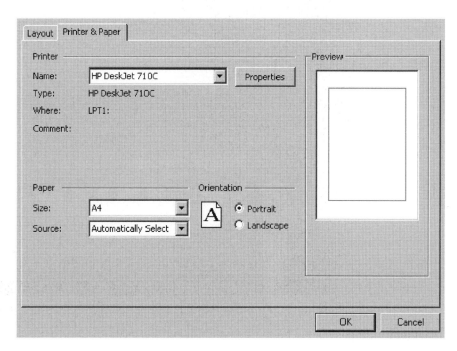

**Figure 6.3** *Printer & Paper window*

(**Note**: In earlier versions of Publisher the paper size is shown in the Paper Size box under File, Page Set-up.... To change this setting you must go to the Print Set-up option on the main menu and change the size of the paper in the Paper Size: field. A4 size is 210 x 297 mm.)

### Introducing layout guides

When a new, blank publication opens it appears similar to a new Word document, but there are some significant differences. You will first notice pink and blue lines surrounding the page. These are known as layout guides and they provide guides for text and image frames in a publication. Layout guides are part of the master page, which means they are repeated on every page of the document, providing consistency throughout the publication (see Figure 6.4).

(**Note**: In earlier versions of Publisher the Wizard may still be present when a new document is opened. Using wizards is not a requirement for New CLAIT so it can be hidden once a new publication is created. To close the Wizard click on the Hide Wizard button on the bottom left of the screen.)

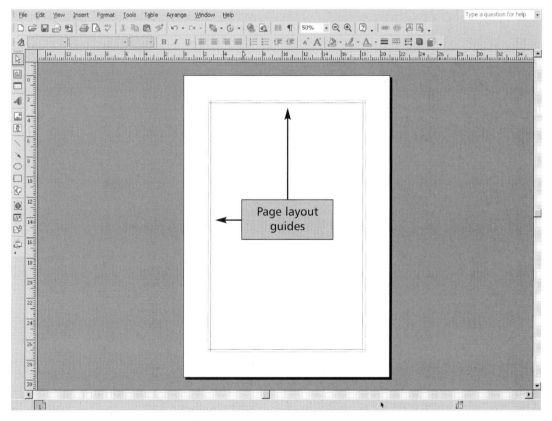

**Figure 6.4** *Page layout guides*

Now have a go at creating a new publication based on an A4 layout.

> ## Build-up Exercise 7: Stage 1
>
> **Open** Publisher.
>
> **Select** Blank Publication.
>
> (For Publisher 2000 users, Press the Create button and then the Hide Wizard button once the new document has been created.)
>
> **Select** Paper, Size: as A4 210 x 295 mm.
>
> **Save** your publication as Community_Lectures.
>
> **Close** the publication.

Unlike a wordprocessing document, text does not go straight onto the page. The page is in two parts: background and foreground. Work done on a background page (i.e. the master page) is repeated on every page of your publication whereas work on the foreground appears only on the current page. (To switch from foreground to background using Publisher 2000 use View, Go to Background on the main menu. In Publisher XP the background is in use when Master Page on the View menu is selected.)

You will know whether you are working on the background or foreground because in the bottom left of the screen you will see either the letter R (or the letters R and L) if you are working on the background, or alternatively a number if you are working on the foreground. If your publication has more than one page there will be more than one number (see Figure 6.5).

**Figure 6.5** *Foreground and Background view*

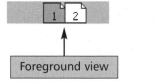
Foreground view

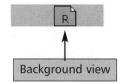
Background view

### Setting margins

For New CLAIT you will need to know how to set the margins in a publication. To ensure that the document is printed correctly you should be aware of your printer's limitations. To find out the minimum settings you can use WordPad, a text editing application supplied with your Windows operating system. WordPad operates in a very similar way to a full wordprocessing application but does not have all of its functionality. The dialogue box for setting the margins in WordPad is shown in Figure 6.6.

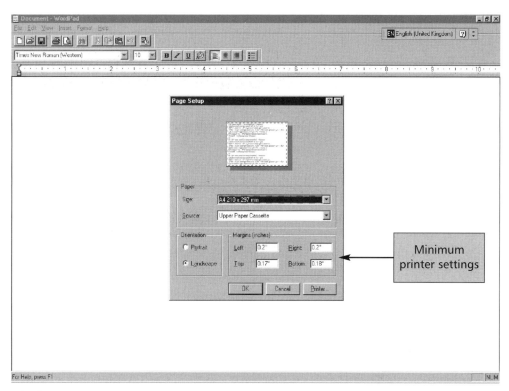

**Figure 6.6** *Setting the margins in WordPad*

Complete the following exercise to determine the minimum print area for the margins on your printer.

**Try it out**

On the Windows taskbar:

**Click** the Start button.

**Select** Accessories.

**Click** WordPad.

**Select** Page Set-up from the File option on the main menu.

**Set** the Left, Right, Top and Bottom margin boxes to zero. The margins will then be reset automatically to the minimum margin that is supported by your printer.

**Note** the minimum margins.

**Create** a new publication in Publisher.

**Select** Master Page on the View menu.

**Click** Layout Guides on the Arrange menu.

**Enter** the minimum margins for Left, Right, Top and Bottom under Margin Guides.

Notice how the guidelines move to the edge of the preview page (see Figure 6.7).

As with margins in Word, the layout guidelines can be adjusted using the drag technique. To adjust the guidelines you must first go to the <u>M</u>aster Page view. By placing the cursor over the guideline and holding down the Shift key, you can drag the lines to the required position. As the Shift key is pressed and the cursor is over the guideline it will change to the following shape:

ADJUST

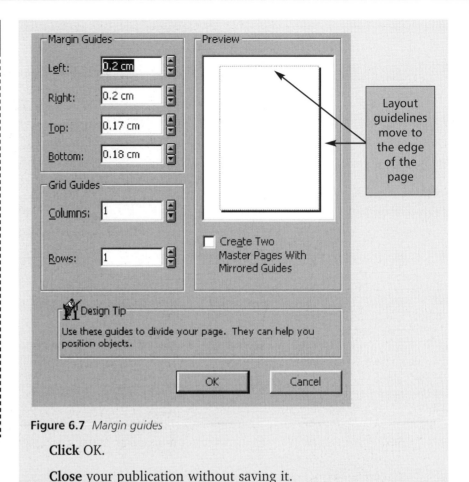

**Figure 6.7** *Margin guides*

**Click** OK.

**Close** your publication without saving it.

---

## Build-up Exercise 7: Stage 2

**Open** Community_Lectures.

**Set up** the master page/template for the page as follows:

Note: the page should already be set for A4.

| | |
|---|---|
| Page orientation: | portrait |
| Set left and right margins to: | 2.5 cm |
| Set top and bottom margins to: | 2.0 cm. |

**Save** your publication.

---

## Changing the layout guides

For a one-page publication, consistency in not really an issue. However, for documents that have more than one page it is important to ensure the whole document is consistent in terms of layout and style. Using the layout guides is a very useful way of ensuring that consistency of layout is maintained. Have a look at Figure 6.8.

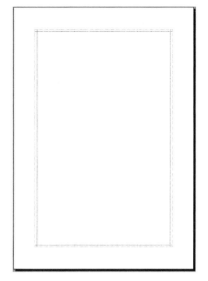

**Figure 6.8** *The layout guide*

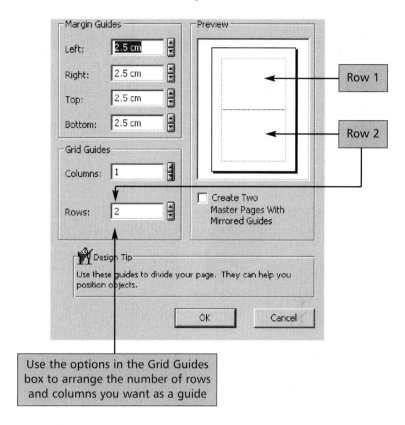

Use the options in the Grid Guides box to arrange the number of rows and columns you want as a guide

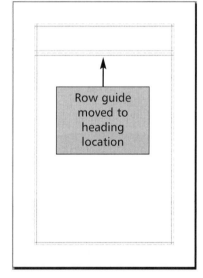

Row guide moved to heading location

**Figure 6.9** *Moving row guide*

Say you wanted a guide to show exactly where the heading should be placed, and also guides for two columns. By using Layout Guides… under the Arrange option on the main menu you can add both rows and columns to the publication template. In Figure 6.8 two rows have been created. Now the row position can be altered to accommodate the positioning of the heading. Remember, this is just a guideline and you can't place text onto the page until you have created a text box. Using the drag technique, the first row can be moved to the required heading location (see Figure 6.9).

## Build-up Exercise 7: Stage 3

**Open** Community_Lectures.

**Create** two rows.

**Adjust** the first row so that the bottom edge is 6 cm from the top.

Use the ruler guide at the left-hand side to measure 6 cm.

**Save** the publication.

Your page should now look like Figure 6.10 overleaf.

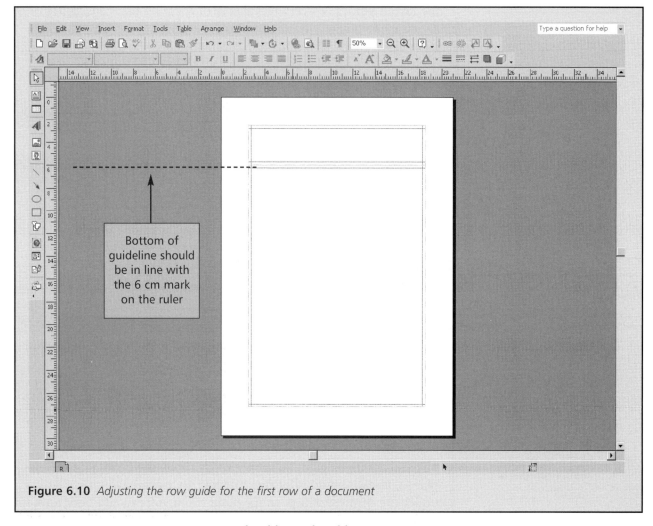

**Figure 6.10** *Adjusting the row guide for the first row of a document*

You should now be able to:

- create a new publication document
- set up the document to an A4 page layout
- understand the concept of layout guides
- set the page margins for the document appropriate for the minimum settings of your printer
- change the layout guides.

## Formatting a publication

### New CLAIT

### Creating text areas and text frames

Now that the publication has a general framework in terms of the page size, margins and orientation, you can look at setting up the page to accept text and graphics. You will need to determine whether the frames to be inserted need to be consistent throughout the publication. In this instance the first page will contain the heading which will not be repeated on subsequent pages, so the foreground page will be used. To place a text box on either the master page or your foreground page, first select the text box symbol from either the menu or toolbar, as shown in Figure 6.11.

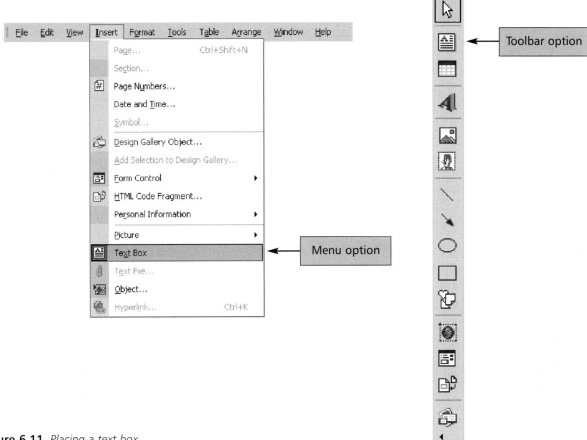

**Figure 6.11** *Placing a text box*

Once the text box symbol has been selected the cursor is moved so that it is over the place on the page of the publication at the point where the text box is to start. As the cursor is placed over the publication, its shape will change to a cross hair ─|─ (see Figure 6.12).

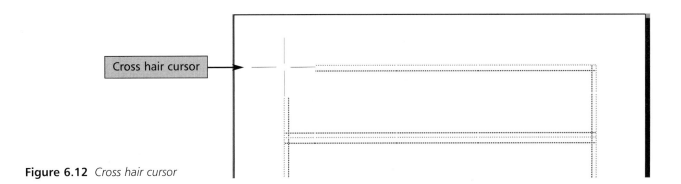

**Figure 6.12** *Cross hair cursor*

The cursor is now dragged to create the text box to the desired size over the area prepared for the heading. Once the mouse button is released the text box is completed and the cursor will flash in the text box waiting for text input (see Figure 6.13).

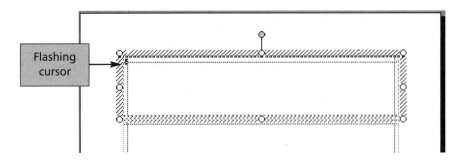

**Figure 6.13** *The cursor will flash in the text box*

The text can now be input and sized accordingly. First, input the text you want for the heading. Highlight the text and format alignment, size and weight (e.g. normal or bold), as shown in Figure 6.14.

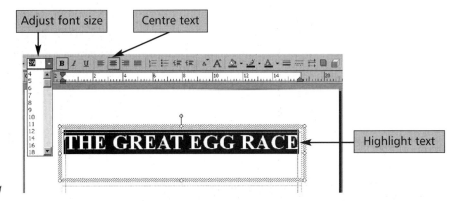

**Figure 6.14** *Formatting the heading*

**Try it out**

Create a new publication with the following set-up:

| | |
|---|---|
| Page: | A4 |
| Page orientation: | portrait |
| Set left and right margins to: | 2.25 cm |
| Set top and bottom margins to: | 2.50 cm. |

**Change** the layout grid to 2 rows.

**Position** the first row to accommodate the heading, with the bottom guideline at 6 cm on the page.

**Insert** a text box to accommodate a heading the full width of the layout guidelines.

**Type** in the following heading and change format as shown:

SEPTEMBER VILLAGE NEWSLETTER

## GENERAL TIP

For horizontal alignment use the Alignment icon on the toolbar. For vertical alignment use the right-hand mouse button to bring up the Format Text Box dialogue box. Then select the Text Box tab (see Figure 6.15).

**Format** font:   sans-serif (Font styles are covered on page 238. For the purposes of this exercise use Arial.)

**Format** text alignment as:

Horizontal:   centre
Vertical:       centre.

**Save** your publication as Test_1.

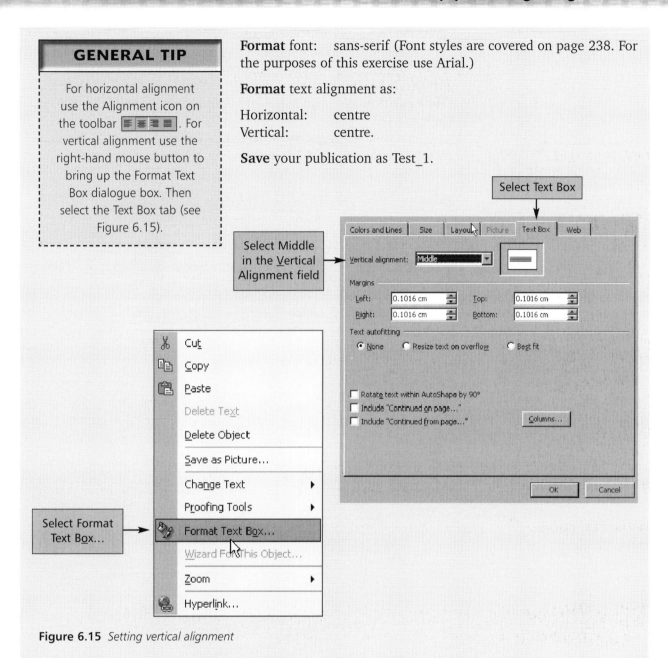

Select Text Box

Select Middle in the Vertical Alignment field

Select Format Text Box...

**Figure 6.15** *Setting vertical alignment*

## Formatting columns in a text box

In addition to being able to insert text and graphic boxes, for New CLAIT you will also need to be able to format the text boxes so that text can flow into more than one column. To achieve this, the same Format Text Box dialogue box as above is used. On that dialogue box you will see a command button named Columns.... Once this is pressed a new dialogue box appears called Columns. Here you have the option to select the number of columns you want to use and also any spacing needed between the columns. Have a look at Figure 6.16. If you are using Office 2000, right-click on the text frame and from the menu list select Change Frame from the primary list and Text Frame Properties...

from the secondary list. The number of columns and their spacing can be entered into the Columns section of the dialogue box, immediately below the Margins section. Changing the vertical alignment of text in the Office 2000 version is achieved by selecting Format, Align Text Vertically from the main menu and then choosing one of the options from the list.

Once your selections are accepted, by clicking on the OK button the text box will be divided into two columns. Now try this out.

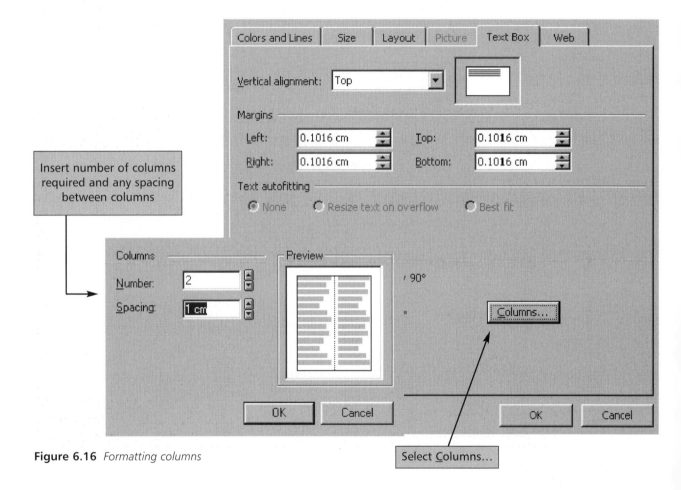

**Figure 6.16** *Formatting columns*

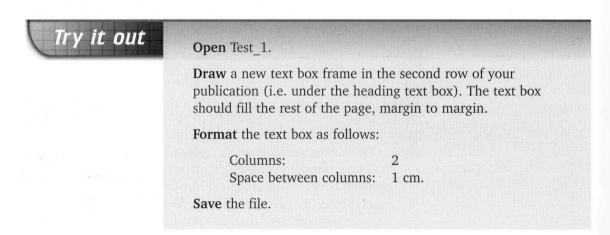

**Open** Test_1.

**Draw** a new text box frame in the second row of your publication (i.e. under the heading text box). The text box should fill the rest of the page, margin to margin.

**Format** the text box as follows:

Columns: 2
Space between columns: 1 cm.

**Save** the file.

## Importing text into a text frame

Text can either be typed directly into a text box or imported from a text file. For New CLAIT you are required to be able to import a text file into a publication. The good news is that you don't have to type the text yourself as this is provided as a pre-prepared file. The procedure for importing a text (or graphics) file is very straightforward. Once the text box has been placed in your publication you can use Insert, Text File... from the main menu or, if it is on your toolbar, the Text File icon ⬚. By selecting the menu option or clicking the icon, the following dialogue box will appear for you to select the file to be imported (Figure 6.17).

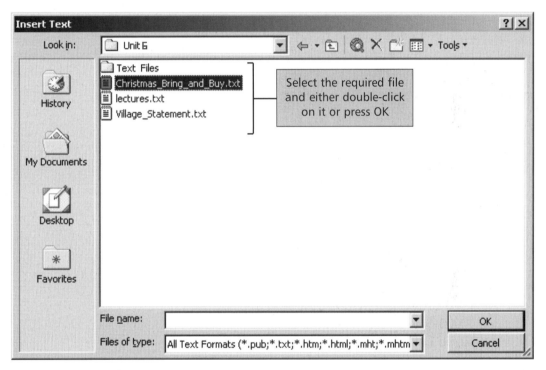

**Figure 6.17** *Selecting the file to be imported*

Once the file to be imported has been selected, either press the OK button or double-click on the file to import it into the text box.

(**Note:** Ensure the text box in the publication is highlighted and the cursor is flashing in the box.)

### Try it out

**Open** Test_1.

**Select** your two-column text box under the heading text box. This should fill the rest of the page from margin to margin.

**Select** Insert, Text File... (or **Press** the Text File Import icon).

**Highlight Christmas_bring_and_buy.txt** (located on the CD).

**Press** OK.

Your publication should now look like Figure 6.18.

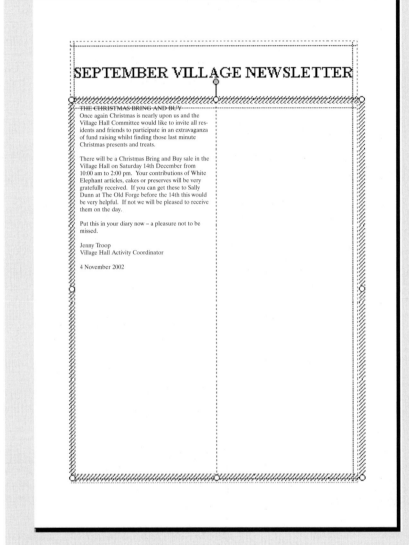

**Figure 6.18** *Importing text into a text frame*

**Save** Test_1.

You should now be able to:

- create a text box and position it as specified
- format the text in a text frame
- modify the layout guides to create columns
- import a text file

Now return to the Build-up exercise and put some of this into practice.

## Build-up Exercise 7: Stage 4

**Set-up** the page layout in newsletter format (two-column text) and include a page-wide heading text box:

The specification for the columns is:

| | |
|---|---|
| Columns: | 2 |
| Column widths: | equal (this should be the default in Publisher 2000 and Publisher XP) |

Space between columns: 1 cm.

**Type** the following heading: MAKE A DIFFERENCE.

**Increase** the font size of the heading so that the text extends across the full width of both columns of text.

**Import** the text file on the CD called **Lectures.txt** so that it begins at the top of the left-hand column, below the heading.

**Save** the publication file.

Your publication should now look like Figure 6.19.

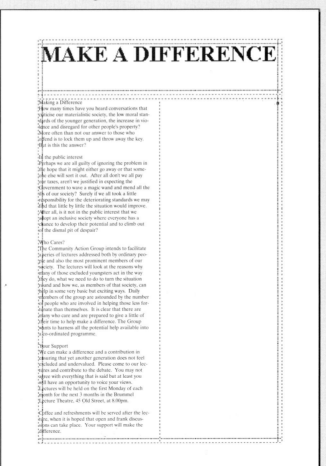

**Figure 6.19** *Text file with text frame inserted*

## Displaying text effectively

### Formatting font styles and sizes

So far you have either typed words into the publication (the heading) or imported text from an external file. At the beginning of this unit it was emphasised that the purpose of using desktop publishing packages was to make an impact with the visual appearance of the document. If you simply accept the default fonts and formats then you may as well use wordprocessing software. The appearance of any publication can be enhanced significantly by varying the style, weight and size of the fonts used. The variety and type of fonts available for DTP and other packages is enormous and font types can run into thousands. Indeed, the choice is so big that it is sometimes difficult to decide which ones should be used.

### Serif and sans-serif fonts

New CLAIT requires that you are able to change the style and size of fonts in a publication. Fonts are basically *serif* or *sans-serif* types, meaning the letters either have tails or they don't. Times New Roman is a serif font. If you look at the 'T' of Newsletter in the heading of the Test_1 exercise, you will see it has small 'tails' on the top bar and at the base of the downstroke. Have a look at Figure 6.20 to see the difference between serif (with tails) and sans-serif (without tails). 'Sans' in French means without, which might help you remember the difference between the two.

This font
is serif
and has tails

This font is
sans-serif
and has no tails

**Figure 6.20** *Serif and sans-serif fonts*

### Font size

Not only do fonts come in different types and styles but many, although not all, are sizeable. You will recall that when you entered your heading text in the heading text box, Publisher gave you a default font size that was really not suitable to stand out as an eye-catching heading. To change the font size the text must first be selected (or highlighted). Once the font has been selected you can use the Font Format box on the toolbar shown in Figure 6.21, or the Font dialogue box in Figure 6.22 which can be found by selecting Font... from Format on the main menu.

**Figure 6.21** *The Font Format box*

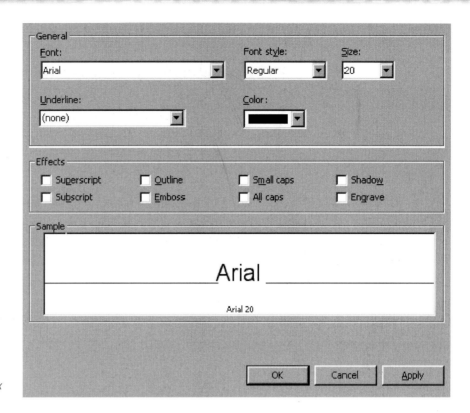

**Figure 6.22** *The Font dialogue box*

Now return to the file Test_1.

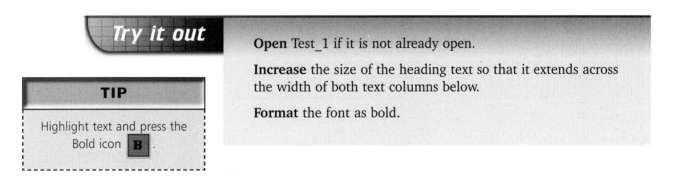

**Try it out**

**Open** Test_1 if it is not already open.

**Increase** the size of the heading text so that it extends across the width of both text columns below.

**Format** the font as bold.

**TIP**

Highlight text and press the Bold icon **B** .

### New CLAIT

### Formatting paragraphs and text

It is unlikely that an imported text file will produce the style of text that you want for the final version of your publication. If the file imported is purely a text file it will not have any formatting such as bold or underlining and therefore any formatting needed will have to be done within the publication itself.

If you look at the text file imported into Test_1 you can see that the font is small and would certainly fail to attract anyone's attention if the publication was to be printed in its present format. In terms of formatting text, you will need to be able to:

- apply alignment and justification
- set the paragraph spacing and/or first line indentation
- resize text
- balance the columns so that the text fits the area of the publication.

You have already seen how text can be resized. Aligning and justifying text in a text box is fundamentally no different from aligning and justifying text in a Word document. Remember that to format any text you must first highlight the text to be formatted. All the formatting you will be required to do can be achieved by using the formatting toolbar or the appropriate formatting dialogue box accessed through the main menu. Have a look at Figure 6.23.

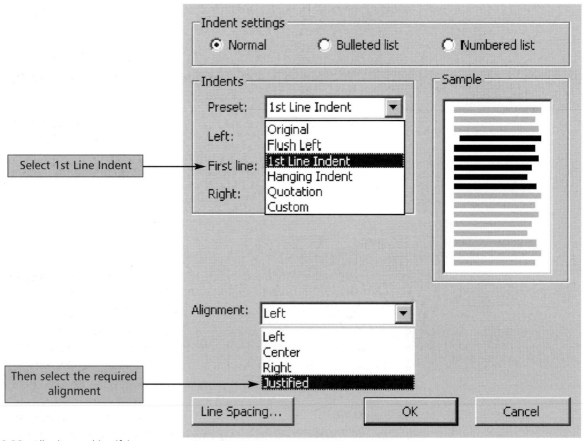

**Figure 6.23** *Aligning and justifying text*

This is the dialogue box accessed by selecting Format, Indents and Lists on the main menu. However, you can only open it once the text to be formatted has been highlighted. If the text is not highlighted then the option is greyed out and not available. Now have a go at some formatting of the text in the file Test_1.

## Try it out

**Open** Test_1.

**Highlight** the text where it starts 'Once again Christmas....' down to 'Put this in your diary now – a pleasure not to be missed.'. Do not include:

> Jenny Troop
> Village Hall Activity Coordinator
> 4 November 2002

or the main heading.

**Select** Indents and Lists... from Format on the main menu.

**Select** 1st Line Indents from the Indents box and Justified from the Alignment: field.

**Press** OK.

**Highlight** all the text excluding the paragraph heading (using Ctrl+A).

**Select** a font size of 18 and a sans-serif font type (e.g. Arial).

**Highlight** the paragraph heading THE CHRISTMAS BRING AND BUY.

**Select** a font size to make the paragraph heading larger than the main text but smaller that the main heading (e.g. 22).

**Save** your publication.

### GENERAL TIP

To highlight all text within a frame use the keyboard shortcut Ctrl+A. Alternatively, if only part of the text is to be highlighted, press the left-hand mouse button and, while it is still held down, drag the pointer over the text to be highlighted.

You should now be able to:

- format the size, alignment and spacing of fonts.

## New CLAIT

## Using graphic files

In addition to importing text files, New CLAIT requires that you are also able to import basic graphic files into a publication. For the formal assignment you will be provided with the image that has to be imported. Most of the time when you use Publisher you will either be importing a clip art file (supplied with the Office Suite) or a graphic file available on your hard disk or a CD. In this unit you will cover both importing a clip art file and a file provided from an external source (namely the CD that accompanies this book). To insert a clip art picture or graphic file is as easy as, if not easier, than inserting text. Publications are significantly enhanced through the use of pictures, graphs, clip art and other forms of graphics. The number of clip art pictures that are available to you on the hard disk will depend very much on how many were loaded when the software was installed. If you only have a limited number on disk you can always add more to your hard disk or alternatively access your clip art files directly from the CD that came with Microsoft Office.

### Importing clip art

Remember that everything in a publication is contained within a frame. Publisher 98 and 2000 operate in a very slightly different way from Publisher XP, however the principles are exactly the same. In any of these versions of Publisher there are basically two ways of importing your file. Option one is to use the object toolbar. This toolbar is present in all versions of the software. Have a look at Figure 6.24.

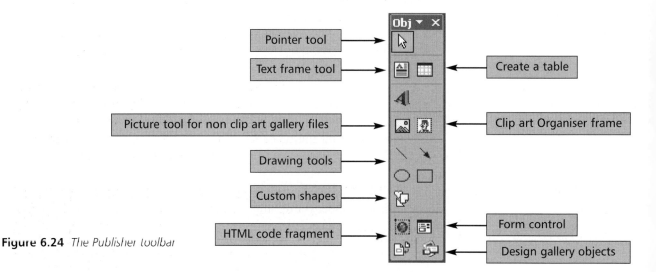

**Figure 6.24** *The Publisher toolbar*

From this toolbar you can import pictures from either the Clip Art Gallery or a file. In Publisher XP clicking on the Clip Art icon will bring up a search box on the left of the screen as shown in Figure 6.25.

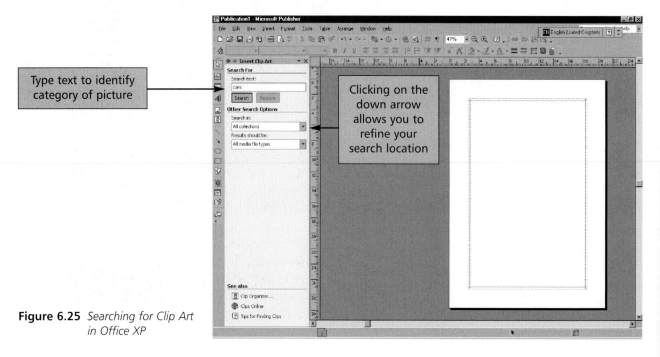

**Figure 6.25** *Searching for Clip Art in Office XP*

The Search text: box allows you to type in a category, e.g. car, woman, house, etc. Beneath this box are two further fields – Search in: and Results should be:. In the Search in: box you can specify the catalogue where the picture might be found and the Results should be: box further refines the search to file types such as clip art, photograph, movie, etc. More often than not the default category of Seeking all is used unless you are searching through a very large library of images. By pressing the Search button, Publisher will find any pictures relating to the text entered. Here, for example, the search text is Cars and after pressing the Search button Publisher displays the results of the search as shown in Figure 6.26.

The picture can be inserted into the publication either by double-clicking on it or using the arrow to the right of the picture and selecting Insert.

If you have an earlier version of Publisher you will need to draw a frame on the document by clicking on the Clip Organiser button and then moving the cursor over to the publication and literally dragging out a frame to the desired size. Once the mouse button is released the Clip Art Gallery box shown in Figure 6.27 will appear.

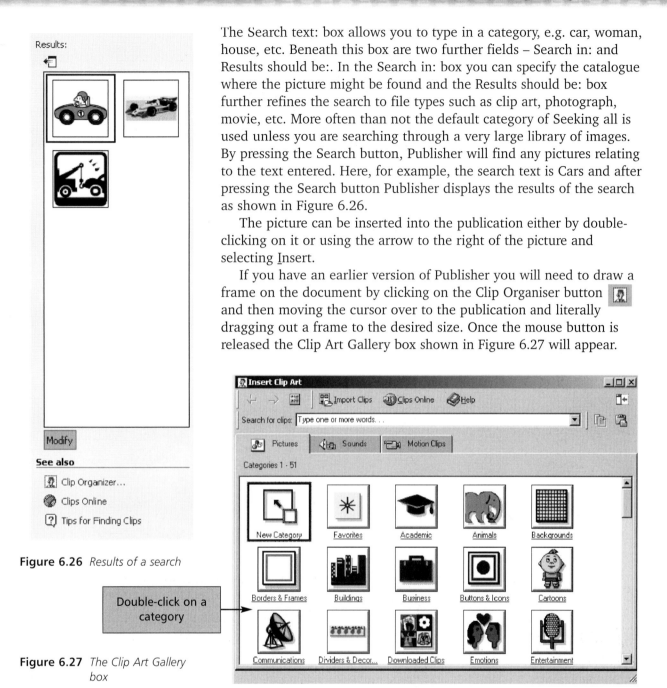

**Figure 6.26** *Results of a search*

Double-click on a category

**Figure 6.27** *The Clip Art Gallery box*

You can now click on a category or type in some text in the Search for clips: field. Once the selection is shown in the main window the picture can be inserted into the document by either double-clicking on it or using the right-hand mouse button and selecting Insert Clip (Figure 6.28).

Click here

Press the Insert Clip button

**Figure 6.28** *Inserting Clip Art into a document; Publisher 2000 version*

### Importing a non-clip art graphic file

To import a graphic file you can either use the Picture Frame icon 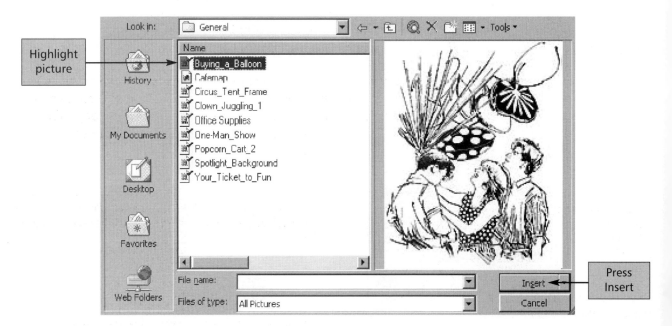 on the objects toolbar or use the Insert, Picture, From File... option on the main menu. Using the Picture Frame icon allows you to place the picture frame in a specific area of the publication. After selecting the icon move the cursor over to the publication and draw a frame, using the drag technique, starting at the point where you want the picture to appear. Once the mouse button is released the Insert Picture dialogue box appears (see Figure 6.29) from which you can find and select the graphic file you want to use. Highlight the file and press the Insert button to place the graphic in the publication document. If the Insert, Picture, From File... option is used, the Insert Picture dialogue box will automatically appear and, once the file has been selected, the picture will be placed in the publication without the need to draw a frame first. Since, in the majority of cases, you will probably want to reposition or resize the picture before completing the publication, it is a matter of personal preference which option you use.

**Figure 6.29** *Inserting a picture*

### Picture frame properties

Placing an image into a frame where there is already text will displace the text in the frame. Publisher XP provides a picture formatting facility that allows you to determine how the text should 'wrap' in relation to the text, i.e. 'top and bottom', 'through', 'square' and so on.

To format the image or picture, first select the picture and then, using the right-hand mouse button, select Format Picture... from the drop-down menu. A dialogue box appears with six tabs along the top of the box. Selecting the Layout tab offers a number of styles for wrapping the text around the image (see Figure 6.30).

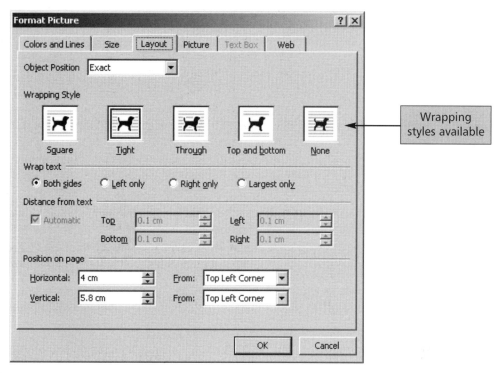

**Figure 6.30** *The Format Picture dialogue box in Publisher XP*

By clicking on one of the wrapping style options and pressing the OK button, you can position the image in relation to the text according to the selection made. Clearly, the wrapping style you choose depends largely on the style of the document, as well as personal preference.

Look at Figure 6.31 below.

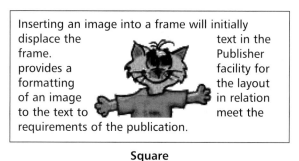

**Square**

**Figure 6.31** *Wrapping styles*

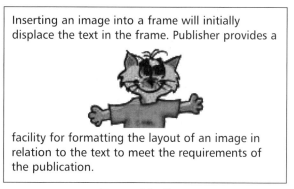

**Top and bottom**

The left-hand picture shows the text wrapped around all four sides of the image, and the right-hand picture shows the text wrapped around the top and bottom only.

**Note:** For Office 2000 users, right-click on the image and select Change Frame in the first menu list and then Picture Frame Properties... in the second list. A different dialogue box to that shown in Figure 6.30 appears (see Figure 6.32).

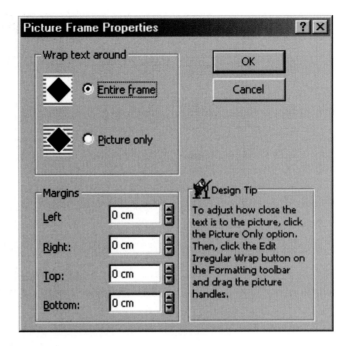

**Figure 6.32** *The Format Picture dialogue box in Office 2000*

The options are more limited than those offered with Office XP, allowing you to wrap text around the entire frame or the picture only.

**Try it out**

**Open** Test_1 if it is not already open.

**Import** the image **Bring_and_buy.jpg** from the CD.

## Manipulating text and images

### Moving and resizing frames

Being able to manipulate text and images to balance a page is a New CLAIT requirement. For images, this means being able to resize and move an imported picture.

Sometimes, even though you prepare your publication style before inserting text and graphics, the end result is not always exactly what you want. Frames can be moved into any position required and resized. Take a look at Figure 6.33 on page 247.

Say that you wanted to place the owl and the cat in the boat. Clearly the boat needs to be bigger and the animals probably a bit smaller. When you click on an image, drag handles appear and you can see the cursor's pointer change which then allows you to resize or move the object using the icons shown on the left.

Start by selecting the owl. The drag handles appear and initially the move symbol is shown. If you move the cursor to the bottom-right drag handle the cursor pointer changes to the resize symbol.

RESIZE

MOVE

THE OWL AND PUSSY CAT WENT TO SEA

**Figure 6.33** *Images as imported, awaiting resizing*

With the left-hand mouse button held down, you can now drag the picture to the desired size. Then you can do the same with the cat and finally enlarge the boat to a size that will accommodate both the owl and the cat.

The next stage is to move each of the picture objects so that the animals appear to be in the boat. If you move the cursor over the object, the move symbol appears. You can then click using the left-hand mouse button and drag the images to their new location. The end result then looks something like Figure 6.34 on page 248.

Having now seen how easy it is to resize and move an image, try it out in this exercise.

## Try it out

**Open** Test_1 if it is not already open.

**Move** the image you recently imported so that it is immediately above the paragraph heading THE CHRISTMAS BRING AND BUY.

**Resize** the image so that it spans the width of the first column.

**Figure 6.34** *The images resized and in their new location*

## Balancing columns

Posters and publications of a similar type will be enhanced if the images and text fill the space provided by the page. New CLAIT requires that you are able to balance (or fit) the text and graphics into the space available so that the overall finished document seems balanced and that text is no more than two lines from the bottom of the page. There are some sophisticated ways to achieve this but generally for most people it is a matter of experimenting with different sizes of font. In Test_1 you have now made the graphic the correct size and placed it in the position required. However, this has still left quite a few lines empty at the bottom of the second column.

### Try it out

**Open** Test_1.

**Adjust** the font size of the body text so that it fills the two columns of the text box. In this exercise you should find that Arial point size 20 is about right.

Your final publication should now look like Figure 6.35.

**SEPTEMBER VILLAGE NEWSLETTER**

A Christmas bonanza not to be missed

**THE CHRISTMAS BRING AND BUY**

Once again Christmas is nearly upon us and the Village Hall Committee would like to invite all residents and friends to participate in an extravaganza of fund raising whilst finding those last minute Christmas presents and treats.

There will be a Christmas Bring and

Buy sale in the Village Hall on Saturday 14th December from 10:00 am to 2:00 pm. Your contributions of White Elephant articles, cakes or preserves will be very gratefully received. If you can get these to Sally Dunn at The Old Forge before the 14th this would be very helpful. If not we will be pleased to receive them on the day.

Put this in your diary now — a pleasure not to be missed.

Jenny Troop
Village Hall Activity Co-ordinator

4 November 2002

**Figure 6.35** *The final publication*

Now put what you have learnt together and finish off the Build-up exercise.

## Build-up Exercise 7: Stage 5

**Open** Community_Lectures.

**Format** the text as follows:

| | |
|---|---|
| Font: | sans-serif |
| Paragraph: | first lines indented |
| Text: | fully justified. |

**Import** the image **Robber.jpg** from the accompanying CD and place it in the bottom right-hand corner of the second column.

## Build-up Exercise 7: Stage 6

**Re-format** the text to size 12.

**Increase** the size of the paragraph headings so that they are larger than the body text (14 recommended) and make the text bold.

**Re-format** the last sentence starting 'Your support...' so that the text is larger than the paragraph heading but smaller than the main heading (16 recommended). Make the text bold.

**Indent** the first line of each paragraph (do not include the paragraph headings).

**Move** the image so that it is below the main heading and immediately above the first paragraph heading.

**Resize** the image to an appropriate size and balance the text in the columns so that there is no more than one line space between the last line of the second column and the bottom of the text box.

You should now be able to:

- import clip art
- import an image file
- understand picture frame properties
- move and resize an image
- balance text in columns.

### Using box and line features

Being able to separate text and graphics by the use of boxes and lines is a New CLAIT requirement.

To enhance your publication further you can separate text and graphics by using boxes and lines. You may remember that when you were looking at creating a page-wide heading earlier in this unit, the objects toolbar provided the text frame tool used to draw the text box on the publication. This toolbar (shown in Figure 6.24 on page 242) also provides the drawing tools.

### Enclosing text frames with borders

To enclose a text box with a line (or rectangle) you can do one of two things:

- change the property of the box so that the border has a line
- insert a second box around the text you want to separate.

The first option is to give the actual frame a border. To change the property of the frame use the right-hand mouse button while the cursor is over the text box and then select Format Text Box.... The Format Text box will appear as shown in Figure 6.36.

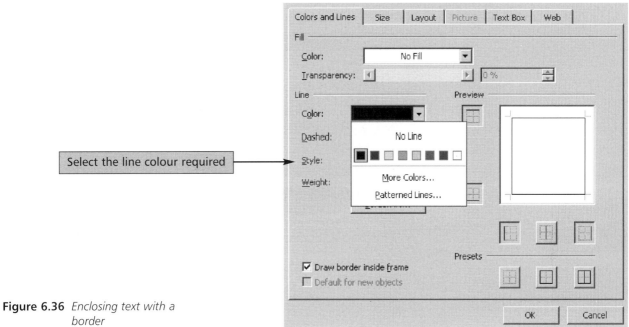

**Figure 6.36** *Enclosing text with a border*

Select the line colour required

Select the style and colour of line required and then press OK.

The second option is more flexible as it allows you to have any size box around the selected text. In this case the rectangle drawing tool is selected from the objects toolbar, as shown previously in Figure 6.24. Using the left-hand mouse button drag a text box around the text to be enclosed.

## Formatting lines and borders

In the previous section you learnt how to create a border around a frame. Lines can also be drawn simply by using the line drawing tool on the drawing toolbar ⬊. To draw a line, select the line drawing tool and click and hold down the left-hand mouse button at the point where the line is to start on the page. With the left-hand mouse button still depressed, drag the line to the required length and release the mouse button.

Lines and borders can be formatted in terms of both style and weight (thickness). In Office XP, to format a line or border first click on it using the right-hand mouse button. Whether you have selected a line, text box or picture frame will determine which option from the menu list is selected. The options are shown below:

| Line: | Select Format AutoShape... |
|---|---|
| Text box border: | Select Format Text Box... |
| Picture: | Select Format Picture... |

In each case the format dialogue box will appear and will be named Format Text Box, Format AutoShape or Format Picture, depending on which object is to be formatted. Figure 6.37 shows the Format AutoShape dialogue box.

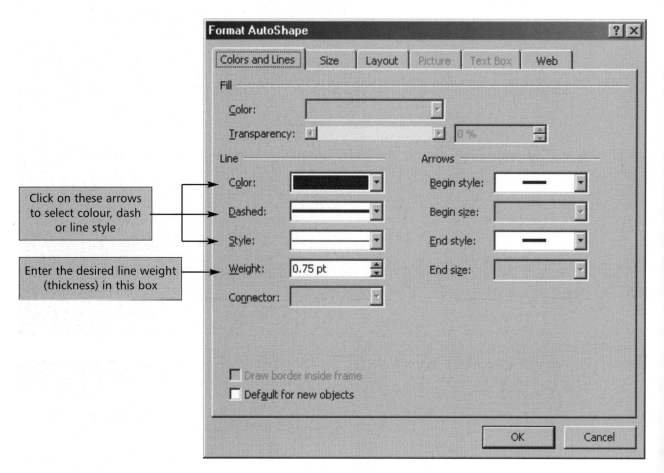

Click on these arrows to select colour, dash or line style

Enter the desired line weight (thickness) in this box

**Figure 6.37** *The Format AutoShape dialogue box*

Having selected the style and weight required, press the OK button in the bottom right of the box to format the line. Changing the format and style for borders around text boxes or pictures is carried out in exactly the same way.

Note: For Office 2000 users the procedure is slightly different. For a line, first select the line using the right-hand mouse button, then choose the Change Line option from the first menu list and Line Border Style from the second menu list. Selecting the More Styles… option from the third list will bring the Line dialogue box (Figure 6.38 on page 253) into view. The same procedure is followed for text boxes and pictures, but in the first menu list the Change Frame option is selected instead of Change Line.

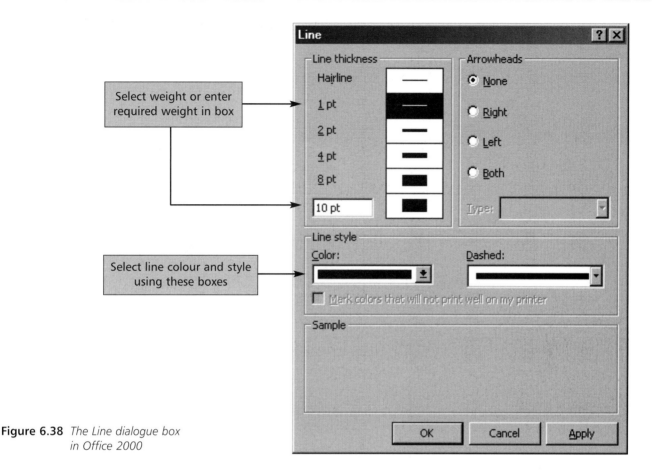

Select weight or enter required weight in box

Select line colour and style using these boxes

**Figure 6.38** *The Line dialogue box in Office 2000*

---

**Try it out**

**Create** a new publication.

**Draw** a line from the left-hand guideline to the right guideline.

Using the right-hand mouse button:

**Click** on the line.

**Select** Format AutoShape....

**Change** the Color: to blue.

**Change** the Weight: to 5 pt.

**Close** the publication without saving it.

---

**TIP**

To draw the border use the rectangle drawing tool from the objects toolbar ensuring that the border does not overlap any text (see Figure 6.24, page 242).

---

**Build-up Exercise 7: Stage 7**

**Draw** a single border around the two columns of text and the graphic to separate the main body of your publication from the heading.

Your final publication should now look like Figure 6.39.

# MAKE A DIFFERENCE

### Making a Difference

How many times have you heard conversations that criticise our materialistic society, the low moral standards of the younger generation, the increase in violence and disregard for other people's property? More often than not our answer to those who offend is to lock them up and throw away the key. But is this the answer?

### In the public interest

Perhaps we are all guilty of ignoring the problem in the hope that it might either go away or that someone else will sort it out. After all don't we all pay our taxes, aren't we justified in expecting the Government to wave a magic wand and mend all the ills of our society? Surely if we all took a little responsibility for the deteriorating standards we may find that little by little the situation would improve. After all, is it not in the public interest that we adopt an inclusive society where everyone has a chance to develop their potential and to climb out of the dismal pit of despair?

### Who Cares?

The Community Action Group intends to facilitate a series of lectures addressed both by ordinary people and also the most prominent members of our society. The lectures will look at the reasons why many of those excluded youngsters act in the way they do, what we need to do to turn the situation round and how we, as members of that society, can help in some very basic but exciting ways. Daily members of the group are astounded by the number of people who are involved in helping those less fortunate than themselves. It is clear that there are many who care and are prepared to give a little of their time to help make a difference. The Group wants to harness all the potential help available into a co-ordinated programme.

### Your Support

We can make a difference and a contribution in ensuring that yet another generation does not feel excluded and undervalued. Please come to our lectures and contribute to the debate. You may not agree with everything that is said but at least you will have an opportunity to voice your views. Lectures will be held on the first Monday of each month for the next 3 months in the Brummel Lecture Theatre, 45 Old Street, at 8.00pm. Coffee and refreshments will be served after the lecture, when it is hoped that open and frank discussions can take place.

**Your support will make the difference.**

**Figure 6.39** *The final text with borders*

## Setting up a publication template

Setting up a publication's style is time consuming and if the style is being used on a regular basis it clearly does not make sense to go through the set-up process every time you start a new publication. As with other Office applications, Microsoft provides a solution whereby you can save a template and use it as many times as required. Assume that you regularly use a style that has the following characteristics:

Page size:     A4
Text frames:   header box
               two-column text box.

You can set up this as a template and then include it as a standard template that can be used each time it is needed. Follow this Try it out exercise:

**Try it out**

Create a new publication.

Set the page layout properties to A4, portrait.

Set the margins as follows:

|              |        |
|--------------|--------|
| left margin:   | 2.5 cm |
| right margin:  | 2.5 cm |
| top margin:    | 2 cm   |
| bottom margin: | 2 cm.  |

Insert a heading text box.

Insert a main text box with two columns.

Save the publication using File, Save As... on the main menu.

Select Publisher Template (*.pub).

Type A4_2column in the Save as type: field.

Press Save.

The next time you want to use this template just select New from the menu and then select A4_2column from the My Templates folder.
You should now be able to:

- separate text and graphics using frame formatting and shapes
- create a Publisher template.

**New CLAIT**

## Printing your work

Printing the publication is the same as printing any other document. Use Print on the File option of the main menu. Now print the final version of your publication.

**Build-up Exercise 7: Stage 8**

Open Community_Lectures.

Print your publication.

Save the file.

Close the application.

You should now be able to:

- use and format lines and borders
- print your publication.

That completes all the assessment objectives needed for New CLAIT desktop publishing.

Now complete Practical Assignment 6. Once you have completed the assignment check your work against the solution in Part 3 near the end of the book.

## Unit 6 Desktop publishing using Publisher

### Scenario

You are the Clerk to the Parish Council for Burberry-on-the-Hill responsible for the Council's administrative affairs.

The Chairman has asked you to prepare a poster that can be circulated to the village residents asking them to submit final comments on the draft village statement, and inviting them to a presentation on 11 October.

| Assessment objectives | Stage | |
|---|---|---|
| 1a 5a | 1 | Create a new single-page publication. |
| 2a | 2 | Set up the master page or template for the page as follows: |

|  |  |  |
|---|---|---|
| Page size | A4 | |
| Page orientation | portrait | |
| Top/bottom margins | 2.5 cm | |
| Left/right margins | 2.5 cm. | |

| Assessment objectives | Stage | |
|---|---|---|
| 5b | 3 | Save the master page/template. |
| 2c 2d | 4 | Set up the page layout in a newsletter format, to include a page-wide heading above two columns of text. |

|  |  |  |
|---|---|---|
| Columns widths | equal | |
| Space between columns | 0.5 cm. | |

| Assessment objectives | Stage | |
|---|---|---|
| 2e 3c | 5 | Enter the heading SAVING OUR VILLAGE at the top of the page using a sans-serif font. |
| 4e | 6 | Increase the size of the heading so that it extends across the full width of both columns of text. |
| 3a | 7 | Import the text file **Village_statement.txt** from the CD so that it begins at the top left-hand column, below the heading. |
| 2e 4a | 8 | Format the body text to be left-aligned, in a serif font. |
| 3b | 9 | Import the image **Village_square.jpg**, and place it at the bottom of the right-hand column, making sure it does not cover any text. |
| 5d | 10 | Print one composite proof copy of the publication for the Chairman. Make sure your printed publication fits onto one page. |

### Scenario

The Chairman thanks you for your work but has a number of small amendments he would like you to make.

| Assessment objectives | Stage | |
|---|---|---|
| 3d | 11 | Under the heading, draw a single border around the two columns of text and the graphic to separate the article from the heading. Make sure the border does not overlap any text. Your border may extend into the margin area. |

▶▶

| | | |
|---|---|---|
| 2f | 12 | Increase the size of the sub-headings, PROTECTING OUR VILLAGE, THE CONSULTATION PROCESS, VILLAGE PROTECTION and ACT NOW, so that they are larger than the body text, but smaller than the page heading. |
| 4c | 13 | Make the image smaller and move it into the left-hand column immediately below the main heading. Make sure the image does not extend into any margin space. |
| 4a | 14 | Change the body text to be fully justified. |
| 4b | 15 | Format the body text so that the first line of each paragraph is indented. Make sure the sub-headings are not indented. |
| 2f<br>4d<br>4f | 16 | Increase the size of the text so that the columns are balanced at the bottom of the page. Make sure that the heading, sub-headings and body text are still different sizes. |
| 5c<br>5d | 17 | Save and print a composite proof of the publication. Make sure your printed publication fits onto one page. |
| 1a<br>5e | 18 | Close the publication and exit the software securely. |

# UNIT 7

## *Graphs and charts*

For New CLAIT's graphs and charts unit you will learn some of the basic principles in the presentation of data and how to use data modelling software. There are four learning outcomes in this unit and each of these has a number of assessment objectives which are shown below.

## What you need to know about graphs and charts for New CLAIT

For New CLAIT you will need to know how to:

**Identify and use appropriate software correctly**
- Use appropriate application software.

**Produce pie charts, line graphs and bar/column charts**
- Use a pie chart.
- Use a line graph.
- Use a bar/column chart.

**Select and present single comparative sets of data**
- Select a single data set.
- Select a comparative data set.
- Select a subset of a single data set.

**Set numerical parameters and format data**
- Set axes upper and lower limits.
- Select and display data labels.
- Select/enter headings and axes titles.
- Use a legend where appropriate.
- Ensure that comparative data is distinctive.

**Manage and print graph and chart documents**
- Open an existing data document.
- Save a data document.
- Save charts/graphs.
- Print charts/graphs.
- Close a document.

> ### *In this unit you will cover:*
>
> - What are charts and graphs?
> - What is appropriate software?
> - Types of chart
> - Creating different types of chart
> - Setting numerical parameters and formatting the data in a chart
> - Formatting displayed features on charts
> - Managing and printing charts and graphs

## What are charts and graphs?

For the purposes of New CLAIT, charts and graphs means displaying data from a data source in a pictorial form that is easily understood by someone who needs to analyse the information produced from the data.

There is a subtle difference between the terms 'data' and 'information'. Data are the raw text or numbers you enter. You can then use the data to produce reports that allow a viewer to interpret and analyse the underlying information from where the data was collected. You might put a thousand sales records into a spreadsheet or database. These records are built up of individual bits of data, such as the product, town, number of sales, month and so on. These data can then be processed into a format that provides a clearer picture to those who wish to analyse the data. They may wish, for example, to see where the best sales of a product were over a period of time. One of the easiest ways to understand what a set of figures is telling you is to view them pictorially or graphically using charts and graphs.

For New CLAIT you need to be able to produce charts and graphs from a given set of data. You will learn how to select the data used in a chart from a range or ranges in a worksheet. You will also learn how to present the chart or graph in a way that is meaningful to the viewer with appropriate headings and labels that make the information being presented easier to understand.

There are numerous types of charts and graphs but New CLAIT only asks that you can produce three. These are:

- bar charts
- pie charts
- line graphs.

In addition, you will be expected to produce a chart from a single data range and also one that is built from two sets of data for comparison. For example, a single set of data may show the sales by month for a company whereas a comparative chart or graph could show a comparison of sales from the current year with those from the previous year.

## What is appropriate software?

For New CLAIT you can use spreadsheet, database or other statistical modelling software to produce charts and graphs. For this unit, Excel has been chosen as the appropriate software although Access could equally have been used. Spreadsheets can be large and complex but can also help you present all the data in a way that lets a reader absorb the information quickly. Charts are useful in providing an overview of the information presented in a professional and user-friendly way.

There are many different types of chart and each one is designed to display data in a different way. Look at Figure 7.1.

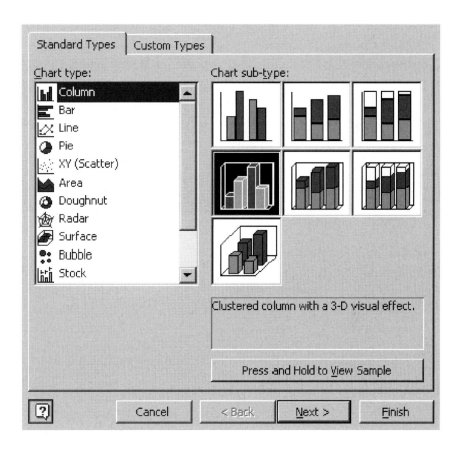

**Figure 7.1** *Standard types of chart*

All Office applications have the capacity to create charts through a Chart Wizard. Figure 7.1 shows just one selection of the chart types available. The left-hand side of the dialogue box displays the type of chart or graph that can be chosen to represent the data. First on the list shown is the column type. By scrolling down the list others can be viewed.

Charts share a number of attributes. They all can have:

- a main chart title
- axes labels
- data labels
- legends.

Depending on the chart type, other attributes may be selected.

A simple chart will represent one set of data. For example, suppose you wanted to show the bookings for The Business Café throughout the year (Figure 7.2).

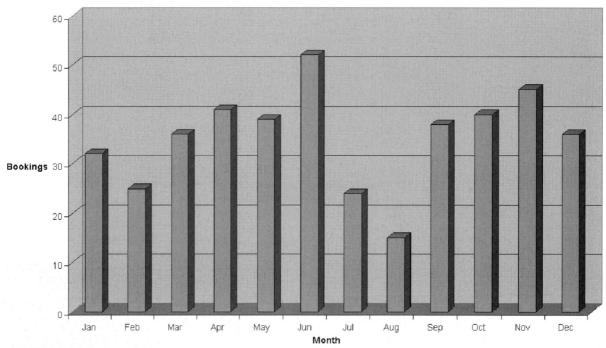

Business Café Bookings for 2002

**Figure 7.2** *A simple chart: Business Café bookings for 2002*

This chart is based on data from a worksheet in Excel and shows the number of bookings for 2002 in The Business Café. The data the chart is using is shown in Table 7.1.

## Types of chart

The type of data and how it is to be presented will determine what style of chart should be used. For example, pie charts depict information in segments like a cake after it has been cut into portions. It is useful for showing at a glance the percentage or proportion one piece has of the whole. Figure 7.2 showed a column chart representing bookings by the month. Had you wanted to see what percentage each month's bookings represented over the whole year you could have produced a pie chart similar to that shown in Figure 7.3. So that you are not confused, Microsoft calls a chart where the data is displayed vertically a column chart, and one where the data is displayed horizontally a bar chart. The method of producing these charts is exactly the same so you will only be using the column chart.

Line graphs tend to be used more when you want to see a pattern of activity or predict a trend, whereas bar/column and pie charts tend to be used more for visual impact. Figure 7.4 shows a line graph to which a trend line has been added. It is clearly not as visually effective from a graphical perspective but still gives the user some very useful information regarding the general trend of bookings.

**Table 7.1** *Business Café bookings for 2002*

| | |
|-----|----|
| Jan | 32 |
| Feb | 25 |
| Mar | 36 |
| Apr | 41 |
| May | 39 |
| Jun | 52 |
| Jul | 24 |
| Aug | 15 |
| Sep | 38 |
| Oct | 40 |
| Nov | 45 |
| Dec | 36 |

**Proportion of Bookings by Month**

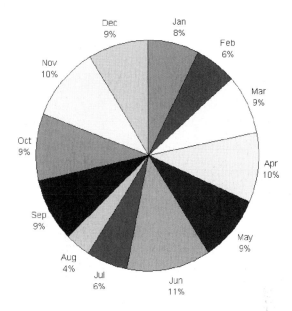

**Figure 7.3** *A pie chart showing the proportion of bookings by month*

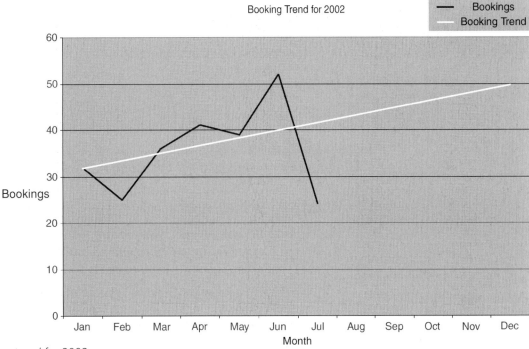

**Figure 7.4** *Booking trend for 2002*

The examples above use only one data set but there may be times when it is important to compare different sets of data. If you take the Business Café bookings, it may be helpful to see whether bookings are better or worse than the previous year. In Figure 7.5 the bookings for 2001 (which was the first year of operation) are compared with those for 2002. Here you can see at a glance that booking performance has improved dramatically.

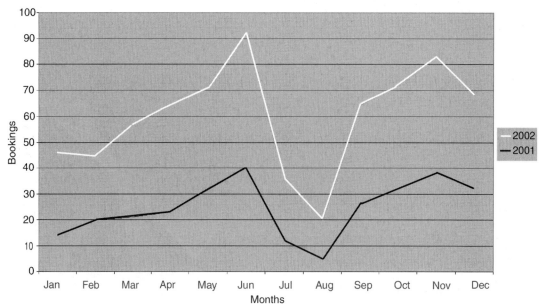

**Figure 7.5** *Comparison of bookings for 2001 and 2002*

You should now be able to:

- understand what charts and graphs are
- select appropriate software to produce charts and graphs
- distinguish between different types of charts and graphs.

## Creating different types of chart

### Creating a pie chart

For New CLAIT you will be expected to produce a pie chart, column chart and line graph. In addition, you will have to select various ranges of data that show a single range, comparative sets of data and a subset of a single range (i.e. part of a range). Now try building a simple pie chart from a single data set.

**New CLAIT**

---

**Try it out**

**Open** the Excel file **Visitors.xls** on the accompanying CD (remember to copy 'Visitors' to your hard or floppy disk, and change the read-only option).

**Highlight** the range of data A3:B7.

**Press** the Chart Wizard icon  .

Alternatively, **Select** Insert, Chart... on the main menu.

The Chart Wizard dialogue box appears.

**Select** Pie.

**Press** the Next> button.

If you are happy with the data range (see Figure 7.6),

**Press** Next> again.

**Data range:** =Sheet1!$A$3:$B$7

**Figure 7.6** *Data range dialogue box*

In the Chart title: box:

**Type** VISITOR INTERESTS.

**Press** the Legend tab and deselect the Show legend check box.

**Press** the Data Labels tab.

**Select** the check boxes Category name and Percentage (see Figure 7.7a–c).

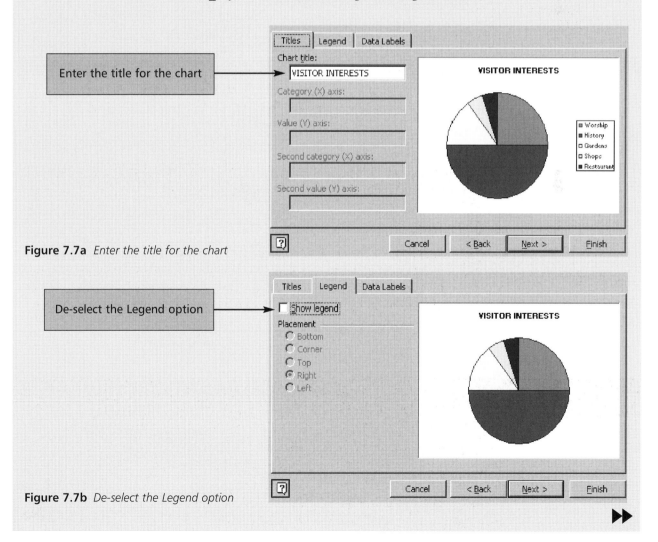

**Figure 7.7a** *Enter the title for the chart*

**Figure 7.7b** *De-select the Legend option*

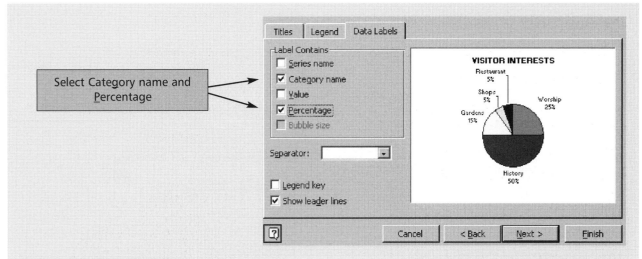

Figure 7.7c *Select Category name and Percentage*

**Note:** If you are using Office 2000, the dialogue box will appear slightly different, as shown in Figure 7.7d.

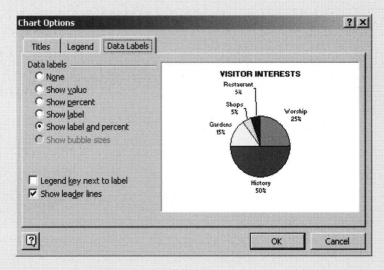

**Figure 7.7d** *The dialogue box in Office 2000*

**Press** Next>.

In the dialogue box shown in Figure 7.8:

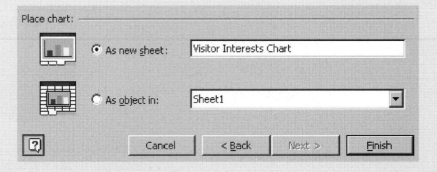

**Figure 7.8** *Place chart dialogue box*

**Select** As new sheet.

**Type** 'Visitor Interests Chart' in the field that has Chart1 as the default text.

**Press** Finish.

**Note:** Choosing 'As new sheet:' will create a new sheet in the workbook, whereas choosing 'As object in:' will create the chart in the current worksheet.

The chart is presented as shown in Figure 7.9.

**Save** the chart and Excel workbook.

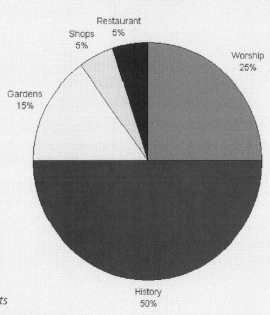

**Figure 7.9** *Visitor interests*

## Creating a column chart using a single set of data

The way a column chart is created is virtually the same as a pie or any other type of chart. In the first Build-up exercise you will create a column chart showing the crime statistics for a city in the Midlands.

---

### Build-up Exercise 8: Stage 1

Copy the file **Crime.xls** from the accompanying CD onto your hard disk or to a floppy disk (remembering to change the 'Read-only' option).

**Open** the file **Crime.xls**.

**Highlight** the data range A1:H6.

**Click** on the Chart Wizard.

**Select** Column as the standard style of chart.

**Select** 'Clustered column with a 3-D visual effect' in the Chart sub-type: box.

▶▶

## GENERAL TIP

Check the data selected in the Data range: box; it should be A1:H6. Don't worry about the $ signs. The range shown should be =Sheet1!$A$1:$H$6. The term '=Sheet1' is telling you that the data selected is in Sheet 1. The range is separated from this by an exclamation mark, !. The range details you are interested in are A1 and H6. Both of these range markers are surrounded by a $ sign. These are related to something called *referencing*. There are two types of referencing – absolute and relative – but you do not need to know about these for New CLAIT.

**Note**: the sub-type description is displayed in a box below the sample sub-types.

**Press** Next>.

If you are happy with the chart data range and display:

**Press** Next> again.

**Type** CRIME STATISTICS JANUARY – JULY in the Chart title box.

**Type** Month in the Category (X) axis: box.

**Type** Incidents in the Value (Y) axis: box.

**Press** Next>.

**Type** CRIME STATISTICS in the As new sheet: box.

**Press** Finish.

**Note**: Excel will now build the chart and insert a new sheet in the workbook called CRIME STATISTICS.

Your completed chart should look similar to Figure 7.10.

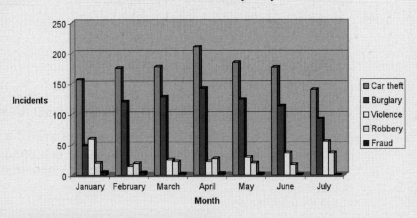

**Figure 7.10** *A column chart for crime statistics, January–July*

**Save** your spreadsheet as BU7a.

**Close** Excel.

### Creating a column chart by selecting a subset from a single set of data

There will be occasions when it is necessary to select specific parts of a single data set from a worksheet. Let's say, for example, you wanted to produce a pie chart that showed the percentage, by category, of one month's sales of different foods being sold in a restaurant, from a data set that contained a range of foods and sales over a six-month period. The data set might look like Figure 7.11.

| | A | B | C | D | E | F | G |
|---|---|---|---|---|---|---|---|
| 1 | Restaurant Sales by Category | | | | | | |
| 2 | | | | | | | |
| 3 | Category | January | February | March | April | May | June |
| 4 | Sandwiches | 2500 | 2300 | 2400 | 2350 | 2600 | 2800 |
| 5 | Baguettes | 1560 | 1700 | 1350 | 1200 | 1460 | 1520 |
| 6 | Toasties | 3200 | 3650 | 3520 | 3100 | 2900 | 2870 |
| 7 | Baked potatoes | 4000 | 4500 | 4750 | 5000 | 5500 | 5410 |
| 8 | Casseroles | 6000 | 6900 | 6750 | 5900 | 5600 | 4700 |
| 9 | Cakes | 4500 | 5000 | 4980 | 4700 | 5600 | 6000 |
| 10 | Total Sales | 21760 | 24050 | 23750 | 22250 | 23660 | 23300 |

**Figure 7.11** *Data set for restaurant sales by category*

Only data required to produce one month's worth of sales is selected by pressing the left-hand mouse button and dragging the section from cell A1 to B9 (Figure 7.12). Note that the column heading has been selected but not the total row.

| | A | B | C | D | E | F | G |
|---|---|---|---|---|---|---|---|
| 1 | Restaurant Sales by Category | | | | | | |
| 2 | | | | | | | |
| 3 | Category | January | February | March | April | May | June |
| 4 | Sandwiches | 2500 | 2300 | 2400 | 2350 | 2600 | 2800 |
| 5 | Baguettes | 1560 | 1700 | 1350 | 1200 | 1460 | 1520 |
| 6 | Toasties | 3200 | 3650 | 3520 | 3100 | 2900 | 2870 |
| 7 | Baked potatoes | 4000 | 4500 | 4750 | 5000 | 5500 | 5410 |
| 8 | Casseroles | 6000 | 6900 | 6750 | 5900 | 5600 | 4700 |
| 9 | Cakes | 4500 | 5000 | 4980 | 4700 | 5600 | 6000 |
| 10 | Total Sales | 21760 | 24050 | 23750 | 22250 | 23660 | 23300 |

**Figure 7.12** *Data selected for one month's worth of sales*

The pie chart is then built on the subset of data selected, shown in Figure 7.14.

In the next exercise you will create a pie chart based on a subset of the data in the Crime.xls spreadsheet.

**MOUSE TIP**

If a different month is required, the first column is selected and then, with the control key pressed down, the additional data can be selected, as shown in Figure 7.13.

**Figure 7.13** *Restaurant sales by category, selecting by month*

| | A | B | C | D | E | F | G |
|---|---|---|---|---|---|---|---|
| 1 | Restaurant Sales by Category | | | | | | |
| 2 | | | | | | | |
| 3 | Category | January | February | March | April | May | June |
| 4 | Sandwiches | 2500 | 2300 | 2400 | 2350 | 2600 | 2800 |
| 5 | Baguettes | 1560 | 1700 | 1350 | 1200 | 1460 | 1520 |
| 6 | Toasties | 3200 | 3650 | 3520 | 3100 | 2900 | 2870 |
| 7 | Baked Potatoes | 4000 | 4500 | 4750 | 5000 | 5500 | 5410 |
| 8 | Casseroles | 6000 | 6900 | 6750 | 5900 | 5600 | 4700 |
| 9 | Cakes | 4500 | 5000 | 4980 | 4700 | 5600 | 6000 |
| 10 | Total Sales | 21760 | 24050 | 23750 | 22250 | 23660 | 23300 |

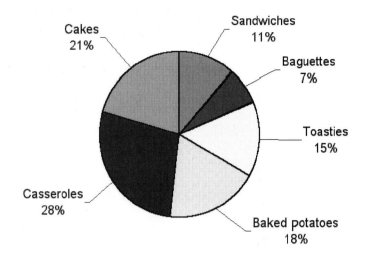

**Figure 7.14** *Pie chart of restaurant sales by category, January*

## Build-up Exercise 8: Stage 2

*Scenario*

You have been asked to produce a pie chart that shows the proportion of the different crimes for April, which appears to have the worst statistics for crime over the seven-month period.

**Open** BU7a.

**Select** cells A1:A6 as the segments that will form part of the pie chart.

**Select** the crime statistics for April.

**Click** on the Chart Wizard icon.

**Select** Pie as the chart type.

**Press** Next>.

**Check** that the data range is correct.

**Press** Next>.

**Type** 'Crime Statistics – April' as the title for your chart.

**Select** the Legend tab and uncheck the Legend box.

**Select** the Data Labels tab and ensure the Category name and Percentage check boxes are checked.

**Press** Next>.

**Select** As new sheet:.

**Type** 'Crime Stats for April' as the new sheet's title.

Press <u>F</u>inish.

**Save** your worksheet as BU7b.

Your pie chart should look like Figure 7.15.

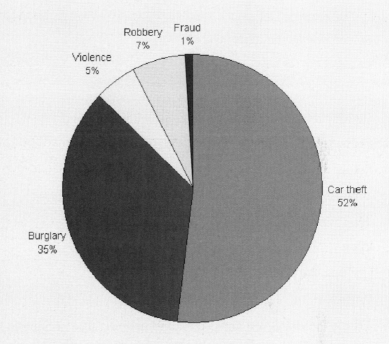

**Figure 7.15** *Pie chart of crime statistics for April*

Here you can see that car theft accounted for 52% of all crime in April, with burglary running a close second at 35%.

## Creating a comparative line graph

The next type of chart you are going to look at is a line graph that compares two subsets of data. You may recall that when the various types of graph and chart were introduced, a line graph allowed the reader to view trends. Line graphs are produced in much the same way as other chart types. In the next Build-up exercise you will produce a comparative line graph.

## Build-up Exercise 8: Stage 3

*Scenario*

Having established the two main crime categories you are required to produce a line graph that compares car theft with burglary for the months January to July.

**Open** BU7b.

**Select** the data that displays both car thefts and burglary for January to July. Include the category heading and the months for these crimes.

**Create** a line graph that compares these two subsets of data from the worksheet.

**Select** Line as the chart type.

**Select** 'Line with markers displayed at each data value' as the chart sub-type.

**Press** Next>.

**Check** that the correct data range is being displayed.

**Press** Next>.

**Select** the Titles tab.

**Type** 'Analysis of Car Theft to Burglary' as the chart title.

**Type** 'Months' as the Category (X) axis title:.

**Type** 'Crime Numbers' as the Value (Y) axis title:.

Ensure that the legend is displayed.

**Press** Next>.

**Create** the chart As a new sheet: and give it a title of 'Burglary and Theft'.

**Press** Finish.

**Save** your worksheet as BU7c.

Your chart should look like Figure 7.16.

You should now be able to:

- create a pie chart
- create a column chart from a single data set
- create a column chart from a subset of data
- create a comparative line graph.

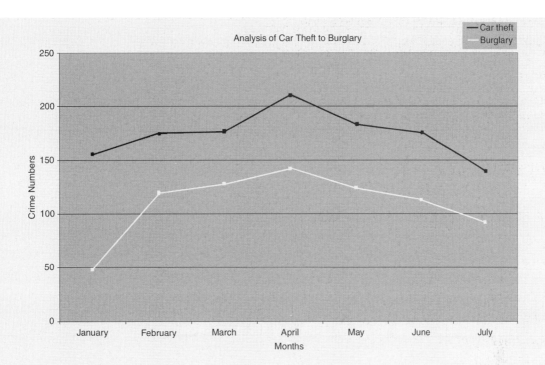

**Figure 7.16** *A comparative line graph – analysis of car theft to burglary*

## New CLAIT

### Setting numerical parameters and formatting the data in a chart

Other than for some special chart types, most have an X and a Y axis. Normally the X axis displays the category or activity being charted while the Y axis displays the values that relate to the data you are charting. When you are setting up a chart display using the Wizard, you can determine the various parameters and formats you want for your chart as you build it. Any of these can be changed at a later time once the chart has been produced.

In the Build-up exercises completed so far you have entered heading and axes titles for your chart and selected the option to display a legend. You can change these at any time. Now try changing some of the default formats in a pre-prepared worksheet.

## Try it out

*Formatting fonts*

**Open** the file called **Shares.xls** on your CD.

**Save** the file as 'Shares' on your own hard drive or floppy disk.

**Select** the 'Share Nos 1' tab to show the prepared column chart based on the data in 'Sheet 1'.

**Highlight** the heading 'Quantity'.

**Replace** the highlighted text with 'Number of Shares Held By Company'.

**Click** in a blank area of the chart to accept the changes.

**Right-click** on the new heading.

**Select** Format Chart Title....

**Select** the Font tab.

**Change** the Font Style to bold.

**Change** the Size of the font to 14.

**Select** Single in the Underline drop-down menu.

**Press** OK.

**Click** outside the title in a blank area of the chart to accept the changes.

### Adding X and Y axes titles

**Select** Chart Options... from the Chart option on the main menu.

**Select** the Titles tab.

**Type** 'Company' in the Category (X) axis: box.

**Type** 'Numbers of Shares' in the Value (Y) axis: box.

**Select** OK.

You can now see that the chart has both an X and Y axis title.

### Removing the legend

Since we only have one subset of data on display – namely the quantity of shares held by the company in its portfolio – and the title is now specific as to what the chart is displaying, there is really no need for a legend. To remove the legend:

**Select** Chart Options... from the Chart option on the main menu.

**Select** the Legend tab.

**Deselect** the Show legend box.

**Press** OK.

### Displaying data labels

Occasionally it is helpful for the viewer of your chart to be able to see the actual values of each category. These values are shown by enabling the Data Labels options.

**Select** Chart Options... from the Chart option on the main menu.

**Select** the Data Labels tab.

**Select** the Show value option.

**Press** OK.

## Setting the axes upper and lower limits

When Excel builds a chart it looks at the range of data in the worksheet and decides on the most appropriate scale to use for the axes. In our current example Excel has decided that the scale should start at 500 and finish at 3500. Having included the data labels on each column of data it is less important to show the numbers of shares at the present interval of 500. An interval of 1000 is quite adequate. Limits can easily be changed or even removed altogether.

To change the scale:

**Right-click** in the Y axis area as shown in Figure 7.17.

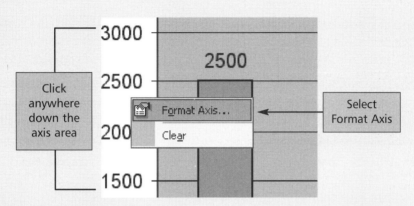

**Figure 7.17** *Changing the scale of a chart*

**Select** F<u>o</u>rmat Axis....

**Select** the Scale tab.

Now have a look at Figure 7.18 in conjunction with the chart itself to understand the elements of the dialogue box.

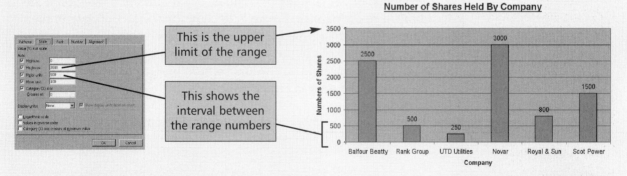

**Figure 7.18** *Elements of the dialogue box for changing scale*

The two you are interested in here are the upper limit of the range and the interval between the numbers in the range. You are going to change the upper limit to 3000 since this is the highest number of shares held in any one company, and the interval between to 1000.

**Type** 3000 in the Ma<u>x</u>imum: field.

**Type** 1000 in the M<u>a</u>jor unit: field, again making sure the Auto box is unchecked.

Press OK.

Your chart should now look like Figure 7.19.

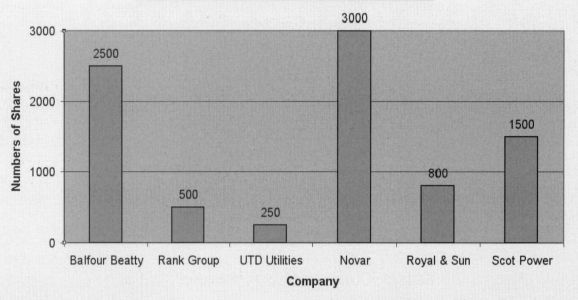

**Figure 7.19** *Completed chart of number of shares held by the company*

## Formatting displayed features on charts

In New CLAIT you would be penalised in an assignment if the data being displayed was not distinctive. A problem can arise in some charts or graphs when the printed copy is not in colour and the fill of segments, or the shading of columns or the lines of a line graph are difficult to distinguish. Figure 7.20 shows two views of data in the Shares files. One shows the quantity of shares by company and the other is a snapshot of the value of the shares over a six-month period. Even with the legend you would be hard pressed to be able to distinguish the data in either chart.

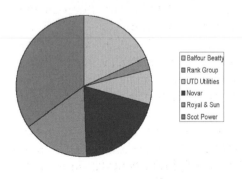

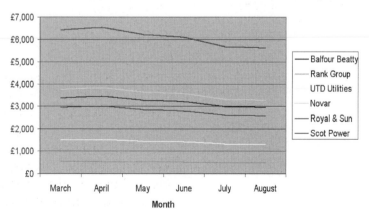

**Figure 7.20** *Distinguishing between data ranges*

Excel allows you to format the fill or style of the graph or chart by changing either the fill (for example to a texture or a pattern) or the weight of a line. Have a look at Figure 7.21.

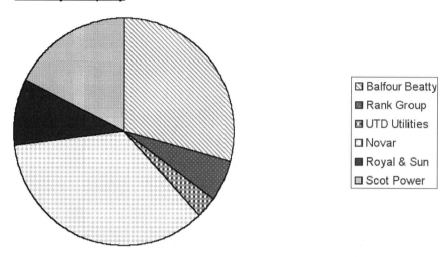

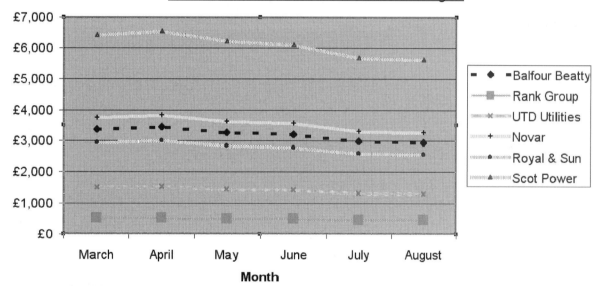

**Figure 7.21** *The same data with styling added to graph and chart*

This figure is basically the same as Figure 7.20 but the fill on the pie chart has been changed to a pattern as opposed to a solid colour and the weight and style of lines in the line graph have also been changed to make them more distinctive and identifiable. To change the style or pattern, bring up the Format Data Series dialogue box by either double-clicking on the selected data or placing the cursor over the data to be changed and selecting Format Data Series (or Format Data Point for a pie chart). In a pie chart this will be a segment, for a column or a bar chart it will be the column(s)/bar(s), or for a line graph it will be the line that you want to change. Press the Fill Effects button in the Area box and then choose the relevant tab depending on what you want to change (i.e. Texture, Pattern, Picture, etc.). (See Figure 7.22.)

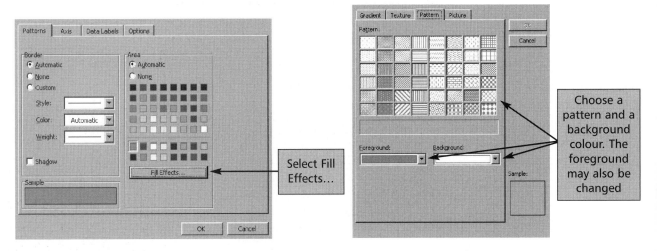

**Figure 7.22** *Changing the style or pattern in a chart*

Now have a go at changing the format of some of the features for the line graph 'Burglary & Theft' you created in BU7c.

---

## Build-up Exercise 8: Stage 4

**Open** BU7c.

**Select** the chart sheet 'Burlary and Theft'.

**Format** the chart title to Arial, bold, point size 16.

**Format** the X Category axis labels to Arial, bold, point size 10.

**Format** the Y Value axis numbers to Arial, bold, point size 10.

**Format** the X Category axis title to Arial, bold, point size 12.

**Format** the Y Value axis title to Arial, bold, point size 12.

**Format** the Burglary data series line so that it is clearly distinct from that of the Car Theft data series line.

**Change** the scale of the Y series values as follows:

      Maximum:   250
      Major unit:   50

**Save** the changes as BU7d.

**Close** the file.

---

**Note**: When formatting titles and labels in a chart you will not be penalised for consistent use of upper, lower, sentence or title case. However, you will be penalised if the case you have chosen is not used consistently within the chart.

You should now be able to:

- format fonts and other attributes in a chart
- show and remove a legend
- display data labels as required
- set the axes upper and lower limits.

**New CLAIT**

## Managing and printing charts and graphs

### Saving a chart or graph

When producing a chart, as you have seen, you have a choice of placing the finished chart either to a new sheet (see page 266) or as an object in the current worksheet. However, this does not save the chart; this must done when saving the whole workbook. By pressing the Save icon on the toolbar or using the File, Save (or Save as...) option on the main menu, the whole of the workbook is saved including any charts that are present in the current worksheet or other worksheets in the same workbook.

### Printing charts and graphs

When placing a chart in a new worksheet you can print the entire chart using Print under the File menu option. It is sometimes useful to use the Print Preview option first to see how your chart will be printed. If you chose to place the chart in the current worksheet the chart must be selected before being printed. If you do not do this then the data, along with the chart, will be printed. Have a look at Figure 7.23.

| Crime | January | February | March | April | May | June | July |
|-------|---------|----------|-------|-------|-----|------|------|
| Car theft | 156 | 175 | 177 | 210 | 184 | 176 | 140 |
| Burglary | 48 | 120 | 128 | 142 | 124 | 113 | 92 |
| Violence | 59 | 14 | 25 | 22 | 29 | 36 | 55 |
| Robbery | 20 | 19 | 22 | 27 | 20 | 17 | 36 |
| Fraud | 5 | 4 | 2 | 3 | 2 | 1 | 0 |

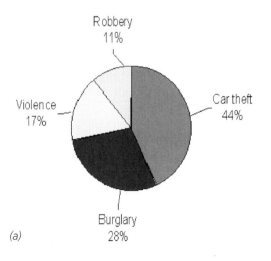

(a)

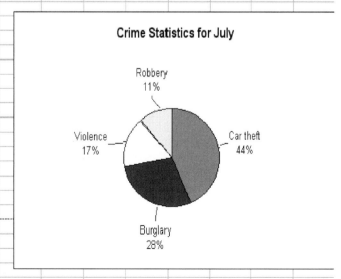

(b)

**Figure 7.23** *(a) Chart has been selected; (b) chart has not been individually selected*

## Build-up Exercise 8: Stage 5

**Open** BU7d.

**Select** the chart sheet named 'Burglary and Theft'.

**Print** the chart.

**Save** the workbook.

   **Close** the application.

Your completed printout should look like Figure 7.24.

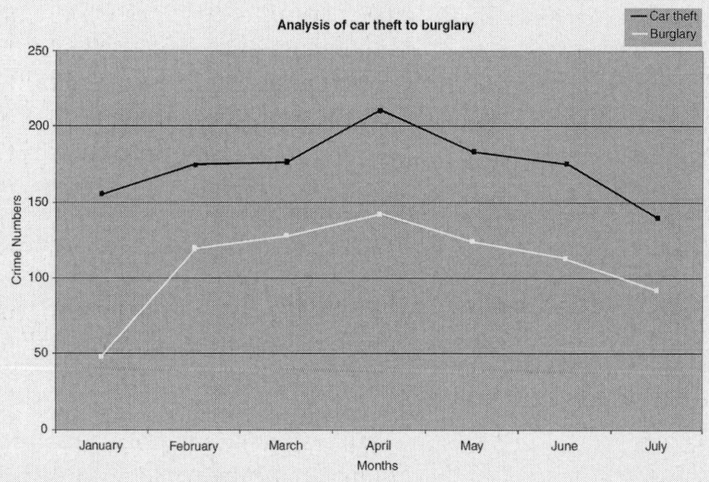

**Figure 7.24** *Print where the chart has been selected*

You should now be able to:

- save a chart or graph
- print a chart or graph.

You have now completed all the assessment objectives required in New CLAIT for charts and graphs.

   Now have a go at Practical Assignment 7. Solutions to this assignment can be found in Part 3.

## Unit 7 Graphs and charts

### Scenario

You are the manager of the local video shop and decide that the time has come to start analysing the level of film hire for video releases from Monday to Sunday.

You decide to produce a pie chart that reflects which film, by percentage, has the greatest appeal, a bar chart that shows the hire per day for each film, a column chart that shows the hire rate for the four most popular films and a comparison line graph for the two most popular films for each day.

| Assessment objectives | Stage | |
|---|---|---|
| 1a<br>5a | 1 | Open the file called **Video_hire.xls** from your accompanying CD.<br>Save the file to your hard disk, giving it the same name. |
| 2a<br>4c<br>4d<br>4e | 2 | Create a pie chart that shows each film being hired by the percentage of the hire for the total week.<br><br>(a) Give the chart the title of 'Hire By Film For The Week'.<br>(b) Ensure that the data is shaded in such a way that it can be clearly identified.<br>(c) Each sector should be labelled with the percentage for the film.<br>(d) Include a legend showing the film names. |
| 5b<br>5c | 3 | Save the file as **Pie_1**. |
| 5d | 4 | Print a copy of the **Pie_1** chart. |
| 2c<br>4c<br>4d<br>4e | 5 | Create a bar chart (horizontal data) that shows the number of hires per day over the week for each film.<br><br>(a) Give the chart the title of 'Hires By Film'.<br>(b) Title the X axis 'Number of Hirers'.<br>(c) Title the Y axis 'Weekday'.<br>(d) Ensure that the data is shaded in such a way that it can be clearly identified.<br>(e) Include a legend placed at the bottom of the chart. |
| 5b<br>5c | 6 | Save the file as **Bar_1**. |
| 5d | 7 | Print a copy of the **Bar_1** chart. |
| 2c<br>4c<br>4d<br>4e | 8 | Create a column chart that shows the four most popular films over the week for each day.<br><br>(a) Give the chart the title of 'Most Popular Four Films'.<br>(b) Give the X axis the title of 'Day Of The Week'.<br>(c) Give the Y axis the title of 'Number Of Hirers'.<br>(d) Insert a legend and position it in the top left of the data area of the chart. |
| 5c | 9 | Save the chart as **Column_1**. |

| | | |
|---|---|---|
| 5d | 10 | Print a copy of the **Column_1** chart. |
| 4a<br>4b | 11 | Format both the X and Y axis titles so that they are bold and font point size is 8.<br>Format the heading as Arial, bold, point size 16 and underlined.<br>Set the maximum Y axis limit to 50 and the major units to 10. |
| 4e | 12 | Change the fill of the data columns so that the comparative data is distinctive. |
| 5c | 13 | Save the chart as **Column_2**. |
| 5d | 14 | Print a copy of the **Column_2** chart. |
| 2b<br>3c<br>4a<br>4c<br>4d | 15 | Create a line graph that compares the most popular films (*The Heist* and *Shrek*) over the week.<br><br>(a) Give the graph a main title of 'Hires For The Two Most Popular Films'.<br>(b) Give the X axis the title of 'Day Of The Week'.<br>(c) Give the Y axis the title of 'Number Of Hirers'.<br>(d) Show the legend at the bottom of the graph.<br>(e) Set the maximum Y axis limit to 50 and the major units to 10. |
| 5c | 16 | Save the chart as **Line_1**. |
| 5d | 17 | Print a copy of the **Line_1** graph. |

*Practical assignment 7 (cont.)*

# 8

# *Computer art using Word*

**New CLAIT**

For New CLAIT's unit on computer art you will learn how to use generic software to produce and then print artwork with images, text and other graphics. You will find out how to introduce images into a document and format their size, position and orientation. In addition, you will learn how to recognise different types of images, how to create simple geometric shapes and how fonts can be used to enhance a picture.

There are five learning outcomes in this unit and each of these has a number of assessment objectives, which are shown below.

## What you need to know about computer art for New CLAIT

For New CLAIT you will need to know how to:

**Identify and use appropriate software correctly**
- Use appropriate application software.

**Import, crop and resize images**
- Import and place bitmapped image(s).
- Crop an image.
- Resize image(s) to fit.
- Create graphic shape(s).

**Enter, amend and resize text**
- Enter text.
- Amend text.
- Resize text to fit.

**Manipulate and format page items**
- Use specified colours.
- Rotate an item.
- Flip an item.
- Copy an item.
- Delete an item.

**Manage and print artwork**
- Create a new document.
- Set artwork size/resolution.
- Save a document.
- Save a document with a new filename.
- Close a document.

> ### In this unit you will cover:
>
> - What is computer art?
> - Types of image files and where they should be used
> - Creating a simple piece of artwork using shapes
> - How to align and evenly distribute objects
> - Creating and using text boxes
> - Learning about fonts
> - Inserting and working with image files
> - Sizing, rotating and colouring shapes and text
> - Managing and printing artwork

## What is computer art?

For New CLAIT computer art is about being able to use appropriate software to create designs or pictures using images, geometric shapes and text. It is also about understanding the differences between different types of image files and how they behave when they are manipulated. During the unit you will learn how to *crop* an image, and resize it to a specified dimension. You will learn how to rotate to a given number of degrees and also how to flip an image.

Designing and using computer art can be great fun and is an extremely useful way of developing your own library of pictures. For example, you may want to create designs for Christmas or birthday cards or design images for a web page, posters or other documents. Have a look at this very simple picture in Figure 8.1.

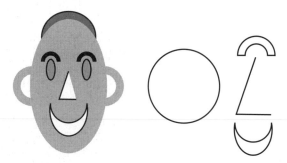

**Figure 8.1** *Simple computer art*

The face is made up entirely of the four drawing shapes shown on the right of the picture. Each of these shapes is available on the drawing toolbar. For this unit you will use Word to produce a number of designs and images, but you could just as easily use Publisher, PowerPoint or other applications that support graphical work.

## Types of image files and where they should be used

### File types

There are fundamentally two types of graphic file:

- bitmap (also referred to as raster) files
- vector files.

Bitmap graphics are composed of pixels while vector graphics are composed using paths. It is easier to explain this by showing examples of both types. Have a look at Figure 8.2.

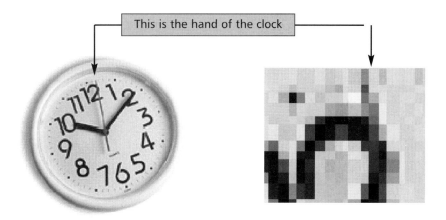

This is the hand of the clock

**Figure 8.2** *The picture of the clock is actually made up of tiny coloured squares known as pixels*

In Figure 8.2 is a picture of a clock. At normal size it looks fine but if it is enlarged you can see that it is made up of hundreds of small squares of colour known as pixels (or bits).

Now look at Figure 8.3.

**Figure 8.3** *An example of a vector graphic*

Instead of squares of colour the image is made up of lines (or paths). In the early days of computer graphics most were of the vector variety, partly because they require less storage space than bitmaps.

The advantage of bitmap images is that you have more control over editing the detail in a picture (provided you have the time and patience). For example, you can change each colour square in a good image editing package. Indeed, if you want to try this out open the Paint program that comes with Windows, open a bitmap picture and, by using View Bitmap in conjunction with the zoom facility, edit the pixels and their colour. Alternatively, by simply starting a new file in Paint and using View Bitmap, you can build your own picture. This is beyond the requirements for New CLAIT but it can give you endless hours of fun.

Generally speaking, bitmaps are more suitable, in terms of detail, for photographs whereas vector images are better in design drawing and creating clip art images. You can enlarge either type of image but if you size the bitmap image too much it becomes 'chunky' which does not happen to the same extent in vector images.

### File formats

There are literally dozens of different graphic file formats. The most common are shown in Table 8.1 below:

**Table 8.1**  *Graphic file formats*

| Format | Designed for | Used for |
|---|---|---|
| BMP (Bitmap) | On-screen displays | Desktop or wallpaper |
| EPS (Encapsulated Post Script) | Line art and vector graphics | Clip art images |
| GIF (Graphic Interchange Format) | Line art and vector graphics | Internet graphics and allows transparency |
| JPG or JPEG (Joint Photographic Experts Group) | Websites and low-resolution graphics | Web images |
| TIFF (Tagged Image File Format) | Bitmap images and high-resolution graphics | Printing photographs and occasional line art |

The format you use will very much depend on what you are trying to achieve, the quality of reproduction needed and how important it is to minimise the file size. For example, if you were preparing images for a web page, .jpg or .gif files are likely to be more suitable.

### Learning about drawing tools

For New CLAIT you will need to be able to draw basic shapes such as squares, circles, rectangles, ellipses, and triangles, and straight, curved and freehand lines. Nearly all the tasks you need to carry out can be done by using the drawing toolbar (which by default is located at the bottom left of the screen). This toolbar is made up of three main elements:

- drawing tools
- AutoShapes
- formatting and editing tools.

Figure 8.4 shows the first of these: the Drawing icons.

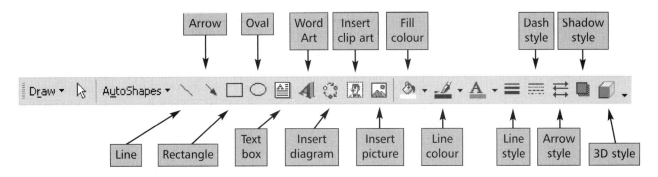

**Figure 8.4** *The Drawing icons*

As the name suggests, AutoShapes provides a wide range of shapes, from simple lines and arrows through to flowchart shapes, stars and banners. Figure 8.5 shows all the options under each menu item.

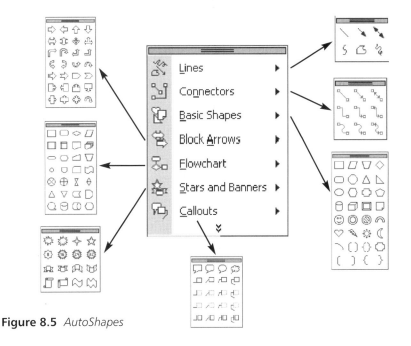

**Figure 8.5** *AutoShapes*

Group
Ungroup
Regroup
Order
Grid...
Nudge
Align or Distribute
Rotate or Flip
Text Wrapping
Reroute Connectors
Edit Points
Change AutoShape
Set AutoShape Defaults

Once you have drawn an object and placed it on the page it can be formatted and edited in a variety of ways. If you have several objects that you want to behave as one you can group them. You can also rotate and flip an object. Once an AutoShape has been inserted onto a page it can be edited in a variety of ways. Lines can also be manipulated by editing points referred to as nodes. All these actions can be selected from the Draw menu options shown in Figure 8.6.

These, then, are the drawing tools Microsoft provides for most of its applications within the Office suite.

## Creating a simple piece of artwork using shapes

If you are using Word XP to produce drawings or designs you will find that it appears to operate slightly differently from earlier versions of Word. When you insert a drawing object in Word XP, a drawing canvas is placed around it. The drawing canvas helps you arrange a drawing in

**Figure 8.6** *Draw menu options*

your document. However, if you do not want to use the drawing canvas you can drag the objects out of the canvas and then delete the canvas by pressing the canvas frame and pressing the Delete button. The canvas simply allows you to keep all parts of a drawing together, which is helpful if you have several objects in the drawing. When you want to reposition the canvas the objects will move with the whole canvas frame.

Now produce a few simple shapes to get used to working with the drawing toolbar.

**Try it out**

**Open** a new Word document.

Ensure the drawing toolbar is on display. If it is not:

**Select** <u>V</u>iew, <u>T</u>oolbars.

**Select** Drawing.

The drawing toolbar will appear at the bottom of the screen but you can drag it to any position and then resize it if you wish.

**Click** on the Rectangle icon on the drawing toolbar ⬜ .

The drawing canvas will appear as shown in Figure 8.7.

Create your drawing here.

**Figure 8.7** *The drawing canvas*

Using the mouse, **move** the cursor to the top left of the drawing canvas. Notice how the cursor changes shape to a cross hair as it moves from the toolbar to the document.

**Press** the left-hand mouse button and, while still pressing, drag and draw a rectangle shape in the canvas.

**Release** the mouse button.

You should now have a rectangle with eight drag handles (see Figure 8.8). At the top of the rectangle is an additional small line leading to a green circular handle. This is called the free rotate handle.

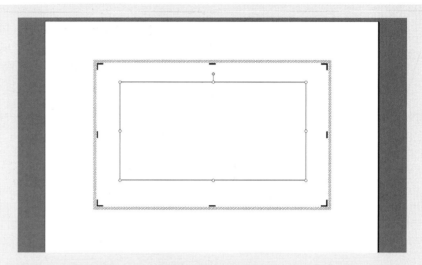

**Figure 8.8** *Document with drag handles*

Note: In earlier versions of Office the Free Rotate icon ↻ is only on the toolbar. To use free rotate, select the object and then select the Free Rotate icon. Once free rotate has been selected, it must be deselected before any resizing of the frame can take place.

**Place** the cursor over the rotate handle and, using the mouse, rotate the rectangle around 90 degrees. Notice how the canvas now automatically adjusts to the new orientation of the rectangle.

**Click** in the centre of the rectangle and drag it towards the right-hand side of the canvas, leaving about an inch of clear space from the right edge of the rectangle and the edge of the canvas.

**Place** the cursor over the central lower (or upper) drag handle until a double-headed arrow appears and, using the drag technique, reduce the height of the rectangle by about 2 cm.

**Move** the cursor to the centre of the rectangle (notice how the shape of the cursor now changes to a cross with arrow ends at the four points).

**Drag** the rectangle back to the centre of the canvas.

Using the drag points on the canvas (see Figure 8.9) drag the canvas sides to the size of the rectangle.

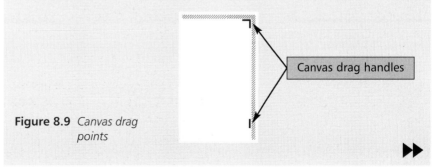

Canvas drag handles

**Figure 8.9** *Canvas drag points*

▶▶

**Click** on the Oval icon on the toolbar and, with the Shift key
depressed, use the left-hand mouse button to draw a circle in
the top of the rectangle with the apex of the circle about 2 cm
from the top of the rectangle.

**Click** on the Oval drawing tool again and draw a second circle
about half the size of the first and place it below the top circle.

Your picture should now look like Figure 8.10.

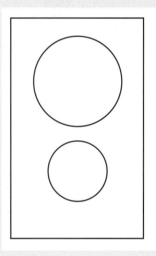

**Figure 8.10** *The finished drawing*

**Save** the document as 'Speaker'.

## How to align and evenly distribute objects

Being able to align objects is not strictly a New CLAIT requirement but
it is included here as one of the formatting and editing tools on the
drawing toolbar.

Have a look at Figure 8.11.

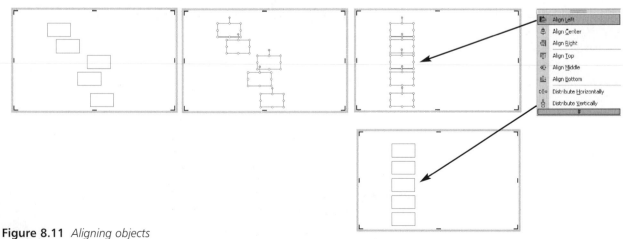

**Figure 8.11** *Aligning objects*

Here five rectangles have been created in various parts of the drawing canvas. You could spend a long time trying to line them up and distributing them equally either horizontally or vertically within the frame. However, Microsoft provides an easy way of doing this. First, select each of the objects (the five rectangles) then press the D<u>r</u>aw button on the drawing toolbar, select <u>A</u>lign or Distribute and choose Align <u>L</u>eft. The rectangles are then all aligned to the left. To distribute the spacing evenly between each of the rectangles you choose, from the <u>A</u>lign or Distribute menu option, Distribute <u>V</u>ertically. Now try this out.

## Try it out

**Open** a new Word document.

**Click** on the A<u>u</u>toShapes button.

**Select** <u>B</u>asic Shapes.

**Click** on the isosceles triangle.

**Move** the cursor over the page.

**Drag** a triangle out in the drawing canvas (or on the page if you are using an earlier version of Word). Your triangle should be about 2 cm in height.

**Click** the right-hand mouse button over the triangle.

**Select** <u>C</u>opy.

**Click** the right-hand mouse button.

**Select** Paste.

**Repeat** Paste four times in all.

**Select** all the objects. (You can only lasso all the objects if they are within the drawing canvas.)

**Click** on the D<u>r</u>aw button of the drawing toolbar.

**Select** <u>A</u>lign or Distribute.

**Select** Align <u>C</u>entre.

You should now have a picture similar to Figure 8.12.

> ### MOUSE TIP
>
> When using the drawing frame in Office XP, the easiest way to select all the objects is to click on the left-hand mouse button outside the objects area and then drag a box shape around all the objects that have to be selected.
>
> For Office 2000, hold down the Shift key and, while it is still held down, click each object using the left-hand mouse button.

**Figure 8.12** *The final drawing*

You should now be able to:

- create shapes using the drawing tools on the toolbar
- rotate an object
- resize a shape(s)
- move a shape(s)
- copy a shape
- align and distribute a selection of shape objects.

## Build-up Exercise 9: Stage 1

**Open** a new Word document.

**Create** a cube shape using the cube from the AutoShapes selection.

**Copy** the cube.

**Paste** two further cubes into the canvas (onto the page if an earlier version is being used).

**Move** the cubes so that they form three steps.

**Adjust** the first and second cubes' heights so that the base of all three cubes appears to be on one line across.

Your picture should look similar to Figure 8.13. For the moment the scale is not important and it does not matter if your steps are slightly larger or smaller than those shown.

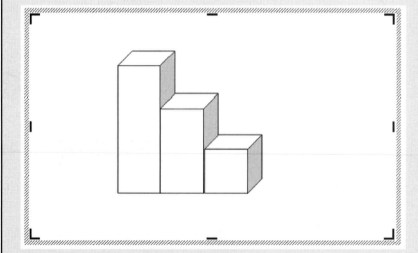

**Figure 8.13** *Cubes*

**Save** your picture as BU9a.

## Creating and using text boxes

When text is required as part of an overall picture it cannot be typed into the picture as it can in a normal Word document. Text to be included in a graphic must be placed in a text box which is itself a graphic object. Microsoft provides a text box facility on the drawing toolbar 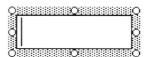. The box is placed into the canvas in just the same way as any other object. The Text Box icon is selected and dragged out to a suitable size:

Then it is simply a matter of typing in the text. Once the text has been inserted it can be modified and formatted in much the same way as it would be in any other situation. Clicking outside the box accepts the changes. By default, the text box has a line around it and a solid white fill, but these, together with other properties, can be re-formatted.

To change the properties of the box, right-click on the edge of the text box as shown in Figure 8.14 and select Format Text Box....

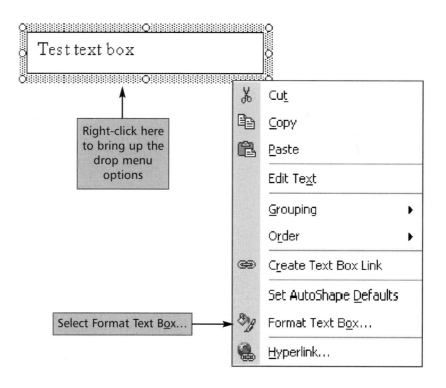

**Figure 8.14** *Test text box*

When the dialogue box shown in Figure 8.15 appears, the selections are made as required for both the line around the box and the fill. If you want the underlying graphic to show through the text, then select 'No Fill' in the Color: field.

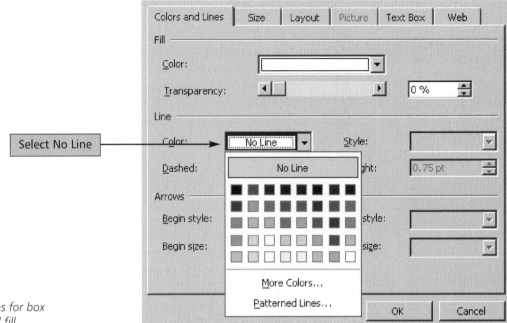

**Figure 8.15** *Selections for box lines and fill*

## Learning about fonts

Any document can be enhanced by the type, size or colour of the fonts being used. However, there are significant difference between some fonts that you see on a screen (sometimes referred to as screen fonts) and those that eventually appear on the hard copy. Like picture images, fonts are created using bitmap or vector graphics. Have a look at Figure 8.16.

**Figure 8.16** *Vector and bitmap graphics*

Fonts created using an object orientated graphics language (vector fonts) such as PostScript or TrueType are known as scalable. They have a number of advantages, not least that the higher the resolution capability the better they look. Bitmap fonts are made up of hundreds of dots and if these are enlarged (as opposed to rescaled) the image becomes less clear.

Some fonts are not scalable and these are often referred to as fixed-point fonts. Others, such as Times New Roman, are scalable. Fonts are measured in points. One point is about 1/72 of an inch. Modern software makes it incredibly easy to resize (or rescale) a font. On the formatting toolbar you have two drop-down menu boxes (see Figure 8.17).

One menu option allows you to select the font while the other offers a range of sizes. With a scalable font you can either choose one of the sizes in the list or alternatively you can type in your own size. For example, the size only goes up to 72 points. If you were preparing a poster you may well want something larger. In this case you can type in the size wanted.

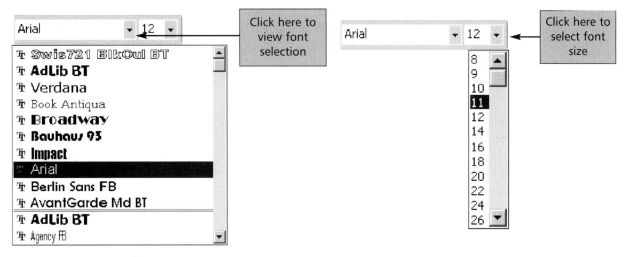

**Figure 8.17** *Choosing a font size*

**Try it out**

**Open** a new blank Word document.

**Select** Impact as the font.

**Type** in 200 as the required size.

**Type** CAT.

View your work and then **close** the file without saving.

**New CLAIT**

### Editing text in a text box

Once you have created a text box and entered text it is a simple matter to edit the text, or the font type or size. First the text box is selected by clicking in the box area. Select the text (either all of it or the part that you wish to change) and, using the formatting toolbar, make the appropriate changes. In the next Try it out exercise you will create a text box and then change the text, font and the size of the text box itself.

**Try it out**

**Open** a new Word document.

**Create** a text box using the drawing toolbar.

**Type** the following text into the box using the default font and size 12: 'Computer Art Using Word'.

**Centre** the text using the Centre icon on the formatting toolbar:

**GENERAL TIP**

To format the box with no line, click on the box frame using the right-hand mouse button. Select Format Drawing Canvas.... In the dialogue box under Line, select No Line.

**Resize** the text box to a suitable size to fit the text.

**Highlight** the text in the box.

**Select** a different font from the Font selection box (e.g. Broadway).

**Change** the font size to 20.

**Change** the font to bold.

**Resize** the text box using the drag handles so that the text is on one line and fits the text box.

**Format** the text box so that it has no line around the box.

Your text box should now look similar to Figure 8.18.

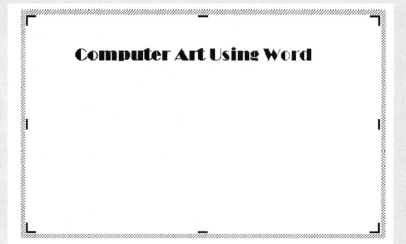

**Figure 8.18** *Resizing text and text box*

You should now be able to:

- create a text box and enter text
- amend the text
- format the text's font, size and alignment
- resize a text box
- format a text box property.

## Build-up Exercise 9: Stage 2

**Open** BU9a.

**Create** a text box and position it centrally at the bottom of the steps.

**Type** the following text into the text box: 'Climbing the Career Ladder'.

Change the font style to Impact, bold, size 14.

Resize the text box to ensure that all the text is on one line.

Align the text so that it is central in the text box.

Change the text box properties so that it has no line around the box.

Save your document as BU9b.

## Inserting and working with image files

As you have already seen, image files come in a vast variety of formats and the type which you use will depend largely on what you want to achieve. However, generally speaking you will normally use either a .jpg, .gif or .bmp type of file. You have already seen the difference between bitmap and vector type files so now you will learn how to manipulate an image once it has been inserted into a document file.

### Inserting a clip art image

To insert a clip art image select Insert, Picture, Clip Art... from the main menu. Alternatively you can use the Insert Clip Art icon 🖼 on the drawing toolbar. In Office XP the Insert Clip Art task pane will appear to the right of your screen. Enter a suitable name in the Search text: field and press Search. Office will go away and look for all the pictures related to your search criteria. The number of pictures returned will depend on the images stored on your hard disk. Select the appropriate picture from the Results: of your search, and clicking on the arrow to the right of the picture selected will bring up a menu list. Select Insert from the menu list and the clip art will be inserted into your document.

Note: if you are using Office 2000 follow the same procedure as above, but instead of a task pane Word will show you the Clip Art gallery. Select one of the categories in the gallery or alternatively type a search word in the Search for clips: field. Pressing the Enter key will return all the pictures related to your search criteria. Once you have found the picture you want to use either double-click on the picture or, using the right-hand mouse button, click on the picture and select Insert from the menu offered.

### Flipping an object

Within the selection of formatting tools on the drawing toolbar is one that allows you to flip (or mirror) an image. Have a look at Figure 8.19. The clip art on the left is the original picture. The one on the right has been flipped horizontally.

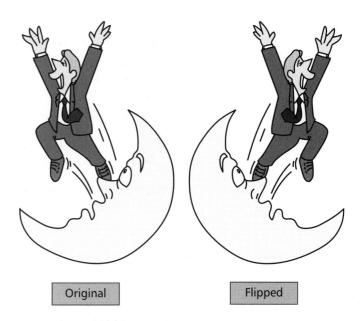

**Figure 8.19** *Original and flipped Clip Art images*

| Original | Flipped |
|---|---|

To flip a picture, first select it and then click on the D<u>r</u>aw menu option of the toolbar, select Rotate or Fli<u>p</u> and choose whether you want to flip <u>H</u>orizontally or <u>V</u>ertically.

**Note:** If you are using Word 2000 you cannot flip a clip art image using the drawing tools. However, there are a number of ways in which you can flip an image and re place it in your document. One way is to first copy (or open) the image and paste it into Microsoft Photo Editor, rotate the image and then copy and paste it back to the Word document. The following procedure can be used:

**Option 1**
- Open a new Word document.
- Insert a clip art image using the menu or toolbar technique.

Using the right-hand mouse button:
- Right-click on the image.
- Select Edit Picture.
- Click on the Select Objects icon � on the drawing toolbar.
- Using the lasso technique, drag the cursor around the picture to select all the individual parts of the image.
- From the Draw menu list select Group.
- From the Draw menu list select Rotate and Flip....
- Select Flip Horizontal.
- Click Close Picture.

**Option 2**
- Open a new Word document.
- Insert the required clip art image using the technique outlined above.
- Copy the image to the clipboard using the Ctrl+C keyboard option (Ctrl+C) or Edit, Copy from the main menu.
- Open Microsoft Photo Editor by choosing Programs, Microsoft Office Tools, Microsoft Photo Editor from the Start menu.
- Select File, New from the menu.

- Press OK.
- Select Edit, Paste from the menu.
- Select Image, Rotate from the menu.
- Select the Mirror radio button in the orientation section.
- Press OK.
- Select Edit, Copy from the menu.
- Return to your Word document.
- Select Edit, Paste from the main menu. The image will be pasted into the document, horizontally flipped.

While clip art images cannot be flipped automatically in Word 2000, normal drawing objects, such as shapes, can be flipped using the Rotate and Flip option from the Draw toolbar menu list.

### Cropping images

There will be occasions when you have an image that includes parts that you don't want or need. Cropping allows you to reduce the amount of a picture that is shown on the screen or printed. Cropping does not remove that part of the picture but simply restricts the amount viewed and printed. Have a look at Figures 8.20a and 8.20b.

**Figure 8.20a** *Cacti*          **Figure 8.20b** *Cropped cacti*

The picture on the left is the original and the picture to the right has been cropped to remove the tumbleweed.

To crop a picture, first select it so that the drag handles appear. Also, by selecting the picture the picture toolbar appears (see Figure 8.21).

**Figure 8.21** *Picture toolbar*

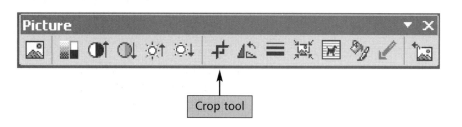

Crop tool

**Figure 8.22** *Move crop tool over handle*

Select the Crop tool and move it over the drag handle where you want to crop the picture. Next, with the left-hand mouse button held down, drag the Crop tool to the point where the picture is to be cropped (see Figure 8.22).

Release the mouse button and, if necessary, repeat the process on one of the other handles if another part of the picture is to be cropped. Remember this does not cut that part of the picture off, it simply hides the cropped part from view. When the Crop tool has been selected, it must be deselected before the image can be resized or moved. Now have a go at cropping a picture.

**Try it out**

**Open** a new Word document.

**Insert** the picture on the CD called **Painters.jpg**.

To insert the picture use Insert, Picture, From File… on the main menu.

**Crop** the picture so that only the boy with the dark top is showing.

Now have a look at Figures 8.23a and b.

**Figure 8.23a** *Uncropped image*

**Figure 8.23b** *Cropped image*

Once you are satisfied,

**Close** the document without saving.

## Positioning an image

When you insert an image into a document, Word, by default, assumes that you want to place it in line with the text. In Word XP, if the file is being placed within the canvas, it is the canvas frame itself that formats to any text in the document. This means that any text you insert will come immediately after the frame of the picture or the canvas. You can, however, format either frame (picture or canvas) to interact with the text in a number of ways, as demonstrated in Figure 8.24.

In line with text

Square with text

Behind text

Tight with text

**Figure 8.24** *Formatting picture frames to interact with text*

By selecting the image and clicking the right-hand mouse button you can then select the Format Picture... option. This will bring up the Format Picture dialogue box (or Format Drawing Canvas... dialogue box) where you can choose how your image is to be presented in the document. Have a look at Figure 8.25.

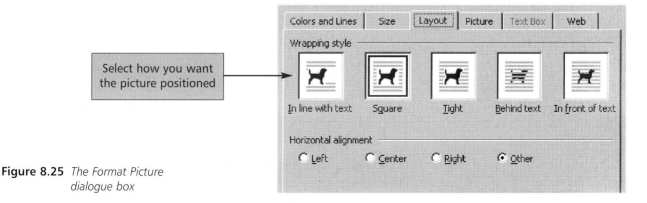

Select how you want the picture positioned

**Figure 8.25** *The Format Picture dialogue box*

Having made one of the selections you can now move the image or canvas around the page. It will interact with the text depending on the selection made.

**Open** the Word file **Eiffel.doc** from the CD.

**Insert** the image file **Eiffel.jpg**.

**Resize** the image to about half of its present size.

**Format** the image using the square option from the Layout tab on the Format Picture dialogue box.

Your document should look similar to Figure 8.26.

The Eiffel tower is a major landmark structure in the middle of Paris. It was originally built in 1889 by Gustav Eiffel. In 1914 its radiotelegraphy centre managed to intercept enemy messages and this was how the infamous spy Mata Hari was caught. During the war the tower was closed but by 1919 it was reopened again to the public and saw around 300,000 visitors. The tower saw many celebrated functions and hosted a gala dinner in 1945 on the 45th birthday of the Duke of Windsor. The tower was again closed during the Second World War but again opened after the war to the public. In 1946 it had over 600,000 visitors.

**Figure 8.26** *Reformatting an image to fit with text*

You should now be able to:

- insert a clip art image
- flip an object
- crop an image
- position an image.

## Build-up Exercise 9: Stage 3

**Open** BU9b.

**Insert** the image **Climber_1.gif** from the CD.

**Flip** the image so that the climber is pointing in the opposite direction.

**Move** the image to the left side of the steps and position it so that the rope appears to be fixed to the top of the steps.

**Insert** the image **Ballman.gif** from the CD.

**Crop** the image so that only the man appears. (i.e. crop the ball).

**Resize** the picture so that it is approximately three times the original size.

▶▶

**Position** the man so that he appears to have climbed the first step.

**Click** outside the canvas to remove it from view.

**Save** your picture as BU9c.

Your picture should now look similar to Figure 8.27.

**Climbing the Career Ladder**

**Figure 8.27** *Manipulating images*

New CLAIT

## Sizing, rotating and colouring shapes and text

### Sizing a shape to a specified dimension

So far you have resized shapes by using the drag handles. This technique is fine but there will be occasions when you need to know the precise size of an object or shape. Let's take a simple shape – a rectangle. You can create the rectangle using the drawing toolbar. The shape is dragged out to the rough size you want. Now you need to size it to a specific dimension: height – 3 cm and width – 5 cm.

To achieve this, the shape (or object) is selected by pressing the right-hand mouse button and selecting Format AutoShape... from the menu selection (or Format, AutoShape... on the main menu). Next select the Size tab on the dialogue box shown in Figure 8.28.

Enter the required height and width where indicated and press OK. The rectangle will then be the exact size you want.

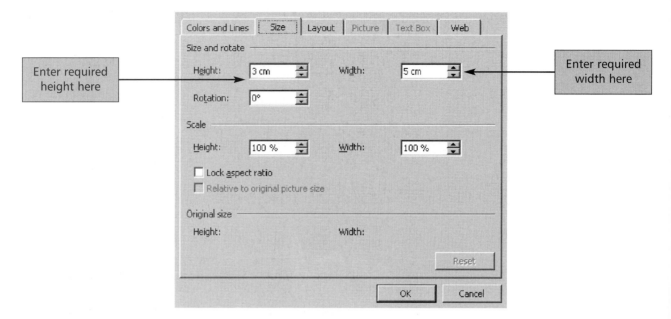

**Figure 8.28** *Sizing a shape to a specified dimension*

### Rotating an image

To rotate an image or a shape enter the number of degrees by which the image or shape is to be rotated in the box immediately below the height box.

### Using colours

Both text and shapes can be coloured using the Fill, Line or Font colour tools on the drawing toolbar or by using the Format Autoshape dialogue box.

To use a fill colour, first select the object to be coloured. Again using the right-hand mouse button, bring up the drop-down menu box and select Format AutoShape... (or use the option from the main menu). Select the Colors and Lines tab as shown in Figure 8.29.

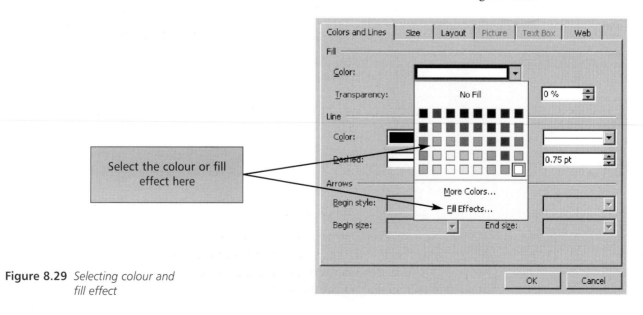

Select the colour or fill effect here

**Figure 8.29** *Selecting colour and fill effect*

Select the colour required and press OK. Your object will then be filled with the appropriate colour (or filling if one of the filling options has been chosen). Another way of changing the colour is to select the object or shape and click on the Fill Color icon on the toolbar (Figure 8.30).

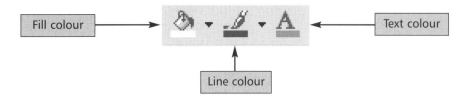

Fill colour → | Line colour | ← Text colour

**Figure 8.30** *The Fill Colour icon on the colour toolbar*

If you want to change the colour of the lines around the box simply use the Line option immediately below the Fill options.

To change the colour of the text, first highlight the text to be coloured and then choose a colour from the Text Colour icon on the drawing toolbar shown above.

## Try it out

**Open** a new Word document.

**Create** a circle 5 cm high and 5 cm across.

**Change** the line colour of the circle to dark blue.

**Change** the fill colour of the circle to light green.

**Create** a text box and insert the following text: 'Not all sun-shaped objects are yellow'.

**Format** the font as Impact, point size 14.

**Resize** the text box so that the text is all on one line.

**Centre** the text in the box.

**Change** the text colour to red.

**Close** the document without saving when you have finished.

You should now be able to:

- size a shape to a specified dimension
- rotate an object to a specified dimension
- use the colouring tools to fill a shape
- change the colour of any given text.

## Build-up Exercise 9: Stage 4

**Open** BU9c.

**Resize** the largest stepping block to 4.5 cm high and 2.28 cm wide.

**Resize** the middle-size stepping block to 2.87 cm high and 2.28 cm wide.

**Resize** the smallest stepping block to 2.06 cm high and 2.28 cm wide.

**Fill** each stepping block with a yellow colour.

**Change** the text colour in the text box to dark blue.

**Reposition** any of the objects as necessary to maintain the picture's integrity (i.e. the position of the images and the baseline across all three cubes).

Your final picture should look similar to Figure 8.31.

**Climbing the Career Ladder**

**Figure 8.31** *The finished picture*

**Save** the file as BU9d.

## Managing and printing artwork

Saving your work is basically the same as saving any Word document. To save the artwork you have created simply use the File, Save option on the main menu. Remember that when you are creating artwork in a specific piece of software such as Word, PowerPoint or Excel, the file is saved in the format of that application. So, for example, artwork drawn in Word will be saved as a Word (.doc) file whereas if it was created in

PowerPoint it would be saved as a PowerPoint (.ppt) file. If you intend to create individual images that can be imported into a document then you would need to use a specialised graphics program and save the image as a .jpg, .gif or other graphic file format. When saving a document for the first time, the Save As dialogue box will appear. However, once a design has been created, in say Word, you can highlight it, copy it and paste it into another Word document or other program. You need to save your files in a logical manner so that you can locate them easily at a later date.

Where you have created a piece of artwork and then later amended it but want to keep both the original and the amended version you will have to use the File, Save As... option. This will bring up the Save As dialogue box which allows you to give the file another name. During this unit you have worked through a number of Build-up exercises. Each time you move on to the next stage you save the document with a different name. You started with BU9a and in the next stage you saved that file as BU9b and so on. In the final Build-up exercise of this unit you are going to resave file BU9d and then print your work.

---

### Build-up Exercise 9: Stage 5

**Open** BU9d.

**Print** the document using the File, Print... option from the main menu.

**Save** this file as BU9_Final.

(Note: It is sometimes worthwhile to use the Print Preview option before printing so that you can view how your work will look on paper before actually making a hard copy.)

**Close** the file.

**Exit** the application.

---

That completes all the objectives you will need for New CLAIT. Now complete the Practical Assignment below. A solution to this assignment can be found in Part 3.

## Unit 8 Computer art using Word

### *Scenario*

You are a graphics assistant working for a toy manufacturer. Your boss has told you that there is to be a toy fair in a few weeks time and she would like you to prepare the graphics for advertising labels.

An outline of the required label is shown below:

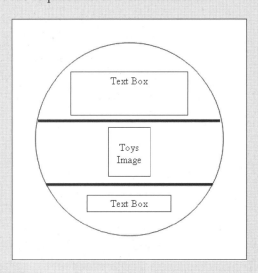

| Assessment objectives | Stage | |
|---|---|---|
| 1a<br>2d<br>4a<br>5a<br>5b | 1 | Create a new piece of artwork based on the above label. Draw a square 10 cm wide and 10 cm high. Fill the background as black. |
| 5d<br>4a<br>5b | 2 | Inside the square create a circle 8 cm by 8 cm and position it so that it is centralised both horizontally and vertically within the square. Set the background colour to yellow. |
| 2a<br>2b<br>2c<br>4b<br>4c | 3 | Import the image **Toys.gif** from the CD and position it in the centre of the circle.<br>Resize the image so that it is 2.03 cm high and 2.5 cm wide.<br>Crop the image so that only the child is showing.<br>Rotate the image by 10 degrees to the right.<br>Flip the image. |
| 2d | 4 | Insert a text box at the top of the circle.<br>Set the size of the text box to: 1.8 cm high and 4.97 cm wide.<br>Set the colour fill to the same as the circle (i.e. yellow). |
| 3a | 5 | Enter the following text in green inside the text box:<br><br>**Toy Fair 25–27 October 2002**<br>**In**<br>**The Fulerton Hall** |

| | | |
|---|---|---|
| 2d | 6 | Insert a text box at the bottom of the circle.<br>Set the size of the text box to 0.85 high and 3.55 cm wide.<br>Set the colour fill to green. |
| 3a<br>3b | 7 | Enter the following text in white inside the text box:<br><br>**Admission Free**<br><br>Centre text within the box.<br>Set the line colour of the box to black. |
| 2d | 8 | Insert a 3pt black line above and below the image so that they meet the edge of the circle. |
| 5c<br>5e | 9 | Save the artwork using the filename **CA_Practical_Exercise**.<br>Print one copy of the artwork. |

# Web pages using FrontPage

The New CLAIT web pages unit has five required learning outcomes. Each learning outcome has a number of assessment objectives and these are linked to specific aspects of knowledge and understanding. Unit 9 of this book addresses all requirements of New CLAIT for web pages and provides some additional information over and above that required for the qualification to give you a broader understanding of the subject.

## What you need to know about web pages for New CLAIT

For New CLAIT you will need to know how to:

### Import and place text and image files
- Insert a text file.
- Insert and place an image.

### Amend and format web pages
- Align page items.
- Use three different font sizes.
- Change background colour.
- Emphasise text.
- Edit text.
- Control text flow.

### Insert relative, external and e-mail hyperlinks
- Link pages.
- Insert an external link.
- Insert an e-mail link.
- Test links.
- Insert link text.
- Retain original data and formatting.

### Manage and print web pages
- Create a new document.
- Save a document.
- Print web pages.
- Print HTML source code.
- Close a document.

> **In this unit you will cover:**
>
> - What are web pages?
> - The jargon – what does it mean?
> - Getting familiar with FrontPage
> - Creating your first web page
> - Creating a website framework
> - Enhancing web pages
> - Organising a web
> - Importing and positioning images in a web page
> - Hyperlinks
> - Managing and printing web pages

You will learn how to complete all the above objectives and additional aspects of relevant software that is used both for creating and publishing web pages on the Internet. Assessment objectives required for New CLAIT will be indicated in relevant paragraphs throughout the unit. The complete syllabus relating to New CLAIT objectives can be found in Appendix 1.

## What are web pages?

If you completed Unit 3 on electronic communications you will have already gained some understanding of the Internet and how to find information either using search techniques or typing in the URL for specific websites. Now you will be learning a little more about how sites are built and managed. If electronic communications was not one of the optional units you have chosen to complete, don't worry because you will learn everything you need to know about web pages for New CLAIT in this unit.

A web page can be a part of a website or can be a site in its own right. When you sign up with an *Internet Service Provider* (*ISP*) you will normally be allocated a certain amount of space on the ISP's *server* to keep your own website. The amount of space allocated will vary according to the type of provider and the amount you are paying for the service. If your ISP is providing a free service the space allocated will be relatively small, typically between 5 MB and 20 MB. In general terms this means you will only be able to have a relatively simple site containing mainly text and not much in the way of graphics. Nevertheless, it will probably be enough for personal needs. For example, you may want to build a website to keep family and friends informed about what you are doing or a simple site for advertising a home craft industry. Browsing the Internet for information is one thing, developing your own web page and publishing it on the World Wide Web makes you a part of the Internet. Have a look at Figure 9.1.

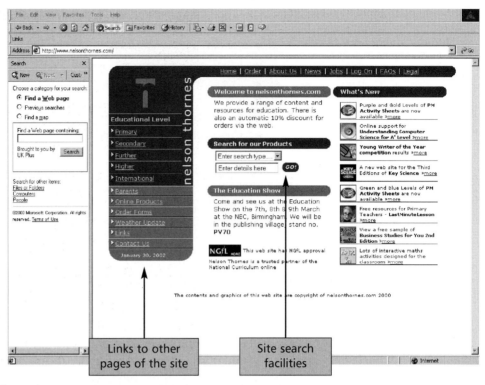

**Figure 9.1** *A typical website home page*

This is a fairly typical website home page. It has general information about what the site contains, links to other pages (areas) of the site and a site search facility. For example, here you are looking at Nelson Thornes' own website. In the Search box you can select the type of search wanted and then enter the search criteria in the box below. So, for example, as Nelson Thornes is a publisher, you would expect to search for book information such as title, author, ISBN, etc. Have a look at Figure 9.2.

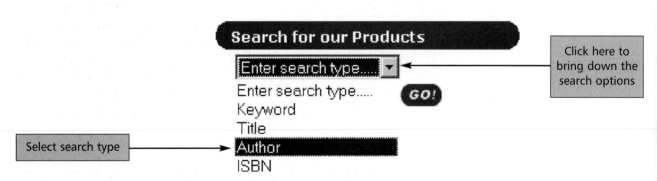

**Figure 9.2** *Searching for a product*

In this example, 'author' was selected and Kane used as the author. The site then searches for any page with a reference to Kane. The book is selected and a further page covering details of the book is shown (see Figure 9.3). Clearly this is a sophisticated professional site but it gives you an idea of what is meant by web pages.

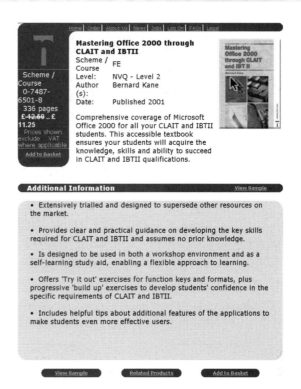

**Figure 9.3** *Web page showing details of a product*

The underlying code for building web pages is known as *Hypertext Markup Language* or *HTML* for short. HTML uses *tags* which ensure the page is formatted properly for the Web. Although learning HTML is not complicated you will be pleased to know that most modern text and web design applications will automatically convert your standard text into HTML. More of this shortly.

## The jargon – what does it mean?

As you may well have found already, the Internet and the services provided for and through the Internet, is a perfect vehicle for coming across jargon. Such words as *browser*, *domain*, *File Transfer Protocols*, *Hypertext Markup Language (HTML)*, *Hypertext Transfer Protocols (HTTP)*, *meta-tags*, *tags*, *URLs* and *WYSIWYG* are just a very small selection of jargon words that mean something to those who deal with web design all the time. You will not need to know any of these in detail although some knowledge of their existence and what they mean in broad terms will be helpful in completing this unit. A list of definitions to these and other terms can be found in Appendix 3.

### HTML

In the 1960s the principle of using hypertext was developed as a means of linking data together, and it took many years before this concept was applied to the Internet. Hypertext Transfer Protocols, or HTTP for short, were developed to do this. It marked the birth of the World Wide Web as we know it today. However, there lacked a common language that allowed text and objects in web pages to be viewed consistently, so Hypertext Markup Language (HTML) came along and provided all developers with a way to design and format web pages that could be viewed consistently by anyone using the Internet irrespective of their browser. Nowadays you can use a variety of software applications to develop web pages. Some of these are specifically designed for the purpose such as Microsoft FrontPage, which this unit concentrates on because it forms part of the Microsoft applications suite. You can also use basic text editing software such as a wordprocessing application or even a basic text editor such as Notepad – if you know what you are doing.

Have a look at this text, which might quite easily form part of a web page.

> **The Business Café**
> This site contains details of the services provided by The Business Café.
>
> Whatever your needs we will find a way to meet them.
>
> **Contact:**

If you type this in as normal text in Word and then save it as an HTML file you can view the source code that has been created. Look at Figure 9.4a.

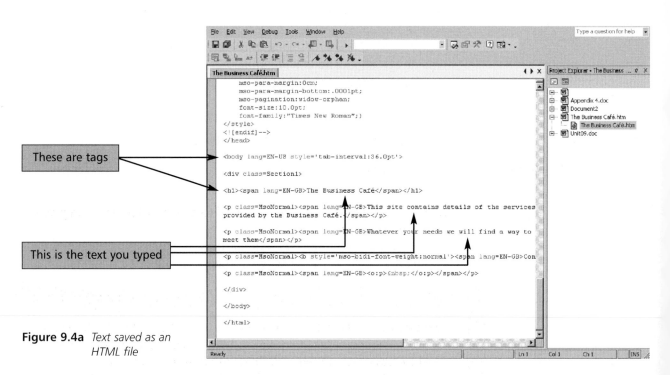

**Figure 9.4a** *Text saved as an HTML file*

Before you start to panic you will not be expected to know anything about writing HTML source code for New CLAIT. However, you will need to appreciate the basic mechanisms of a web page and the effects of editing code on the browser display. You will also need to understand some of the fundamental *tags* that form the HTML language and will be asked to print out a copy of HTML code for web pages. This is not really as complicated as it sounds. You will already be familiar with viewing the unprintable format symbols in a Word document. With these you can see where there is a paragraph break with the ¶ symbol, a line break or space. Reading HTML tags is really not, in principle, that dissimilar. For New CLAIT there are two things you need to keep in mind. First, that there should not be any superfluous paragraph breaks, and second that there should not be any superfluous line breaks. In HTML terms the paragraph and line breaks are identified as follows:

<p>        paragraph break
<br>       line break

Have a look at the HTML in Figure 9.4b. The three lines of text are separated by a superfluous number of paragraph breaks (<p>), which would not be acceptable.

The <p> indicates a new paragraph

```
<p>The beginning of the story</p>
<p> </p>
<p> </p>
<p> </p>
<p>The middle of the story</p>
<p> </p>
<p> </p>
<p> </p>
<p>The end of the story</p>
```

These would be your lines of typed text

**Figure 9.4b** *The <p> indicates a new paragraph*

Now have a look at Figure 9.4c.

**Figure 9.4c** *Text with the right number of paragraph breaks inserted*

```
<p>The beginning of the story</p>
<p>The middle of the story</p>
<p>The end of the story</p>
```

Here you can see that the lines of text have no superfluous paragraph breaks between them.

**New CLAIT**

## Hypertext links

One function of web design you will need for New CLAIT is knowing how to create links between pages. Although this may sound a bit daunting it is in fact a very simple operation thanks to the sophistication of modern software. You cover links in more detail later, but have a go at an exercise to give you some idea about links. For the Build-up exercises in this unit you will use Microsoft FrontPage, but for simply demonstrating how to create a link you will use Word. Bear in mind, of course, that you don't have to create links just for web pages; this is also useful if you want to link various documents that have nothing whatever to do with the Internet or World Wide Web.

**Try it out**

**Open** Word.

**Select** Blank Web Page as the new document.

**Type** in the following text:

This is an exercise to create a link to a second page.

Page 2

**Save** the page as 'Page 1'.

**Create** a new document, again based on the Web Page template.

**Type** in the following text:

This is the second page with a link back to page 1.

Page 1

**Save** the page as 'Page 2'.

**Highlight** the text 'Page 2' on web page 1.

**Click** the right mouse button and the drop-down menu list in Figure 9.5 appears:

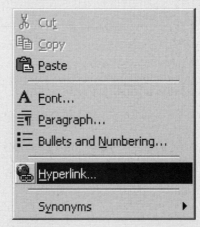
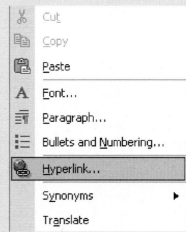

**Figure 9.5a** *Drop-down menu for Word 2000 users*

**Figure 9.5b** *Drop-down menu for Word XP users*

On the menu list:

**Select** Hyperlink....

**Press** File... under Browse for:.

**Select** Page 2 (remember you want to link to page 2).

**Press** OK (notice how the file selected now says Page 2.htm, indicating that this is a web link using hypertext).

**Press** OK a second time.

The stages of this process are shown in Figures 9.6a and 9.6b.

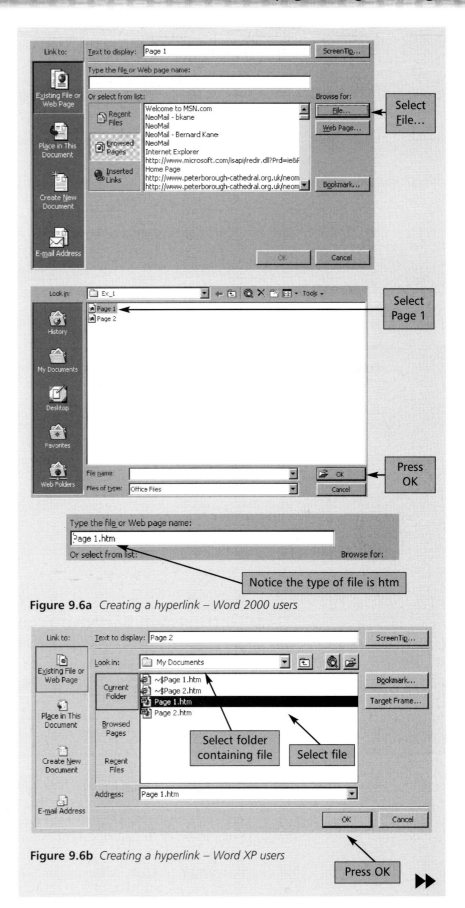

Figure 9.6a *Creating a hyperlink – Word 2000 users*

Figure 9.6b *Creating a hyperlink – Word XP users*

There are small variations depending on the version of Word you are using. With Word XP the operation is completed in the same window but to activate the link you will have to place the cursor over the link and press Ctrl+click using the left-hand mouse button.

Now repeat this process on page 2 but this time you will select page 1 as the link page.

**Press** the hyperlink and you will be taken to page 1.

**Press** 'Page 1' on page 1 and you will be taken to page 2.

You have now linked two web pages. Once the link has been established the text supporting the link is underlined (see Figure 9.7).

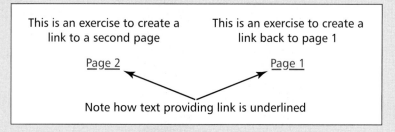

**Figure 9.7** *Two linked web pages*

## Getting familiar with FrontPage

For your assignments in New CLAIT you will be using Microsoft FrontPage. Using a web designing tool can save you both time and a lot of heartache. While Word and other text editing programs will allow you to produce HTML documents, you may well face problems further down the line if you are not familiar with the complexities of web design and various protocols. The reality is that using a special type of software such as FrontPage may save you considerable frustration later on.

Remember that a website is a collection of web pages that will have a variety of links depending on what the website has been designed to do. Some links will be internal to the site itself and others may well point the user to other sites (or internal company publications and documents). When you open FrontPage for the first time there will be elements that are familiar to you and others that are perhaps new. Have a look at the FrontPage window in Figure 9.8.

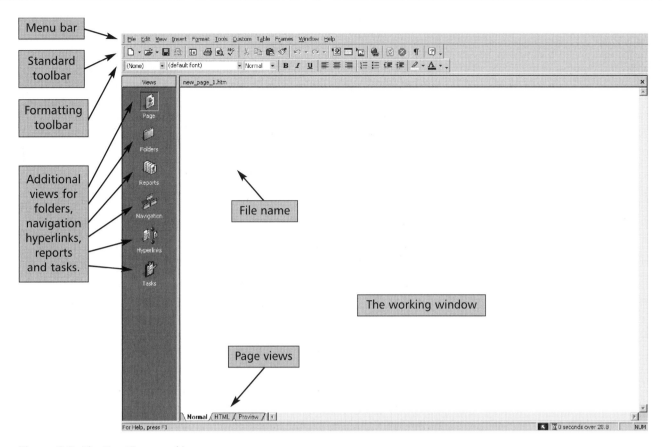

**Figure 9.8** *The FrontPage working window*

As you will have noticed in other Office applications, there is much about this window which is familiar. You have the menu and toolbars at the top of the screen and the working window or display area in the middle. This is the area where all the work is done and it is not that dissimilar from the work area found in Word or other text editing programs. For New CLAIT you will not be expected to create pages as these will be provided for you to edit and modify. However, you are expected to have an overall understanding of the structure of a web and HTML page which is a fundamental part of a website. As has already been mentioned, websites can be made up of single or multiple pages. Have a look at Figure 9.9.

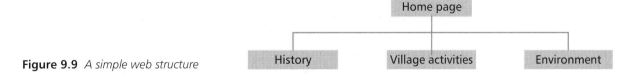

**Figure 9.9** *A simple web structure*

This represents the structure of a website consisting of four pages. All websites have a home page and in the example above you will see there is the home page with a number of supporting pages about the history of the village, village activities and a page on the environment.

## File management

Each page in a website is a file in its own right and it is therefore important that you are able to keep all files relating to your website together. On the left-hand side of the work area is a column entitled Folders List. If this is not on view for any reason go to the Yiew option on the main menu and select Fold<u>e</u>r List. You should see a list of the files and folders for the site currently being designed. Have a look at Figure 9.10.

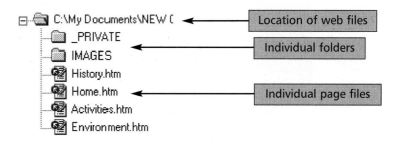

**Figure 9.10** *Folder list for a website*

This looks very similar to a view you may see in Windows Explorer and indeed to a large extent this is exactly what you are seeing. At the top of the structure you have the root or parent folder. This identifies where your site files are being stored. In this case they are shown as being stored on the C drive but they could equally be on the web server. Under the root directory or folder are sub-folders. These contain files relating to the website such as images and other multimedia files that may form part of your site. FrontPage also creates its own files that support various functions provided in the software that allow you to administer and edit your website, which is another reason for using an application specifically designed for creating web pages and sites.

## Views

Perhaps something that may be new or unfamiliar to you is the column on the far left of the screen. This contains icons that allow web files to be viewed from a number of different perspectives (see Table 9.1). The first called Page is the default view that is seen when FrontPage is opened. As the name suggests, this shows the page view and is where pages are built up or edited. Second is the Folder icon and again, as the name suggests, this allows details of the folders and files that form the website to be viewed. The Reports icon gives information on all aspects of a website such as picture, hyperlinks, pages that are slow to download or component errors. The Navigation icon gives a view of the structure of the website and also allows you to drag, drop, remove or rename pages. Hyperlinks gives a picture of the status of all the internal and external links for a website. It also shows whether they are active, confirmed or have broken links. Finally there is a Tasks icon which shows a list of tasks that need to be done to complete or maintain a website. You can add a task (or aide-memoire) by selecting T<u>a</u>sk from the <u>E</u>dit menu option. This is not something that is required for New CLAIT but it is nevertheless a very useful way of remembering

**Table 9.1** *View icons in FrontPage*

| | |
|---|---|
| | Page |
| | Folder |
| | Reports |
| | Navigation |
| | Hyperlinks |
| | Tasks |

what needs to be done, particularly if you have to develop your website over a period of time and forgot where you were on the last occasion you worked on the site.

Now that you have an overview of the FrontPage screen you can begin to work on a few pages for the site.

## Designing and building a simple web page

The first thing to remember about websites is that you are designing something that could potentially be seen by millions of people. Once a site has been published on the WWW it is available for all to see. In reality this is probably unlikely if you are building something fairly simple for a specific purpose, such as promoting your own local business, or designing a website for your village or even a private family website. However, whatever your audience, the principles are the same. Any site should have:

- clarity of purpose
- consistency in format and design
- accuracy in terms of detail
- up-to-date information.

### Clarity of purpose

The overriding question that any designer should ask is: what message or information am I intending to give to my audience? If the designer is not clear from the outset what his or her website is for, then it is very unlikely that the message will get across to those who are viewing the site.

### Consistency in format and design

If a site becomes too cluttered then again the message will become unclear and the likelihood is that the viewer will become frustrated. The inevitable result is that the viewer is unlikely to return to the site. The secret is to keep a site as simple as possible and to ensure there is consistency in terms of format (e.g. font, colour, etc.) throughout.

### Accuracy in terms of detail

People seldom comment on correct information, but if information is inaccurate it will be noticed and this will be remembered above anything else. Designers should check the details on their site before publishing it.

### Up-to-date information

Information on websites can become out of date quickly, and it is therefore essential that they are reviewed on a regular basis. Websites that have out-of-date information are unlikely to be revisited.

You should now have a broad understanding of:

- what web pages are
- the jargon that surrounds the designing of websites and pages
- HTML
- the general layout of the FrontPage screen
- the importance of managing web files
- the principles of web design.

## Creating your first web page

New CLAIT

### Importing a text file into a web page

When FrontPage is opened it will display a screen with 'new_page_1.htm'. This is like opening Word and being presented with the default template for a new document based on the Normal template (see Figure 9.11).

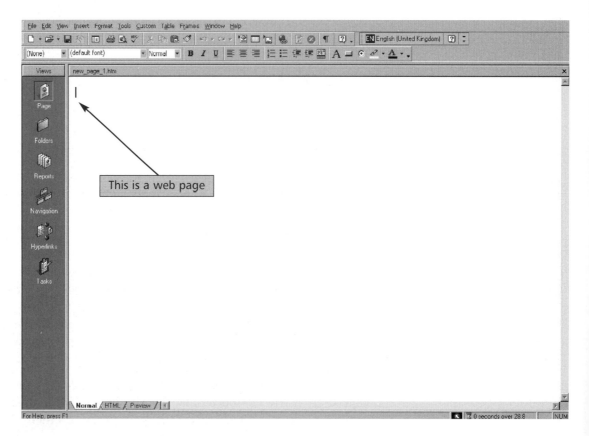

This is a web page

**Figure 9.11** *A default web page in FrontPage*

When you create a new website (as opposed to a page that can be imported into a website) FrontPage also creates folders and files that will be associated with the website. You therefore have a choice of creating your web pages separately and then importing them later into a website or creating the website and developing pages within it. For New CLAIT you will be asked to use pre-prepared web pages and also to import text and images into a web page. So, for example, you may be provided with a text file that needs to be imported into a web page. To import a text file open a new web page document and use the Insert, File... option from the main menu. The simplest way of seeing how this works is to try it out.

**Try it out**

Open FrontPage.

Select Insert, File... from the main menu (the dialogue box shown in Figure 9.12 appears).

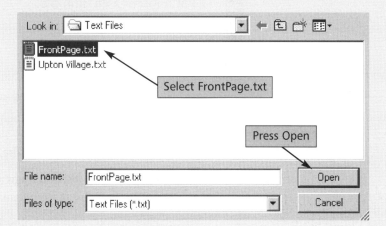

**Figure 9.12** *Importing a text file*

Select **FrontPage.txt** from the Text Files sub-folder of the folder for Unit 9 on the accompanying CD.

Click Open. The Convert Text dialogue box appears (see Figure 9.13).

Select Formatted Paragraphs.

Press OK.

The text file will then be imported into the new web page.

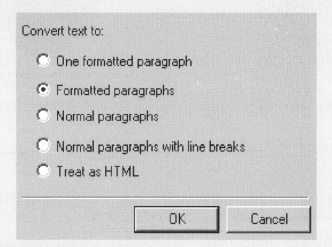

**Figure 9.13** *The Convert text dialogue box*

Save your file as Ex_2.

**New CLAIT**

### Inserting an .htm file

Inserting a pre-prepared .htm document into a web page is carried out in exactly the same way as importing a text file. However, if the file is .htm then the formatting will be imported as well as the text. Have a go at importing an .htm file.

**Try it out**

**Open** FrontPage.

**Select** Insert, File... from the main menu.

**Find** and select **Holiday_choice.htm** from the Web Files sub-folder in the Unit 9 folder on the accompanying CD.

Your page should now look like Figure 9.14.

**Choosing the right holiday for you**

Whether you are intending to travel to the other side of the globe or to your nearest coastal destination we have the right holiday for you.

First select your preferred destination:

UK & Ireland

Europe

Far East

Americas

Australia

Africa

**Figure 9.14** *Inserting an .htm file*

Notice how the formatting and picture have been imported as a new web page.

## Creating a website framework

Although for New CLAIT you are only expected to work on web pages, it is nevertheless easier using FrontPage to work with these pages within the framework of a website itself. The reason for this is mainly that you can then see from the views what is actually going on. This is particularly true when it comes to looking at links you have created between the pages. You can create websites using a number of different styles that come with FrontPage. Here you will look at two options. First, creating a simple new web framework where you can build the pages as you go along or import them. However, if you already have a number of pre-prepared web pages, you can get FrontPage to build your framework using these pre-prepared pages.

To create a basic framework is no more difficult than opening a new page. When FrontPage is opened, as you have already seen, it starts by showing you a new page. If you then select File, New and instead of choosing Page..., selecting Web... will bring up the dialogue box shown in Figure 9.15.

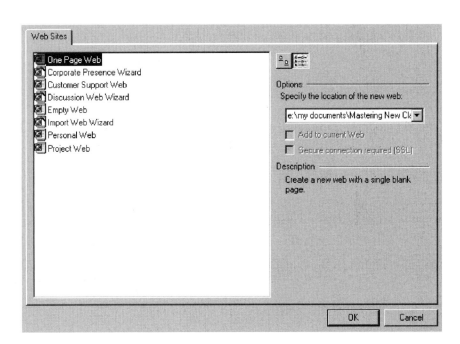

**Figure 9.15** *Creating a basic website framework*

In the field on the right of the dialogue box you can type in the location of your new website. After selecting One Page Web on the left, FrontPage then prepares the basic framework for your website. Once it has completed its work it will show the structure of folders and files on the left of the screen under Folders List.

### Creating a web framework using the Import Web Wizard

The method described above for creating a new web framework is fine if you intend to build your own pages as you go along. However, FrontPage also gives you the opportunity of building a web framework using previously created web pages. Since you are not expected to build your own pages for New CLAIT, for the Build-up exercise that follows you will use the Wizard to help build a site based on web pages provided for you.

## Build-up Exercise 10: Stage 1

### Scenario

You work for a local training company who has a contract with the Learning Skills Council. The Council is keen to provide help in job searching and recruitment techniques for those who either have not had a job previously or are unsure about how to set about applying for a job. A number of unformatted web pages have already been prepared for you and you have been asked to set up the framework of a website.

**Note:** You will be using the source files from your CD. Copy these files to an appropriate folder on your hard disk (Web Page Recruitment) and change the properties so that they are not read-only. (If necessary refer back to Unit 1, page 36.) You will be using the following files from the CD:

**Web Page (.htm) files to be used:**

- The_Advertisements.htm
- The_Application.htm
- The_Interview.htm
- The_Right_Job.htm
- The_Secrets.htm

### WEB TIP

**Naming a website**

Unlike other applications in the Office suite, in FrontPage the location of the website is also the name of that site. So, for example, if you chose C:\My documents\My Webs\test1, FrontPage would build a framework under the folder name of C:\My documents\My Webs\test1. The last part of the address will become the filename for the website; in this case 'test1'.

**Open** FrontPage.

**Select** File, New, Web... from the menu options.

This time instead of choosing the One Page Web option,

**Select** Import Web Wizard.

In the Options field on the right of the dialogue box,

**Type** in the location where you want your new web to be stored.

**Type** 'Web 2' as the Web folder name. For example C:\My Documents\Websites\ Web 2.

**Press** OK.

The dialogue box shown in Figure 9.16 will appear.

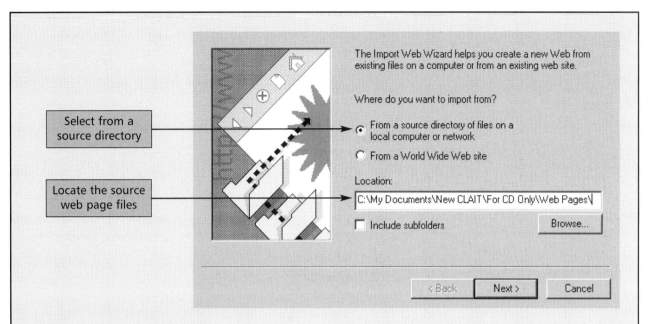

**Figure 9.16** *Setting up a new website framework*

**Select** the radio button indicating that files will be taken from a source directory where you stored the files from the CD.

**Select** the Browse button to identify the location of the web pages to be imported.

**Press** Next.

FrontPage will now show you the files available to import from the source directory to your web (see Figure 9.17).

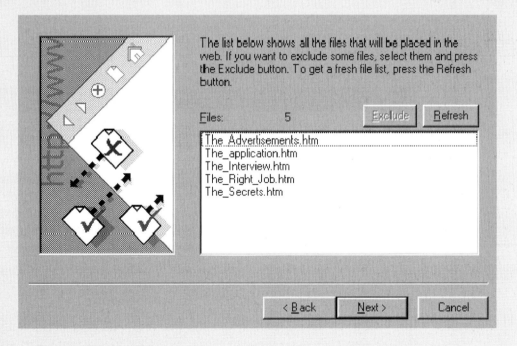

**Figure 9.17** *Contents of source directory*

**Press** Next.

**Press** Finish.

You should now see the folders and files FrontPage has built for you in the folders list shown in Figure 9.18.

**Figure 9.18** *Folder list for the website*

**Note:** When you open FrontPage a new page is generated automatically but is not saved automatically. You will learn about Index.htm and home pages later in this unit so for now click on the Close button ✕ to the top right of the new page 1. This will close and remove the page, leaving only those pages imported to your website. To view an imported web page, double-click on the required .htm file in the Folders List pane.

To Save any changes that may have been made, select <u>F</u>ile, <u>S</u>ave from the main menu or alternatively click on the Save icon 🖫 on the toolbar.

**Save** your web.

**Close** the file.

## Enhancing web pages

So far you have imported unformatted .txt and .htm files into a website framework. Clearly an important aspect of designing a web is to ensure it is sufficiently attractive to the user for them to want to view the whole site. A site that looks dull and boring is unlikely to arouse much enthusiasm so the next thing you need to do is make the web attractive. This can be achieved in a number of ways. The text can be emphasised, and the font, type, alignment and style changed. In addition, images and other multimedia files can be used, the background colour changed, or a background image inserted.

### Emphasising the font on a web page

One of the easiest ways to improve your web page is to change the size, style and emphasis of the font. Changing a font's size, style, emphasis or colour is handled in exactly the same way as in any other application. First the font is selected and the changes made using the

Font dialogue box, which is accessed through Format, Font on the main menu or by using the icons on the formatting toolbar. Both these are shown in Figure 9.19.

You can also use the built-in formats on the toolbar shown in Figure 9.20. Select the format required (e.g. Heading 3) and then change the font name and size in the boxes next to the style.

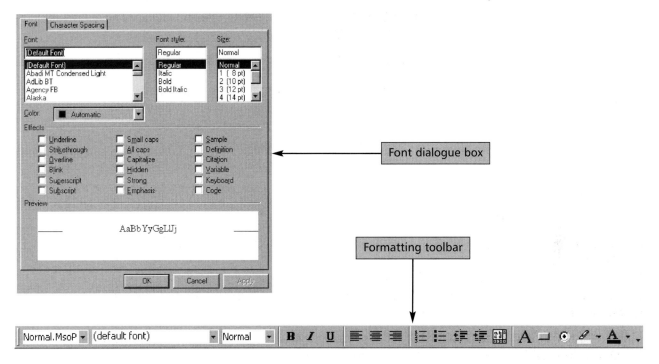

Font dialogue box

Formatting toolbar

**Figure 9.19** *Font dialogue box and formatting toolbar*

**Figure 9.20** *Built-in formats on the toolbar*

---

## Build-up Exercise 10: Stage 2

**Open** Web 2.

You decide that you want to emphasise the headings on each page.

**Format** the heading text for each page so that it is bold, 18 points and a different font from the rest of the text.

**Format** the font style for the bullet points on each of the five pages in the web as italic.

**Press** Save.

### Inserting text into a web page

Inserting text is similar to inserting text in a normal wordprocessing document. First the cursor is positioned at the point where the text is to be inserted and then the required text is typed in the normal way. Now add some text to The_Interview page of the website.

---

**Build-up Exercise 10: Stage 3**

**Open** Web 2.

**Click** on The_Interview.htm web page.

**Type** the following after the last bullet point:

'Remember this is a two-way process so have your questions well thought out in advance.'

**Highlight** the text and embolden it.

**Press** Save.

---

### Aligning text

As you will probably realise by now, formatting and editing text in a FrontPage web page is much the same as doing so in another text editing program. For example, if you wanted to align text centrally in a Word document you would place the cursor at the beginning of the text and align it using the toolbar icons. Exactly the same applies in a web page in FrontPage. Now align the text you input to The_Interview page centrally.

---

**Build-up Exercise 10: Stage 4**

**Position** your cursor at the beginning of the line in the page in The_Interview.htm that starts 'Remember this is a two ...'.

**Press** the Centre icon from the toolbar.

**Press** Save.

---

You should now be able to:

- import a text file
- insert an .htm file
- create a simple web framework
- view HTML tags
- insert text into a web page
- enhance aspects of a web page
- align text as directed.

**New CLAIT**

## Using colours, patterns and pictures

Any website can be enhanced not only by the information it contains and the style of font, but also by the use of colours and patterns. FrontPage has a number of built-in themes that can be applied to a web page. Alternatively, you can set a background colour or picture (or both) to your own design.

### Built-in themes

To view the themes that are available, select Format, Theme... on the menu and those available are shown in the dialogue box that appears on the screen (see Figure 9.21).

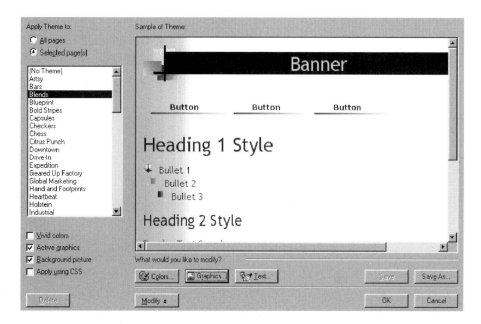

**Figure 9.21** *Selecting a theme for the website*

When selecting a theme you can make it apply to the current page only or to all pages. This option is in the top left of the box Apply Theme to:. Scrolling down the options in the selection box allows you to choose the most appropriate theme for your web. For example, were you to select the theme 'Blends' for Web 2, it would look something like Figure 9.22 on page 332.

One thing to bear in mind is that if you have already determined the font you want or other formatting, you will need to ensure the theme is modified to reflect the fonts and formatting you are using. You can change the theme fonts or other attributes by pressing the up arrow on the Modify button at the bottom of the box and selecting the Colors, Graphics or Text buttons. Depending on which button is pressed, a further formatting dialogue box will appear for you to make the changes required.

### Background pictures and colours

If you don't want to use one of the themes provided by FrontPage, you can enhance your web by formatting the background with a colour, picture or both. When using a coloured background, a picture or indeed a mixture of the two, it is important that the colours or pictures used

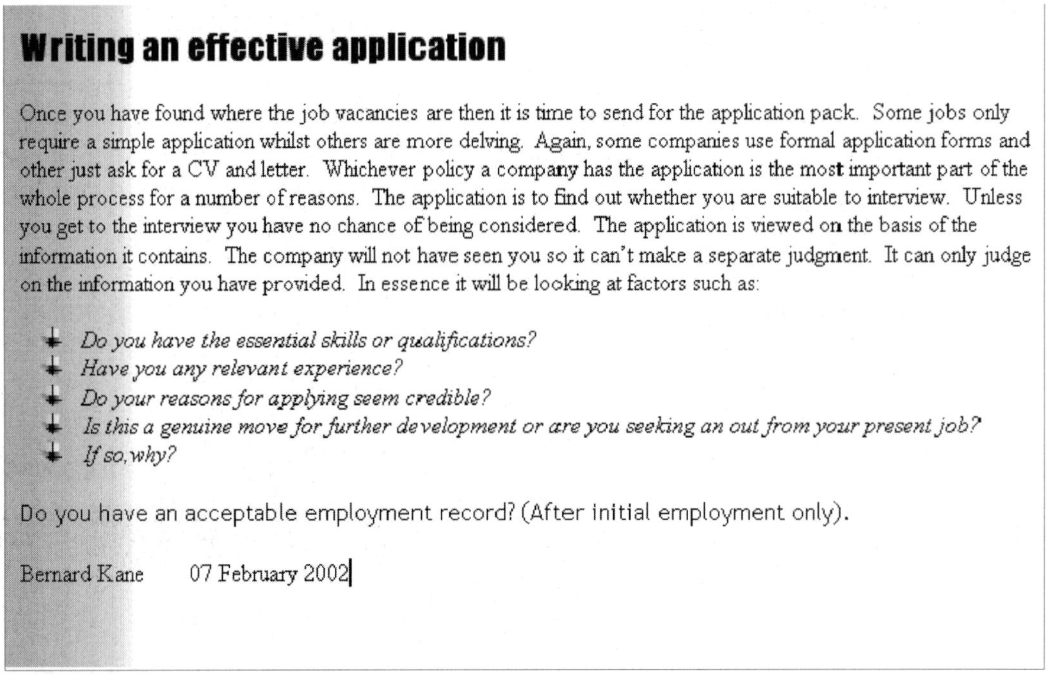

## Writing an effective application

Once you have found where the job vacancies are then it is time to send for the application pack. Some jobs only require a simple application whilst others are more delving. Again, some companies use formal application forms and other just ask for a CV and letter. Whichever policy a company has the application is the most important part of the whole process for a number of reasons. The application is to find out whether you are suitable to interview. Unless you get to the interview you have no chance of being considered. The application is viewed on the basis of the information it contains. The company will not have seen you so it can't make a separate judgment. It can only judge on the information you have provided. In essence it will be looking at factors such as:

- *Do you have the essential skills or qualifications?*
- *Have you any relevant experience?*
- *Do your reasons for applying seem credible?*
- *Is this a genuine move for further development or are you seeking an out from your present job?*
- *If so, why?*

Do you have an acceptable employment record? (After initial employment only).

Bernard Kane     07 February 2002

**Figure 9.22** *Selecting an appropriate theme for a web*

do not obscure the text on the page. For the New CLAIT assignment your options are limited to a tiled background or a colour. Colours are determined by specifying a hexadecimal code such as Hex={FF,33,00} which is red. Don't worry about these codes as you would only use them if you were already familiar with hexadecimal coding. Fortunately FrontPage makes changing the background very easy. Try changing the background of a page in a new web.

### Try it out

**Create** a new web based on a single page.

**Open** and place the cursor in the Index.htm page.

**Right-click** the mouse button to show the menu list.

**Select** Page Properties... and the dialogue box in Figure 9.23 will appear (see page 309).

**Select** Background.

**Select** <u>M</u>ore Colours... and choose a colour from the palette.

**Press** OK and you will be returned to index.htm with its new colour.

To change the background back simply go back to the Background, put the colour back to Automatic and press OK.

▶▶

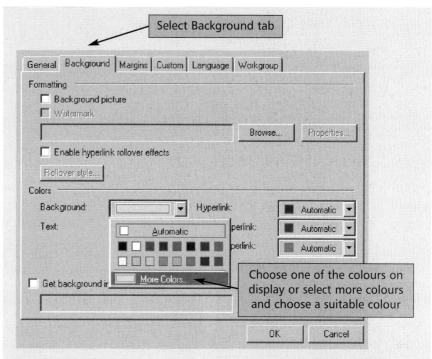

**Figure 9.23** *Changing the background of a page in a new web*

To format the background using a picture, bring up the Page Properties... box again. This time:

**Click** in Background Picture.

**Press** Browse....

**Press** the Select Files icon to locate the picture you want to use.

**Press** OK twice.

Notice that the picture is embedded, and if you now type text into the page it is printed over the background picture. With an inserted picture, the text would move depending on the properties given to the picture frame.

These stages are shown in Figure 9.24.

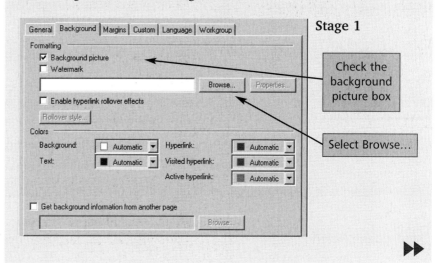

If you are changing the background colour for a web with more than one page, use the 'Get background information from another page' box at the bottom of the Page Properties dialogue box. Click in the check box and press the Browse button. FrontPage will show you the pages available in the current web from which to choose the background.

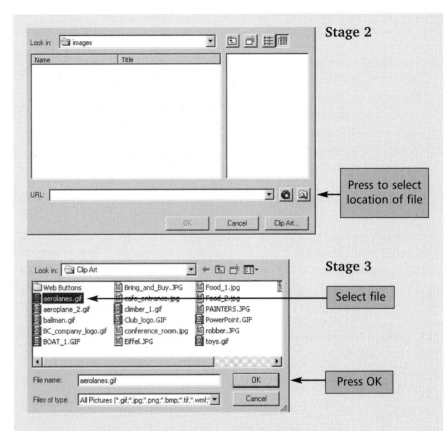

Stage 2

Press to select location of file

Stage 3

Select file

Press OK

**Figure 9.24** *Inserting text over the background picture*

Now try changing the background of the page using the **Aeroplanes.gif** file on your accompanying CD. First put Background colour back to Automatic in the Colours box.

## Build-up Exercise 10: Stage 5

**Open** Web 2.

**Format** the background colour of each page, making sure that the colour is consistent for each page.

**Press** Save.

You should now be able to:

- use background colours and pictures to enhance the page
- use the built-in themes that come with FrontPage.

### Organising a web

Although understanding how a web is organised is not formally part of the New CLAIT syllabus, it may help your general understanding of web structure and design. Setting up a formal structure for your web helps you in a number of ways. First, it helps you to remember how your website is set up; which pages belong where and what they are related to. Second, it allows you to set up navigation bars that link various pages together. You will be looking at links shortly, but for now it is enough to know that having a structure will help you in designing your site and ensuring those who are using it can move around the site easily.

### Setting up a web structure

By selecting the Navigation view in the Views column, FrontPage will show what your current structure looks like. Clearly, if you have not set up a structure yet there will be nothing to see. Had you opened a new web, FrontPage would, by default, have given you a home page. The .htm file in the folders list will show this as Index.htm which is the actual name of the file. In your current web, no home page yet exists so you must first introduce one. Once you have created a home page you can begin to build the structure for our website.

## Build-up Exercise 10: Stage 6

**Open** Web 2.

**Select** Navigation view.

Your screen should look similar to Figure 9.25.

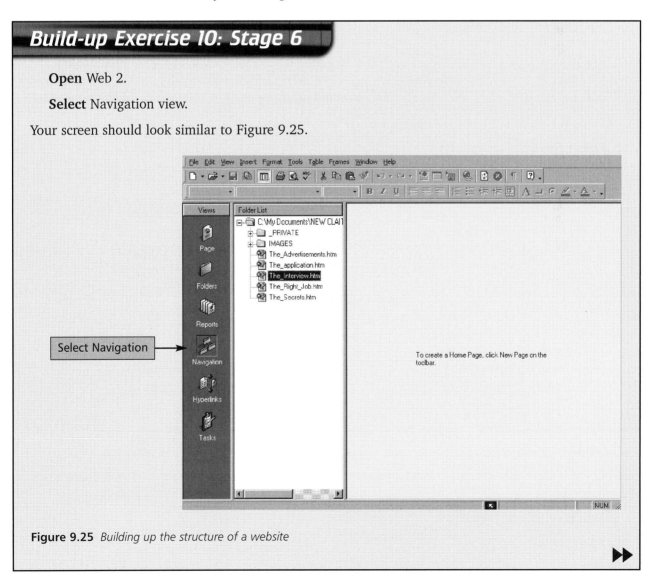

**Figure 9.25** *Building up the structure of a website*

**Click** the New Page icon  to insert a home page.

Holding the left-hand mouse button down,

**Drag** The_Secrets.htm file onto the navigation page and, once you see the link appear, release the mouse button. Your Navigation view should now look like Figure 9.26.

**Figure 9.26** *Navigation view*

**Drag** the remaining files into the structure in the following order:

**The_Right_Job.htm**
**The_Advertisements.htm**
**The_Application.htm**
**The_Interview.htm**

Notice how the name of each page is not the filename, but is the same as the heading on each page. Although there is nothing wrong with this it is difficult to see the page name in full. You can change the name by right-clicking on each page and selecting the Rename option on the menu list.

**Press** the right-hand mouse button over the First Page box.

**Select** Rename.

**Type** Secrets.

Now rename the remaining pages as follows:

The Job
Adverts
Applications
Interviews

Your structure should now look like Figure 9.27.

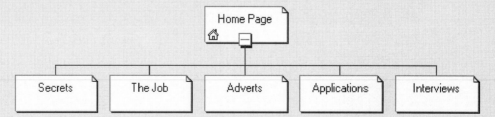

**Figure 9.27** *A web structure*

**Open** your new home page, Index.htm, and change the background colour to match each of the other pages.

**Double-click** on HomePage.

**Save** the web and pages.

**New CLAIT**

## Editing a web page

You may recall that earlier in the unit, on pages 313–5, HTML was discussed, and the need to avoid superfluous spacing between text and paragraphs. An experienced web designer who is familiar with HTML can edit pages from the HTML code to ensure the page is viewed in the way it is intended. However, for most of us this is unnecessarily complex, and editing text and formats in the Normal view for the page is much easier. HTML can play its part in terms of being able to see at a glance where extra lines or paragraph breaks have been inserted, as referenced on page 315.

In the web you have been building throughout this unit there is no obvious additional spacing. However, if you look at the HTML view you can see that on some pages the bullet points have additional breaks between them. It would be neater if these were removed. In addition, for the purposes of completing assignments you will be asked to insert your name, centre number and date on any pages that are being assessed. In the next part of the Build-up exercise you will re-format the bullet points and add text to each page.

## Using HTML tags to view formatting

At the beginning of this section you learnt about HTML and how the source code could be viewed, and you were given a basic understanding of tags and what they represented. You can also view and use HTML tags in the Normal view, and this will help you understand how changing the format of a page automatically changes the underlying HTML source code. Viewing the tags in the Normal view is perhaps less intimidating than trying to read through the source code itself.

HTML tags can be viewed in graphical form in the Normal view by selecting <u>V</u>iew, Reveal T<u>a</u>gs from the main menu or using the keyboard shortcut Crtl+/. Have a look at Figure 9.28a and b.

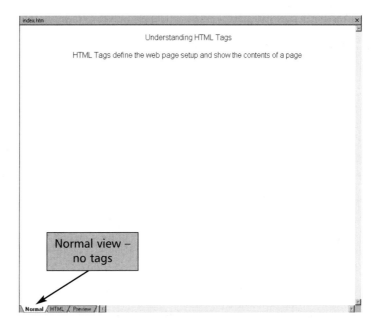

**Figure 9.28a** *Normal view*

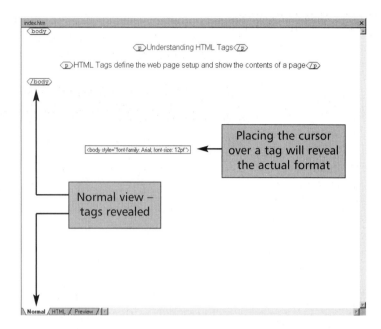

**Figure 9.28b** *Normal view with tags revealed*

Figure 9.28a is the Normal view and Figure 9.28b shows the Normal view with the HTML tags revealed. By placing the cursor over one of the tags you can see the format for that section. As an example, in Figure 9.28 you can see that the text is in Arial, font size 12 pt.

If the text 'Understanding HTML Tags' is formatted as a heading style, emboldened and underlined, the tags will change automatically to show this (see Figure 9.29).

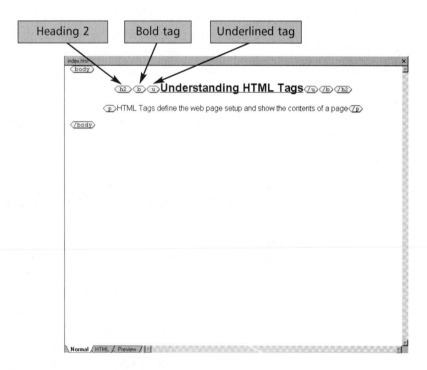

**Figure 9.29** *Normal view with tags revealed, showing heading style*

By highlighting the text on the page and then selecting the HTML tab for viewing the code you will be able to see the source code for this format. Although it is not essential to highlight the text first, it helps to identify the actual code you are interested in when viewing in the source code. This is particularly so if the page is full of text and graphics that would make it harder to see a specific area of code.

When you import a web page the formatting you expect to see may not in fact appear. This is particularly so with bullet lists. You can check this by placing the cursor on one of the bullet points and see whether the Bullet icon on the toolbar is highlighted. If it is not, then place the cursor at the beginning of the first point to be included in the bullet list and, after backspacing to remove the 'apparent' bullet symbol, press the Bullet icon. Next place the cursor in front of the second bullet point and repeat the process. When the Bullet icon has been pressed the item will automatically find the right position in the list.
Alternatively, you can remove the bullet symbol, highlight all the lines that are to become a bullet list and then press the Bullet icon on the toolbar (see Figure 9.28).

## Build-up Exercise 10: Stage 7

**Open** Web 2 if it is not already open.

**Re-format** the bullet lists for each page where there appears to be a space between each point (Figure 9.30).

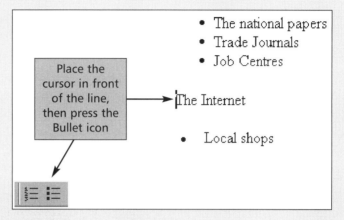

**Figure 9.30** *Re-formatting a bullet list*

**Open** each page individually, except Index.htm, and type your name and the date under the last piece of text.

On the page The_Interview.htm:

**Left align** the new text.

**Press** Save.

## Importing and positioning images in a web page

Importing images into a web page is very similar to importing images into any other application that supports image files. However, there is one very important difference. When you use images, FrontPage assumes that they are part of the website and therefore they must be available to the site when the site is published. When you build your web you are probably using image files that are stored on your hard disk. If the image file is not stored with your web, when it is published the web folder will not know where to find the file – particularly if it is still on your hard disk. You will have noticed that when FrontPage prepares the website framework it includes two folders – 'Private' and 'Images'. The images folder is where you store all the image files used in the website. Normally you would prepare the images you want to use and import them into the web folder in preparation for using them on a particular page. To import your files you first select the images folder and then go to File, Import on the main menu. After selecting Import, the dialogue box in Figure 9.31 appears.

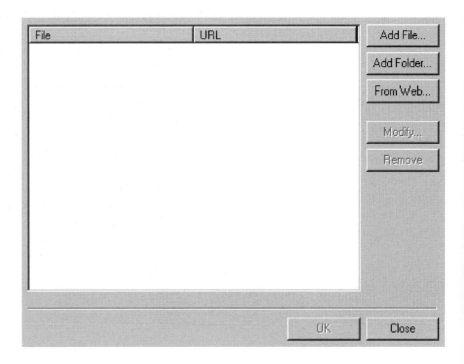

**Figure 9.31** *Importing image files*

By pressing the Add File... button you are shown a further dialogue box called 'Add File to Import List'. Locate the folder and files you want to import (see Figure 9.32).

**Figure 9.32** *Locating the folder and files for import*

Press the Open button and the files are placed in the Import box. After pressing OK the files are imported to the images folder where they will be available for you to use in your website. However, this is not the end of the story. Although it is quite legitimate for you to keep the images imported into the images folder, a large website might use many different types of image. For example, as you will see shortly, one way of making your site more user friendly is to use buttons and while you can create 'hover buttons' within FrontPage that you can then use to link other parts of the web, these are fairly basic and you may want to create your own more exciting buttons in one of the many graphics packages that help you build web images. These are still images and must be stored in the web folders.

In addition to buttons you may want normal pictures to enhance your website. As in any file management system, it is sensible to create a clear filing structure for your image and other files. You can easily accomplish this by creating a sub-folder in the images folder. To do this, simply click using the right-hand mouse button on the images folder, select New Folder and give it an appropriate name.

Now have a go at creating a new folder and importing the button images needed for the website. These buttons will form some of the internal links for the site. Links are covered in the next section so don't worry about them now.

## Build-up Exercise 10: Stage 8

**Open** Web 2.

**Click** on the images folder in the Folders box using the right-hand mouse button.

**Select** New Folder.

**Type** Buttons as the name of the folder.

**Select** the Buttons folder.

Using File, Import on the main menu:

**Add** the following .jpg files, which can be found in the Unit 9 folder on the CD to the Buttons folder you have just created:

**Home.jpg**
**Secrets.jpg**
**Right_job.jpg**
**Where_is_the_job.jpg**
**The_Interview.jpg**
**Writing_the_application.jpg**

**Press** Save.

### Inserting images onto a web page

You will hardly be surprised to learn that there are a number of ways you can insert an image onto a web page. Here you will look at just two – dragging and inserting an image using the menu bar.

### Inserting images by dragging

Having built the pages and imported the button images, you now need to place the relevant buttons on each page in the web. In the Buttons sub-folder under Images you can see the .jpg files that are contained in the folder. To move them onto the web page is simply a matter of clicking on the file and, while holding the left-hand mouse button down, dragging the image to the desired location on the page.

### Inserting images using the menu bar

First the cursor is placed where the image is to be inserted. Then select Insert, Picture, From File..., locate the file from the appropriate folder and press the OK button. The image will be inserted at the place where the cursor is positioned. If this is not the correct place then select the image and drag it to a different location on the page.

You will notice that moving an image around a page is not as easy as in some other applications. Positioning graphics on a web page can be either simple or relatively complex, but essentially you can tell FrontPage how you want an image to behave in terms of both its position on the page and other text. Using the Format, Position features from the main menu gives you a number of options for wrapping style (i.e. how the image behaves in relation to text) and positioning style (i.e. whether the position is absolute or relative to text). Once you have placed the image on the page, click on it to select it and then select Format, Position... to make the Position dialogue box shown in Figure 9.33 appear.

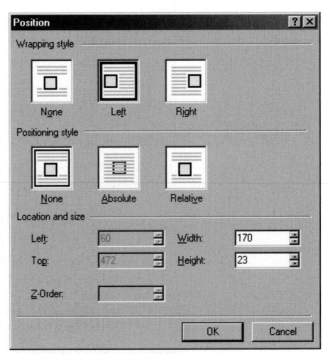

**Figure 9.33** *The Position dialogue box*

Using the Absolute option under Position style, you can move an image to any part of the page you want. Simply select the Absolute option, press OK and, with the cursor positioned over the image, click the left-hand mouse button and drag the image to the desired location.

The Z-Order option determines the layer of the image. A zero value means the image will be in front of any text or object, and minus values place the image behind them. While this is beyond the scope of New CLAIT, you may wish to experiment to see how an image reacts to different settings.

Now you are going to insert the buttons from the buttons folder onto the pages of the web. The buttons should be inserted just above your name. To ensure there is sufficient space, place the cursor at the beginning of the name line and insert a line break.

## Build-up Exercise 10: Stage 9

**Open** Web 2.

Using either the insert or drag method, place the buttons on the pages as shown in Figure 9.34.

| Web Page | Buttons | | |
|---|---|---|---|
| The_Secrets | | The Right Job | HOME |
| The_right_job | Where is the job? | Secrets | HOME |
| The_advertisements | Writing the application | Secrets | HOME |
| The_application | The Interview | Secrets | HOME |
| The_interview | | Secrets | HOME |

**Figure 9.34** *Web page buttons*

**Insert** the following text as the headings for the home page (Index.htm). The format is Impact, 24 points.

**Be a Successful Applicant**

**for**

**Your Chosen Job**

Using either the insert or drag method, place the buttons on the pages as shown in Figure 9.35.

**Figure 9.35** *Placing buttons on the page*

**Press** Save.

You should now be able to:

- organise the structure of a web
- edit a web page
- import images.

## Hyperlinks

On page 315 you saw how useful it can be to build links into documents to be able to move from one page to another, or indeed from one paragraph to another. Web pages have a number of different types of links. There are links internal to the website allowing you to move effortlessly from one page to another, there are external links which allow you to move from one website to another, and there are also links that allow you to send e-mail to a selected site or individual. We will look at each of these in turn.

### Internal links

A hyperlink is an instruction created in HTML that becomes embedded in a web page. The instruction tells the browser to display another page (or another site, if it is an external link). A link has two elements: the link itself and the target or file/page that the user will see when the link is activated.

Internal links allow users to move around a website. Take the website you have been building in the Build-up exercises. You can see that it would not be very helpful if, having built all the pages and published the website on the Internet, users could not access all the pages. There are a number of ways you can achieve this, but perhaps the simplest is to use words, phrases or images in a page that direct the user, on clicking the word, phrase or image to a different part of the web.

In FrontPage, creating links is child's play. Links are created by selecting the letter, word, phrase or image that is to be used in the link. In the last Build-up exercise you inserted a number of buttons. It is these buttons that are going to provide the links that allow users to navigate around the website. Follow this Build-up exercise to create links from the home page to other pages in the site.

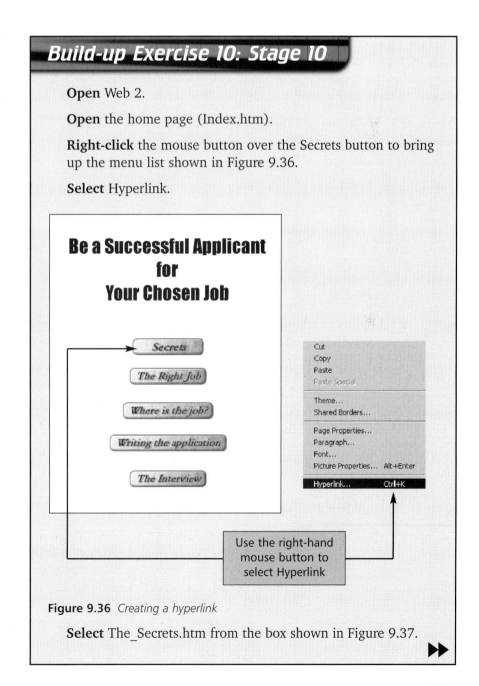

## Build-up Exercise 10: Stage 10

**Open** Web 2.

**Open** the home page (Index.htm).

**Right-click** the mouse button over the Secrets button to bring up the menu list shown in Figure 9.36.

**Select** Hyperlink.

**Be a Successful Applicant for Your Chosen Job**

Secrets

The Right Job

Where is the job?

Writing the application

The Interview

Cut
Copy
Paste
Paste Special

Theme...
Shared Borders...

Page Properties...
Paragraph...
Font...
Picture Properties...   Alt+Enter

Hyperlink...          Ctrl+K

Use the right-hand mouse button to select Hyperlink

**Figure 9.36** *Creating a hyperlink*

**Select** The_Secrets.htm from the box shown in Figure 9.37.

▶▶

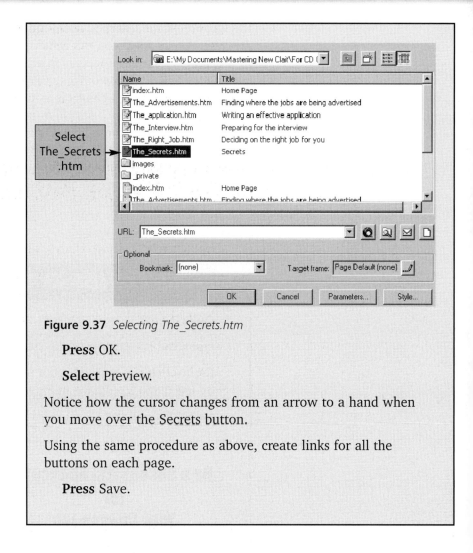

**Figure 9.37** *Selecting The_Secrets.htm*

**Press** OK.

**Select** Preview.

Notice how the cursor changes from an arrow to a hand when you move over the Secrets button.

Using the same procedure as above, create links for all the buttons on each page.

**Press** Save.

### External links

On most websites you will find links to other sites that contain similar information. Creating external links follows a similar procedure to creating internal ones, but this time you will need to know the URL (address) of the site to which you want to link. You will create a link to two sites. One of the sites, The Microsoft Network, can be viewed off-line (i.e. you do not need to be connected to the Internet to be able to view the MSN browser, although you cannot use any of the links within the browser unless you are connected or have arranged for that page to be viewed off-line).

### Views available when creating web pages

FrontPage provides three views of your work when working in Page view:

- Normal
- HTML
- Preview.

By default FrontPage opens in Normal view where you create, develop and amend your web page. By selecting the HTML tab at the bottom of the Page view window, you can view or edit the HTML code created automatically by FrontPage as you build your web page. To see how your web page will look through an Internet browser, select the Preview tab.

## Build-up Exercise 10: Stage 11

**Open** Web 2.

**Open** the home page (Index.htm).

**Position** the cursor immediately below the last button, which should be 'The Interview'.

**Press** the down arrow to give you a line space.

**Type** 'Other useful sites:'.

**Left align** this text.

**Press** the down arrow.

**Type** 'The Microsoft Network'.

**Highlight** the text.

**Press** the right-hand mouse button.

**Select** Hyperlink.

In the field titled URL:, after http://

**Type** www.msn.com.

**Press** OK.

**Press** Save.

**Press** the down arrow.

**Type** 'Nelson Thornes Publishers'.

**Create** a link to the Nelson Thornes website using the following URL:

www.nelsonthornes.com

**Press** Save.

Notice that when a link is created the text turns to a blue colour and is underlined. This usually indicates that the text has a hyperlink property.

**Select** Preview.

**Press** The Microsoft Network link to view this browser page.

This is the default URL for the browser and can be viewed off-line.

**Press** the Nelson Thornes link. Notice that this is not a site that has been set to be viewed off-line and therefore you are asked whether you want to go on-line to view the site.

**Press** Normal view.

**Press** Save.

### E-mail links

More often than not visitors to your website may have additional information they want from you or your organisation. In addition, you may well want feedback from your visitors on what they think about the site or how they think it could be improved and so on. It is extremely helpful and useful to the web designer to have an e-mail link facility that enables this type of feedback to take place. FrontPage provides a hyperlink specifically for you to be able to do this.

## Build-up Exercise 10: Stage 12

**Open** Web 2.

**Open** the home page (Index.htm).

**Position** the cursor at the end of the link line to Nelson Thornes Publishers.

**Press** the down arrow to create a new line.

**Type** the following text: 'Please e-mail us to gain more information on how to be a successful applicant:'.

**Press** the down arrow.

**Select** Insert, Hyperlink... from the main menu (Keyboard shortcut is Ctrl+K).

In the Create Hyperlink dialogue box:

**Select** the icon that looks like a closed envelope .

A second dialogue box appears, like the one in Figure 9.38.

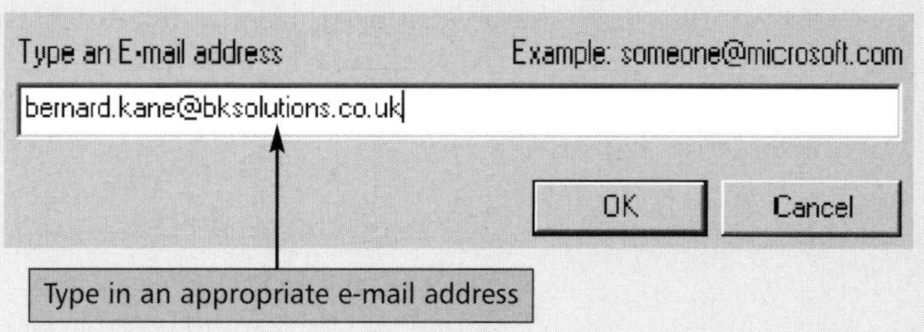

Type an E-mail address      Example: someone@microsoft.com

bernard.kane@bksolutions.co.uk

OK     Cancel

Type in an appropriate e-mail address

**Figure 9.38** *Creating an e-mail link facility*

**Type** in a suitable e-mail address. You can use your own or someone@microsoft.com.

**Press** OK.

Make sure your cursor is at the end of the link text then:

**Press** the down arrow.

**Type** your name and the date under the Mail to: link.

**Centre-align** this text.

**Press** Save to save the changes to the page.

FrontPage will automatically insert a mail to: e-mail link. In the example it looks like this:

mailto:bernard.kane@bksolutions.co.uk.

**Select** Preview.

**Press** the Mail to: link and an e-mail editing page will appear with the address you set for the link.

You should now be able to:

- create an internal website link
- create a link to an external site
- create an e-mail link.

## Managing and printing web pages

### Saving your web

You will have noticed that after completing each Build-up exercise you were asked to press the Save icon. This captures the work or amendments made for the page in the current view. Sometimes, if you have been working on a number of pages during a session it is difficult to remember which pages have been saved and which have not.

FrontPage will always know whether there is unsaved work, and when you close the application it will offer you the opportunity of saving each element of the website. It is always wise to press the OK button when asked if you want to save a piece of work.

### Viewing your web from the browser

Websites are made up of various parts, from folders created by FrontPage itself to folders, pages or other files you have created and imported. You must remember when you get to the stage of publishing your website on the Internet that it is self-contained, and unless the Web knows where to find the elements of the site, it will not work. Always make sure you have imported whatever elements the site needs.

However, you can always see how your website works by viewing it from the Internet Explorer browser (or whatever browser you choose to use). To view your web, open Internet Explorer and in the Address box type the location of your web, which is on your hard disk. In this case the web address is 'E:\My Documents\Mastering New Clait\For CD Only\Unit 9\Webs\Web 2\index.htm'. To view your Web 2, you will need to type in the full address to which you saved your website. Alternatively you can find the home page file in Windows Explorer and by double-clicking on the Index.htm file, the software will recognise that it is a web file and open it. If you look at Figure 9.39 you will see the home page shown in Internet Explorer.

You can now test all the links in the web to ensure that they work.

### Printing your web pages

New CLAIT requires that you print your web pages from the browser. It is not acceptable to print from the Preview mode of the web designing software such as FrontPage. To print a web page, open the web in the browser you are using (in this case it is Internet Explorer). Use File, Print or alternatively use the Print Preview... under the menu options and press Print....

## Build-up Exercise 10: Stage 13

**Open** Web 2 in Internet Explorer (Figure 9.39).

**Print** each of the six pages.

Your pages should look similar to Figure 9.40.

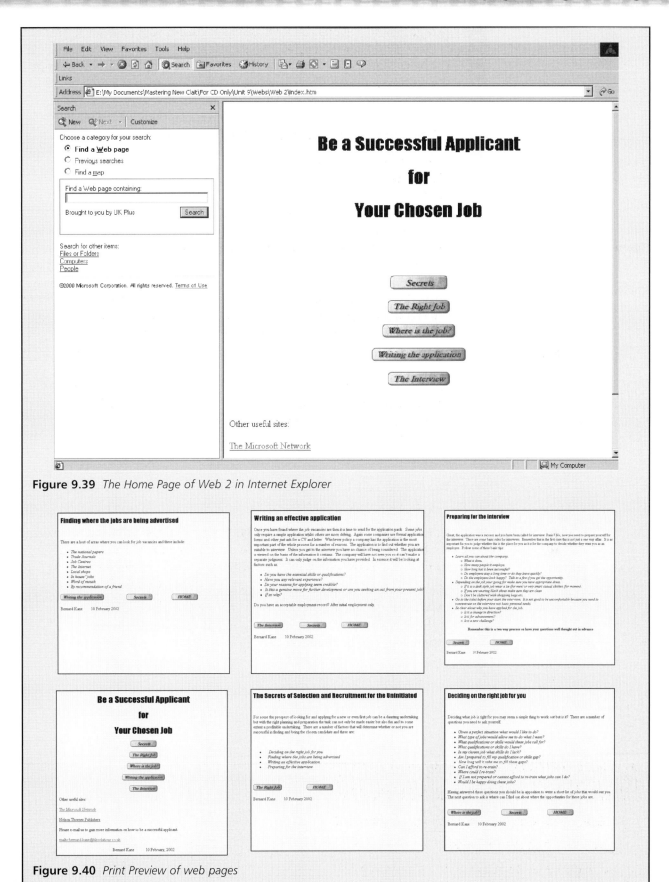

**Figure 9.39** *The Home Page of Web 2 in Internet Explorer*

**Figure 9.40** *Print Preview of web pages*

**New CLAIT**

## Printing your HTML code

For New CLAIT, HTML code can be printed from either the browser or the editing software. To print your HTML code, open the web pages in FrontPage and select the HTML tab as shown in Figure 9.41.

The HTML code will be shown and you can then use either File, Print to print directly or the Print Preview... option if you wish to format the page in a different way other than default. It is usually best to look at your printout through the Print Preview before printing so that you know exactly what is going to print.

**Figure 9.41** *The HTML tab*

---

### Build-up Exercise 10: Stage 14

**Open** Web 2 if it is not already open.

**Print** the HTML code for each page in your web.

**Save** your web files.

---

You should now be able to:

- save your web pages
- view web pages using a browser
- print individual web pages
- print the HTML code for a web page.

You have now completed all the assessment objectives required in New CLAIT for web pages.

Now have a go at Practice Assignment 9. Solutions to this assignment can be found in Part 3.

**Practical assignment 9**

### Unit 9 Web pages using FrontPage

### Scenario

You are the seminar co-ordinator for The Business Café at Peterborough Cathedral. Your boss has asked if you would help him develop a website for the Café to advertise the business on the Web. Luckily some of the work has already been done in preparing the web pages (which can be found on the CD).

| Assessment objectives | Stage | |
|---|---|---|
| 1a | | Your first job is to link a number of pages that have already been prepared. The pages are:<br><br>**About_us.htm**<br>**Location&Facilites.htm**<br>**Facility_charges.htm**<br><br>Open each of these pages. |
| 3a<br>3e<br>5b | 1 | On the **About_us.htm** page after 'Individual rooms, or the whole building, can be booked for either full or half days', insert the following text aligned to the left:<br><br>Location and Facilities<br>Facility Charges<br><br>Save the amended **About_us.htm** page. |
| 3e<br>5b | 2 | (a) On the **Location&Facilities.htm** page on a new line after the text '… in your own room or in the lounge', insert a new line and type 'Home'.<br>(b) On the **Facility_charges.htm** page on a new line after the text 'Other conferencing accessories are available on request', insert a new line and type 'Home'.<br>Save both these pages. |
| 4a<br>4d<br>4e<br>5b | 3 | Create links in the **About_us.htm** page as follows:<br><br>Link the text 'Location and Facilities' to **Location&Facilities.htm**.<br>Link the text 'Facility Charges' to **Facility_charges.htm**.<br>Link the text 'Home' on the 'Location and Facilities' page to the **About_us.htm** page.<br>Link the text 'Home' on the 'Facility Charges' page to the **About_us.htm** page.<br><br>Save the amended pages.<br><br>On the page **About_us.htm** create a new line after the text 'Ring 01733-347239 or' and enter your name.<br>On the page **Location&Facilities.htm** create a new line after the hyperlink text Home and enter your name.<br>On the page **Facility_charges.htm** create a new line after the hyperlink text Home and enter your name.<br><br>Save the changes you have made to each of the web pages.<br><br>Test the links to the pages. |

▶▶

| | | |
|---|---|---|
| 3b 3d 5b | 4 | On the **About_us.htm** page, format the font for 'if ..., ...then' and 'The Business Café' to point 24, italic, bold and set the colour for 'if...' and '...then' to green. |
| | | Format the font of all other text, excluding hyperlinks, which should remain Normal (12 point), to Times New Roman, point 14. |
| | | On the **Location&Facilities.htm** page set the heading 'Location and Facilities' font to point 24, italic and bold and set the colour to green. |
| | | Format the remaining text, excluding the hyperlink, which should remain Normal (12 point), to Times New Roman, point 14. |
| | | On the **Facilities_charges.htm** page set the heading 'Facility Charges' font to point 24, italic and bold and set the colour to green. |
| | | Format the remaining text, excluding the hyperlink, which should remain Normal (12 point), to Times New Roman, point 14. |
| | | Save the changes made to each page. |
| 4c | 5 | After the text 'Ring 01733-347239 or' on **About_us.htm**, insert an e-mail (mail to:) link: |
| | | Business.Cafe@peterborough-cathedral.org.uk |
| 3c | 6 | Change the background colour of each of the three pages: |
| | | **About_us.htm** **Location&Facilities.htm** **Facility_charges.htm** |
| | | Make sure the colour of the background is different from that of the text and that each page has the same colour. |
| 2b | 7 | On the **About_us.htm** page insert the image from the CD called **Café_entrance.jpg**, sizing and positioning it to the right-hand side of the page lying between the 'if...' and '...then' text at the top of the page. |
| | | To the right of the paragraph below headed 'The Business Café' insert and resize the picture **Conference_room.jpg**. |
| | | Save the changes to each of the pages. |
| 2a 3e 5a 5b | 8 | You decide that you need a new page to include some of the catering services offered. Create a new web page. Insert the text file **Menus.txt** from the CD. Save the page with the name **Menus.htm**. |
| 3b 3f 3c 5b | 9 | Format the text 'Finger Buffet' in the default font point size 24, bold and italic. Format the text 'Menu A' and 'Menu B' in the default font point size 14, bold. The remaining text should be formatted in the default text point size 12. Format the background colour as the same as the other three pages. Save the changes made to the page. |

▶▶

| 3a | 10 | Centre the heading and all body text. |
|---|---|---|
| 3e<br>3a<br>4a<br>3f<br>5b | 11 | After the text '£6.50 per delegate' enter the text 'Home'.<br>Create a link to the page **About_us.htm.**<br>After the 'Home' page link enter your name on a new line.<br>Centre align your name.<br>Save the changes made to the page. |
| 2b | 12 | Insert the image from the CD called **Food1.jpg**, sizing and positioning it to the right-hand side of the heading 'Finger Buffet'.<br>Insert the image from the CD called **Food2.jpg**, sizing and positioning it to the left-hand side of the heading 'Finger Buffet'. |
| 3e<br>4a<br>4d | 13 | On the **About_us.htm** page create a new line above the text 'For further information, to view our facilities, or to make a booking please:'.<br>Insert the text 'Menus'.<br>Create a link to the **Menus.htm** page.<br>Save the changes made to the page. |
|  |  | Stage 13 is optional. If you do not intend to create a web file go to Stage 14. |
| 5a<br>2a | 14 | Create a new web file (as opposed to a new web page).<br>Import web pages:<br><br>**About_us.htm**<br>**Location&Facilites.htm**<br>**Facility_charges.htm**<br>**Menus.htm** |
|  |  | Remember pages must be printed from a web browser. The HTML code may be printed from either a browser or the FrontPage editor. |
| 5c | 15 | Print each of the pages:<br><br>**About_us.htm**<br>**Location&Facilites.htm**<br>**Facility_charges.htm**<br>**Menus.htm** |
| 5d | 16 | Print the HTML code for each of the pages:<br><br>**About_us.htm**<br>**Location&Facilites.htm**<br>**Facility_charges.htm**<br>**Menus.htm** |
| 5b<br>5e | 17 | Save all files.<br>Close FrontPage. |

# UNIT 10

# *Presentation graphics using PowerPoint*

In New CLAIT there are five broad learning outcomes for you to attain certification in presentation graphics. Each learning outcome has a number of assessment objectives that will be covered as you progress through the unit. Learning how to use presentation graphics can be great fun and at the same time useful, whether you need the skills at work or for home use.

## What you need to know about presentation graphics for New CLAIT

For New CLAIT you will need to know how to:

### Identify and use presentation graphics software correctly

### Set up a slide layout/template
- Create text areas/text frames.
- Apply a background.
- Insert graphic(s).

### Format text style
- Use specific font sizes.
- Use bullets.
- Apply alignment.
- Apply enhancements.

### Enter and edit data
- Create a new slide.
- Insert text.
- Delete text.
- Replace specified text.
- Promote and demote text.

### Manage and print presentation files
- Create a new presentation.
- Save the document.
- Print out slides.
- Print out audience notes/thumbnails.
- Close a document.

- What are presentation graphics?
- Getting familiar with PowerPoint
- Creating your first presentation
- Introducing the master slide
- Entering text
- Editing and replacing text
- Printing presentation slides, notes and thumbnails

## What are presentation graphics?

If you completed Unit 7 you will have seen how desktop publishing software can help create eye-catching posters, cards and other styles of document that can grab people's attention on a particular topic or subject. Presentations do a similar job in so far as they help to portray information to an audience in a graphical format. Presentations can be given either by using slide transparencies and projecting them using an overhead projector onto a screen, or simply providing an audience with printed copies of the various aspects of a talk.

Have a look at the pictures in Figure 10.1. It shows a number of ways in which presentation software can be used effectively to present information to an audience. In 'A' the presentation is being projected electronically directly from a laptop computer. In 'B' the individual slides of the presentation have been printed on transparencies and projected using an overhead projector. More often than not hard copies of a presentation, as shown in 'C', will be given to delegates or alternatively PowerPoint offers a facility whereby slides can be reproduced together with accompanying notes, as shown in 'D'.

### Some differences between versions of PowerPoint

As you will have seen in other units, different versions of software packages can vary, though normally only slightly. Generally speaking, with Microsoft applications development is gradual and, while new versions often have additional functionality as well as improvements in terms of presentation, usually you will find that the principles regarding their use are pretty much the same. Since most people tend not to buy new software as soon as a new version comes onto the shelves, both here and in other units any major differences between the latest XP and earlier versions will be pointed out to ensure you are able to complete the requirements stipulated by OCR.

For example in PowerPoint 97 and 2000 the first screen you see is a dialogue box, which asks you to select one of four options:

- AutoContent Wizard
- Design Template
- Blank presentation
- Open an existing presentation.

Have a look at Figure 10.2.

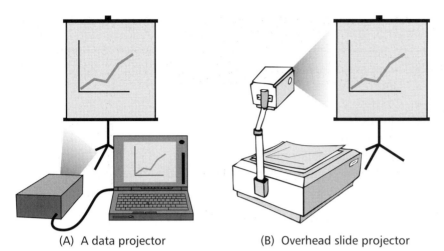

(A) A data projector        (B) Overhead slide projector

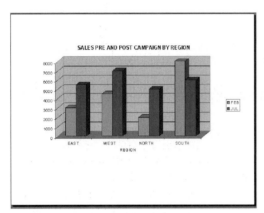

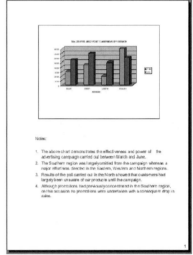

(C) Hard copy without notes        (D) Hard copy with notes

**Figure 10.1** *Using presentation software*

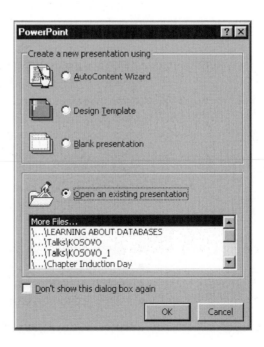

**Figure 10.2** *PowerPoint 97 and 2000: first dialogue box*

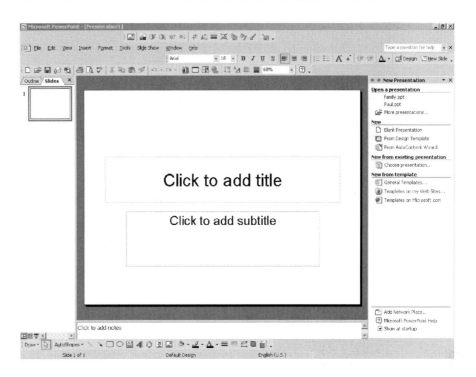

**Figure 10.3** *PowerPoint XP: Title Slide*

By contrast, if you are using PowerPoint XP the program will automatically open with a new presentation and a slide layout called, not surprisingly, 'Title Slide'. Have a look at Figure 10.3.

Don't worry about the various boxes and names at this stage, as all this will become clear as you go through the unit and start using the program. Assuming you are happy with the slide layout proposed by PowerPoint (XP), by closing the New Presentation selection box on the right of the screen or pressing OK on the Layout box shown in earlier versions (Figure 10.4), this will bring you back to a point where both the XP and earlier versions of the program appear more or less the same. Have a look at Figure 10.5.

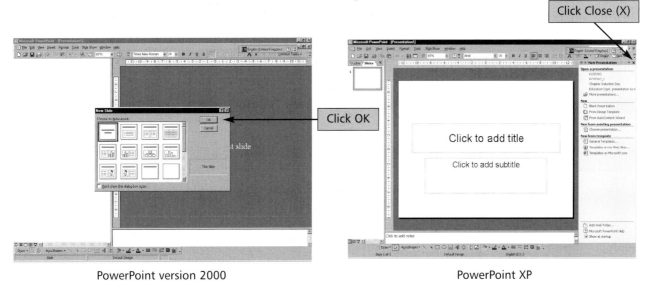

PowerPoint version 2000      PowerPoint XP

**Figure 10.4** *Choosing a slide layout in PowerPoint 2000 and PowerPoint XP*

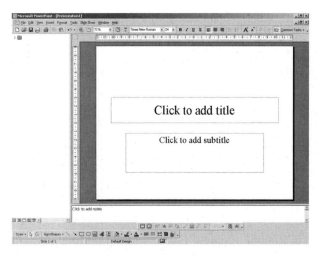

PowerPoint version 2000

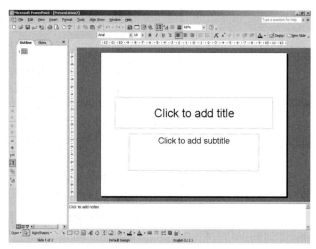

PowerPoint XP

**Figure 10.5** *Choosing the slide layout for PowerPoint 2000 and PowerPoint XP*

Other than the number of toolbars on view there are few differences. In PowerPoint XP, on the window to the left of the screen there is a small picture of a slide with two tabs on the top of the window labelled Outline and Slides. In earlier versions only the Outline view is available. Since this unit only covers the Outline view this is of little consequence.

## Getting familiar with PowerPoint

The basic skills needed for building presentations in PowerPoint have largely been covered in other parts of this book. As with most Windows applications, once you have grasped some of the basic concepts and become familiar with a new screen you will find that gaining presentation skills is both relatively easy and, more importantly, very enjoyable.

### Some concepts

A presentation is normally built up of more than one slide and PowerPoint offers a number of differing layouts. PowerPoint XP offers a few more variations on a theme, but for all practical purposes the options are more or less the same. Sometimes you may well find that none of the layouts offered suit your needs, in which case the software offers complete flexibility to design your own customised slide layouts. For New CLAIT you will use layout templates provided by Microsoft. Have a look at Figure 10.6.

Although the Slide Layout boxes differ in style slightly between versions, overall they are very similar. Slide layouts comprise either text or a combination of text and other graphic- or multimedia-type files. Below are a number of variations you can include within a slide:

- text
- text and pictures
- text and charts
- text and graphs
- pictures and any combination of the above.

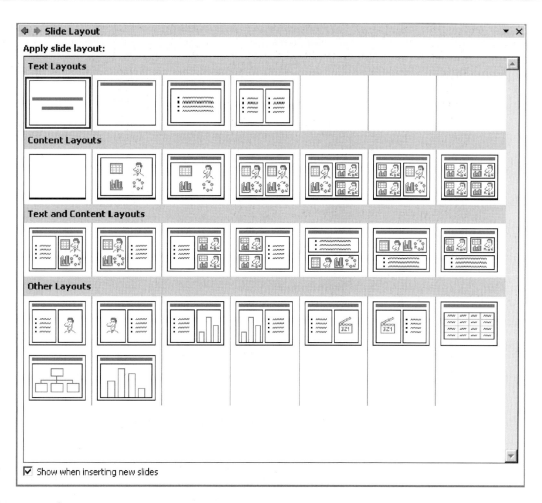

**Figure 10.6** *Slide layout templates, XP version*

The complexity of a slide will also depend on the purpose of the presentation and how it is intended to be delivered. For example, if you are using a computer and data projector it may be appropriate to include sound and/or video files to enhance the impact of the presentation. Clearly it would not make sense to include these if you were simply using transparencies of hard copies of slides.

## The PowerPoint screen

If you have already completed earlier units on Word or Publisher you will find that much of the PowerPoint screen is familiar. Like all Office applications, you have a menu bar, toolbars that can be brought into view, and a work area. In PowerPoint the work area contains the current template being worked on. Have a look at Figure 10.7.

To add a new slide to your presentation simply select Insert on the main menu and then New Slide. A new slide will be inserted together with the Layout selection box on the right of the screen (see Figure 10.8).

**Note:** If you are using an earlier version than XP, after selecting Insert, New Slide, the Layout selection box will appear in the centre of the screen and will disappear once a selection has been made (Figure 10.9).

---

**DESIGN TIP**

Because PowerPoint offers such a wide selection of options for enhancing a presentation you should avoid trying to include too many text styles, colours or other features in one presentation. An over-busy presentation can be irritating to your audience. Keep your presentation as simple as is necessary to get the message across effectively.

Menu bar  Toolbar  Slide  Text box

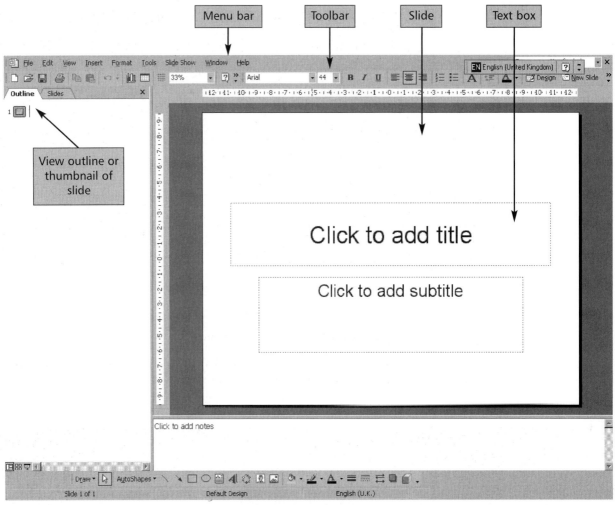

View outline or thumbnail of slide

Click to add title

Click to add subtitle

Click to add notes

**Figure 10.7** *The PowerPoint screen*

To insert a new slide select Insert, New Slide

New Slide          Ctrl+M
Duplicate Slide
Slide Number
Date and Time...
Symbol...
Comment
Slides from Files...
Slides from Outline...
Picture
Diagram...
Text Box
Movies and Sounds
Chart...
Table...
Object...
Hyperlink...          Ctrl+K

Click to add title

• Click to add text

**Figure 10.8** *Inserting a new slide*

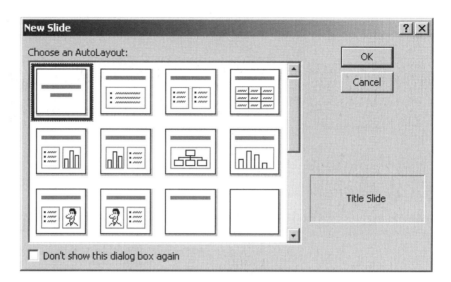

**Figure 10.9** *Choosing an AutoLayout, pre-XP version*

## Creating your first presentation

Now try and create a very simple presentation to help you get familiar with the way that PowerPoint works.

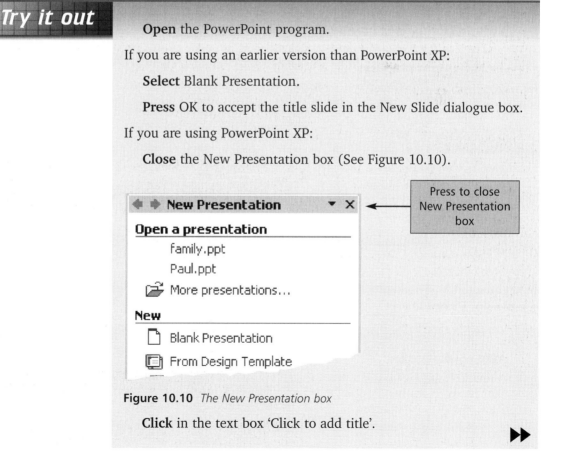

**Try it out**

**Open** the PowerPoint program.

If you are using an earlier version than PowerPoint XP:

**Select** Blank Presentation.

**Press** OK to accept the title slide in the New Slide dialogue box.

If you are using PowerPoint XP:

**Close** the New Presentation box (See Figure 10.10).

**Figure 10.10** *The New Presentation box*

**Click** in the text box 'Click to add title'.

When you see the cursor flashing:

**Enter** the following heading: MY FIRST PRESENTATION.

**Click** in the text box 'Click to add subtitle'.

**Enter** the following subtitle: By [enter your name].

**Click** outside the text boxes in a blank area of the screen for the text to be accepted.

Your presentation should now look like Figure 10.11.

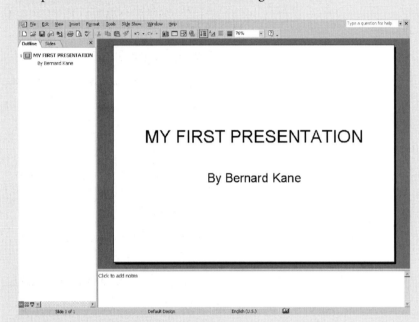

**Figure 10.11** *Creating a presentation*

### TEXT TIP

Notice how on the left of the window you can see an outline of the slides. In PowerPoint XP you will see two tabs. The one named Slides is for viewing a thumbnail of the slide and the other is for viewing the text outline. Once you have inserted a new slide you can type the text for the slide in the outline box and it will automatically appear on the slide itself. The first line you type will go into the heading frame. By pressing the Ctrl+Enter key the cursor will tab to the next text frame.

You are now going to insert a new slide with a different layout.

On the main menu:

**Select** Insert, New Slide.

The Slide Layout dialogue will appear.

**Select** the layout with a heading and bullets.

(Note: This is called 'bullet text' in 98 and 2000 versions and 'title and text' in the XP version.)

**Click** in the heading text frame and type: What I will learn in this unit.

**Click** in the second text box and type the following bullet points:

- How to set up a slide layout
- How to format text
- How to enter and edit data
- How to manage and print presentations

**Click** outside the text frame.

You have now created two slides.

**Insert** a new slide with the title and text layout (or bulleted list for earlier versions).

**Click** in the outline box on the left of the screen next to the new slide image.

**Enter** the following text: Applications I have learnt.

Notice how the heading text also appears in the slide.

**Press** Crtl+Enter (a bullet point should appear under the heading text).

**Type** in the following bullet points:

- Word
- Access
- Publisher
- Excel
- Internet Express and Explorer
- PowerPoint
- FrontPage

These bullet points should now have appeared in the second frame on the slide.

**Save** your presentation as Exercise_1.

## Viewing your presentation

As you have already seen, slides can be presented in a variety of ways, from hard copy to projection using an overhead projector or data projector. In addition, you can view your presentation on the screen. Viewing a presentation, or an individual slide, on the screen is a handy way of checking the presentation.

To view a presentation from the beginning you need to ensure the first slide is showing on the screen. There are a number of ways to return to the first slide. You can use the scroll bar or click on the Slide Sorter View icon 𝄜. Double-clicking on the first slide or simply clicking on the slide you want to start from and then selecting Normal from View on the main menu will bring the desired slide on the screen in edit mode. The presentation can then be viewed by selecting Slide Show followed by View Show on the menu or clicking on the Slide Show icon at the bottom left of the screen 🖵. Now have a go at viewing your presentation. To move from one slide to the next press the left-hand mouse button.

**Try it out**

**Open** Exercise_1.

**Click** on the Slide Sorter icon on the bottom left of the screen and the screen should look like Figure 10.12.

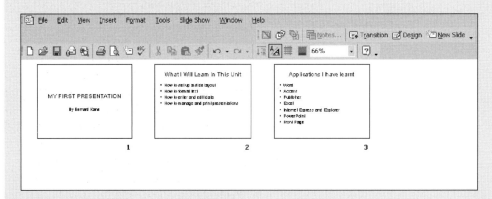

**Figure 10.12** *My First Presentation screen*

**Select** Slide 1.

**Click** on the Slide Show icon on the bottom left of the screen (or select View Show from Slide Show on the menu bar).

**Press** the left mouse button to move through the presentation.

At the end of the presentation you will see a black screen with a notice telling you that you are at the end of the slide show.

**Press** the Esc key (or click on the screen) to return to the slide sorter.

**Save** your presentation.

**Close** Exercise_1.

You should now be able to:

- understand the basic concepts of building a presentation
- understand the PowerPoint screen
- create a simple presentation
- view a presentation.

## Introducing the master slide

A very important aspect of presentation design is the need for consistency. For New CLAIT you are expected to understand the importance of consistency within a slide show and one of the easiest ways to ensure this is to use the master slide. This slide forms the template for your whole presentation and will ensure that text at all levels (i.e. headings, sub-headings, bullet text, body text) is consistent. So, for example, if you want your headings in a sans-serif font (see page 238) and a size of 36 points, this can be set in the master slide. Once you have set this in the master slide, headings in each slide of your presentation will follow those in the master slide by default. You can, of course, change this manually for each slide if needed. Many organisations have a corporate style for all their correspondence and publicity material. This is often referred to as the house style. In New CLAIT you will be asked to set up your presentation according to a certain house style. The house style will dictate the style required for each layout of slide. For example, you may be asked to ensure that the font is bold or italic, text is left aligned or centred, some text is indented, and so on.

### Setting up the master slide

First have a look at the master slide in PowerPoint. To view the master slide go to View, Master, Slide Master on the main menu. The master slide does not look that much different from a normal slide layout. However, once set up this will become the template style for all the slides in your current presentation.

Have a look at Figure 10.13.

**Figure 10.13** *Setting up the master slide template*

There are a number of specific areas in the basic template you can change:

- titles or headings
- object (and text levels)
- date, footer and number boxes.

You can also add additional text boxes or graphics to the master slide where you want these to appear on every slide. If you completed the desktop publishing unit you will recall that a publication had a foreground and a background and that anything on the background was carried forward to each page of the publication. The master slide can be viewed as the equivalent to the background.

### Heading or title

By clicking in the heading or title text frame at the top of the master slide you can set the style, size, colour, weight or alignment of the font required for each heading or title.

### Object (and text levels)

In the main body of each slide, in addition to being able to set the format and alignment of the font, you can set a number of levels which can then be selected as you add text to the slide. For example, you may not want to have all the levels as bullet points. Each can be changed individually in the slide itself, but once the master is set the levels can be selected based on the defaults set up in the master slide. If this is confusing it will become clear once you go through an exercise.

### Date, footer and number boxes

At the bottom of the master slide are specific areas for date fields, footers or numbers. In the footer, for example, you might want to put your name or a company logo.

## Build-up Exercise 11: Stage 1

*Scenario*

You are the Secretary of the Longhurst Model Club. The President of the club has been asked to give a talk to the local youth club on the benefits of modelling and how to get started. He has heard how easy it can be to create a slide presentation using PowerPoint. He has no idea himself how to use this program but knows you do and has asked if you would do a few transparencies for him based on his notes.

**Create** a new presentation with a title slide as the first slide layout.

**Open** the master slide.

### GENERAL TIP

Use the menu options <u>V</u>iew, <u>M</u>aster, <u>S</u>lide Master.

> **Click** in the title area text frame. The default title 'Click to edit Master title style' should be highlighted when you click on the text.

Note: Office 2000 users will find that clicking on the text frame only selects the frame. The text does not need to be highlighted in the title frame to change the font or format.

Using Format, Font on the main menu:

> **Select** a different sans-serif font (e.g. Impact).
>
> **Select** Regular as the style.
>
> **Select** 48 as the size.
>
> **Click** in the 'Object area for Autolayouts'.
>
> **Click** on the first level where it says 'Click to edit Master text styles'.

Note: In Office 2000 the text will not be highlighted by clicking on each level. To change the font or format, first highlight the text for each level.

> **Select** a serif font (Dutch801 Rm BT or Times New Roman).
>
> **Type** 30 in the Font Size box.
>
> **Press** Enter.
>
> **Click** on the second level text to highlight it.
>
> **Select** the same font as you did for the first level.
>
> **Select** 24 for the font size.
>
> **Click** on the third level text.
>
> **Select** a different sans-serif font from the one displayed (e.g. Tahoma or similar).
>
> **Select** 20 for the font size.
>
> **Select** 16 for the fourth level font. Leave the font type as the default.
>
> **Select** 14 as the fifth level font. Leave the font type as the default.
>
> **Close** the master slide.

Note: In Office XP the master slide can be closed by clicking on the Close Master View toolbar button or using the View, Normal options on the main menu. In Office 2000, close the mini toolbar which appears on the screen.

> **Save** your presentation with the name 'Model_Building'.

## Master slide footers

The Date, Footer and Number boxes at the bottom of the master slide are all footers and can be formatted either individually or by using the Header and Footer dialogue (see Figure 10.14).

This box is accessed by using View, Header and Footer... on the main menu or clicking the Header and Footer icon on the toolbar (XP version only).

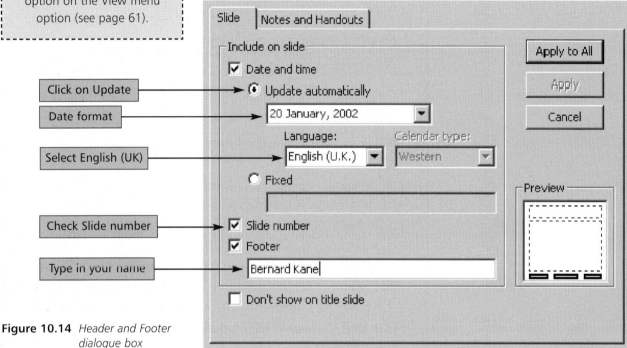

**Figure 10.14** *Header and Footer dialogue box*

In the Header and Footer box there are a number of options you are interested in:

- date and time
- language
- slide number
- footer.

Selecting the Update Automatically button will ensure that whenever you run your presentation the current date will be shown on the slide.

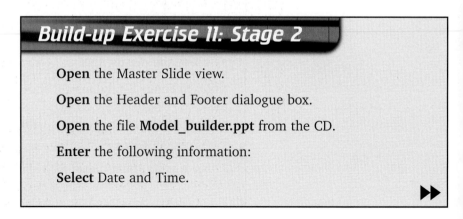

### Build-up Exercise II: Stage 2

**Open** the Master Slide view.

**Open** the Header and Footer dialogue box.

**Open** the file **Model_builder.ppt** from the CD.

**Enter** the following information:

**Select** Date and Time.

**Select** date format, as shown in Figure 10.14.

**Select** Language as English (UK).

**Select** Slide number.

**Select** Footer and type in your name.

**Press** Apply to All.

Note: PowerPoint offers you the opportunity to apply the headers and footers required to all the slides. The single Apply button is disabled in the master slide since the master formats apply to each slide in the presentation. You do, however, have the option of omitting the headers and footers from the title slide.

**Select** each of the text boxes (date area, footer area and number area).

Using the Font icon options on the toolbar:

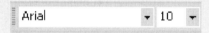

**Change** the font size to 10.

**Close** the master slide.

Notice how the first slide reflects the changes you have made in the master slide, with the new font and the addition of the date, name and slide number at the bottom.

**Save** your presentation.

You should now be able to:

- understand what the master slide is and why it is used
- set up a master slide
- set up headers and footers in a master slide

New CLAIT

## Master slide graphics and backgrounds

For New CLAIT you will need to understand how to insert graphics into a presentation and also how to use backgrounds on slides. Neither of these skills is particularly difficult and indeed learning how to use backgrounds and playing with graphics can be a lot of fun.

First you will learn how to insert an image from a file. Remember that any graphics file inserted on the master slide will be reproduced on every slide in your presentation, whereas a graphic inserted directly into an individual slide will only appear on that particular slide.

Inserting images into your presentation is achieved by either using the options on the main menu or using the From File or Clip Art icon on the toolbox. The steps you need to take to insert an image are, first,

**GENERAL TIP**

To insert a new slide use Insert, New Slide from the main menu.

to decide whether it needs to be placed on the master slide or will apply only to an individual slide. Once this decision has been made select Insert, Picture and then From File... from the menu and highlight the image to be used. Finally press the Insert button as shown in Figure 10.15a. The Insert Picture dialogue box has a number of views available and therefore your box may differ slightly depending on what view has been selected. For users of Office 2000 the Insert dialogue box is slightly different from the XP version and is shown in Figure 10.15b.

Select the folder containing the required image

Select the required image

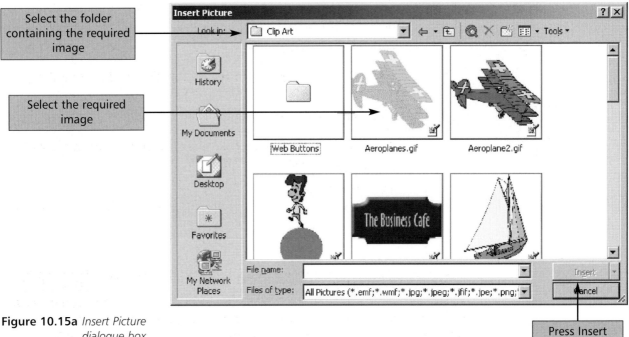

Press Insert

**Figure 10.15a** *Insert Picture dialogue box*

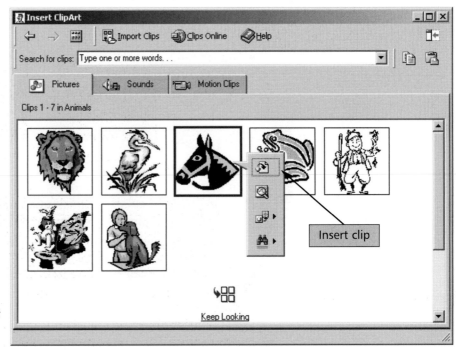

Insert clip

**Figure 10.15b** *Office 2000 Insert Clip Art dialogue box*

## Try it out

**Create** a blank presentation.

**Accept** the default title layout.

**Open** the master slide.

**Insert Aeroplane2.gif** from the CD.

**Place** the image in the top right-hand corner of the master slide.

**Close** the master slide.

**Insert** a new slide.

**Save** your presentation as Exercise_2.

Notice how your aeroplane image appears automatically on the new slide.

**Open** the Master Slide view.

**Resize** the image **Aeroplane2.gif** so that it is approximately half the size of the original image.

**Save** your presentation.

**New CLAIT**

### Slide backgrounds

You can further enhance your presentation by incorporating a colourful background to each slide. PowerPoint offers a wide variety of backgrounds for you to choose from. Once you get more familiar with the software you can also create your own personalised backgrounds. Backgrounds come in a variety of different styles. Have a look at Figure 10.16a.

Single colour

Gradient colour

Texture

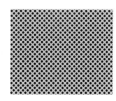
Pattern

Picture

**Figure 10.16a** *Background styles*

The style of background you choose is entirely a matter of personal preference. However, whatever you choose you should take account of

**RESIZING TIP**

To resize an image click on the image to be resized using the left-hand mouse button. When the resize or drag handle appears, click on a corner handle and drag the image to the required size.

To resize an image but keep the centre of the image in the same position, hold down the Crtl key as the image is resized.

the content of the presentation and in particular make sure that the font can always be clearly seen over the background colour. It would, after all, be a shame to spoil a perfectly good presentation by having a background that was too busy, or where the colour was so dark (or light) that the impact of what you were actually trying to say was lost.

It is also advisable, and indeed a requirement for New CLAIT, to maintain consistency throughout your presentation by setting the background in the master slide. This will ensure that the same background appears in every slide of your presentation. However, OCR recognises that not all centres will have colour printing facilities for students to use, and therefore it is more than likely that for assignment work you will only be required to set a background as white. As you will see later, you can always change the default master slide settings for any objects in a slide (see Figure 10.16b). To give you experience and practice in setting different backgrounds, the following exercise allows you to experiment with coloured backgrounds.

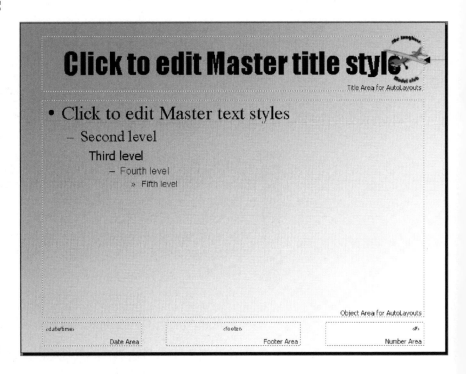

**Figure 10.16b** *Click to edit default master slide settings*

In the previous Try it out exercise you placed a picture of an aeroplane in the top right-hand corner of the slide. What background would be appropriate?

To set the background for a slide or complete presentation, use Format, Background on the main menu. A Background dialogue box appears, as shown in Figure 10.17 (page 375).
Decide whether the background is to be a single colour or whether you will use a style offered through the Fill Effects… option in the drop-down list. If you want to use a single colour you can either choose one of the colours in the selection offered or press the More Colours… option and use the Colours box to customise the background colour as shown in Figure 10.18.

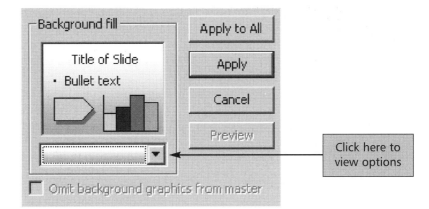

**Figure 10.17** *Background dialogue box*

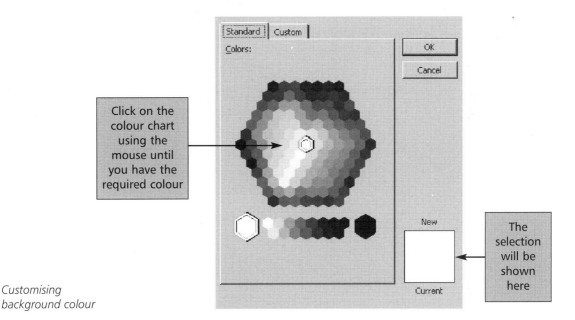

**Figure 10.18** *Customising background colour*

Fill effects offer you a range of options, from a one- or two-colour graded effect to a textured or patterned effect. Alternatively, you can insert a picture you created or one from a selected source. Have a look at Figure 10.16a again. Having selected one of the options, the Apply button is pressed and the results can be reviewed. (Note: If you were setting the background for an individual slide and not the master slide, you have the choice of applying to that slide or all the slides in the presentation.)

**Try it out**

**Open** Exercise_2 if it is not already open.

**Go to** the master slide.

**Select** Format, Background from the main menu.

▶▶

**Select** Fill Effects....

**Select** Two colours.

**Select** Horizontal from Shading Styles.

**Press** OK and the Apply to All button.

Note: Pressing the Apply to All button will override any colour that has been applied to a single slide.

**Close** the master slide.

This sequence is shown in Figure 10.19 below.

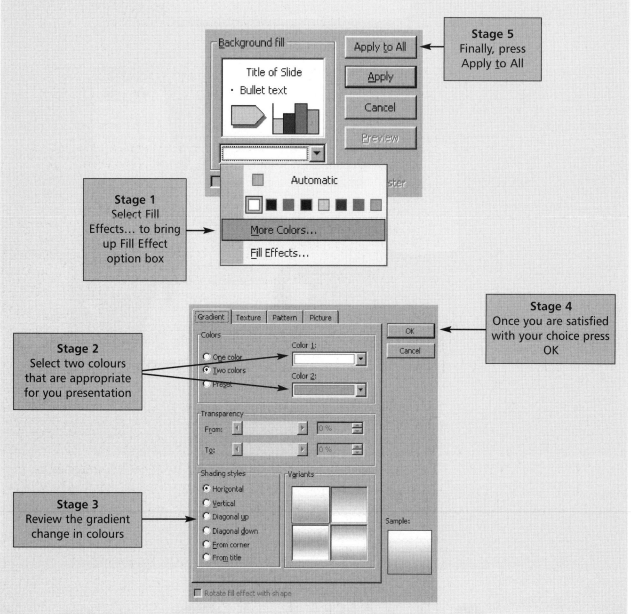

**Figure 10.19** *Formatting the background*

Your background should now look similar to Figure 10.20.

**Figure 10.20** *Preview background*

**Save** the presentation.

Having already inserted a second slide into the presentation you can see that both slides have the same background. Now return to the Build-up exercise.

## Build-up Exercise 11: Stage 3

**Open** the file **Model_builder.ppt** from the CD.

**Open** the Master Slide view.

**Insert** the image **Club_logo.gif** from the CD.

**Position** the image in the top right-hand corner of the master slide.

**Select** Background from the Format menu.

**Select** Fill Effects.

**Select** Two colours in the Colours box (first colour should be white and second colour a sky blue).

**Select** Diagonal up from the Shading Styles box.

**Select** in the Variants box the choice of blue in the top-left corner moving to white in the bottom-right corner.

**Press** OK and the Apply button.

**Close** the master slide.

Your first slide should look similar to Figure 10.21.

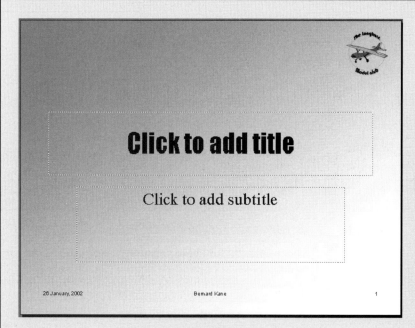

**Figure 10.21** *Formatting your first slide*

Save your presentation as Model_Building.

You should now be able to:

- insert an image into a slide or master slide
- move an image's position
- resize an image
- format a slide background.

## Entering text

So far you have concentrated on the format and layout of a presentation using the master slide as the template for all the slides in the presentation.

Since all formats on the master slide will be repeated on every slide in the presentation, you will need to know how to insert, delete and replace text on individual slides. You will also be expected to know how to use bullet point frames in a slide and then promote or demote text as appropriate.

You have already seen that PowerPoint offers a range of slide layouts to help build up a presentation (See Figures 10.6 and 10.9). It is beyond the scope of this book to review all of them but you should experiment with some of the layouts to get familiar with the options they offer to enhance your presentation. You will, however, look at some of those that are most commonly used; the title slide; the title and text slide ('bulleted list' for users of PowerPoint 98 or 2000); the title, text and clip art slide ('text & clip art' for users of PowerPoint 98 or 2000).

### The title slide

Most presentations will start with an opening title slide. This will show the audience the subject of the presentation and possibly the name of the presenter or the organisation involved. In Exercise_1 you created a simple slide and then viewed the presentation. You are now going through a similar exercise to reinforce what you learnt at the beginning of this unit. Try setting up a title slide.

**Try it out**

**Create** a new presentation and accept or select the title slide as the first slide.

**Click** on the text frame that says 'Click to add title'.

When you see the cursor flashing and waiting for you to enter text:

**Enter** the following heading: LEARNING HOW TO USE POWERPOINT.

**Click** on the text frame that says 'Click to add subtitle'.

**Enter** the following subtitle: An application in Microsoft Office.

**Click** outside the frame for the text to be accepted.

**Save** your presentation as Exercise_3.

### The title and text slide

Each slide in a presentation will normally, but not necessarily always, have a title at the top of the slide. The remaining data can be in any number of formats but one very common layout is 'title and text' where the text element of the slide is in bullet point format. The principle for using this slide layout is very much the same for a wordprocessed document. Once you have clicked on the 'Click to add text' frame you will notice a bullet has been inserted and the cursor is flashing alongside waiting for text to be input. Once you have entered the text for the first bullet point simply press Enter and a second bullet point will be inserted.

The easiest way of learning how to do this is to try it out.

**Try it out**

**Open** Exercise_3.

**Insert** a new slide based on the title and text layout (bulleted list for 98 and 2000 users).

**Click** on the title text frame and add the following text: The Benefits of PowerPoint.

**Click** on the frame that says 'Click to add text'.

**Enter** the following bullet points:

- Creation of presentations made easy
- Variety of layouts and styles
- Point and click technology
- Professional finishes

**Save** your presentation.

## The title, text and clip art slide

The title, text and clip art slide layout is used in very much the same way as the title and text slide layout. The main difference is that the text element is narrower and there is an additional frame for you to add a clip art image or picture file. The title and bullet text is inserted in exactly the same way as before. To add an image, double-click on the clip art frame. For PowerPoint XP users, you will be shown a picture box that includes all your images, whether they are clip art pictures that came with the software or pictures you have saved on your hard disk. For users of PowerPoint 98 or 2000, you will see the traditional Clip Art dialogue box where you can select an image from the Gallery or alternatively import your own image file to insert.

### Try it out

**Open** Exercise_3 if it is not already open.

**Insert** a new slide based on the title, text and clip art layout.

**Enter** the following text for the heading: Creating your first presentation.

**Enter** the following bullet points in the appropriate text frame (see Figure 10.22):

- Select blank presentation
- Enter a title
- Enter a subtitle
- Insert a new slide
- Enter title and text
- Insert a new slide with a graphics frame
- Enter title, text and image.

**RESIZING TIP**

Notice how PowerPoint will automatically word wrap the text if the bullet point is too long for the frame size. If you don't want to bunch your text up like this you can resize the text frame. To resize the frame, simply click on the frame itself. When you see the drag handles select one and drag the frame to the desired size (see Figure 10.22).

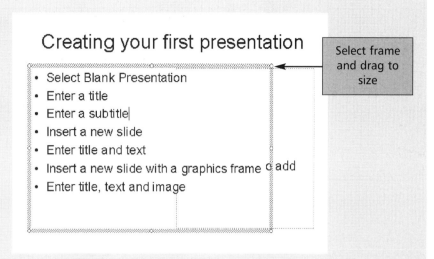

**Figure 10.22** *Resizing the frame*

**Double-click** on the clip art frame.

**Insert** the **PowerPoint.gif** image from the CD.

Note: If you have resized your text frame make sure that the text does not overlap the image. If necessary, resize the frame again to ensure it is clear of the image.

Your slide should now look similar (depending on which image you selected) to Figure 10.23.

**Figure 10.23** *The finished slide*

If necessary, the image can be resized and repositioned using the techniques you covered earlier in this unit.

**Save** your presentation.

New CLAIT

## Editing and replacing text

Earlier you set up a master slide and changed some of the defaults in terms of font size and style, and various other features. Whenever you start a new presentation it will be based on Microsoft's default settings for PowerPoint. You can, of course, set up your own templates and save them for use in other presentations but again this goes beyond the requirements for New CLAIT. Remember that in New CLAIT a key objective is to ensure consistency in terms of font style and slide layout. However, the content of your slides, providing it is not part of the master slide, can be changed or edited, and being able to edit or replace specific text is a New CLAIT objective.

### Editing text

Editing text is done in very much the same way as in a normal wordprocessing document. The text to be edited or deleted is first highlighted and the relevant editing completed. Alternatively you can place the cursor in front of the text to be altered and press the Delete button to remove the text. New text can then be entered. A third way is to place the cursor at the end of the text and press the backspace key, which will have the same effect.

**Try it out**

Open Exercise_3.

**Edit** the first bullet point on Slide 3 so that it reads: Open PowerPoint. Highlight the text and then either overtype the highlighted text or press the Delete key and type in the new text.

- **Open PowerPoint**

**Insert** a new bullet point after the first bullet point.

**Enter** the following text: Accept the default title slide. Do this by placing the cursor at the end of the first bullet point and press Enter.

New CLAIT

### Replacing text

You may recall, if you completed the wordprocessing unit, that text can be replaced by using the Replace… function found on the Edit item of the main menu. PowerPoint has exactly the same function available. Once this is selected the dialogue box shown in Figure 10.24 (page 383) appears.

The text to be found and replaced is entered in the top box Find what: and the text which will replace it is put in the bottom box

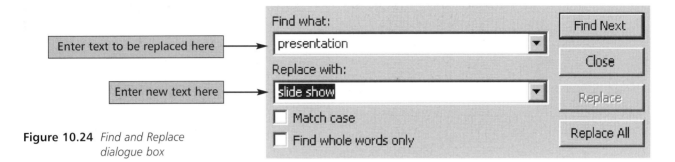

Enter text to be replaced here →

Enter new text here →

**Figure 10.24** *Find and Replace dialogue box*

Replace with:. The user has the choice of either replacing each occurrence one by one by pressing the Find Next button or replacing all occurrences at once using the Replace All button. Once PowerPoint has found all the occurrences of the word or phrase you will see the dialogue box shown in Figure 10.25.

**Figure 10.25** *The Find and Replace feature*

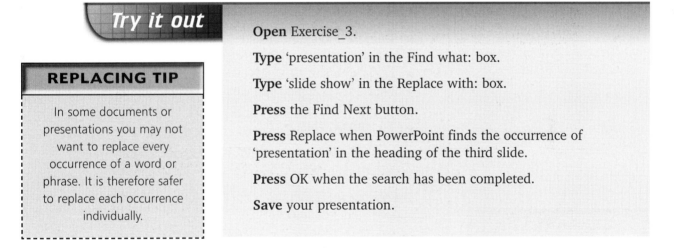

**Try it out**

**Open** Exercise_3.

**Type** 'presentation' in the Find what: box.

**Type** 'slide show' in the Replace with: box.

**Press** the Find Next button.

**Press** Replace when PowerPoint finds the occurrence of 'presentation' in the heading of the third slide.

**Press** OK when the search has been completed.

**Save** your presentation.

**REPLACING TIP**

In some documents or presentations you may not want to replace every occurrence of a word or phrase. It is therefore safer to replace each occurrence individually.

Now return to the Build-up exercise and put some of these newly learnt skills to the test in the model club's presentation.

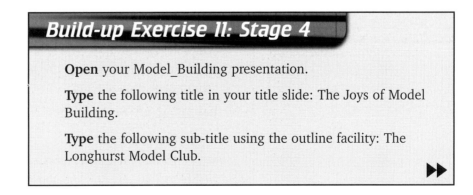

**Build-up Exercise 11: Stage 4**

**Open** your Model_Building presentation.

**Type** the following title in your title slide: The Joys of Model Building.

**Type** the following sub-title using the outline facility: The Longhurst Model Club.

▶▶

**Insert** a new slide based on the title and text slide layout (or bulleted list depending on the version of your software).

**Type** the following heading by clicking on the frame and typing directly in the text box: Six Reasons to be a Modeller.

Note: If you find that the image you inserted on the master slide is obscured by the text heading, return to the master slide and alter the position or size of the image.

**Enter** the following bullet points into the text box:

- Modelling is creative and constructive
- Modelling is relaxing and reduces stress
- Modelling is challenging and rewarding
- Modelling is educational and stimulating
- Modelling helps improve your social life
- Modelling can be profitable

**Insert** a new slide based on the title, text and clip art layout.

**Type** the following heading: Getting started on your first model.

**Enter** the following bullet points in the bullet text frame:

- Don't be too ambitious
- Choose a simple model to start with
- Make sure you have the proper tools
- Find a space where you can do your modelling
- Read all the instructions carefully
- Be patient, don't rush.

**Replace** the word 'modelling' with 'model making' (eight occurrences in all).

**Delete** the second bullet point in the third slide 'Choose a simple model to start with'.

**Insert** the following text at the beginning of the last bullet point: Have fun but.

**Change** the capital 'B' of 'Be patient' to lower case.

**Insert** the picture **Boat1.gif** from the CD.

**Resize** the boat so that it is approximately twice the original size and position it so that it is in the bottom right of the slide. Ensure that none of the text in the bullet list is obscured by the picture.

**Resize** the text frame so that each bullet point is on one line.

**Save** your presentation.

---

### GENERAL TIP

After highlighting and deleting the text, press the Backspace key to remove the bullet point and a second time to remove the line space.

## Promoting and demoting text

When you set up your master slide you will remember that the text frame had a number of levels and each level had different font sizes. When you are creating a presentation it can be very useful to be able to use the various levels without the need to re-format the text every time you want to make a change. Promoting and demoting text is carried out in exactly the same way. Type in the text and then select the text to be promoted or demoted. Using the Promote and Demote icons from the outlining toolbar, the text level can be changed by clicking on the right button to promote or left button to demote. Have a look at Figure 10.26.

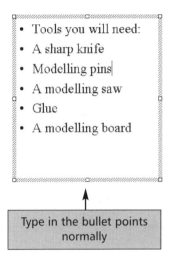

Type in the bullet points normally

Highlight the text to be demoted or promoted

Press the demote or promote arrow on the toolbar

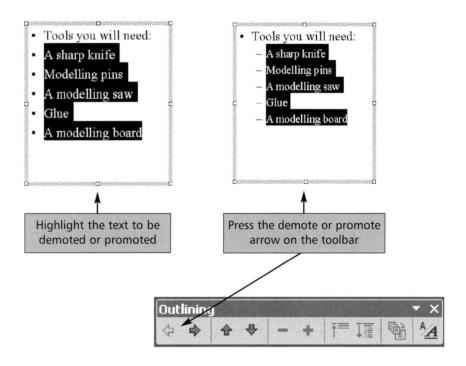

**Figure 10.26** *Using the Promote and Demote icons*

As is the case with most functions in the Office suite of applications, you can achieve the same result in a variety of different ways. For example, once the text has been highlighted you can also use the Tab key or the Promote/Demote icon ⬅ ➡ to demote text. (If only one bullet point is to be promoted/demoted, there is no need to highlight the text.) Alternatively, you can select the text in the Outline view (see the Text Tip on page 364) and use either the Tab key or the indent arrows on the formatting toolbar. Note that if the icon is not on the formatting toolbar, you can place it there using Customise… from the View, Toolbars option on the menu.

## Build-up Exercise 11: Stage 5

**Open** the Model_Building presentation.

After the bullet point 'Make sure you have the proper tools' on slide 3:

**Insert** the following new bullet points:

- A sharp knife
- Modelling pins
- Glue.

**Highlight** these three bullet points.

**Press** the demote arrow (the demote arrow is the one that points to the right).

**Resize** the boat image so that it does not obscure any text.

**Save** your presentation.

### Aligning and enhancing text

You may well have come across the term alignment in other parts of this book. The principles for aligning text are the same in PowerPoint as in other applications. Text is left aligned, right aligned, centre aligned (or in the case of a paragraph of text, justified). Generally speaking, text and titles in presentations are left aligned but there may well be occasions when this is not what you want.

Normally you would set up your alignment and text format in the master slide to ensure you had consistency across all slides. As you saw earlier, you can devise your own personal styles for a presentation or, in the case of, say, a company, you may be told what the house style for that organisation is. Table 10.1 is a typical way of informing the designer what the relevant house style should look like.

**Table 10.1** *Presentation of house style*

| Frame | Style | Emphasis | Font size | Font type | Bullets | Alignment |
|-------|-------|----------|-----------|-----------|---------|-----------|
| Title | Title | Bold | 40 | Sans-serif | No | Left |
| Main | 1st level | Bold | 30 | Sans-serif | Yes | Left |
| Main | 2nd level | None | 20 | Serif | Yes | Left |
| Main | 3rd level | Italic | 14 | Serif | No | Centre |

By transposing these instructions into the master slide it would look like Figure 10.27:

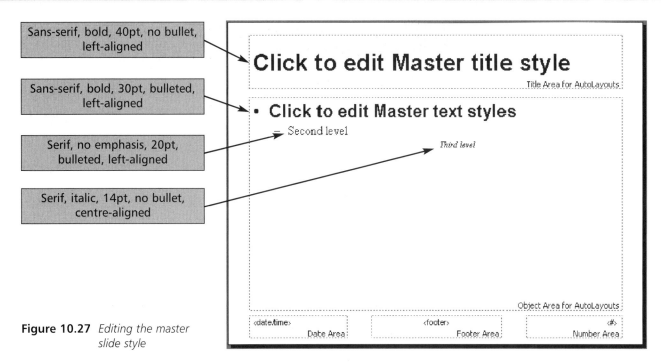

Sans-serif, bold, 40pt, no bullet, left-aligned

Sans-serif, bold, 30pt, bulleted, left-aligned

Serif, no emphasis, 20pt, bulleted, left-aligned

Serif, italic, 14pt, no bullet, centre-aligned

**Figure 10.27** *Editing the master slide style*

You should now be able to:

- enter text into text boxes on slides
- insert bullet points into a slide
- resize a text frame
- edit and replace text
- promote and demote text
- align and emphasise text.

## Build-up Exercise 11: Stage 6

### Scenario

Having looked at your presentation, the President of the club has asked if you can make a few changes to its format. First he would like all the headings aligned to the left and underlined. Also he would like the heading slightly smaller. He would like the first level text (not the titles) to be in italic and bold.

**Open** the Model_Building presentation.

**Open** the master slide.

**Select** the main heading and make sure it is left-aligned and underlined. To underline the text first highlight it and then press the Underline icon on the toolbar.

**Change** the title line font to 40.

**Change** the first level text to italic font and embolden it. To embolden the line, select it and press the Bold icon on the toolbar.

**Save** your presentation.

**New CLAIT**

### Creating new text frames

In addition to changing the default settings of text frames already present in the master slide, you can also create new frames. Inserting a text frame in PowerPoint is basically the same as inserting a text frame in any other Office application. First you create the frame using the Text Box tool on the drawing toolbar [⬚]. To create the frame click on the Text Box tool, move your cursor over the master or other slide where the box is to be positioned and click and hold the left-hand mouse button. The pointer will change shape to a cross wire (+). Dragging with the mouse, the box can be drawn to the required shape and size. When the mouse button is released the cursor will start flashing in the box to await the input of text (Figure 10.28).

Cursor will flash to await input of text

**Figure 10.28** *Creating new text frames*

After the text has been inserted the text and box style can be re-formatted. To change the text's font, select the text box and then change the font style and/or its size by using the Font box on the formatting toolbar (Figure 10.29). You can, of course, also use Format, Font... on the main menu.

Select font and font size

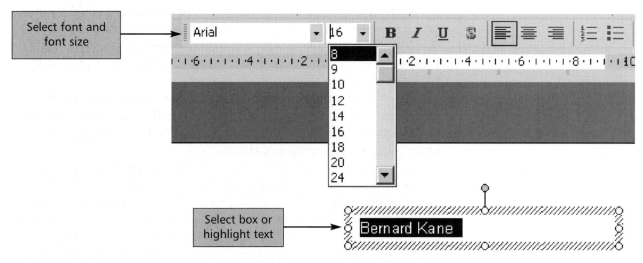

Select box or highlight text

**Figure 10.29** *Choosing font and font size*

Remember that a frame (or any object) placed on the master slide will be seen on all slides in the presentation. An object drawn on an individual slide will only be seen on that particular slide.

## Build-up Exercise II: Stage 7

*Scenario*

The President of the club has reminded you that it would be a good idea to have the club's address and telephone number on each slide and has asked if this can be done.

**Open** your Model_Building presentation.

**Open** the Master Slide view.

**Insert** a text box in the bottom left-hand corner of the master slide and enter the following text:

14 St Princes Street – Tel: 01732-566427

**Format** the text as follows:

Font:         sans serif
Font size:     8
Font weight:  normal.

**Save** your presentation.

### Inserting audience notes on slides

New CLAIT

Presentations are designed to draw the audience's attention to the main points of the speaker's talk, and the bulleted topics shown on the slides are there to summarise and reinforce what the speaker is saying. So while printed copies of slides can be a useful reminder of the broader points made in a presentation, they will lack some of the important detail that the speaker covered. PowerPoint allows you to add notes to your slides so that when the slide is printed off the notes can also be seen and reviewed at a later date.

To insert notes for a slide, there is an option under View on the main menu called Notes Page. By clicking this view option you will see both a picture of the slide and below it a text frame where you can enter your notes, as shown in Figure 10.30.

In addition to providing an 'aide-memoire' for the audience, notes can also be used by the speaker to remind him or her of the main points of the slide and their talk. When typing notes for a slide, you may find it helpful to enlarge the text by using the zoom facility on the standard toolbar, or selecting View, Zoom... from the main menu.

This page also has a Master view similar to the slide master. It is not a requirement for New CLAIT that you are able to set up the notes master but you may like to have a look at this view and experiment on setting up your own notes master. For now, however, it is sufficient for you to know how to insert audience notes on a slide and subsequently print them onto hard copy. Have a go at inserting some notes into the Model_Building presentation.

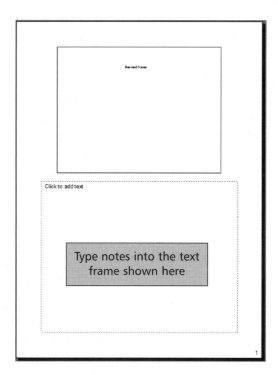

**Figure 10.30** *A slide and text frame*

## Build-up Exercise II: Stage 8

**Open** your Model_Building presentation.

**Select** Notes Page on the <u>V</u>iew menu.

**Click** on the notes text frame.

**Type** the following notes for each relevant slide.

Note: This presentation can be found on your accompanying CD. If you do not want to type all the notes you can copy them from the notes page on the **Model_builder.ppt** file and paste them into your own note pages. The zoom button will enable you to zoom into text when typing on a notes page, to make it clearer to read.

*Slide 1*
Notes:
1 If you are interested in learning more about the Longhurst Model Club you can contact the Secretary on Tel: 01732-566427 or write for an application pack to: The Secretary, Longhurst Model Club,14 St Princes Street.

2 Subscriptions are £10 annually and include a variety of benefits including: use of the model boating lake, a flying area for aero modellers, use of the model club's modelling benches, locker space and invitations to a number of social events laid on for members.

*Slide 2*
Notes:
1 Model making is a hobby that will give enormous satisfaction to everyone who engages in this pastime, whether they are 9 or 90.

2   Models can be built from kits or the more experienced modeller can draw their own plans and purchase the required materials.

3   Models are generally quite expensive and so it is better that the beginner starts with a basic model that will be within his or her capability. It is better to complete a simple model well than finish a complicated model incorrectly. If it is an aeroplane and it has not been finished properly it probably won't fly.

4   Once you have become more experienced you may find that you can build your models and then sell them to people who like to use them but not build them.

*Slide 3*

Notes:

1   You will find that it is better to find a room or a space where you do not have to move your model every time you finish for the day. A model that is being constantly moved is more likely to be damaged. Also you are less likely to lose important parts.

2   Before you start your model make sure you have all the necessary tools. Often manufacturers will include a list of required tools in the kit. Depending on which type of model you are building, some kits will come with basic needs such as pins, glue and sand paper. However, this is more the exception than the rule.

3   Always read the instructions very carefully before you start. Very often the beginner will be anxious to get started quickly and find later on that a certain task should have been done earlier. It is too late to go back once the wood or plastic has been cut and glued.

4   Joining a local model club can be very useful. If you get stuck there are always more experienced modellers there to help. You can share notes and also when it comes to using your model (if it is a working model) it is more fun to do this with other people.

**Save** your presentation.

Your completed slide show, together with notes, should now look similar to Figure 10.31.

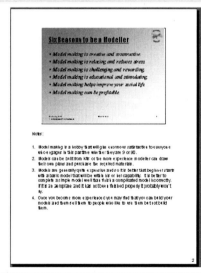
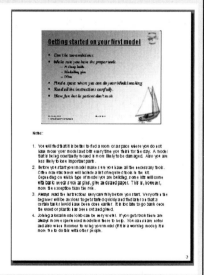

**Figure 10.31** *Presentation*

New CLAIT

## Printing presentation slides, notes and thumbnails

A requirement of New CLAIT is that you are able to print the results of your work in a number of ways. You will need to print the full slide, the notes page and thumbnails.

On page 366 you were introduced to the Slide Sorter view of a presentation 🔲. From this view it is perhaps easier to determine which slides you want printed. To determine the print required, select File and then Print... from the main menu and the PowerPoint Print dialogue box will appear. In Figure 10.32 you can see the various print options that are available. Note that in Office 2000 there is no Print Preview button.

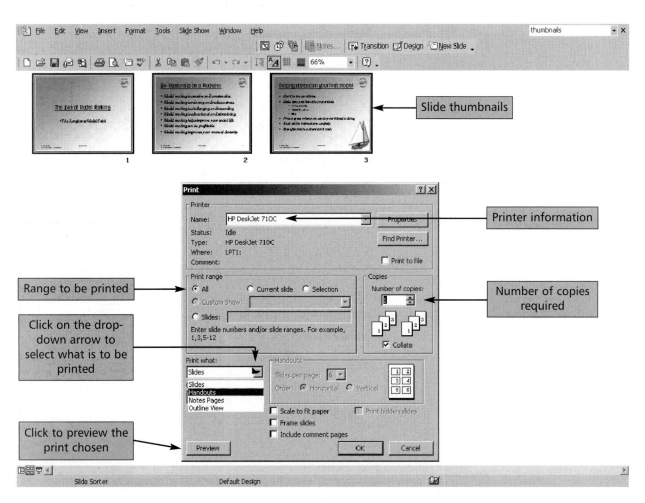

**Figure 10.32** *Print options in PowerPoint*

**Note:** When Handouts is selected in the Print what... box, the Handouts area of the Print dialogue box is activated, allowing the user to choose how many slides are printed to the page.

There are effectively five areas you need to review: Printer, Print range, Copies, Print what and Handouts.

**PRINTING TIP**

Printing in black and white will save your toner and printer ink. To print colour slides in black and white, select the Pure Black and White option from the Colour/Grayscale: box at the bottom of the Print dialogue box.

- The printer will be the default printer.
- The print range allows you to print all the slides, a selection or the current highlighted slide.
- Copies determines the number of copies that will be printed.
- Print what gives you the choice of printing the full slide (Slides), the notes pages (which includes a view of the slide as well as the notes) or a Handouts version of the slides. It can be extravagant on printer toner or ink to print full versions of all slides. The Handouts selection allows you to print a number of slides on one page. Up to nine slides can be printed per page. If you select the three slides per page option a space is provided on the right-hand side of each slide for notes to be written by the person receiving the handout. Finally, you can print an outline of your presentation.

Figure 10.33 shows the type of print you might expect from each of these options.

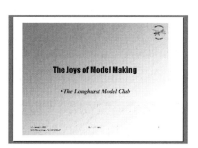

Slide · Handout

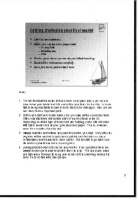

**Figure 10.33** *Types of print available*

Notes · Outline

You should now be able to:

- create and insert audience notes for a slide
- print:
  individual slides
  slides and their accompanying notes
  thumbnails of slides
  a presentation outline.

## Build-up Exercise 11: Stage 9

**Open** your Model_Building presentation.

**Print** Slide 1 as a full slide.

**Print** Slides 1–3 in handout form with three slides per page.

**Print** Slide 3 in page notes form.

**Save** your presentation.

**Close** the presentation.

**Close** the application.

That completes all you need to know for presentation graphics in New CLAIT. Now have a go at Practical Assignment 10. Solutions to this assignment can be found in Part 3.

## Unit 10 Presentation graphics using PowerPoint

### Scenario

You are the administrator for a small group of retail and services businesses operating in a city in the East Midlands. Your group has just set up a new service business providing discreet seminar and training facilities for companies and organisations in the local area.

Your Managing Director has been asked to give a presentation to the local Chamber of Commerce outlining the benefits of this new business and he would like you to produce a short, three-slide presentation to use with his talk.

| Assessment objectives | Stage | |
|---|---|---|
| 1a<br>2a<br>2b<br>2c<br>3a<br>3b<br>3c<br>3d<br>4b<br>4e<br>5a | 1 | Set up the master slide with the following:<br><br>(a) Create a page-wide title frame at the top of the page.<br>(b) Create a page-wide main frame below the title frame.<br>(c) Set up the following house style: |

| Frame | Style | Font | Size | Emphasis | Bullets | Align |
|---|---|---|---|---|---|---|
| TITLE | Title | Sans-serif | 40 | Bold | No | Left |
| MAIN | 1st level | Sans-serif | 30 | Bold | Yes | Left |
| MAIN | 2nd level | Serif | 20 | Italic | Yes | Centre |

(d) Insert the **BC_company_logo.jpg** (from the CD) at the top right of the slide. Change image size to:

Width:   2.5 cm
Height:   1.25 cm.

Adjust the title frame so that the image does not overlap the title text frame.

(e) Footer should contain the date, your name and the slide number. Font is to be serif and the size 8 points.

(f) Insert a new text frame centred above your name and enter the company name of 'The Business Café'.

(g) Format the background with the two colours pale blue to white on a diagonal up gradient.

| | | |
|---|---|---|
| 5b | 2 | Save the master slide as **BC_1**. |
| 3a<br>3b<br>3c<br>3d<br>4a<br>4b<br>4e | 3 | In the title slide (Slide 1) enter the title:<br><br>'The Business Café'<br><br>In the main text frame enter:<br><br>'We look after you so you can look after your business.' |

| | | |
|---|---|---|
| 3a<br>3b<br>3c<br>3d<br>4a<br>4b<br>4e | 4 | Insert a new slide based on the title and text layout ('bulleted list' for earlier versions than XP).<br>Type in a title for this slide of:<br><br>'Key facilities offered'<br><br>Enter the following points at the levels shown: |

| | |
|---|---|
| Fully equipped seminar rooms | Level 1 |
| OHPs, data projection and video units | Level 2 |
| White boards and flip charts | Level 2 |
| Video conferencing | Level 2 |
| Outstanding catering hospitality | Level 1 |
| Sandwiches to | Level 2 |
| Full à la carte menu | Level 2 |
| Very competitive prices | Level 1 |

| | | |
|---|---|---|
| 3a<br>3b<br>3c<br>3d<br>4a<br>4b<br>4e | 5 | Insert a new slide based on the title and text layout ('bulleted list' for earlier versions than XP).<br>Type in a title for this slide of:<br><br>'Prices for all pockets'<br><br>Enter the following points at the levels shown: |

| | |
|---|---|
| Room charge | Level 1 |
| £100 per room per day | Level 2 |
| £20 per room per hour | Level 2 |
| Discounts for two rooms or more | Level 1 |
| Two rooms 10% | Level 2 |
| Three rooms 12.5% | Level 2 |
| Free equipment use | Level 2 |
| Hospitality | Level 1 |
| Ranging from £2.50 to £10.00 per head | Level 2 |

| | | |
|---|---|---|
| 5b | 6 | Save the presentation |
| 5c | 7 | Print each slide – one per page. |
| | | You show your presentation to the Managing Director who thanks you but asks if you can make a few small amendments. |
| 4c | 8 | On Slide 2 delete the word 'Catering' in the second Level 1 bullet point. |
| 4d | 9 | Replace the word 'Hospitality' with 'Gourmet Food' (twice in all). |
| 4e<br>4d | 10 | In Slide 3, promote 'Free equipment use' to Level 1.<br>Amend the line to read 'Free use of equipment'. |
| 4b | 11 | On Slide 2, after 'Very competitive prices' add the following bullet point:<br><br>'We will meet any price in the area like for like' (Level 2). |
| 5d | 12 | Print a set of audience notes with three thumbnail slides per page. |

▶▶

Stage 13 is optional. It is not a New CLAIT requirement.

13    Open Slide 1 in Notes Page view and enter the following notes:

'For full details and a priced business pack please contact:'

Bernard Kane
The Business Café
34 Barker Road
Westley
WT4 3DE

E-mail: business.cafe@training-solutions.co.uk
Tel:    01774-654845
Fax:    01774-654846

The Business Café is open Monday–Saturday all year round and is only closed on the following days:

Christmas Day
Boxing Day
New Year's Day
Good Friday

14    Print the Notes Page of Slide 1 with both slide and notes on view.

5b      15    Save and close your amended presentation and exit the application.

# Part 3

# Solutions to
# Practical assignments

# Practical assignment 1: Using a computer

**Meeting.doc (Stage 6)**

> Meeting of the Nature Conservation Society
> in
> Naphood Village Hall
> on
> Saturday 21 December 2002
> at
> 7.00pm
>
> There will be a meeting of the Naphood Nature Conservation Society to discuss the recent proposals for the election of a new committee to take forward the project of designing and building of a bird watching hut in the 'Danford Copse', 2 miles north of the village of Naphood.
>
> All members of the society are warmly welcome and are asked to confirm with the Secretary whether they will be able to attend by Friday 13th December.
>
> Those attending are asked to bring some refreshments for a post-meeting supper. Further details can be obtained from Hilary Greeves (Hospitality Member) on Naphood 234216.
>
> Thank you
>
> John Green
> Secretary
>
> Bernard Kane          1 September 2002

**PE1_Print_2 (Stage 12)**

> Myname@ourbusiness.co.uk
>
> Item JG/50: 60% discount
>
> Bernard Kane    1 September 2002

# Practical assignment 2: Wordprocessing using Word

**PE2_Print_1 (Stage 6)**

Marketing Report – 2002

The Caster Seminar Centre opened in June 2002 and despite a slow start in attracting new business to the centre there has, over the last two months, been a significant upturn in both enquiries and bookings.

Returns on our internal questionnaire reveal that there are a lot of companies who have chosen to use their conference and meetings room space for additional office space rather than relocating. This is partly due to the significant increase in rented commercial accommodation.

There is clearly a market for our service and providing we target our publicity material effectively the centre should be able to increase its turnover by at least 50% over the coming year. With sales, excluding hospitality, running at £3,000 per month this would offer the opportunity of increasing our take to £4,500 by June 2003.

The plan is to prepare a professional flyer advertising our services and send it to over 800 companies in the local area. The survey conducted on the accommodation we currently use indicated that at least 10% of local companies would be prepared to use the Caster Seminar Centre for training and meetings. Our present clientele only covers around 30 companies or 3.75% of the potential market.

Our competitors, who offer an inferior service, are attracting between 5% and 10% of the market so there is an opportunity to increase market share. We are now working on a formal marketing plan, which will be available for review in about three weeks

Bernard Kane          1 September 2002

**PE2_Print_2
(Stage 17)**

---

**Marketing Report – 2002**

The Caster Seminar Centre opened in June 2002 and despite a slow start in attracting new business to the centre there has, over the last two months, been a significant upturn in both enquiries and bookings.

Returns on our internal questionnaire reveal that there are a lot of organisations who have chosen to use their conference and meetings room space for additional office space rather than relocating.

There is clearly a market for our service and providing we target our publicity material effectively the centre should be able to increase its turnover by at least 50% over the coming year. With sales, excluding hospitality, running at £3,000 per month this would offer the opportunity of increasing our take to £4,500 by June 2003. The plan is to prepare a professional flyer advertising our services and send it to over 800 organisations in the local area.

The survey conducted on the accommodation we currently use indicated that at least 10%

of local organisations would be prepared to use the Caster Seminar Centre for training and

meetings. Our present clientele only covers around 30 organisations or 3.75% of the potential

market. Early indication from our surveys suggests that the 'Service' and 'Professional' sectors

are the most likely organisations to use our facilities.

Our competitors, who offer an inferior service, are attracting between 5% and 10% of the market so there is an opportunity to increase market share.

We are now working on a formal marketing plan, which will be available for review in about three weeks.

Bernard Kane          1 September 2002

---

## Practical assignment 3: Electronic communication

**Training.doc (Stage 2)**

---

**BK Solutions Mail**

| | |
|---|---|
| **From:** | "BK Solutions Mail" <bernard.kane@bksolutions.co.uk> |
| **To:** | "Bernard Kane" <bernard.kane@bksolutions.co.uk> |
| **Sent:** | 10 March 2002 19:34 |
| **Attach:** | Training_1.doc |
| **Subject:** | IT Training |

Dear Colleague

The Personnel Department has agreed that we can submit a request for IT training following the installation of our new computers and software. Please see the attached document and let me have your views.

Bernard Kane

### IT Training for Medical Secretaries

Following the installation of our new computers and software I am trying to establish what training is required to enable us to make the most of this new equipment. I would be grateful if you could fill in the form below and I will then use this information to recommend a suitable programme of training for us all.

| Application | Current proficiency level (please indicate a level of 0 – 5 with '0' being no knowledge and 5 expert). | If training is required what skills would you like to include? |
|---|---|---|
| Word | | |
| Excel | | |
| Access | | |
| PowerPoint | | |
| Publisher | | |
| Outlook | | |
| Internet Explorer | | |
| FrontPage | | |

Please may I have your responses back by the end of the week? If you have any queries I can be contacted on Ext. 56. Thank you.

**From:**        **(Name)**       **Department:**
**Date:**

## Tariffs (Stage 5)

| Time | Price |
|------|-------|
| | |
| Full Day | £750 |
| Half Day | £400 |
| 2-day course | £1000 |
| 3-day course | £1500 |
| Additional days (over 3 days) | £500 |
| Individual hourly rate (by agreement) | £100 |
| What the price includes: | • Initial assessment<br>• Agreed learning outcomes<br>• Full resource pack<br>• Performance feedback<br>• Venue and facilities<br>• Buffet lunch and tea/coffee as appropriate |
| Special rates are available for longer programs involving three or more applications. For more details why not contact us: | mailto:bernard.kane@bksolutions.co.uk |

## Internet_defs (Stage 6)

The NETWORK: Internet – the name given to the collective electronic network of computers and computer networks, which are inter-connected throughout the world – started with the ARPAnet at the US Dept. of Defense.

USENET – the name given to the computer network that carries newsgroups. Newsgroups are arranged in hierarchies based loosely on subject matter. The USENET is often confused with the INTERNET in the news media – started by two students at Duke University.

WorldWideWeb – WWW – W3, the name given to the collection of computers that serve information in hypertext format to the INTERNET. Invented by Dr Tim Berners-Lee, at the European Center for Nuclear Research (CERN), who wrote the first hypertext transfer protocol daemon (HTTPD) and the first hypertext markup language (HTML) browser, as a way to allow nuclear physicists to exchange working papers over the INTERNET.

HTTPD – Hypertext Transfer Protocol Daemon, a computer program that manages the transfer of hypertext and multimedia documents over the INTERNET.

HTML – Hypertext Markup Language, the text markup language used to insert tags, which allow a Web browser to correctly display a hypertext document. HTML1, HTML+, HTML2 and HTML3 are versions of HTML in use at this time. HTML is a subset of the Standard Generalized Markup Language (SGML), first invented to display legal texts and now the world standard for large documentation projects.

VRML – Virtual Reality Modeling Language, a tagging language for conveying three-dimensional information over the Internet using a VRML browser.

Hypertext links – Hypertext documents that contain links to other documents within them – footnotes are a form of hypertext link.

E-mail (Stage 7)

---

**BK Solutions Mail**

| | |
|---|---|
| **From:** | "BK Solutions Mail" <bernard.kane@bksolutions.co.uk> |
| **To:** | <Personnel@myhospital.org.uk> |
| **Cc:** | <ConsultantA@myhospital.org.uk> |
| **Sent:** | 10 March 2002 17:39 |
| **Attach:** | Tariffs.doc |
| **Subject:** | IT Training |

Dear Mrs Jones

I have now consulted with all my colleagues concerning the proposed IT training. The general consensus is that training in a variety of Word functions and PowerPoint presentations would be most useful.

My research indicates that we would need two days' training at a cost of £1,000 for ten of us. That equates to £50 per day each, which seems very reasonable.

I have attached relevant details of costs from the company.

**Bernard Kane**

---

# Practical assignment 4: Spreadsheets using Excel

## PE4_Print_1 (Stage 5)

| STOCK | HOLDING | CURRENT PRICE | COST | DIVIDEND | PAYMENT DATES | VALUE |
|---|---|---|---|---|---|---|
| BAE SYSTEMS | 270 | 4.25 | 341.05 | 2.1 | NOV | 1147.5 |
| PERSIMMON | 1250 | 2.07 | 3308 | 6 | OCT | 2587.5 |
| UNILEVER | 332 | 4.4175 | 1614.99 | 3.1 | DEC | 1466.61 |
| BAA | 397 | 5.615 | 2255.27 | 1.9 | JAN | 2229.155 |
| NATIONAL GRID | 520 | 5.565 | 3000 | 2.8 | JAN | 2893.8 |
| BARCLAYS | 160 | 17.12 | 3186 | 6.7 | OCT | 2739.2 |
| LLOYDS | 240 | 6.425 | 2256 | 3.7 | OCT | 1542 |

Bernard Kane          01-Sep-02

## PE4_Print_2 (Stage 12)

| STOCK HELD | HOLDING | CURRENT PRICE | COST PRICE | COST | DIVIDEND | PAYMENT DATES | VALUE |
|---|---|---|---|---|---|---|---|
| BAE SYSTEMS | 270 | £4.55 | £1.26 | £341.05 | 2 | NOV | £1,228.50 |
| PERSIMMON | 1250 | £2.07 | £2.65 | £3,308.00 | 6 | OCT | £2,587.50 |
| UNILEVER | 500 | £4.42 | £3.23 | £1,614.99 | 3 | DEC | £2,208.75 |
| BAA | 397 | £5.62 | £5.68 | £2,255.27 | 2 | JAN | £2,229.16 |
| BARCLAYS | 160 | £17.12 | £19.91 | £3,186.00 | 7 | OCT | £2,739.20 |
| LLOYDS | 240 | £6.43 | £9.40 | £2,256.00 | 4 | OCT | £1,542.00 |

## PE4_Print_3 (showing formulae) (Stage 13)

| STOCK HELD | HOLDING | CURRENT PRICE | COST PRICE | COST | DIVIDEND | PAYMENT DATES | VALUE |
|---|---|---|---|---|---|---|---|
| BAE SYSTEMS | 270 | 4.55 | =E2/B2 | 341.05 | 2.1 | NOV | =B2*C2 |
| PERSIMMON | 1250 | 2.07 | =E3/B3 | 3308 | 6 | OCT | =B3*C3 |
| UNILEVER | 500 | 4.4175 | =E4/B4 | 1614.99 | 3.1 | DEC | =B4*C4 |
| BAA | 397 | 5.615 | =E5/B5 | 2255.27 | 1.9 | JAN | =B5*C5 |
| BARCLAYS | 160 | 17.12 | =E6/B6 | 3186 | 7 | OCT | =B6*C6 |
| LLOYDS | 240 | 6.425 | =E7/B7 | 2256 | 3.7 | OCT | =B7*C7 |

## Practical assignment 5: Databases using Access

### Computers.mdb (Stage 4)

| | MAKE | TYPE | PROCESSOR | RAM | DISPLAY | HARD DISK | PRICE | STOCK | VALID TILL |
|---|---|---|---|---|---|---|---|---|---|
| | TINY | PC | 1.8 GHz | 512 | 17" CRT | 40 GB | £999.00 | 50 | 20/06/02 |
| ▶ | TINY | PC | 1.0 GHz | 128 | 17" CRT | 30 GB | £799.00 | 25 | 20/06/02 |
| | TINY | LT | 1.2 GHz | 256 | 14.1" TFT | 20 GB | £999.00 | 30 | 20/06/02 |
| | TINY | LT | PENTIUM III | 512 | 14.1" TFT | 30 GB | £1,299.00 | 15 | 20/06/02 |
| | FUJITSU | PC | 1.47 GHz | 256 | 15" TFT | 60 GB | £1,198.00 | 50 | 10/08/02 |
| | FUJITSU | PC | PENTIUM 4 | 128 | NOT SUPPLIED | 20 GB | £499.00 | 20 | 10/08/02 |
| | TIME | LT | CELERON 900 | 256 | 14.1" TFT | 20 GB | £988.00 | 50 | 20/08/02 |
| | TIME | PC | AMD Athlon XP | 512 | 17" SVGA | 40 GB | £999.00 | 120 | 20/08/02 |
| | MAA | PC | 1.8 GHz | 512 | 17" SVGA | 60 GB | £1,100.00 | 5 | 15/06/02 |
| | MAA | PC | 1.2 GHz | 256 | 21" SVGA | 40 GB | £999.00 | 5 | 15/06/02 |
| | IBM | LT | CELERON 900 | 128 | 13.3" TFT | 15 GB | £1,182.00 | 10 | 20/07/02 |
| | IBM | LT | PENTIUM III | 128 | 13.3" TFT | 15 GB | £1,568.00 | 10 | 20/07/02 |
| | IBM | LT | 1.2 GHZ | 128 | 15" TFT | 48 GB | £2,788.00 | 15 | 20/07/02 |
| | COMPAQ | PC | PENTIUM 4 | 256 | 21" CRT | 50 GB | £999.00 | 20 | 10/07/02 |
| | COMPAQ | PC | 1.2 GHz | 512 | 17" SVGA | 60 GB | £1,099.00 | 20 | 10/07/02 |
| | IBM | LT | 800 MHz | 128 | 12.1" TFT | 20 GB | £2,205.00 | 10 | 20/07/02 |
| | ALLBITS | PC | 1.0 GHz | 256 | 17" CRT | 40 GB | £899.00 | 2 | 31/08/02 |
| ✱ | | | | 0 | | | £0.00 | 0 | |

Record: ⟨⟨ ⟨ | 2 | ⟩ ⟩⟩ ⟩✱ of 17

### Database query (Stage 6)

| | MAKE | TYPE | RAM | HARD DISK | PRICE |
|---|---|---|---|---|---|
| ▶ | ALLBITS | PC | 256 | 40 GB | £899.00 |
| | COMPAQ | PC | 512 | 60 GB | £1,099.00 |
| | COMPAQ | PC | 256 | 40 GB | £999.00 |
| | FUJITSU | PC | 128 | 20 GB | £499.00 |
| | FUJITSU | PC | 256 | 60 GB | £1,198.00 |
| | IBM | LT | 128 | 48 GB | £2,788.00 |
| | IBM | LT | 128 | 15 GB | £1,568.00 |
| | IBM | LT | 128 | 15 GB | £1,182.00 |
| | IBM | LT | 128 | 20 GB | £2,205.00 |
| | TIME | PC | 512 | 40 GB | £999.00 |
| | TIME | LT | 256 | 20 GB | £988.00 |
| ✱ | | | 0 | | £0.00 |

Record: ⟨⟨ ⟨ | 1 | ⟩ ⟩⟩ ⟩✱ of 11

**Database query (Stage 7)**

| | MAKE | PROCESSOR | HARD DISK | PRICE |
|---|---|---|---|---|
| | TINY | PENTIUM III | 30 GB | £1,299.00 |
| | TINY | 1.2 GHz | 20 GB | £999.00 |
| | TIME | CELERON 900 | 20 GB | £988.00 |
| | IBM | CELERON 900 | 15 GB | £1,182.00 |
| ▶ | IBM | PENTIUM III | 15 GB | £1,568.00 |
| * | | | | £0.00 |

Record: |◀ ◀ | 5 | ▶ ▶| ▶* | of 5

**Database query (Stage 8)**

| | MAKE | TYPE | PROCESSOR | STOCK | VALID TILL |
|---|---|---|---|---|---|
| ▶ | TINY | LT | PENTIUM III | 15 | 20/06/02 |
| | TINY | PC | 1.0 GHz | 25 | 20/06/02 |
| | TINY | LT | 1.2 GHz | 30 | 20/06/02 |
| | TIME | LT | CELERON 900 | 50 | 20/08/02 |
| | TINY | PC | 1.8 GHz | 50 | 20/06/02 |
| | TIME | PC | AMD Athlon XP | 120 | 20/08/02 |
| * | | | | 0 | |

Record: |◀ ◀ | 1 | ▶ ▶| ▶* | of 6

## Practical assignment 6: Desktop publishing using Publisher

**Composite proof copy (Stage 10)**

# SAVING OUR VILLAGE

**PROTECTING OUR VILLAGE**
Many of you will know that the Parish Council decided last year that it was in the village's interest to adopt a Village Statement to ensure that the historic setting of our village and the important environmental features that surround it are taken into account by the City Council in the event of any future developments.

**THE CONSULTATION PROCESS**
Thanks to the very hard work of a number of people who have been involved in this project the second draft of our statement is now nearing completion. As the statement was being prepared many of you have already expressed your views on what should be included. However, before the Parish Council finalises the statement it would like to give all the residents of Burberry-on-the-Hill a further opportunity to comment on the document so that any additional views or concerns can be considered and, where appropriate, be included in the document.

**VILLAGE PROTECTION**
Although the village statement has no statutory teeth, the City Council is bound to take account of the impact any developments may have on our local environment. We know through the Council's Local Plan that it wishes to see further developments in villages close to the city. Indeed, some developments have already started in two neighbouring villages, Stanton and Reedley. These developments have been the focus of a great deal of criticism by both local residents and visitors to our area. If they were adopted in Burberry the consequences could be disastrous. We have a number of sites of special scientific interest protecting rare flora and fauna, which could be at risk from unsympathetic developments.

**ACT NOW**
The statement will be finalised and submitted at the end of October. On Friday 11 October members of the Parish Council will be giving a final presentation on the document in the Village Hall at 8:00 pm to which all residents are invited. If you are unable to attend this meeting make sure you have your say before it's too late - ring 01776-325647 or send comments to The Old Forge, Main Street, Burberry-on-the-Hill.

John Freeman
Chairman Parish Council

**Final publication
(Stage 17)**

# SAVING OUR VILLAGE

## PROTECTING OUR VILLAGE

Many of you will know that the Parish Council decided last year that it was in the village's interest to adopt a Village Statement to ensure that the historic setting of our village and the important environmental features that surround it are taken into account by the City Council in the event of any future developments.

## THE CONSULTATION PROCESS

Thanks to the very hard work of a number of people who have been involved in this project the second draft of our statement is now nearing completion. As the statement was being prepared many of you have already expressed your views on what should be included. However, before the Parish Council finalises the statement it would like to give all the residents of Burberry-on-the-Hill a further opportunity to comment on the document so that any additional views or concerns can be considered and, where appropriate, be included in the document.

## VILLAGE PROTECTION

Although the village statement has no statutory teeth, the City Council is bound to take account of the impact any developments may have on our local environment. We know through the Council's Local Plan that it wishes to see further developments in villages close to the city. Indeed, some developments have already started in two neighbouring villages, Stanton and Reedley. These developments have been the focus of a great deal of criticism by both local residents and visitors to our area. If they were adopted in Burberry the consequences could be disastrous. We have a number of sites of special scientific interest protecting rare flora and fauna, which could be at risk from unsympathetic developments.

## ACT NOW

The statement will be finalised and submitted at the end of October. On Friday 11 October members of the Parish Council will be giving a final presentation on the document in the Village Hall at 8:00 pm to which all residents are invited. If you are unable to attend this meeting make sure you have your say before it's too late - ring 01776-325647 or send comments to The Old Forge, Main Street, Burberry-on-the-Hill.

John Freeman
Chairman Parish Council

# Practical assignment 7: Graphs and charts

## Pie_1 (Stage 3)

### Hire By Film For The Week

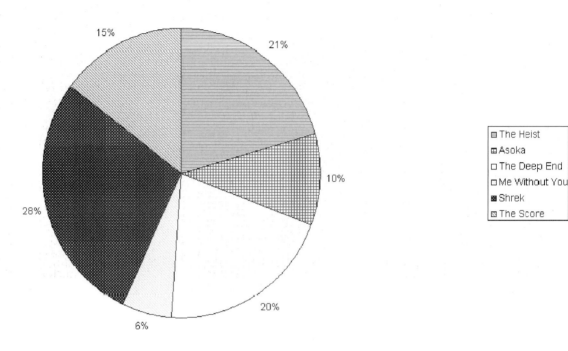

## Bar_1 (Stage 6)

### Hires By Film

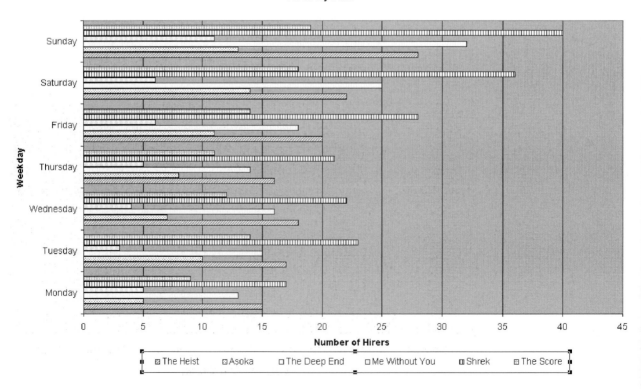

## Column_1 (Stage 9)

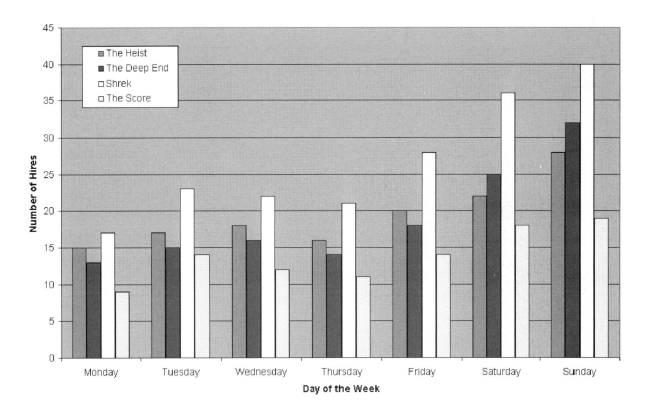

Most Popular Four Films

## Column_2 (Stage 13)

# Most Popular Four Films

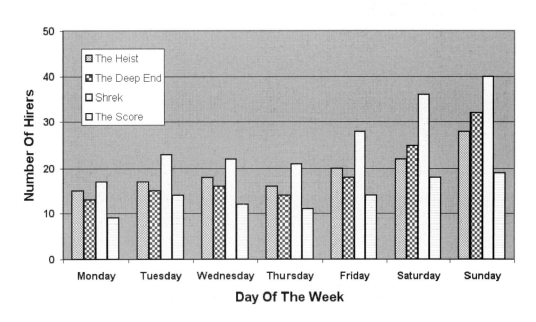

Line_1 (Stage 16)

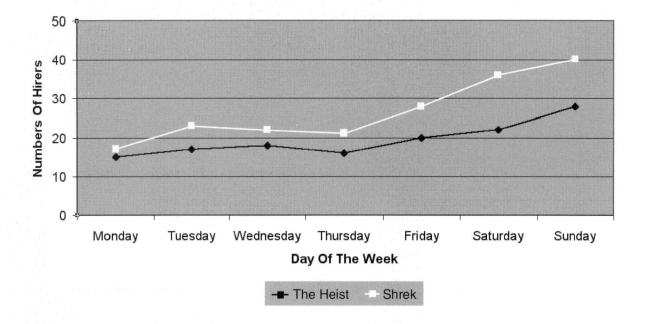

## Practical assignment 8: Computer art using Word

CA_Practical_Exercise
(Stage 9)

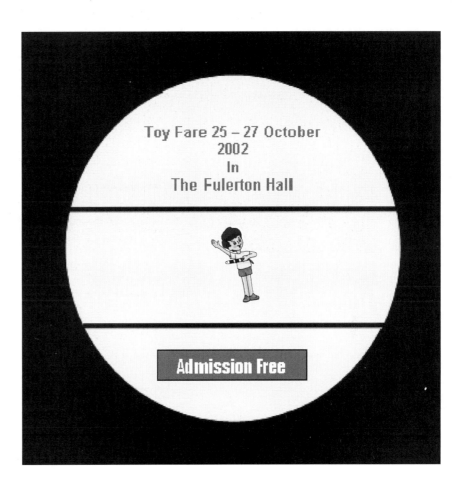

# Practical assignment 9: Web pages using FrontPage

**About_us.htm**
**(Stage 1)**

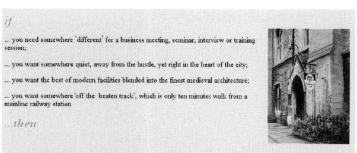

*if*

... you need somewhere 'different' for a business meeting, seminar, interview or training session;

... you want somewhere quiet, away from the hustle, yet right in the heart of the city;

... you want the best of modern facilities blended into the finest medieval architecture;

... you want somewhere 'off the beaten track', which is only ten minutes walk from a mainline railway station

*...then*

### The Business Cafe

at Peterborough Cathedral is what you are looking for

The Business Cafe is situated in the heart of the City in the beautiful and tranquil Cathedral precincts, only ten minutes walk from the mainline station and close to NCP car parks. Parking within the Cathedral grounds can be arranged with prior notice.

We have four well-appointed rooms with videos, overhead projectors, flip charts and whiteboards. A full catering and hospitality service is also available at very competitive rates.

Individual rooms, or the whole building can be booked for either full or half days.

Location and Facilities

Facility Charges

Menus

For further information, to view our facilities, or to make a booking please:

Ring 01733-347239 or mailto Business Cafe@peterborough-cathedral.org.uk

Bernard Kane

**Location&Facilities.htm (Stage 2a)**

## *Location & Facilities*

The Cathedral's Meeting and Conference Centre can provide discreet, high-quality seminar, training and meeting facilities to businesses and other organisations.

We are uniquely situated at 24 Minster Precincts, on the south side of the Cathedral close and next to the Cathedral itself.

The building itself dates in part from the late 13th century with the remainder being 14th and 15th century additions. Originally, it formed part of the Abbot's range of the medieval monastery but its original purpose is not known.

The facilities of No. 24 have been brought up to date, allowing us to cater for all modern conferencing requirements without detracting from the character of the building.

We have four well-equipped rooms, with videos, overhead projectors, flip charts, whiteboards and telecommunication facilities.

Each room can accommodate 12 people when configured as a board room or 15 when set up theatre-style.

Our rooms can be set for your individual requirements and your catering and hospitality needs are served by our experienced staff either in your own room or in the lounge.

Home

Bernard Kane

**Facility_charges.htm (Stage 2b)**

*Facility Charges*

Room Hire

Full Day   –   £100.00

Half Day   –   £75.00

Hours of Business   –   08:00 to 13:00, 13:30 to 18:30

We are able to vary our opening hours to suit a client's needs.

Accessories included:

- Flip charts
- Whiteboards
- Overhead Projector and Screen
- Video Player and VDU.

Other conferencing accessories are available on request.

Home

Bernard Kane

**Menus.htm (Stage 12)**

 *Finger Buffet*

**Menu A**

Sandwiches
Crolines
Vol-au-Vents
Samosas

£5.95 per delegate

**Menu B**

Sandwiches
Crolines
Vol-au-Vents
Samosas
Turkey & Cranberry Sausage Rolls

£6.50 per delegate

Home

Bernard Kane

## HTML code: About_us.htm (Stage 16)

```
html>

<head>
<meta http-equiv="Content-Type" content="text/html; charset=windows-1252">
<meta name="GENERATOR" content="Microsoft FrontPage 4.0">
<meta name="ProgId" content="FrontPage.Editor.Document">
<title>About Us</title>
</head>

<body bgcolor="#FFFFCC">

<p><i><font size="6" color="#00CC00"><b>if...<img border="0" src="images/cafe_entrance.jpg" width="207" height="283"
align="right"></b></font></i></p>
<p><font size="4">.<font face="Times New Roman">.. you need somewhere
'different' for a business meeting, seminar, interview or training session;</font></font></p>
<p><font size="4" face="Times New Roman">... you want somewhere quiet, away from
the hustle, yet right in the heart of the city;</font></p>
<p><font size="4" face="Times New Roman">... you want the best of modern
facilities blended into the finest medieval architecture;</font></p>
<p><font size="4" face="Times New Roman">... you want somewhere off the 'beaten
track', which is only ten minutes walk from a mainline railway station</font></p>
<p><font size="6" color="#00CC00"><b><i>...then</i></b></font></p>
<p> </p>
<p><b><font face="Arial" size="6">The Business Cafe</font></b></p>
<p><font size="4">at Peterborough Cathedral is what you are looking for<span style="left: 463; top: 485; position:
relative"><img border="0" src="images/conference_room.jpg" width="249" height="222" align="right"></span></font></p>
<p><font size="4">The Business Cafe is situated in the heart of the City in the
beautiful and tranquil Cathedral precincts, only ten minutes walk from the main
line station and close to NCP car parks.  Parking within the Cathedral
grounds can be arranged with prior notice.</font></p>
<p><font size="4">We have four well appointed rooms with videos, overhead
projectors, flip charts and white white boards.  A full catering and
hospitality service is also available at very competitive rates.</font></p>
<p><font size="4">Individual rooms, or the whole building can be booked for
either full or half days.</font></p>
<p><a href="location&amp;facilities.htm" style="color: #0000FF"><font size="3">Location
and Facilities</font></a></p>
<p><a href="facility_charges.htm" style="color: #0000FF">Facility
Charges</a></p>
<p><a href="Menus.htm"><font color="#0000FF">Menus</font></a></p>
<p><a href="index.htm">The Business Cafe</a></p>
<p><font size="4">For further information, to view our facilities, or to make a
booking please:</font></p>
<p><font size="4">Ring 01733-347239 or </font><a href="mailto:Business.Cafe@peterborough-cathedral.org.uk"><font
size="3">mailto:Business.Cafe@peterborough-cathedral.org.uk</font></a></p>
<p><font size="4">Bernard Kane</font></p>

</body>

</html>
```

**HTML code: Location&Facilities.htm (Stage 15)**

```
<html>

<head>
<meta http-equiv="Content-Type" content="text/html; charset=windows-1252">
<meta http-equiv="Content-Language" content="en-us">
<title>Location and Facilities</title>
<meta name="GENERATOR" content="Microsoft FrontPage 4.0">
<meta name="ProgId" content="FrontPage.Editor.Document">
</head>

<body bgcolor="#FFFFCC">
<p><font size="6" color="#00CC00"><i><b>Location &amp; Facilities</b></i></font></p>
<p><font size="4">The Cathedral's Meeting and Conference Centre can provide
discreet, high quality seminar, training and meeting facilities to businesses
and other organisations.</font></p>
<p><font size="4">We are uniquely situated at 24 Minster Precincts, on the south
side of the Cathedral close and next to the Cathedral itself.</font></p>
<p><font size="4">The building itself dates in part from the late 13th century
with the remainder 14th and 15th century additions. Originally, it formed part
of the Abbot's range of the medieval monastery but its original purpose is not
known.</font></p>
<p><font size="4">The facilities of no 24 have been brought up to date allowing
us to cater for all modern conferencing requirements but without detracting from
the character of the building.</font></p>
<p><font size="4">We have four well-equipped rooms, with videos, overhead
projectors, flip charts, whiteboards and telecommunication facilities.</font></p>
<p><font size="4">Each room can accommodate 12 people when configured as a board
room or 15 when set up in a theatre-style.</font></p>
<p><font size="4">Our rooms can be set for your individual requirements and your
catering and hospitality needs are served by our experienced staff either in
your own room or in the lounge.</font></p>
<p><a href="About_us.htm"><font color="#0000FF">Home</font></a></p>
<p><font size="4">Bernard Kane</font></p>
</body>

</html>
```

### HTML code: Facility_charges.htm (Stage 15)

```
<html>

<head>
<meta http-equiv="Content-Type" content="text/html; charset=windows-1252">
<meta http-equiv="Content-Language" content="en-us">
<title>Facility Charges</title>
<meta name="GENERATOR" content="Microsoft FrontPage 4.0">
<meta name="ProgId" content="FrontPage.Editor.Document">
</head>

<body bgcolor="#FFFFCC">
<p><font size="6" color="#00CC00"><i><b>Facility Charges</b></i></font></p>
<p><font size="4">Room Hire</font></p>
<p><font size="4">Full Day    -    £100.00</font></p>
<p><font size="4">Half Day    -    £75.00</font></p>
<p><font size="4">Hours of Business    -    08:00
to 13:00, 13:30 to 18:30</font></p>
<p><font size="4">We are able to vary our opening hours to suit a client's needs</font></p>
<p><font size="4">Accessories included:</font></p>
<ul>
  <li><font size="4">Flip charts</font></li>
  <li><font size="4">White boards</font></li>
  <li><font size="4">Overhead Projector and Screen</font></li>
  <li><font size="4">Video Player and VDU</font></li>
</ul>
<p><font size="4">Other conferencing accessories are available on request.</font></p>
<p><a href="About_us.htm"><font color="#0000FF" size="3">Home</font></a></p>
<p><font size="4">Bernard Kane</font></p>
</body>

</html>
```

## HTML code: Menus.htm (Stage 15)

```
<meta http-equiv="Content-Type" content="text/html; charset=windows-1252">
<meta http-equiv="Content-Language" content="en-us">
<title>Menus</title>
<meta name="GENERATOR" content="Microsoft FrontPage 4.0">
<meta name="ProgId" content="FrontPage.Editor.Document">
</head>

<body bgcolor="#FFFFCC">
<div align="center">
 <center>
 <pre><font size="3"><img border="0" src="images/Food_1.jpg" width="109" height="89"
align="right"></font><b><i><font size="6" color="#00CC00"><img border="0" src="images/Food_2.jpg"
width="103" height="83" align="left">Finger Buffet</font></i></b></pre>
 </center>
</div>
<div align="center">
 <center>
 <pre><font size="4"><b>Menu A</b></font></pre>
 </center>
</div>
<div align="center">
 <center>
 <pre><font size="3">Sandwiches
Crolines
Vol-au-Vents      Samosas</font></pre>
 </center>
</div>
<div align="center">
 <center>
 <pre><font size="3">£5.95 per delegate</font></pre>
 </center>
</div>
<div align="center">
 <center>
 <pre><b><font size="3">Menu B</font></b></pre>
 </center>
</div>
<div align="center">
 <center>
 <pre><font size="3">Sandwiches
Crolines
Vol-au-Vents
Samosas
Turkey &amp; Cranberry Sausage Rolls</font></pre>
 </center>
</div>
<div align="center">
 <center>
 <pre><font size="3">£6.50 per delegate</font></pre>
 </center>
</div>
<div align="center">
 <center>
 <pre><a href="About_us.htm"><font color="#0000FF">Home</font></a></pre>
 </center>
</div>
<p align="center">Bernard Kane</p>
</body>

</html>
```

## Practical assignment 10: Presentation graphics using PowerPoint

Slide 1 (Stage 3)

Slide 2 (Stage 4)

Slide 3 (Stage 5)

**Audience notes
(Stage 12)**

**Notes Page of Slide 1
(Stage 14)**

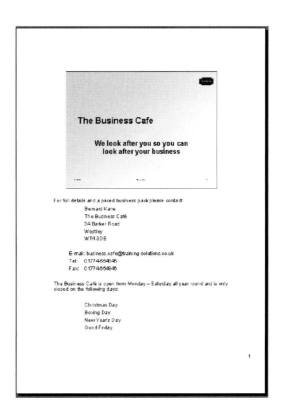

# *Appendices*

*The New CLAIT syllabus*
*Office keyboard shortcuts*
*Glossary*

# Appendix 1
# *The New CLAIT syllabus*

Throughout this book you have been working towards achieving all the requirements laid down by OCR for achieving OCR's Level 1 Certificate for IT Users (New CLAIT). Listed below are the specific learning outcomes and assessment objectives for each unit offered in the New CLAIT programme.

## Unit 1 Using a computer

### 1 Identify and use a computer workstation and system software.

| Assessment objectives | Knowledge and understanding |
|---|---|
| a Switch on computer and monitor safely<br>b Use a personal computer and printer to produce a document<br>c Navigate the operating system<br>d Load application software<br>e Use an input device to enter data<br>f Shut down operating system | ■ Identify, distinguish between and be able to operate hardware and software.<br>■ Understand the generic components of common operating systems and their functions (windows, icons, buttons, menus, pointer, cursor, toolbars, etc.).<br>■ Identify and distinguish between software elements (applications, data files/documents, directories/folders).<br>■ Appreciate the advantages of a Graphic User Interface in using IT (WYSIWYG etc.).<br>■ Appreciate safe working practice in using a computer (location and positioning of workstation, chair, screen, keyboard) to reduce risk of strain-type injuries. |

### 2 Locate and access data on a computer.

| Assessment objectives | Knowledge and understanding |
|---|---|
| a Gain access to data using a login and/or password<br>b Use file search facilities<br>c Find a specified file | ■ Appreciate the need for security in the production of documents, and the risks and consequences of unauthorised access to computers and networks (viruses, secure data, computer misuse, etc.).<br>■ Understand simple login procedures.<br>■ Understand how to change a password and be aware of good practice in selecting passwords.<br>■ Understand how to locate data and files using the features of the system software. |

### 3 Input small amounts of unformatted text, numbers and symbols.

| Assessment objectives | Knowledge and understanding |
| --- | --- |
| a Enter text<br>b Enter numbers<br>c Enter symbols<br>d Amend an existing document | ■ Appreciate the need for accurate data input.<br>■ Understand how to use a keyboard or other input device to enter text, numbers and symbols (=~/#.,:@?!~&%÷*), including use of the 'shift' key and 'return' or 'enter' key.<br>■ Understand the role of the cursor and mouse/pointer combination in selecting the edit point. |

### 4 Print a document using the default printer settings.

| Assessment objectives | Knowledge and understanding |
| --- | --- |
| a Switch on printer safely<br>b Load paper<br>c Print document | ■ Understand the safe use of the selected print facility.<br>■ Understand how to load paper correctly.<br>■ Understand the use of default print facilities. |

### 5 Manage documents and data.

| Assessment objectives | Knowledge and understanding |
| --- | --- |
| a Create a new document<br>b Open an existing document<br>c Save an existing document<br>d Save a document with a new filename<br>e Close document<br>f Delete document | ■ Understand generic document management terms and operations (file menu, new, open, save, save as, close).<br>■ Understand how to navigate filing systems from within generic open/save dialogues.<br>■ Understand the need to save documents on a regular basis and the reasons for saving with a new filename. |

## Unit 2 Wordprocessing

### 1 Identify and use wordprocessing software correctly.

| Assessment objectives | Knowledge and understanding |
| --- | --- |
| a Use appropriate application software | ■ Identify appropriate software (e.g. wordprocessor).<br>■ Understand correct procedures for using chosen software.<br>■ Appreciate the differences between wordprocessing software and text editors (WYSIWYG, formatting, presentation). |

### 2 Use an input device to enter and edit text accurately.

| Assessment objectives | Knowledge and understanding |
| --- | --- |
| a Enter text in paragraphs<br>b Insert text<br>c Move text<br>d Delete text<br>e Replace specified text | ■ Understand the use of an input device to enter text.<br>■ Appreciate the need for accuracy and the importance of checking output against expectations.<br>■ Understand the use of common editing tools (text selection, drag & drop, cut, copy & paste, delete & backspace, search & replace) and appreciate their various advantages/disadvantages. |

## 3   Select fonts and simple text formatting.

| Assessment objectives | Knowledge and understanding |
|---|---|
| a  Change font<br>b  Change font size<br>c  Emphasise text<br>d  Set text alignment/justification | ■ Distinguish between common typefaces and understand how to select them.<br>■ Understand how to set and amend font sizes.<br>■ Understand how to apply emphasis (bold, italic, underline).<br>■ Understand the use of left and centre alignment.<br>■ Understand how to fully justify text and appreciate the effect this has on text spacing. |

## 4   Format basic paragraph and document properties.

| Assessment objectives | Knowledge and understanding |
|---|---|
| a  Set/amend margins<br>b  Insert paragraph breaks<br>c  Amend line spacing | ■ Understand automatic word wrap, and the significance of paragraph breaks.<br>■ Be aware of common wordprocessing conventions and the relevance of 'house style' (e.g. line spaces after paragraphs, spacing after punctuation).<br>■ Understand the major layout and formatting functions of wordprocessors (paragraph breaks, line spacing, margins). |

## 5   Manage and print wordprocessing documents.

| Assessment objectives | Knowledge and understanding |
|---|---|
| a  Create a new document<br>b  Save document<br>c  Save document with new filename<br>d  Print document<br>e  Close document | ■ Understand document management in the chosen software (file menu, new, save, save as, close).<br>■ Understand how to print a document from the chosen software using default print settings. |

## Unit 3 Electronic communication

## 1   Identify and use e-mail and browsing software.

| Assessment objectives | Knowledge and understanding |
|---|---|
| a  Use appropriate application software | ■ Identify appropriate software for the task (e.g. web browser, software, e-mail software).<br>■ Understand correct procedures for using chosen software. |

## 2   Transmit and receive e-mail messages and attachments.

| Assessment objectives | Knowledge and understanding |
|---|---|
| a  Create new message<br>b  Access incoming message<br>c  Reply to message<br>d  Forward message<br>e  Copy message<br>f  Access attached file<br>g  Attach file to e-mail message<br>h  Recall stored e-mail address | ■ Appreciate the implications of using e-mail for business communication (dating, filing, sender's details).<br>■ Understand the structure of an e-mail storage system (mailbox).<br>■ Distinguish between different ways of sending e-mail (reply, forward, compose).<br>■ Appreciate the need for accuracy in addressing.<br>■ Understand facilities to attach documents and to access attachments. |

### 3 Navigate the World Wide Web.

| Assessment objectives | Knowledge and understanding |
| --- | --- |
| a Access specified web page(s)<br>b Navigate the World Wide Web using hyperlinks | ■ Understand website navigation using browser software.<br>■ Understand the component parts of an Internet address (URL).<br>■ Understand the basic structure of web sites. |

### 4 Use search techniques to locate data on the Web.

| Assessment objectives | Knowledge and understanding |
| --- | --- |
| a Use a site-specific (local) search engine<br>b Use a general web search engine<br>c Locate web page(s) containing required data<br>d Save data from web page | ■ Identify and distinguish between different types of search engines.<br>■ Appreciate the need to pursue searches beyond the search results page(s).<br>■ Appreciate the need to select material relevant to the query.<br>■ Appreciate the effect of company policy and relevant legislation on the selection of appropriate material. |

### 5 Manage and print electronic documents.

| Assessment objectives | Knowledge and understanding |
| --- | --- |
| a Store web address (URL)<br>b Delete e-mail message<br>c Store e-mail address<br>d Store e-mail attachment<br>e Print message(s) and attachmen<br>f Print web page(s) | ■ Understand document management in the chosen software (file menu, new, save, save as, close) and the differences from generic document management terms (e.g. mailbox, folders, saving externally).<br>■ Understand how to print a document from the chosen software using default print settings.<br>■ Understand facilities for storage and recall of e-mail addresses.<br>■ Appreciate the need to manage e-mail messages (save, delete, back-up).<br>■ Understand the use of Internet address (URL) storage facilities. |

## Unit 4 Spreadsheets

### 1 Identify and use spreadsheet software correctly.

| Assessment objectives | Knowledge and understanding |
| --- | --- |
| a Use appropriate application software | ■ Identify appropriate software for the task (e.g. spreadsheet).<br>■ Understand correct procedures for using chosen software.<br>■ Appreciate the differences between spreadsheet software and alternatives (formulae, automatic recalculation). |

### 2 Use an input device to enter and edit data accurately.

| Assessment objectives | Knowledge and understanding |
| --- | --- |
| a Insert text and numerical data<br>b Insert row/column<br>c Delete row/column<br>d Amend text and numerical data | ■ Understand the use of an input device to enter data.<br>■ Appreciate the need for accuracy and the importance of checking output against expectations.<br>■ Understand the software's tools for adding and deleting rows and columns and appreciate the difference between deleting, hiding and clearing.<br>■ Understand how to amend data. |

## 3 Insert, replicate and format arithmetical formulae.

| Assessment objectives | Knowledge and understanding |
|---|---|
| a Use formulae that produce correct results<br>b Replicate formulae (fill)<br>c Recalculate data | ■ Understand the structure of a formula and the use of mathematical operators ($+,-,*,/$) and brackets.<br>■ Understand how to fill/replicate down a column or along a row and appreciate the effects on relative cell references.<br>■ Appreciate that amending data may cause an automatic recalculation of the results of formulae based on that data. |

## 4 Use common numerical formatting and alignment.

| Assessment objectives | Knowledge and understanding |
|---|---|
| a Align text<br>b Align numerical data<br>c Display as integer (to 0 decimal places)<br>d Display as decimal (to two decimal places)<br>e Display as currency (to include £ sign) | ■ Appreciate common conventions for the display of spreadsheet data.<br>■ Understand the left, right and centre alignment of cell data.<br>■ Understand how to format numerical data to display in integer and/or in two decimal place format and appreciate the difference between the data that is shown and the data that is used for calculations.<br>■ Understand how to format numerical data to display a £ sign and appreciate that currency data is not always presented to two decimal places. |

## 5 Manage and print spreadsheet documents.

| Assessment objectives | Knowledge and understanding |
|---|---|
| a Create a new spreadsheet<br>b Save spreadsheet<br>c Save spreadsheet with new filename<br>d Print with formulae showing in full<br>e Print with data showing in full<br>f Close spreadsheet | ■ Understand document management in the chosen software (file menu, new, save, save as, close).<br>■ Understand how to print a document from the chosen software using default print settings.<br>■ Understand how to set the spreadsheet to print with the formulae showing and appreciate the changes to the display that may result.<br>■ Understand how to change column width and appreciate the need to leave additional space for differences in printer output. |

## Unit 5 Databases

## 1 Identify and use database software correctly.

| Assessment objectives | Knowledge and understanding |
|---|---|
| a Use appropriate application software | ■ Identify appropriate software for the task (e.g. database).<br>■ Understand correct procedures for using chosen software.<br>■ Appreciate the differences between databases and spreadsheets (live data handling, multiple views [forms], flexible query/search/present facilities). |

## 2 Use an input device to enter and edit data accurately.

| Assessment objectives | Knowledge and understanding |
|---|---|
| a Create new records<br>b Enter data<br>c Delete record<br>d Amend data<br>e Replace specified data | ■ Understand the use of an input device to enter data.<br>■ Appreciate the need for accuracy and the importance of checking output against expectations.<br>■ Understand the software's tools for adding and deleting records and appreciate the effects on the database.<br>■ Understand how to amend an existing record.<br>■ Appreciate the advantages of a search & replace tool over manual editing of multiple items in a large database. |

## 3 Create simple queries/searches on one or two criteria.

| Assessment objectives | Knowledge and understanding |
|---|---|
| a Select data on one criterion<br>b Select data on two criteria<br>c Present only selected fields | ■ Understand the software's facility for producing simple database queries/searches/filters and how to save them for later use.<br>■ Understand the use of $=<,>,<=,>=$ in search criteria.<br>■ Understand the use of the software's query or filter facility to select a subset of data matching one and two criteria (text, numbers & date).<br>■ Understand how to select which fields will be presented/printed. |

## 4 Present selected data sorted alphabetically, numerically and by date.

| Assessment objectives | Knowledge and understanding |
|---|---|
| a Sort data alphabetically<br>b Sort data numerically<br>c Sort data by date | ■ Understand how to present data sorted alphabetically and numerically (both ascending and descending) and by date. |

## 5 Manage and print database files.

| Assessment objectives | Knowledge and understanding |
|---|---|
| a Open an existing database<br>b Save data<br>c Save query/filter<br>d Print data in table format<br>e Close database | ■ Understand the document management techniques for the chosen software and the differences from generic document management terms (e.g. automatic saving of data).<br>■ Understand how to print a table from the chosen software using default print settings.<br>■ Understand how to present and print the results of a query/filter as an unformatted tabular report. |

## Unit 6 Desktop publishing using Publisher

## 1 Identify and use appropriate software correctly.

| Assessment objectives | Knowledge and understanding |
|---|---|
| a Use appropriate application | ■ Identify appropriate software for the task (e.g. DTP/page layout software).<br>■ Understand correct procedures for using chosen software.<br>■ Appreciate the differences between DTP software and wordprocessors (e.g. text flow, image control, purpose). |

## 2 Set up a standard page layout and text properties.

| Assessment objectives | Knowledge and understanding |
|---|---|
| a Set page size/orientation<br>b Set margins<br>c Create text areas/text frames<br>d Set column widths/spacing<br>e Use serif/sans-serif fonts<br>f Use multiple font sizes | ■ Understand the use of master pages, templates or equivalent.<br>■ Understand how to set page size and margins.<br>■ Understand the use and control of text frames or equivalent.<br>■ Distinguish between serif and sans-serif typefaces and understand how to select them.<br>■ Understand how to set and amend text sizes. |

## 3 Import and place text and image files.

| Assessment objectives | Knowledge and understanding |
|---|---|
| a Import text file(s)<br>b Import image(s)<br>c Enter heading<br>d Use line or border feature | ■ Understand the means by which text files and images can be imported and placed in the publication.<br>■ Understand how to enter small amounts of text.<br>■ Understand the basic graphic capabilities of DTP software and how to use lines and/or borders to separate areas of text. |

## 4 Manipulate text and images to balance page.

| Assessment objectives | Knowledge and understanding |
|---|---|
| a Apply alignment and justification<br>b Set paragraph spacing and/or first line indent<br>c Move/resize image<br>d Resize text<br>e Fit headline text to page width<br>f Balance columns | ■ Understand the use of left and centre alignment and of full justification.<br>■ Appreciate common DTP conventions such as first line indents and understand how to use them consistently.<br>■ Understand how to manipulate images (move, resize).<br>■ Understand how to fit text to a specified width.<br>■ Understand the common requirement for text in columns to be balanced or fit to a specific area and how to adjust text size and spacing in order to achieve this. |

## 5 Manage publications and print composite proofs.

| Assessment objectives | Knowledge and understanding |
|---|---|
| a Create new publication<br>b Save master page/template<br>c Save publication<br>d Print composite proof(s)<br>e Close publication | ■ Understand the document management techniques for the chosen DTP software and the differences from generic document management terms (e.g. master pages).<br>■ Understand how to print composite proofs from the chosen software using default print settings. |

## Unit 7 Graphs and charts

### 1 Identify and use appropriate software correctly.

| Assessment objectives | Knowledge and understanding |
|---|---|
| a Use appropriate application | ■ Identify appropriate software for the task (e.g. spreadsheet/database/statistical software).<br>■ Understand correct procedures for using chosen software.<br>■ Appreciate the differences between data modelling software and purely graphical alternatives (e.g. live data modelling). |

## 2 Produce pie charts, line graphs and bar/column charts.

| Assessment objectives | Knowledge and understanding |
|---|---|
| a Use pie chart<br>b Use line graph<br>c Use bar/column chart | ■ Distinguish between pie charts, line graphs and bar/column charts and understand how to create and format them. |

## 3 Select and present single and comparative sets of data.

| Assessment objectives | Knowledge and understanding |
|---|---|
| a Select single data set<br>b Select comparative data set<br>c Select subset of single data set | ■ Understand how to select a variety of data sets for display in graphical form, using contiguous data.<br>■ Understand how to compare two sets of similar data using line graphs and bar/column charts. |

## 4 Set numerical parameters and format data.

| Assessment objectives | Knowledge and understanding |
|---|---|
| a Set axes upper and lower limits<br>b Select and display data labels<br>c Select/enter headings and axes titles<br>d Use a legend where appropriate<br>e Ensure comparative data is distinctive | ■ Understand how to amend the graph/chart to display specific upper and lower limits for continuous data.<br>■ Understand how to amend default /automatic formatting where necessary.<br>■ Distinguish between titles, axes titles, legends and labels and understand how to set and amend them.<br>■ Appreciate the need for a legend to correctly identify comparative data sets.<br>■ Appreciate the need to ensure comparative data is distinctive, and the effects of printing coloured graphs in grey. |

## 5 Manage and print graph and chart documents.

| Assessment objectives | Knowledge and understanding |
|---|---|
| a Open existing data document<br>b Save data document<br>c Save charts/graphs<br>d Print graphs/charts<br>e Close document | ■ Understand the document management techniques for the chosen software and the differences from generic document management terms (e.g. saving charts, tables, data).<br>■ Understand how to print from the chosen software using default print settings. |

# Unit 8 Computer art

## 1 Identify and use appropriate software correctly.

| Assessment objectives | Knowledge and understanding |
|---|---|
| a Use appropriate application software | ■ Identify appropriate software for the task (e.g. bitmapped, paint or vector-based draw software).<br>■ Understand correct procedures for using chosen software.<br>■ Appreciate the differences between bitmap and vector-based graphics and their uses and limitations (e.g. edit modes, scalability). |

## 2 Import, crop and resize images.

| Assessment objectives | Knowledge and understanding |
|---|---|
| a Import and place bitmapped image(s)<br>b Crop image<br>c Resize image(s) to fit<br>d Create graphic shape(s) | ■ Recognise common bitmap file formats (e.g. .jpg, .gif) and understand how to import/paste an existing image file into artwork.<br>■ Understand the chosen software's basic image manipulation facilities (crop, resize).<br>■ Understand how to create simple geometric and freehand shapes using the chosen software (e.g. squares, circles, rectangles, ellipses, triangles, straight and curved lines, freehand lines). |

## 3 Enter, amend and resize text.

| Assessment objectives | Knowledge and understanding |
|---|---|
| a Enter text<br>b Amend text<br>c Resize text to fit | ■ Understand the chosen software's text editing and manipulation facilities (create, amend, resize).<br>■ Appreciate the difference between scalable and non-scalable text (bitmap/vector). |

## 4 Manipulate and format page items.

| Assessment objectives | Knowledge and understanding |
|---|---|
| a Use specified colours<br>b Rotate item<br>c Flip item<br>d Copy item<br>e Delete item | ■ Understand how to apply colour to text and graphics using the chosen software (e.g., fill, object properties, etc.).<br>■ Understand how to isolate and manipulate text and graphic items (e.g. rotate [180°, 90° clockwise, 90° anti-clockwise], flip horizontal/vertical, copy & paste, delete/erase). |

## 5 Manage and print artwork.

| Assessment objectives | Knowledge and understanding |
|---|---|
| a Create new document<br>b Set artwork size/resolution<br>c Save document<br>d Save document with new filename<br>e Print artwork<br>f Close document | ■ Understand the document management techniques for the chosen software (file menu, open, save, save as, close).<br>■ Understand how to specify the size of artwork (in metric measurements) and appreciate the relationships between screen size, print size and resolution.<br>■ Understand how to print from the chosen software using default print settings. |

## Unit 9 Web pages

## 1 Identify and use appropriate software correctly.

| Assessment objectives | Knowledge and understanding |
|---|---|
| a Use appropriate application software | ■ Identify appropriate software for the task (e.g. HTML editor/text editor and browser software).<br>■ Understand correct procedures for using chosen software.<br>■ Appreciate the differences between WYSIWYG, HTML editing software and text editors (e.g. automation, interface, speed) and the disadvantages of exporting DTP and wordprocessing files as HTML. |

## 2 Import and place text and image files.

| Assessment objectives | Knowledge and understanding |
| --- | --- |
| a Insert text file<br>b Insert and place image | ▪ Understand how to import/insert text and images into a web page using the chosen software. |

## 3 Amend and format web pages.

| Assessment objectives | Knowledge and understanding |
| --- | --- |
| a Align page items<br>b Use three different font sizes<br>c Change background colour<br>d Emphasise text<br>e Edit text<br>f Control text flow | ▪ Appreciate the basic mechanism of web page formatting (HTML, tags).<br>▪ Understand how to emphasise text (bold, italic).<br>▪ Understand how to set the font size for specified text.<br>▪ Understand how to set the background colour and distinguish between background colour and background image.<br>▪ Understand the alignment of page items to the left, right and centre. |

## 4 Insert relative, external and e-mail hyperlinks.

| Assessment objectives | Knowledge and understanding |
| --- | --- |
| a Link pages<br>b Insert external link<br>c Insert e-mail link<br>d Test links<br>e Insert link text<br>f Retain original data and formatting | ▪ Understand the correct use and format of basic hypertext links.<br>▪ Understand the correct use of external hyperlinks using http: and mailto:.<br>▪ Appreciate the need to test that hyperlinks function correctly.<br>▪ Appreciate the effects of editing HTML code on the browser display.<br>▪ Appreciate the need to 'refresh or 'reload' web pages after editing. |

## 5 Manage and print web pages.

| Assessment objectives | Knowledge and understanding |
| --- | --- |
| a Create new document<br>b Save document<br>c Print web pages<br>d Print HTML source code<br>e Close document | ▪ Understand the document management techniques for the chosen software (file menu, open, save, save as, close).<br>▪ Appreciate the basic structure of an HTML page.<br>▪ Understand how to print from the chosen browser software using default print settings.<br>▪ Understand how to print the HTML source code using the chosen software. |

## Unit 10 Presentation graphics

## 1 Identify and use presentation graphics software correctly.

| Assessment objectives | Knowledge and understanding |
| --- | --- |
| a Use appropriate application software | ▪ Identify appropriate software for the task (e.g. presentation graphics).<br>▪ Understand correct procedures for using chosen software.<br>▪ Be aware of presentation graphics conventions and the relevance of house style (e.g. words per frame). |

## 2 Set up a slide layout/template.

| Assessment objectives | Knowledge and understanding |
| --- | --- |
| a Create text areas/text frames | ■ Understand the importance of consistency within a slide show. |
| b Apply background | ■ Understand how to insert graphics into a presentation. |
| c Insert graphic | ■ Understand the use of backgrounds. |

## 3 Format text style

| Assessment objectives | Knowledge and understanding |
| --- | --- |
| a Use specified font sizes | ■ Understand how to set and amend font sizes. |
| b Use bullets | ■ Understand how to apply emphasis (bold, italic, underline). |
| c Apply alignment | ■ Understand the use of left and centre alignment. |
| d Apply enhancement | ■ Understand the use of bullet points. |

## 4 Enter and edit data.

| Assessment objectives | Knowledge and understanding |
| --- | --- |
| a Create frames | ■ Understand the use of the mouse, pointer and cursor/prompt in selecting the edit point. |
| b Insert text | ■ Understand the use of common editing tools (text selection, cut, copy & paste, delete & backspace) and appreciate their various advantages/disadvantages. |
| c Delete text | |
| d Replace specified text | ■ Appreciate the advantages of a search & replace tool over manual editing of multiple items. |
| e Promote/demote text | ■ Understand the use of first level and second level text, and the concept of promotion and demotion. |

## 5 Manage and print presentation files.

| Assessment objectives | Knowledge and understanding |
| --- | --- |
| a Create new presentation | ■ Understand the document management techniques for the chosen software (file menu, open, save, save as, close). |
| b Save document | |
| c Print slides | ■ Understand how to print from the chosen software using default print settings. |
| d Print audience notes/ thumbnails | ■ Understand how to produce audience notes and thumbnail printouts. |
| e Close document | |

# Appendix 2
# Office keyboard shortcuts

## Microsoft Word shortcuts

**Create, view and save documents**

| Command | Keystrokes |
| --- | --- |
| Create a new document of the same type as the current or most recent document | Ctrl+N |
| Open a document | Ctrl+O |
| Close a document | Ctrl+W |
| Split the document window | Alt+Ctrl+S |
| Remove the document window split | Alt+Shift+C |
| Save a document | Ctrl+S |

**Find and replace text**

| Command | Keystrokes |
| --- | --- |
| Find text, formatting, and special items | Ctrl+F |
| Repeat find (after closing Find and Replace window) | Alt+Ctrl+Y |
| Replace text, specific formatting, and special items | Ctrl+H |
| Go to a page, bookmark, footnote, table, comment, graphic, or other location | Ctrl+G |
| Go back to a page, bookmark, footnote, table, comment, graphic, or other location | Alt+Ctrl+Z |
| Browse through a document | Alt+Ctrl+Home |

**Undo and redo**

| Command | Keystrokes |
| --- | --- |
| Cancel an action | Esc |
| Undo an action | Ctrl+Z |
| Redo or repeat an action | Ctrl+Y |

**Editing text and graphics**

| Command | Keystrokes |
| --- | --- |
| Delete one character to the left | Backspace |
| Delete one word to the left | Ctrl+Backspace |
| Delete one character to the right | Delete |
| Delete one word to the right | Ctrl+Delete |

| | |
|---|---|
| Cut selected text to the clipboard | Ctrl+X |
| Undo the last action | Ctrl+Z |
| Cut to the spike | Ctrl+F3 |

**Copy and move text**

| Command | Keystrokes |
|---|---|
| Copy text or graphics | Ctrl+C |
| Display the Office clipboard | Ctrl+C, Ctrl+C |
| Move text or graphics | F2 (then move the insertion point and press Enter) |
| Create AutoText | Alt+F3 |
| Paste the clipboard contents | Ctrl+V |
| Paste the spike contents | Ctrl+Shift+F3 |
| Copy the header or footer used in the previous section of the document | Alt+Shift+R |

**Change font size**

| Command | Keystrokes |
|---|---|
| Change the font | Ctrl+Shift+F |
| Change the font size | Ctrl+Shift+P |
| Increase the font size | Ctrl+Shift+> |
| Decrease the font size | Ctrl+Shift+< |
| Increase the font size by 1 point | Ctrl+] |
| Decrease the font size by 1 point | Ctrl+[ |

**Function keys**

| Command | Keystrokes |
|---|---|
| Get Help or the Office Assistant | F1 |
| Move text or graphics | F2 |
| Insert an AutoText entry (after Microsoft Word displays the entry) | F3 |
| Repeat the last action | F4 |
| Choose the Go To command (Edit menu) | F5 |
| Go to the next pane or frame | F6 |
| Choose the Spelling command (Tools menu) | F7 |
| Extend a selection | F8 |
| Update selected fields | F9 |
| Activate the menu bar | F10 |
| Go to the next field | F11 |
| Choose the Save As command (File menu) | F12 |

## Printing and previewing documents

| Command | Keystrokes |
| --- | --- |
| Print a document | Ctrl+P |
| Switch in or out of print preview | Alt+Ctrl+I |
| Move around the preview page when zoomed in | Arrow keys |
| Move by one preview page when zoomed out | Page up or Page down |
| Move to the first preview page when zoomed out | Ctrl+Home |
| Move to the last preview page when zoomed out | Ctrl+End |

## Microsoft Excel shortcuts

### Menus and toolbars

| Command | Keystrokes |
| --- | --- |
| Select the menu bar, or close an open menu and sub-menu at the same time | F10 or Alt |
| When a toolbar is selected, select the next or previous button or menu on the toolbar | Tab or Shift+Tab |
| When a toolbar is selected, select the next or previous toolbar | Ctrl+Tab or Ctrl+Shift+Tab |
| Open the selected menu, or perform the action for the selected button or command | Enter |
| Display the Shortcut menu for the selected item | Shift+F10 |
| Display the Control menu for the Excel window | Alt+Spacebar |
| When a menu or sub-menu is open, select the next or previous command | Down arrow or Up arrow |
| Select the menu to the left or right. When a sub-menu is open, switch between the main menu and the sub-menu | Left arrow or Right arrow |
| Select the first or last command on the menu or sub-menu | Home or End |
| Close an open menu. When a sub-menu is open, close only the sub-menu | Esc |
| Display the full set of commands on a menu | Ctrl+Down arrow |
| Show or hide the standard toolbar | Ctrl+7 |

### Displaying and using windows

| Command | Keystrokes |
| --- | --- |
| Switch to the next program | Alt+Tab |
| Switch to the previous program | Alt+Shift+Tab |
| Display the Windows start menu | Ctrl+Esc |
| Close the selected workbook window | Ctrl+W or Ctrl+F4 |

| | |
|---|---|
| Restore the window size of the selected workbook window | Ctrl+F5 |
| Switch to the next pane in a worksheet that has been split (Window menu, Split command) | F6 |
| Switch to the previous pane in a worksheet that has been split | Shift+F6 |
| When more than one workbook window is open, switch to the next workbook window | Ctrl+F6 |
| Switch to the previous workbook window | Ctrl+Shift+F6 |
| When a workbook window is not maximised, perform the Move command (on the Control menu for the workbook window). Use the arrow keys to move the window, and when finished press Esc | Ctrl+F7 |
| When a workbook window is not maximised, perform the Size command (on the Control menu for the workbook window). Use the arrow keys to resize the window, and when finished press Esc | Ctrl+F8 |
| Minimise a workbook window to an icon | Ctrl+F9 |
| Maximise or restore the selected workbook window | Ctrl+F10 |
| Copy a picture of the screen to the clipboard | PrtScn |
| Copy a picture of the selected window to the clipboard | Alt+Print screen |

**Using dialogue boxes**

| Command | Keystrokes |
|---|---|
| Move to the next option or option group | Tab |
| Move to the previous option or option group | Shift+Tab |
| Switch to the next tab in a dialog box | Ctrl+Tab or Ctrl+Page down |
| Switch to the previous tab in a dialog box | Ctrl+Shift+Tab or Ctrl+Page up |
| Move between options in an open drop-down list, or between options in a group of options | Arrow keys |
| Perform the action for the selected button, or select or clear the selected check box | Spacebar |
| Open the selected drop-down list | Alt+Down arrow |
| Perform the action for the default command button in the dialog box (the button with the bold outline, often the OK button) | Enter |
| Cancel the command and close the dialog box | Esc |

**Preview and print**

| Command | Keystrokes |
| --- | --- |
| Display the Print dialog box | Ctrl+P or Ctrl+Shift+F12 |
| Use the following keys in print preview (to get to print preview, press Alt+F, then press V) | Arrow keys |
| Move around the page when zoomed in | Page up or Page down |
| Move by one page when zoomed out | Ctrl+Up arrow or Ctrl+Left arrow |
| Move to the first page when zoomed out | Ctrl+Down arrow or Ctrl+Right arrow |

**Working with worksheets**

| Command | Keystrokes |
| --- | --- |
| Insert a new worksheet | Shift+F11 or Alt+Shift+F1 |
| Move to the next sheet in the workbook | Ctrl+Page down |
| Move to the previous sheet in the workbook | Ctrl+Page up |
| Select the current and next sheet. To cancel selection of multiple sheets, press Ctrl+Page down or, to select a different sheet, press Ctrl+Page up | Shift+Ctrl+Page down |
| Select the current and previous sheet | Shift+Ctrl+Page up |
| Rename the current sheet (Format menu, Sheet sub-menu, Rename command) | Alt+O H R |
| Move or copy the current sheet (Edit menu, Move or Copy Sheet command) | Alt+E M |
| Delete the current sheet (Edit menu, Delete Sheet command) | Alt+E L |

**Moving around worksheets**

| Command | Keystrokes |
| --- | --- |
| Move one cell up, down, left, or right | Arrow keys |
| Move to the edge of the current data region | Ctrl+arrow key |
| Move to the beginning of the row | Home |
| Move to the beginning of the worksheet | Ctrl+Home |
| Move to the last cell on the worksheet, in the bottom most used row of the right most used column | Ctrl+End |
| Move down one screen | Page down |
| Move up one screen | Page up |
| Move one screen to the right | Alt+Page down |
| Move one screen to the left | Alt+Page up |

| | |
|---|---|
| Switch to the next pane in a worksheet that has been split (Window menu, Split command) | F6 |
| Switch to the previous pane in a worksheet that has been split | Shift+F6 |
| Scroll to display the active cell | Ctrl+Backspace |
| Display the Go To dialog box | F5 |
| Display the Find dialog box | Shift+F5 |
| Repeat the last Find action (same as Find Next) | Shift+F4 |
| Move between unlocked cells on a protected worksheet | Tab |

**Selecting cells, rows, columns and objects**

| Command | Keystrokes |
|---|---|
| Select the entire column | Ctrl+Spacebar |
| Select the entire row | Shift+Spacebar |
| Select the entire worksheet | Ctrl+A |
| With multiple cells selected, select only the active cell | Shift+Backspace |
| With an object selected, select all objects on a sheet | Ctrl+Shift+Spacebar |
| Alternate between hiding objects, displaying objects, and displaying placeholders for objects | Ctrl+6 |

**Entering data**

| Command | Keystrokes |
|---|---|
| Complete a cell entry and select the cell below | Enter |
| Start a new line in the same cell | Alt+Enter |
| Fill the selected cell range with the current entry | Ctrl+Enter |
| Complete a cell entry and select the previous cell above | Shift+Enter |
| Complete a cell entry and select the next cell to the right | Tab |
| Complete a cell entry and select the previous cell to the left | Shift+Tab |
| Cancel a cell entry | Esc |
| Move one character up, down, left, or right | Arrow keys |
| Move to the beginning of the line | Home |
| Repeat the last action | F4 or Ctrl+Y |
| Create names from row and column labels | Ctrl+Shift+F3 |
| Fill down | Ctrl+D |
| Fill to the right | Ctrl+R |
| Define a name | Ctrl+F3 |

| Insert a hyperlink | Ctrl+K |
| Activate a hyperlink | Enter (in a cell with a hyperlink) |
| Enter the date | Ctrl+; (semicolon) |
| Enter the time | Ctrl+Shift+: (colon) |
| Display a drop-down list of the values in the current column of a list | Alt+Down arrow |
| Undo the last action | Ctrl+Z |

**Edit data**

| Command | Keystrokes |
| --- | --- |
| Edit the active cell and position the insertion point at the end of the cell contents | F2 |
| Start a new line in the same cell. | Alt+Enter |
| Edit the active cell and then clear it, or delete the preceding character in the active cell as you edit cell contents | Backspace |
| Delete the character to the right of the insertion point, or delete the selection | Delete |
| Delete text to the end of the line | Ctrl+Delete |
| Display the Spelling dialog box | F7 |
| Edit a cell comment | Shift+F2 |
| Complete a cell entry and select the next cell below | Enter |
| Undo the last action | Ctrl+Z |
| Cancel a cell entry | Esc |
| When the AutoCorrect Smart Tag is displayed, undo or redo the last automatic correction | Ctrl+Shift+Z |
| Copy the selected cells | Ctrl+C |
| Display the Microsoft Office clipboard (multiple copy and paste) | Ctrl+C, Ctrl+C |
| Cut the selected cells | Ctrl+X |
| Paste copied cells | Ctrl+V |
| Clear the contents of the selected cells | Delete |
| Delete the selected cells | Ctrl+- (hyphen) |
| Insert blank cells | Ctrl+Shift++ (plus) |

**Formatting data**

| Command | Keystrokes |
| --- | --- |
| Display the Style dialog box | Alt+' (apostrophe) |
| Display the Format Cells dialog box | Ctrl+1 |

| | |
|---|---|
| Apply the General number format | Ctrl+Shift+~ |
| Apply the Currency format with two decimal places (negative numbers in parentheses) | Ctrl+Shift+$ |
| Apply the Percentage format with no decimal places | Ctrl+Shift+% |
| Apply the Exponential number format with two decimal places | Ctrl+Shift+^ |
| Apply the Date format with the day, month and year | Ctrl+Shift+# |
| Apply the Time format with the hour and minute, and AM or PM | Ctrl+Shift+@ |
| Apply the Number format with two decimal places, thousands separator, and minus sign (–) for negative values | Ctrl+Shift+! |
| Apply or remove bold formatting | Ctrl+B |
| Apply or remove italic formatting | Ctrl+I |
| Apply or remove underlining | Ctrl+U |
| Apply or remove strikethrough | Ctrl+5 |
| Hide the selected rows | Ctrl+9 |
| Unhide any hidden rows within the selection | Ctrl+Shift+( (opening parenthesis) |
| Hide the selected columns | Ctrl+0 (zero) |
| Unhide any hidden columns within the selection | Ctrl+Shift+) (closing parenthesis) |
| Apply the outline border to the selected cells | Ctrl+Shift+& |
| Remove the outline border from the selected cells | Ctrl+Shift+_ |

## Microsoft Access shortcuts

**General keys**

| Command | Keystrokes |
|---|---|
| To open a new database | Ctrl+N |
| To open an existing database | Ctrl+O |
| To quit Microsoft Access | Alt+F4 |

**Printing and saving**

| Command | Keystrokes |
|---|---|
| To print the current or selected object | Ctrl+P |
| To open the Print dialog box | P or Ctrl+P |
| To open the Page Setup dialog box | S |

| To cancel Print Preview or Layout Preview | C or Esc |
|---|---|
| To save a database object | Ctrl+S or Shift+F12 or Alt+Shift+F2 |
| To open the Save As dialog box | F12 or Alt+F2 |

**Finding or replacing data**

| Command | Keystrokes |
|---|---|
| To open the Find tab in the Find and Replace dialog box (Datasheet view and Form view only) | Ctrl+F |
| To open the Replace tab in the Find and Replace dialog box (Datasheet view and Form view only) | Ctrl+H |
| To find the next occurrence of the text specified in the Find and Replace dialog box when the dialog box is closed (Datasheet view and Form view only) | Shift+F4 |

**Menus and toolbars**

| Command | Keystrokes |
|---|---|
| To show the shortcut menu | Shift+F10 |
| To make the menu bar active | F10 |
| To show the program icon menu (on the program title bar) | Alt+Spacebar |
| With the menu or sub-menu visible, to select the next or previous command | Down arrow or Up arrow |
| To select the menu to the left or right, or, when a sub-menu is visible, to switch between the main menu and the sub-menu | Left arrow or Right arrow |
| To select the first or last command on the menu or sub-menu | Home or End |
| To close the visible menu and sub-menu at the same time | Alt |
| To close the visible menu; or, with a sub-menu visible, to close the sub-menu only | Esc |
| To select the next or previous toolbar | CTRL+Tab or Ctrl+Shift+Tab |
| When a toolbar is active, to select the next or previous button or menu on the toolbar | Tab or Shift+Tab |
| When a menu on a toolbar is selected, to open the menu | Enter |
| When a button is selected, to perform the action assigned to a button | Enter |

**Working with data**

| Command | Keystrokes |
|---|---|
| To extend one character to the right | Shift+Right arrow |
| To extend one word to the right | Ctrl+Shift+Right arrow |
| To extend one character to the left | Shift+Left arrow |
| To extend one word to the left | Ctrl+Shift+Left arrow |
| To select the next field | Tab |
| To switch between Edit mode (with insertion point displayed) and Navigation mode | F2 |
| To switch between selecting the current record and the first field of the current record, in Navigation mode | Shift+Spacebar |
| To extend selection to the previous record, if the current record is selected | Shift+Up arrow |
| To extend selection to the next record, if the current record is selected | Shift+Down arrow |
| To select all records | Ctrl+A or Ctrl+Shift+Spacebar |
| To copy the selection to the clipboard | Ctrl+C |
| To cut the selection and copy it to the clipboard | Ctrl+X |
| To paste the contents of the clipboard at the insertion point | Ctrl+V |
| To delete the selection or the character to the left of the insertion point | Backspace |
| To delete the selection or the character to the right of the insertion point | Delete |
| To delete all characters to the right of the insertion point | Ctrl+Delete |
| To undo typing | Ctrl+Z or Alt+Backspace |
| To undo changes in the current field or current record; if both have been changed, press Esc twice to undo changes, first in the current field and then in the current record | Esc |

**Find a record**

| Command | Keystrokes |
|---|---|
| To move to the record number box; then type the record number and press Enter | F5 |

**Moving between fields and records**

| Command | Keystrokes |
| --- | --- |
| To move to the next field | Tab or Right arrow |
| To move to the last field in the current record, in Navigation mode | End |
| To move to the previous field | Shift+Tab, or Left arrow |
| To move to the first field in the current record, in Navigation mode | Home |
| To move to the current field in the next record | Down arrow |
| To move to the current field in the last record, in Navigation mode | Ctrl+Down arrow |
| To move to the last field in the last record, in Navigation mode | Ctrl+End |
| To move to the current field in the previous record | Up arrow |
| To move to the current field in the first record, in Navigation mode | Ctrl+Up arrow |
| To move to the first field in the first record, in Navigation mode | Ctrl+Home |

## Microsoft PowerPoint shortcuts

**Creating and editing presentations**

| Command | Keystrokes |
| --- | --- |
| Create a new presentation | Ctrl+N |
| Insert a new slide | Ctrl+M |
| Make a copy of the selected slide | Ctrl+D |
| Open a presentation | Ctrl+O |
| Close a presentation | Ctrl+W |
| Print a presentation | Ctrl+P |
| Save a presentation | Ctrl+S |
| Run a presentation | F5 |
| Quit PowerPoint | Alt+F4 |
| Find text | Ctrl+F |
| Replace text | Ctrl+H |
| Insert a hyperlink | Ctrl+K |
| Check spelling | F7 |

**Moving around in text**

| Command | Keystrokes |
|---|---|
| One character to the left | Left arrow |
| One character to the right | Right arrow |
| One line up | Up arrow |
| One line down | Down arrow |
| One word to the left | Ctrl+Left arrow |
| One word to the right | Ctrl+Right arrow |
| To the end of a line | End |
| To the beginning of a line | Home |
| Up one paragraph | Ctrl+Up arrow |
| Down one paragraph | Ctrl+Down arrow |
| To the end of a text box | Ctrl+End |
| To the beginning of a text box | Ctrl+Home |
| To the next title or body text placeholder. (If it is the last placeholder on a slide, this will insert a new slide with the same slide layout as the original slide.) | Ctrl+Enter |
| To repeat the last Find action | Shift+F4 |

**Running a slide show**

| Command | Keystrokes |
|---|---|
| Perform the next animation or advance to the next slide | N, Enter, Page down, Right arrow, Down arrow, or the Spacebar (or click the mouse) |
| Perform the previous animation or return to the previous slide | P, Page up, Left arrow, Up arrow, or Backspace |
| Go to slide number | [number]+Enter |
| Display a black screen, or return to the slide show from a black screen | B or Period |
| Display a white screen, or return to the slide show from a white screen | W or Comma |
| Stop or restart an automatic slide show | S or Plus sign |
| End a slide show | Esc, Ctrl+Break, or Hyphen |
| Erase on-screen annotations | E |
| Go to the next hidden slide | H |
| Set new timings while rehearsing | T |
| Use original timings while rehearsing | O |

| | |
|---|---|
| Use mouse-click to advance while rehearsing | M |
| Return to the first slide | 1+Enter (or press both mouse buttons for 2 seconds) |
| Redisplay hidden pointer and/or change the pointer to a pen | Ctrl+P |
| Redisplay hidden pointer and/or change the pointer to an arrow | Ctrl+A |
| Hide the pointer and navigation button immediately | Ctrl+H |
| Hide the pointer and navigation button in 15 seconds | Ctrl+U |
| Display the Shortcut menu | Shift+F10 (or right-click) |

## Microsoft Publisher shortcuts

**Edit and format text**

| Command | Keystrokes |
|---|---|
| Find | Ctrl+F or F3 |
| Repeat previous Find | Shift+F4 |
| Find and replace | Ctrl+H |
| Check spelling | F7 |
| Make text bold | Ctrl+B |
| Italicise text | Ctrl+I |
| Underline text | Ctrl+U |
| Make text small capital letters | Ctrl+Shift+K |
| Change text style | Ctrl+Shift+S |
| Change text font | Ctrl+Shift+F |
| Change text size | Ctrl+Shift+P |
| Copy formatting | Ctrl+Shift+C |
| Paste formatting | Ctrl+Shift+V |
| Return character formatting to the current text style | Ctrl+Spacebar |
| Apply or remove subscript formatting | Ctrl+= |
| Apply or remove superscript formatting | Ctrl+Shift+= |
| Increase space between letters in a word (kerning) | Ctrl+Shift+] |
| Decrease space between letters in a word (kerning) | Ctrl+Shift+[ |

| | |
|---|---|
| Increase font size by 1.0 point | Ctrl+] |
| Decrease font size by 1.0 point | Ctrl+[ |
| Increase to the next size in the Font Size box | Ctrl+Shift+> |
| Decrease to the next size in the Font Size box | Ctrl+Shift+< |

**Menus and toolbars**

| Command | Keystrokes |
|---|---|
| Select the menu bar, or close an open menu and sub-menu at the same time | F10 or Alt |
| When a toolbar is selected, select the next or previous button or menu on the toolbar | Tab or Shift+Tab |
| When a toolbar is selected, select the next or previous toolbar | Ctrl+Tab or Ctrl+Shift+Tab |
| Open the selected menu, or perform the action for the selected button or command | Enter |
| Display the Shortcut menu for the selected item | Shift+F10 |
| Display the Window Shortcut menu (Control menu) | Alt+Spacebar |
| When a menu or sub-menu is open, select the next or previous command | Down arrow or Up arrow |
| Select the menu to the left or right. When a sub-menu is open, switch between the main menu and the sub-menu | Left arrow or Right arrow |
| Select the first or last command on the menu or sub-menu | Home or End |
| Close an open menu. When a sub-menu is open, close only the sub-menu | Esc |
| Display the full set of commands on a menu | Ctrl+Down arrow |

**Document and program windows**

| Command | Keystrokes |
|---|---|
| Switch to the next window | Alt+Tab |
| Switch to the previous window | Alt+Shift+Tab |
| Close the active window | Ctrl+W or Ctrl+F4 |
| Restore the size of the active window after you've maximised it | Ctrl+F5 |
| Move to a task pane from another pane in the program window (clockwise direction). You may need to press F6 more than once | F6 |
| Move to a pane from another pane in the program window (counter-clockwise direction) | Shift+F6 |
| When more than one window is open, switch to the next window | Ctrl+F6 |

| | |
|---|---|
| Switch to the previous window | Ctrl+Shift+F6 |
| When a document window is not maximised, perform the Move command (on the Control menu for the window). Use the arrow keys to move the window, and, when finished, press Esc | Ctrl+F7 |
| When a document window is not maximised, perform the Size command (on the Control menu for the window). Use the arrow keys to resize the window, and, when finished, press Esc | Ctrl+F8 |
| Minimise a window to an icon (works only for some Microsoft Office XP programs) | Ctrl+F9 |
| Maximise or restore a selected window | Ctrl+F10 |
| Copy a picture of the screen to the clipboard | Print screen |
| Copy a picture of the selected window to the clipboard | Alt+Print screen |

## Microsoft FrontPage shortcuts

**Working with pages**

| Command | Keystrokes |
|---|---|
| Create a new page | Ctrl+N |
| Open a page | Ctrl+O |
| Create a hyperlink on a page | Ctrl+K |
| Preview a page in a web browser | Ctrl+Shift+B |
| Print a page | Ctrl+P |
| Display non-printing characters | Ctrl+ Shift+8 |
| Display HTML tags | Ctrl+ / |
| Refresh a page | F5 |
| Switch between open pages | Ctrl+Tab or Ctrl+Shift+Tab |
| Close a page | Ctrl+F4 |
| Save a page | Ctrl+S |
| Quit Microsoft FrontPage | Alt+F4 |
| Find text on pages or in HTML | Ctrl+F |
| Replace text on pages or in HTML | Ctrl+H |
| Check spelling on a page | F7 |
| Look up a word in the Thesaurus | Shift+F7 |
| Cancel an action | Esc |

| | |
|---|---|
| Undo an action | Ctrl+Z or Alt+Backspace |
| Redo or repeat an action | Ctrl+Y or Shift+Alt+Backspace |

**Formatting**

| Command | Keystrokes |
|---|---|
| Change the font | Ctrl+Shift+F |
| Change the font size | Ctrl+Shift+P |
| Apply bold formatting | Ctrl+B |
| Apply an underline | Ctrl+U |
| Apply italic formatting | Ctrl+I |
| Apply superscript formatting | Ctrl++ (plus sign) |
| Apply subscript formatting | Ctrl+– (minus sign) |
| Copy formatting | Ctrl+Shift+C |
| Paste formatting | Ctrl+Shift+V |
| Remove manual formatting | Ctrl+Shift+Z or Ctrl+Spacebar |
| Centre a paragraph | Ctrl+E |
| Left-align a paragraph | Ctrl+L |
| Right-align a paragraph | Ctrl+R |
| Indent a paragraph from the left | Ctrl+M |
| Indent a paragraph from the right | Ctrl+Shift+M |
| Apply a style | Ctrl+Shift+S |
| Apply the Normal style | Ctrl+Shift+N |
| Apply the Heading 1 style | Ctrl+Alt+1 |
| Apply the Heading 2 style | Ctrl+Alt+2 |
| Apply the Heading 3 style | Ctrl+Alt+3 |
| Apply the Heading 4 style | Ctrl+Alt+4 |
| Apply the Heading 5 style | Ctrl+Alt+5 |
| Apply the Heading 6 style | Ctrl+Alt+6 |
| Apply the List style | Ctrl+Shift+L |

**Editing and moving text and graphics**

| Command | Keystrokes |
|---|---|
| Delete one character to the left | Backspace |
| Delete one character to the right | Delete |
| Delete one word to the left | Ctrl+Backspace |
| Delete one word to the right | Ctrl+Delete |

| | |
|---|---|
| Cut selected text to the clipboard | Ctrl+X or Shift+Delete |
| Copy text or graphics | Ctrl+C or Ctrl+Insert |
| Paste the clipboard contents | Ctrl+V or Shift+Insert |
| Insert a line break | Shift+Enter |
| Insert a nonbreaking space | Ctrl+Shift+Spacebar |

**Selecting text and graphics**

| Command | Keystrokes |
|---|---|
| One character to the right | Shift+Right arrow |
| One character to the left | Shift+Left arrow |
| To the end of a word | Ctrl+Shift+Right arrow |
| To the end of a line | Shift+End |
| To the beginning of a line | Shift+Home |
| One line down | Shift+Down arrow |
| One line up | Shift+Up arrow |
| To the end of a paragraph | Ctrl+Shift+Down arrow |
| To the beginning of a paragraph | Ctrl+Shift+Up arrow |
| One screen down | Shift+Page down |
| One screen up | Shift+Page up |
| To include the entire page | Ctrl+A |
| Display the properties of a selection | Alt+Enter |
| Insert a table | Shift+Ctrl+Alt+T |
| Select the next cell's contents | Tab |
| Select the preceding cell's contents | Shift+Tab |
| Extend a selection to adjacent cells | Hold down Shift and press an arrow key repeatedly |
| Select a column | Click in the column's top or bottom cell, then hold down Shift and press the Up arrow or Down arrow key repeatedly |

**Menus and toolbars**

| Command | Keystrokes |
|---|---|
| Show the Shortcut menu | Shift+F10 |
| Make the menu bar active | F10 |
| Show the program icon menu | Alt+Spacebar |

| | |
|---|---|
| Select the next or previous command on the menu or sub-menu | Down arrow or Down arrow (with the menu or sub-menu displayed) |
| Close the visible menu and sub-menu at the same time | Alt |
| Close the visible menu, or, with a sub-menu visible, close the sub-menu only | Esc |
| Create an Auto Thumbnail of a selected picture | Ctrl+T |
| Replace text | Ctrl+H |
| Insert a hyperlink | Ctrl+K |
| Check spelling | F7 |
| Cancel a menu or dialog box action | Esc |
| Undo an action | Ctrl+Z |
| Redo or repeat an action | Ctrl+Y |

# Appendix 3
# Glossary

| Term | Explanation |
|---|---|
| Assessment Objective | A required level of competence in a specific skill relating to an application. |
| Bandwidth | When you access the Internet and download information, the data is sent down the line you are using. Your modem will determine the speed at which you can receive the data but the type of connection will determine the maximum speed the data can actually be transmitted. The speed at which data can be sent is described in terms of bits per second. In simple terms the more you are trying to access or download the slower your system will be. Think of water travelling down a pipe. The thicker the pipe the more water can travel down it in a given period of time. Data acts in the same way; the less resistance, the faster the data can travel. The slowest is probably your telephone line. An optic cable can transfer data much faster. |
| BIOS | Basic input/output system. The BIOS gives a computer instructions on how to run programs and also interpret keystroke actions on the keyboard. |
| Boot | A term used when the computer is switched on and the internal system software looks for instructions for starting the machine. |
| Browser | The software you use to look round the World Wide Web. Perhaps one of the most common is Microsoft's Internet Explorer but there are others available, such as Netscape Navigator. |
| Byte | The equivalent of one character of data. |
| Cache | Temporary storage area for in-use data in the computer's memory. These data are lost once the computer is switched off. |
| Command button | A button, normally with an icon picture or letter, that performs a specific action. |
| CPU | Central processing unit – the box containing the electronic elements that together form the main part of a computer. The CPU can also refer to the actual processor chip of the computer. |
| Cursor | A flashing symbol on the screen that displays where text or graphics will be entered. |
| Database | A container for data from which information on a topic or subject can be obtained. |
| Database management system | The system that stores and retrieves information in a database. |
| Relational Database Management System (RDMS) | An application that is capable of creating, organising and editing databases and displaying data as required by the user in different formats, such as reports or queries. |
| Database Window | The window that appears when you open a database or after creating a new database. The window lists all the objects that are contained in the database such as tables, queries, reports, forms, modules and macros. |

| | |
|---|---|
| **Desktop Publisher** | An application that combines wordprocessing, graphics, and design to produce a publication in a desired format and layout. |
| **Desktop** | The initial Windows screen containing task bar and shortcuts to navigate around programs. |
| **Dial-up** | This is the connection made for access to the Internet or to use e-mail facilities. |
| **Disabled** | A facility that is present but is currently not available to the user. |
| **Domain name** | An Internet address, like freeserve.net, that can be registered and owned by an individual or a business. |
| **Download** | The process of transferring files from one computer to another. If you send files from your computer to a server, it is called uploading. |
| **Drag** | A facility whereby using the mouse, windows, pictures or other objects can be dragged (or moved) from one location to another. |
| **Drop-down menu** | A further selection of choices on a menu list. |
| **Element of Certification** | A required level of competence in a general skill relating to an application. |
| **E-mail** | Using a software application to exchange text messages. You can use e-mail to send messages to anyone anywhere in the world, provided they have an e-mail address. |
| **Enabled** | A facility that has been made available to the user. |
| **Event procedure** | Events are related to mouse movements and keyboard actions such as 'on-click', 'on-open' where some other action is expected to happen when the event is used. For example, an event may be 'When the form is opened' and the action may be 'Run this macro'. |
| **Fields** | A single item of information in a record. A field is synonymous with a column in a table. |
| **Floppy drive** | A removable storage data disk – currently holds 1.4 megabytes of data. |
| **Folder** | A container in a specific location to store programs, data and other files and folders. |
| **Forms** | A user-friendly interface for entering data into a table. |
| **FTP** | File Transfer Protocol – this is a method of sending and receiving files over the Internet. |
| **Functions** | Actions built into software that facilitate a broad range of actions available to the user – such functions can include the insertion of dates, fields for forms, tables, etc. |
| **Gigabyte** | The equivalent of 1 000 000 000 characters of data. |
| **Graphical representation of data** | The representation of numerical data, pictures and other graphical files in the form of charts and graphs. |
| **Hard disk** | Permanent storage area for data. |
| **Hard return** | A physical line return input by the user. This is as opposed to the soft return defined below. |
| **HTML** | Hypertext Markup Language. It is the actual language used to insert 'tags' that allow a browser to display a hypertext document in such a way that is readable to all. |
| **Hypertext** | Hypertext itself is contained in documents that contain links to other documents within a website or to other websites. |

| | |
|---|---|
| **Icon** | A picture that represents a program, drive, file or other feature. |
| **Integration** | The ability to use files created in one application in another. |
| **Internet** | This is a name given to the collection of computer networks across the world, which can be accessed by any of us to obtain a huge amount of information on just about any subject you can name. |
| **Internet Service Provider (ISP)** | These are the organisations or companies that allow people to have access to the Internet. |
| **Inbox** | This is where you can view what mail has been sent to you and is the view you will probably use most often. It will continue to show the messages received whether you have read them or not until you decide to archive them or delete them. |
| **IP address** | Computers turn the domain names and URLs into strings of numbers, which are allocated to servers to find their way around the Internet. The numbers are Internet Protocol, or IP, addresses. |
| **ISDN** | Integrated Services Digital Network. Most of us use a normal phone line for access to the Internet. However, dedicated digital lines on a telephone network can be used to connect to remote computers and these are often referred to as ISDN lines. |
| **Justification** | Presenting blocks of text with either the left, right or both edges straight. |
| **Kilobytes** | The equivalent of 1000 characters of data. |
| **Learning outcome** | Learning outcomes are the broad area of competence a student is expected to know in an application or skill. A learning outcome covers a number of assessment objectives. |
| **Load** | A term used when a program is opened. In New CLAIT this is referred to as initialising an application. |
| **Macro** | A set of instructions that, when run, carry out an action such as opening a form, table or report in a database. Macros can also be seen as grouping a set of keyboard actions into one instruction. |
| **Megabyte** | The equivalent of 1 000 000 characters of data. |
| **Memory** | A temporary storage area used by your computer while it is running. |
| **Modem** | A device that converts the computer's digital language into tones that can be transmitted down a cable (usually your telephone line), to be converted back into digital form at the other end. |
| **Module** | A block of programming code that contains one or more procedures. |
| **Motherboard** | A circuit board inside the computer that connects all the electronic parts together. |
| **Newsgroups** | These are message boards where you can talk about all kinds of topics on the Internet. |
| **Non-printable character** | Formatting characters (e.g. hard returns ¶) that can be made visible on the screen but will not be printed with the document. |
| **Parallel port** | A connector at the back of a computer that allows the connection of devices such as a printer. |
| **Partition (of hard disk)** | Creating separate drives on a single hard disk so that each partition effectively becomes a disk in its own right. |

| | |
|---|---|
| **PC** | Personal Computer – the term has become synonymous with a system comprising a central processing unit, visual display unit, keyboard and mouse. |
| **PS/2 connector** | A different type of connector with only a 6-pin plug. |
| **Query** | A method of retrieving specified data from a database. |
| **Record** | The equivalent of a row in a table. A record is the collection of fields that form a file in a database. |
| **Reports** | The result of retrieving data to display information that can be readily understood by the recipient. |
| **Repagination** | The calculation by Word of how much text will fit onto a page and the insertion of a soft page break. |
| **Scanner** | A hardware device that converts pictures and text into a format that can be stored on a disk or computer system. |
| **Scroll bar** | Moveable slide in a window that allows the user to scroll to see information not displayed on the page. |
| **Search engines** | Search engines are the software that actually allows you to search for information across the whole Internet. There are many search engines available for you to use, from those that come with free internet access packs such as Freeserve or others like Altavista, Excite, Google, Lycos and Yahoo. A search engine allows you to put a name or a phrase into the search field and then find information about that item. |
| **Serial port** | A connector that allows the connection of devices such as a modem or mouse to a computer. |
| **Server** | A server is simply another computer that provides the information, files, web pages and other services from a service provider. A server is also used in local area networks within businesses and organisations. Often these networks are referred to as client/server networks. |
| **Shortcut** | A button or menu item that provides quick access to programs or files. |
| **Soft return** | A return automatically inserted by the software when word wrapping is required. |
| **Spreadsheet** | An application that simplifies calculations and allows users to analyse data and generate 'what if' questions. |
| **Tables** | A storage container for raw data that forms part of the overall database structure. |
| **Tags** | A tag is part of HTML. It tells a browser how to display a page on a website. |
| **Taskbar** | A facility to open programs and navigate around a computer. Usually found at the bottom of the screen and contains start button, toolbars, a clock and other features. |
| **Template** | A predefined and formatted frame that can be used to ensure consistency of style in a document, publication, presentation or worksheet. |
| **Title bar** | Informs user of the name of the file and application in use. |
| **Toggle button** | Switches a function on or off. |
| **Toolbars** | A set of buttons that are clicked to perform specific actions such as opening a program, formatting text or inserting a picture. |
| **Tower** | An upright type of computer casing style. |

| | |
|---|---|
| **URL** | Universal Resource Locator. It is the address identifying a particular document on the Web. |
| **USB** | An alternative type of connector to replace the parallel and serial ports. |
| **VDU** | Visual Display Unit. The screen that forms part of the computer system. |
| **Virus** | A virus is a computer program that 'infects' your computer. It can be received by opening an e-mail or using a floppy disk you have been given by someone else. |
| **Window** | A rectangular portion of the screen displaying a program or contents of a folder or disk. |
| **Wordprocessor** | A software application that enables text entry in a variety of formats. |
| **World Wide Web (WWW)** | This is the name given to a collection of computers providing information in hypertext format to the Internet. It comprises websites that are built in a language called Hypertext. |
| **Zip** | A means of compressing large files for easier transfer over the Internet. |

# Index